TELLING OCTOBER

TELLING

OCTOBER

Memory and the Making of the Bolshevik Revolution

Frederick C. Corney

CORNELL UNIVERSITY PRESS   ITHACA AND LONDON

First published 2004 by Cornell University Press
Printed in the United States of America

Library of Congress Cataloging-in-Publication Data
Corney, Frederick C.
    Telling October: memory and the making of the Bolshevik Revolution / Frederick C. Corney.
        p. cm.
    Includes bibliographical references and index.
    ISBN 0-8014-4219-2 (cloth : alk. paper)–ISBN 0-8014-8931-8 pbk.: alk. paper)
    1. Soviet Union—History—Revolution, 1917–1921. I. Title.
    DK265.C643 2004
    947.084'1–dc22

                                                                    2004001141

Cornell University Press strives to use environmentally responsible suppliers and
materials to the fullest extent possible in the publishing of its books. Such materials
include vegetable-based, low-VOC inks and acid-free papers that are recycled,
totally chlorine-free, or partly composed of nonwood fibers. For further information, visit our website at www.cornellpress.cornell.edu.

Cloth printing   10 9 8 7 6 5 4 3 2 1

To my mother and my father

There is a Party slogan dealing with the control of the past . Who controls the present controls the past, said O Brien . Is it your opinion, Winston, that the past has real existence? Does the past exist concretely, in space?

No.

Then where does the past exist, if at all?

In records. It is written down.

In records. And ?

In the mind. In human memories.

In memory. Very well, then. We, the Party, control all records, and we control all memories. Then we control the past, do we not?

—George Orwell, *1984*

Within the overall context of the task of remembering, such colorful accounts of military spectacles and large-scale operations form what might be called the highlights of history which staggers blindly from one disaster to the next. The chronicler, who was present at these events and is once more recalling what he witnessed, inscribes his experiences, in an act of self-mutilation, onto his own body. In the writing, he becomes the martyred paradigm of the fate Providence has in store for us, and, though still alive, is already in the tomb that his memoirs represent. From the very outset, recapitulating the past can have only one end, the hour of deliverance.

—W. G. Sebald, *The Rings of Saturn*

Contents

Illustrations

Preface

"Aberfan," it was remarked in 1984, "has passed into the currency of ordinary language and requires no explanation." The judge who delivered this statement in a libel case pertaining to Aberfan was of course quite wrong. The event is culturally specific and, for those outside of the cultural frame, *requires* explanation. Aberfan is one of my earliest historical memories. I was not *there*, but in my home in southern England, and, like all but a small number of people, experienced it through the mass media. As I engage in this self-conscious act of reminiscence about Aberfan, it acquires an increasing significance for me as a *primary* historical memory. In the act of conveying this personal memory to others, its impact may well depend in part on my storytelling abilities, the choice and specificities of my language, affect, and tone. American acquaintances had not heard of Aberfan, with the exception of one man who had grown up in the coal-mining districts of Pennsylvania, and recognized not the event itself but *its kind.*

And so. At 9:15 on the morning of Friday October 21, 1966, a rain-drenched slag heap slid down first onto a farm cottage, killing all inside, then onto a junior school in the Welsh village of Aberfan, killing 116 children and five teachers. My memory of Aberfan relies neither on my physical proximity to the event, nor even on my ability to remember its specifics. In fact, I could remember precious few of the above details, and turned to written reports to jog—and reinforce—my memory. My memory draws upon impressions, images, and reports that are part of a process of mediation that never ceases. At the time, my personal memory was mediated by local authorities, the press, survivors, the families of victims—all saw different meanings in the event. It was simultaneously an unavoidable act of God or Nature, an avoidable man-made disaster, an indictment of the inequities of Britain's class system, a tale of overwhelming tragedy mitigated by individual acts of heroism and self-sacrifice, and a tale of precognition, which even lent it an element of mystical fatalism. That I was eleven years old at the time, close in age to the children who died, also shaped my memory of Aberfan. I experienced it as a series of gloomy, black-and-white images on television in the company of my family, as stilted and awkward conversations with my friends and teachers, as raw emotion from relatives in the mining industry in the north of England, and even perhaps as part of a more inchoate but collective British experience. Of course, my present act of recollection filters the memory through my accumulated life experiences, through my way of looking at the world now, not then. Nonetheless, this poorly articulated but deeply felt experience of Aberfan is no less powerful for all that. I recall Aberfan, and it recalls *me* to that time and place.

At first blush, my memory of Aberfan might seem to have little to do with the October Revolution. Like individuals, however, societies anchor themselves by the stories they tell about their roots. For individuals and societies alike, these stories are told in the telling. My memory of Aberfan is of interest for the processes by which that mythic memory has been produced. This book is about the production of a larger mythic memory, Russia's October Revolution. Unlike Aberfan, October *has* passed into the currency of ordinary language, perhaps because it inhabited a much broader cultural frame. Like Aberfan, though, the complex processes of October's mediation, of its production as an event of cultural, political, and personal significance, still require explanation. In this sense, the act of remembering Aberfan shares much with the act of remembering the October Revolution.

I have lived with this book for many years. Along the way, many people have shared in it with me and contributed in different ways. I would like to thank Yanni Kotsonis for his friendship and his constant academic support for this project. I benefited enormously from the opportunity to exchange ideas with him and with Peter Holquist at Columbia University. I am indebted to both for their friendship and their insights. My approach to history was shaped in a variety of challenging courses at Columbia. Leopold Haimson's exacting seminars demanded more from me than I knew I possessed, and our sometimes difficult exchanges, I only now realize, have deeply shaped this book. Richard Wortman introduced me to the joys and despairs of historiography and, in ways he may not realize, also helped lay the basis for this study. Mark von Hagen taught me the critical importance of the *kinds* of questions we ask of our materials. Edward Keenan taught me the salutary and disturbing lesson that all sources are contingent and suspect—and the more intriguing for that. In a remarkable seminar with Stephen Kotkin in 1991, I was taken beyond the confines of Russian and Soviet history. He saw where my work was headed before I did, and I thank him for his generous support and encouragement over the years. With Jeffrey Olick and Fitz Brundage, I have had the pleasure of discussing any and all things related to memory and have benefited from the insights of each. I sincerely thank them all.

This book has also benefited in part or in whole from the academic scrutiny and assistance of Fran Bernstein, David Hoffmann, Nadezhda Murav'eva, Cathy Nepomnyashchy, Dan Peris, Ken Pinnow, Dave Spaeder, Chuck Steinwedel, Maria Todorova, Michael Tsin, Amir Weiner, and Luise White. Michael Gorham brought his critical eye to bear on later sections of this work, and they are better for it. I am grateful to him for that, for our perennial discussions about our respective fields, and for his friendship. I also owe a special debt to Donald Raleigh for his generous and constructive commentary as Cornell University Press's "anonymous" reader of my work, to my editor at Cornell, John Ackerman, for his fine editorial critique, and to John Raymond, for his meticulous copyediting of the final manuscript. I would also like to thank Juno Pfeiffer and Yuri Bukhstab of Russian Archives Online and the Russian State Film and Photo Archives at Krasnogorsk for their help in securing permission to use archival photographs, and Joan Neuberger, Richard Taylor, and Grzegorz Cieslewski for their advice about movie stills. On a personal note, I extend my deep gratitude to the Ratych family whose generous support of my academic career has been unstinting. I owe them much. Most of all, I thank my wife, Caroline, for sustaining me with her love, support, and sanity over these long years. Without her, and our daughters Sarah and Rachel, this book would simply not have been written.

This project has received generous funding and support from a number of agencies and institutions that I am pleased to acknowledge: the National Endowment for the Humanities (NEH), the National Council for Eurasian and East European Research (NCEEER), the International Research and Exchanges Board (IREX), Fulbright-Hays, the Harriman Institute at Columbia University, the Department of History at the University of Florida, and the Summer Research Laboratory on Russia, Eastern Europe, and Eurasia at the University of Illinois at Champaign-Urbana.

Part of chapter 1 appeared as "Narratives of October and the Issue of Legitimacy," in *Russian Modernity: Politics, Knowledges, Practices*, edited by David L. Hoffmann and Yanni Kotsonis (New York: Palgrave Macmillan, 2000), and is reprinted with the press's permission.

Dates up to February 1918 refer to the old Julian calendar, which was thirteen days behind the Western calendar. Thereafter they refer to the adopted Western calendar. I use the following translations of territorial divisions in Soviet Russia: region (*oblast'*), territory (*krai*), province (*guberniia*); for the various administrative subdivisions: district (*raion*), county (*uezd*), rural district (*volost'*). St. Petersburg was renamed Petrograd in 1914 and Leningrad in 1924. My usage reflects these changes. I have also used common versions of some well-known Russian names and words, for example, Trotsky, Mayakovsky, Smolny, Bolshevik, although I use precise transliterations in the bibliographic citations.

TELLING OCTOBER

WRITING THE EVENT

Not only did the crisis have its language, but in fact the crisis was language: it is speech which in a sense molded history.
—Roland Barthes on the Parisian student unrest of 1968

"I tell them fairy tales about Bolshevism," wrote Isaac Babel, the novelist, as a young Red Army soldier in Galicia in 1920, "and I captivate all these tormented people."[1] The stories that states tell of their origins always have something of the fairy tale about them. Whether they indeed ultimately become part of a state's tradition or heritage, its foundation narrative, or are rejected as illusion or as Boris Pasternak's "glittering lie," they are, as Babel implied, devices of considerable power both for the teller and the told. The most potent foundation narrative so deeply informs the individual that the individual's very identity, experiences, and memories are inextricably bound up with it. Powerful feelings such as national identity, nostalgia for a state's past achievements, or even a willingness to fight for the essential values or "spirit" embodied in the state often originate in the complex processes required to establish and maintain such a narrative. A foundation tale is only successful insofar as it is able to implicate the individual in the tale. In the best-case scenario, the listener becomes the storyteller, retelling the major elements of the foundation story in conscious and unconscious ways. For the act of telling involves the articulation of personal experience *as a function of* the foundation tale. And what could be truer, as the historian Joan Scott asks, "than a subject's own account of what he or she has lived through?" The individual experience of the foundation event becomes visceral, and the "constructed nature of experience" is forgotten.[2]

Telling October explores just such a manifestation of political and cultural power during the first decade of Soviet Russia. It is the tale of the telling of the

October Revolution of 1917. It is divided into two parts. The first part examines the performance of the October Revolution between 1917 and 1920, as revolutionaries of various stripes—not only Bolsheviks—used official public ceremonies and celebrations to convey to the population the aesthetic and dramatic essence of October. The second part follows the shift in emphasis, with the end of the Civil War (1918–1921), from the theatricalization of October to its institutionalization as historical memory in the course of the 1920s. The shaping of the revolutionary narrative in these years was accompanied by a prodigious state-sponsored program to establish institutions and organizations designed to reinforce and confirm its place in the new regime. This moved the process from a more freewheeling (though scripted) telling of the tale of October to one that was more tightly controlled and narrowly defined. Each part of *Telling October* culminates in a focal moment at which the Communist Party of the Soviet Union (CPSU) and the Soviet state decided to pour considerable time and resources into this process: in 1920, the third anniversary celebrations represented the Soviet state's best effort to find a Bastille for October, to distill it to a single transcendent event; in 1927, the tenth anniversary celebrations represented its best effort to tell an unequivocal narrative of the October Revolution. The construction and institutionalization of October's story also depended on the telling of another, prior story, that of the events from 1903 to 1917. Thus, even as the events of October 1917 were being reshaped as a narrative of revolution, they were being furnished with a *pre*-revolution as a pedigree. This story about the prerevolutionary period portrayed October as the culmination of an organic revolutionary movement within the Russian Empire, directed by a conscious revolutionary agent—the coherent and inspired Bolshevik Party.

The telling of the October Revolution was a sprawling process of suppression and creation. It was neither neat nor efficient but insistent and creative, sometimes brutal, sometimes elegant. Revolutionaries strove to tell a clear and unmistakable tale of revolution, although the tale was also deeply shaped by issues, occurrences, and individuals they could not have expected. The telling of October, then, was also about the limits of storytelling. Still, its success in becoming Bolshevik Russia's foundation event depended on its ability to draw broad sections of the population into the telling, and it created multiple possibilities for individuals to experience October as both a personal and historical foundation event. The conclusion to the book explores some of these possibilities.

FOUNDATION TALES

Successful foundation narratives are commissioned in a complex relationship between rulers and the ruled. Criticism of Britain's past imperialist policies has become an accepted part of dealing with her history, but tales of her former empire, while no longer evoking unbridled fin-de-siècle jingoism in most of the British population, can still stir degrees of nostalgia for an idealized and romanticized past. While Germany and France condemn their periods of Nazi dictatorship and Vichy collaboration, they continue to defend what their states' foundation tales say about their essentially German or French identities.[3] Few states, not even postwar Germany, with the global condemnation of its Nazi past, feel a need to repudiate their entire history *tout court.*

Recent studies of foundation narratives or myths have raised fundamental questions about the ways in which the terms and categories of their articulation have been defined by the social, political, and cultural assumptions of those who framed them, whether foreign conquerors or domestic actors.[4] Several groundbreaking studies of the ideological, political, and cultural reconstitution of the French Revolution across two centuries have shifted attention from the event per se to the complex processes of its constitution as modern France's foundation narrative.[5] Archives, and the primary sources they hold, have come to be seen not as largely unproblematic sources of immediate and original knowledge of the past but as defining tools in an elite's literal production of the past.[6] Language has become used less as a tool for describing the Great Event itself and more as one for analyzing it. Scholars have asked how these events acquired their seemingly self-evident meanings, indeed their very historical significance as past reality.[7] Narrative, language, and other meaning-making processes are recognized as integral parts of this appropriation. "The action of a rioter in picking up a stone," the historian Keith Michael Baker contends in his seminal study of the French Revolution, "can no more be understood apart from the symbolic field that gives it meaning than the action of a priest in picking up a sacramental vessel." These processes are always grand in scale, occurring simultaneously at the archival, symbolic, political, and ideological levels.[8] Their very viability depends on their ability to draw individuals into the process of meaning-making, allowing them to experience the event-in-the-making.

Foundation myths derive their most enduring power from the processes of their telling. Eschewing simplistic comparisons of myth with reality, recent studies focus on the mechanisms of the mythopoetic process through which individuals or groups live the myth, experiencing it as an integral component of their identity.[9] The myth, in the words of the student of mythology Henry Tudor, "explains the circumstances of those to whom it is addressed. It renders their experience more coherent; it helps them understand the world in which they live. And it does so by enabling them to see their present condition as an episode in an ongoing drama.... [It is] not only an explanation, but also a practical argument."[10] Myth informs people and shapes their understanding of past events. As sociologist

Iwona Irwin-Zarecka writes, "How people make sense of the past—intellectually, emotionally, morally—is not reducible… to the 'truth' of their accounts."[11]

Narrative, as I use it in this book, adds important dimensions to this conception of myth. It conveys the notion of dynamism and process, of a story told in the telling, replete with the sense of drama, coherence, and flow shared by all well-told tales. Narrative form should not be dismissed as mere adornment but seen as a device that makes the story itself comprehensible.[12] The power of the narrative form derives from its organization of past events into meaningful stories that are broadly accepted as natural and commonsensical. The form itself, to invoke narrative theorist Hayden White, has content.[13] It also foregrounds both storyteller and audience, and their complex interactions, in a way that myth does not.

OCTOBER AND THE ISSUE OF LEGITIMACY

The foundation tale of the October Revolution has been resistant to such scrutiny because, like no other twentieth-century state, the Soviet Union was engaged in a protracted battle with the West over its perceived legitimacy, a battle that heated up during the Cold War.[14] While generations of Soviet scholars, and several generations of radical Western scholars and literati in the 1930s, 1960s, and beyond, celebrated the Soviet Union as the ultimate fulfillment of the modern state project, conservative and openly anticommunist scholars execrated it as that project's perversion. Scholars viewed every aspect of Soviet history through the prism of (il)legitimacy. For some, Soviet socialism was an admittedly brutal and harsh ideology, but one that derived essential legitimacy from its bold efforts for the first time to give the traditionally suppressed masses a real say in the course of human history. It did so primarily, in their view, through a party apparatus that, for all of its shortcomings, was firmly rooted in those segments of society in whose name it acted.[15] Others have argued that the ideology and the party lost their initial legitimacy only after the brutalizations of the years of the Civil War ushered in the policies of centralization, bureaucratization, terror, and coercion that became the stamp of the Stalinist state.[16]

Others saw socialist ideology itself as fundamentally wrongheaded, its collectivist pretensions doomed to founder on the rock of man's natural individualism. They attributed the passionate support this ideology evoked in many to an illusion, a dream, or a spell, something from which they would in the end awaken. The monopolistic, bureaucratized, and rigidly hierarchical party and state apparatus, they argued, had sustained the elite's illegitimately gained power through a propaganda network of unparalleled power and reach.[17] Party and state had perpetrated, in historian Martin Malia's words, a socialist "Myth-Lie."[18] Scholars offered the avalanche of dry, formulaic studies of Soviet history, and the "fraud" of socialist realism as proof of efforts to preserve the lie.[19] Soviet memory itself had been contaminated, with one scholar calling for the recovery of Russia's "real memory, not the mythologized substitute."[20]

Increasingly, scholars in the East and West view Communist Russia as a state and society that had become hopelessly dichotomized over time. The state, goes the argument, spoke only for itself and in its own interests, across the objections of its own society, in an obfuscatory language that served only to alienate its population. More and more studies detail incidences of resistance or opposition to the state by segments of society from the very beginning of the Soviet era.[21] In this view, Soviet Communism was an empty shell beneath which the peoples of the Soviet Union went about their business. This is a historiographical trend that is being reprised for many of the states of the former Soviet bloc.[22]

At the root of one's view of the fundamental legitimacy or illegitimacy of the Soviet state lies one's view of the foundation event it claimed for itself: the October Revolution. Soviet historians described an act of revolution that laid the sturdy pillars of the new Soviet state. Many Western scholars described a coup d'état by a small band of merciless opportunists, which served as only the shakiest of foundations for an illegitimate and immoral Soviet state.[23] As historian Ronald Suny succinctly puts it, these Western scholars often wrote Soviet history backward from the Great Purges to 1917 "to find what went wrong."[24] Curiously, this approach has helped reify the February Revolution as a spontaneous and leaderless event, a true revolution against which October's illegitimacy came to be measured.[25]

None of this helps us to understand what even the highly critical scholar François Furet has called the "universal spell of October."[26] Like all foundation narratives, the story of October is by definition a *legitimizing* process and merits close scrutiny within that context, but it must be freed from the straitjacket of the (il)legitimacy debate. Soviet Russia's capacity to "mythologize its own history" through such stories, Furet adds, has been one of its "most extraordinary performances."[27] Ignoring or dismissing this mythmaking will not make October a "normal" object of scholarly scrutiny.[28] Rather, only examination of the performance itself can offer a picture of the culture that produced it, and why and how parts of the population came to identify with it so deeply.[29] Such an examination can highlight both the tellers and the told. It can reveal not only the preexisting tales of revolution, the revolutionary scripts that inspired these tellers, but also the ideological problems raised by their attempts to adapt or invoke these scripts in the service of their own tale of October.

REVOLUTIONARY SCRIPTS

Russia's revolutionaries embraced the post-Enlightenment transformation of the term "revolution," moving away from its earlier emphasis on disruption and bloodletting to its modern meaning of, in Baker's words, "a more profound process of transformation, an advance of the human mind frequently qualified in such positive terms as 'juste,' 'sérieuse,' 'grande.' "[30] They looked back to the French Revolution, in which thousands of people learned the new revolutionary lexicon and articulated new possibilities of political action that were inconceivable prior to 1789.[31] In and beyond the nineteenth century, this new revolutionary tradition would be "reimagined by each succeeding generation."[32] "The Bolsheviks were given Jacobin ancestors," writes Furet, "and the Jacobins were made to anticipate the communists."[33] While careful not to fit the events of 1917 into the procrustean bed of the French Revolution, several scholars have studied the ways in which that mythology helped shape the revolutionary mentality of the Russian revolutionaries during the late imperial period.[34] Historian Tamara Kondratieva is undoubtedly correct in her observation that it was difficult to find a Russian revolutionary in 1917 "who would not think of Robespierre, Danton, the Vendée or the French Revolution as a whole."[35] These were symbols of considerable power.

Yet by the first decade of the twentieth century, many of Russia's revolutionaries, and the Bolsheviks in particular, had shifted their sights from the French Revolution as a bourgeois phenomenon to the Paris Commune of 1871 as the first (failed) dictatorship of the proletariat. They retold the tale of the Paris Commune as a truncated revolution in need of completion.[36] It had failed, in the view of leading Bolsheviks, for reasons that must not be repeated in their own forthcoming revolution. The communards, Vladimir Lenin wrote from exile in Geneva in 1908, had failed to see through the carefully orchestrated "bourgeois 'patriotism' " of Versailles, and this had delayed the realization of their true interests, namely to liberate the workers from capitalism.[37] Still under the spell of the bourgeois ideals of the French Revolution, he had argued earlier, the Parisian proletariat attempted to exert moral influence on its enemies instead of annihilating them. Bourgeois power, he concluded, was not amenable to moral suasion but must be annihilated and replaced by the enlightening power of socialist ideology. The enormous power at the disposal of bourgeois ideology, then, could be countered only by a single-minded and ruthless political party capable of making the socialist case to the proletariat.[38] In 1917, Russian socialists of all shades would argue for some form of suppression of the bourgeois press so that their own class conception of democracy could be heard.[39] The attitude of Lenin (and other Bolshevik leaders), however, was uncompromising: "To tolerate the existence of these [bourgeois] newspapers means to cease being a socialist."[40] This attitude lay at the core of Bolshevik propaganda and agitation in the post-October era. It always meant relentless physical suppression of opposing voices and an equally relentless process of persuasion and transformation of people's perceptions of their surroundings.[41]

Lenin's most famous contribution to revolutionary ideology, namely the positing in his 1902 pamphlet *What Is to Be Done?* of a small, conspiratorial organization of professional revolutionaries to act as a revolutionary vanguard, raised serious questions about what constituted a "genuine" revolution, about the relationship between political parties and political action, and about the relationship between elites and the population in whose name they spoke and acted. Lenin believed that the economic and political struggle of the Russian workers could bear fruit only if assisted by enlightened groups in society, with the Russian Social Democratic Labor Party (RSDRP) in the forefront of these groups.[42] He was also, however, very sensitive that such an organization of a "dozen wise men" might be viewed as imposing on the workers "political knowledge and revolutionary experience from outside." The party should not be seen, he argued, as "do[ing] the thinking for all."[43] Indeed, such considerations played a part in the split of the RSDRP into the Bolshevik and Menshevik factions at the party's Second Congress in 1903, and loomed large in the debates and arguments within the socialist movement through 1917. Lenin's socialist opponents warned against forcing the proletariat to confront political power before it was ready. For the Menshevik leader Iulii Martov, Lenin's "cult of 'professional revolutionaries' " was a clear attempt to "force a mass movement into the procrustean bed of a conspiratorial-bureaucratic system."[44]

Lenin's plans for a party of a new type seemed to many political radicals in early twentieth century Russia to offer a script for revolution that was both counterproductive and counterintuitive. All were acutely aware of the recent emergence of their parties, of the often insuperable difficulties of organizing and running them, and of the weak name recognition of these organizations among significant parts of the population. Intermittent and sometimes brutal police repression, especially following the upheavals of 1905, forced many radical leaders to think of their organizations less in terms of political power than in terms of naked survival.[45] Furthermore, many of them were forced into emigration for long periods, where they engaged in a protracted battle there over the ownership and nature of the RSDRP, a battle that must have seemed arcane in the extreme to many of the rank-and-file members who were trying to stay out of the grasp of the tsar's police force (Okhrana)[46] Frequently deprived of significant guidance from their leaders in the émigré centers of Western Europe, the fragmentary and thinly stretched organizations inside Russia were forced to rely on their own resources and local circumstances. Well into 1917, cooperation at the local level among various radical factions and parties, accompanied by frequent switching of members among them, suggests that the ideological, political, and cultural lines dividing Bolshevik from Menshevik, in particular, remained poorly defined in the minds of party members and the broader population.[47] In 1917, after the February Revolution, a new and energetic language of revolutionary politics emerged that involved the volatile—and seemingly arbitrary—application of social labels as political weapons.[48] "Bourgeois," "class," "workers," "proletariat," "class consciousness," "revolutionary," and "Bolshevik" undoubtedly rang strange to many ears at this time.[49] This surely added to the confusion among some of the population over the political choices available to them, a confusion or ambivalence reflected in the elections to the Constituent Assembly held in late 1917.[50]

TELLING THE TALE OF THE OCTOBER REVOLUTION

The October Revolution, then, derived its narrative force from the modern idea of revolution, which invested it with a place in a seemingly inexorable revolutionary tradition. This script could take the Bolsheviks only so far. Moreover, Russian revolutionaries, notably Lenin, added elements that jarred with the traditional revolutionary tale. Still, Lenin and the Bolsheviks undeniably imagined theirs as a working-class revolution, and as nothing less than the ultimate realization of the revolutionary potential of the long nineteenth century. They would conceive and institutionalize Soviet Russia as the ultimate expression of such a revolution.[51] Beyond this broad blueprint, though, the storytellers of October were not clear about the contours of their own revolutionary narrative, its major actors, or even the nature of their audience. Moreover, as they told their tale of October, they would have to resolve the thorny issues they had added to the revolutionary tradition: the role of a party in making a revolution, the relationship between that party and the population in whose name it spoke, the absence of clearly defined political allegiances in much of the population. These issues, of course, all went to the fundamental question of the legitimacy of October as a "genuine" revolution.

These aspects would have to be worked through in the telling; for the October Revolution was not a *description* of events but rather an *argument* for a particular representation of events. The possibilities of representation were also the limits of representation, storytelling being both seductive and reductive.[52] As they told their tales of revolution, Bolsheviks and other revolutionaries selected the dramatic sites and events for their narratives on the basis of their own "revolutionary" experiences and expectations, and on their understanding of the particular matrices of power in Russia. They used terms that were freighted with, for them, positive meaning: *revoliutsiia* (revolution), *vosstanie* (uprising), *perevorot* (overthrow), *perekhod vlasti* (transfer of power). The agents of these events included the *narod* (the people), *massa* (the masses), *dvizhenie* (movement), *partiia* (party), *proletarii* (proletarians), and *raboche-krest'ianskoe pravitel'stvo* (worker-peasant government). Their tales might hinge on what they deemed a pivotal party or mass meeting prior to the October takeover, or on Lenin's return to Russia at the Finland Station in April 1917. They might focus on the Smolny Institute, the seat of the Bolshevik Party (and of the Petrograd Soviet since August 1917), which was the nerve center for the operations of the Military Revolutionary Committee (MRC). In Moscow, they might focus on the Kremlin, where bloody battles took place at the end of October between Red Guards and "junkers" (*iunkery*, or military cadets). They might focus on barricades and street demonstrations rather than on buildings as the legitimate sites of revolutionary power. Their tales might be driven by soldiers and sailors, or Red Guards and Bolsheviks, rather than events.

Alternatively, those who rejected these representations of revolution used a quite different vocabulary—*zagovor* (coup), pogrom, putsch, *avantiura* (adventure), *miatezh* (mutiny)—to describe the events they saw being perpetrated by a *kuchka* (clique) of *avantiuristy* (adventurists) and *zagovorshchiki* (conspirators). They might build their narratives around the Winter Palace, the seat of the Provisional Government, or the Petropavlovsk Fortress, where the government's defenders would languish imprisoned. They might tell tales of heroic junkers and female soldiers, of looted palaces and rampaging mobs. They might choose the Mariinsky Palace, where the Council of the Russian Republic (Preparliament) sat and where the Mensheviks and Socialist Revolutionaries (SRs, members of the Party of Socialist Revolutionaries or PSR, which had grown out of moderate socialist' efforts to address both peasants' and urban workers' needs) moved after quitting Smolny to protest Bolshevik actions. They might choose the Tauride Palace to focus on the State Duma that had resided there since 1906, or perhaps on the Constituent Assembly, which held its only meeting there in January 1918.

Only in the telling, then, would the October Revolution (or the counternarrative of coup d'état for that matter) acquire its ultimate narrative contours, in which the Bolsheviks would attempt to resolve the problematic issues discussed above, most especially the relationship of party to people in a revolution. It was in the telling that it would acquire the coherence, dramatic flow, and explanatory power of a good story. And the breadth and variety of this telling would lend particular force to the story, as individuals experienced it again and again and on various levels in their daily lives. For the October Revolution was told in the newspapers, leaflets, and pamphlets by self-proclaimed revolutionaries of all shades. It could be heard in their daily speeches and addresses, on street corners, in factories and plants, on agit-trains and agit-steamers that took the message to the rest of the country. It was told in history books, class textbooks, and children's stories. It was told in the archives, museums, and libraries dedicated to the preservation, storage, and organization of its physical traces. It was told in "red" funerals, processions, and festivals. It was told in the photographs that soon began to cover the pages of magazines and in the films that filled the cinema screens. Through the steady accretion of multiple forms of "evidence," October became the Soviet Union's originary event. Through regularized performances, particularly on the occasion of anniversary celebrations, October became a ritual of the Soviet state, an oath of allegiance, "manifest, eternal, and untouchable."[53]

In this ambitious and routinized storytelling, then, the October Revolution became an abstraction, a set of revolutionary qualities that, while they drew authority from the revolutionary script of the previous century, were inextricably identified with *this particular* revolution. The Bolsheviks and other revolutionaries were in search of a transcendent "total event" to serve the October Revolution in the way the Storming of the Bastille had served the French Revolution.[54] The "accumulating memory of print" had transformed the French Revolution, as Benedict Anderson put it, into a "concept," a " 'thing'—and with its own name: The French Revolution."[55] So the reification of the October Revolution was a prerequisite both for the process of its subsequent institutionalization and for its passage into popular experience as an event with meaning for individual lives.[56] Only through this process could October 1917 achieve its "magic" transformation from chronological numbers into a historic date heavy with meaning. Historian Robert Berkhofer described the creation of historic dates thus: "1776, 1789, 1917, or 1968. An accumulation of incidents is converted into an event through interpretation, and events are summed through interpretation into renaissances, revolutions, and other shorthand terms for a complex of events or the christening of an era."[57]

Although the telling of October was clearly an ambitious project initiated and energetically promoted by the rulers and intellectual elites of the new regime, it should not be seen as the imposition of a finished narrative on the tabula rasa of the population.[58] The effectiveness of the story relied on the ability of the storytellers to draw in, indeed implicate, the listeners in the telling of the story. They did so by providing individuals with multiple means of experiencing the event and providing the language with which to articulate that experience. The October Revolution would eventually become part of the experienced reality of the population of the USSR, and it would be experienced most enduringly as historical memory. The Parisian communards saw revolution as a "struggle over memory."[59] So too did the Russian revolutionaries. They strove to replace the population's tsarist historical memory with a new revolutionary memory, and provided not only a new chronology of the past few decades but new terms and categories with which to conceive the new past.

Telling October cannot be separated from remembering October, and vice versa. The act of recollection involves an act of interpretation or representation of past events, and the arrangement of those representations into a narrative that at least aspires to coherent meaning.[60] The events of October 1917, therefore, could be vividly remembered *and experienced* by some people as a revolution, and equally vividly by others as a coup d'état. This act is also always a social process. Individuals test, measure, and corroborate their recollections in complex interaction with others, but they always advance with increasing confidence toward a complete and coherent story.[61] In the young Soviet state, recollections were reinforced by the groups in which they were articulated, by the preponderance of "hard evidence" of the event accumulating insistently and publicly, and by the ways in which the language they used resonated with the new revolutionary language of the day. More than this, these recollections were also acts of "awakening" to the possibilities and limitations of the present.[62] Through them, individuals articulated and defined themselves vis-à-vis the new state, and also defined their roles as historical actors in self-consciously historic times. "Memory makes us," anthropologist Elizabeth Tonkin writes, "We make memory."[63]

Part 1
THE DRAMA
OF OCTOBER

THE POWER OF THE STORY

Est-ce donc une rØvolte?
Non, Sire, c est une rØvolution!
—exchange between Louis XVI and the Duc de La Rochefoucauld-Liancourt, after
the Storming of the Bastille

One would think that you are afraid a revolution will break out.
Your Majesty, the revolution has already begun.
—exchange between Tsar Nicholas II and his minister of internal affairs, February
1905

The October Revolution was first proclaimed by the Bolshevik leaders at the
Second Congress of Soviets of Workers' and Soldiers' Deputies in Petrograd on
October 25, 1917. [1] They stressed its ongoing, dynamic nature, the idea that mo-
mentous events were taking place *in the present*, the culmination of a century of
revolutionary progress. [2] "We are experiencing," soon-to-be Commissar of Enlightenment Anatolii Lunacharsky noted at the congress, "a great turnaround in
our history; truly, our revolution is developing according to the type of the great
revolutions." Lev Trotsky, who would soon become the Soviet state's first commissar for foreign affairs, spoke of the "huge masses" that had been involved in
the uprising (*vosstanie)* and praised the "heroism and self-sacrifice" of the soldiers
and workers of Petrograd. The workers' and peasants' revolution, said Lenin,
meant that "the oppressed masses themselves will create power [*vlast'*]." [3] In
proclaiming October at the Second Congress, the Bolsheviks publicly announced
its sanctioning by the legitimate representatives of the workers and soldiers.

These statements were but opening salvos in a concerted effort to "frame
public understanding of events." [4] Even those who were "there," so to speak, only
learned of the "significance" of any particular episode later through such speeches
and through the leaflets, proclamations, and bulletins that inundated Petrograd
and Moscow in those first days after October 25. [5] Patrick Wright, in his study of
contemporary Britain, writes:

> We hear news of this or that particular event through a thematisation which encourages us to understand occurrences (and our relation to them) in the accumulating terms of national identity, culture, history and tradition.... [It is] a publicly instituted sense of identity.... Among its most fundamental elements is a historically produced sense of the past which acts as ground for a proliferation of other definitions of what is normal, appropriate or possible.[6]

Even one of the arrested—and doomed—Provisional Government ministers, the liberal Constitutional Democratic Party (Kadet) member A. I. Shingarev, despite his intense dislike of the Bolsheviks, wrote in his diary in his prison cell in the Petropavlovsk Fortress on December 14, 1917: "I accept the revolution, and not only accept it but welcome it, and not only welcome it but assert it. If someone suggested starting all over again to me, I would not hesitate to say now: 'Let us begin!' "[7]

The press was the primary channel through which individuals came to identify with the October Revolution as a personal or group experience of significance. [8] Whether received as promise or threat, the October Revolution was a practical argument. Those who kept journals or diaries at the time, and who drew heavily on the press barrage, were awed by what they believed they were witnessing. "The impossible is becoming possible, and the unprecedented is turning into a story of catastrophe or, perhaps, a new world phenomenon," the philosopher Vladimir Vernadskii wrote in his diary in the week after October 25. [9]

OF BOLSHEVIKS AND BOLSHEVISM IN 1917

The event was perhaps unprecedented, but it was certainly not unheralded. Whether one viewed it as Russia's calamity or catharsis depended to an extent on one's view of the body politic in the turbulent months preceding the events of October and the possibilities of action it might offer up. It also depended on one's perceptions of these Bolsheviks who had suddenly claimed power in the name of the soviets.

Ever since February 1917, the now-legal radical parties had exploded into life, their leaders forced to confront the realities of political action and the possibilities of future revolution. [10] The socialist parties' fortunes had risen and fallen according to their ability to tap into the popular moods of the times. [11] Yet these moods were mercurial. The parties' leaders, after long years cloistered in the émigré enclaves of Europe, had sometimes encountered undisguised hostility from party activists on their return. George Denike, a Social Democrat who had spent most of his active political life inside Russia, recalled the Menshevik leader Iulii Martov being denounced at a conference as a "Paris *kafeinik* [coffeehouse type]." Martov's group, he added, "decked out in strange clothes, with large hats" were constantly interrupted by interjections from the audience. [12] Notwithstanding the iconic place the Finland Station would ultimately occupy in Soviet revolutionary lore, Lenin's arrival in Russia in April 1917 marked neither an upsurge of popular support for the Bolsheviks nor an undisputed position for him within his own party's central committee, where he would find himself isolated at key points during the next six months. [13] The steady flow of radical agitators from all kinds of public and political organizations who trailed to the provinces armed with books, articles, and pamphlets attested to each party's recognition of the urgent need to explain their party and its policies to the population at large, and to the peasantry in particular. They were countering not only the weak recognition of their parties among the population but also the "official [tsarist] sources" that had tried to cast them, as an early history of the Party of Socialist Revolutionaries put it in early 1917, as "the product of the criminal activity of a clique of madcaps [*sumasbrody*] and scoundrels, who attract enthusiastic but inexperienced young people or ignorant masses." [14] These local activists used a rhetoric of class polarization and mounting crisis that helped to politicize daily life. When local Mensheviks and SRs in power failed to solve the enormous social problems facing their regions, they left behind a perception of a crisis situation in need of urgent and extraordinary remedy. Exposed by the decline in their popular local support, local moderate socialists stepped down, ceding their positions of power to local Bolsheviks who were less reluctant, as historian Michael Hickey puts it in his study of Smolensk, to "replace democratic policies with rule by force." [15]

Indeed, in the course of 1917, one party in particular had forced itself onto the political stage and proclaimed its readiness to rule. The explosion in the membership of the Bolshevik Party (the RSDRP[b], renamed the All-Russian Communist [Bolshevik] Party or VKP[b] in March 1918) from about 20,000 at the beginning of the year to some 350,000 by October had compelled its leaders and opponents alike to contemplate the nature of the party and the political implications of its ideology. [16] Bolshevik leaders raised serious questions about the quality and commitment of their flood of new members and what this signified for the conspiratorial party they knew from the repressive, tsarist period. They strove to impress on local organizations that they were indeed integral parts of a coherent party occupying the center of the political stage, informing them periodically of "the most important events from Piter [Petrograd], in general, and about our party in particular." [17] Still, the opportunities taken at party gatherings in 1917 to quiz local delegates on the history, composition, political positions, and general attitudes of their organizations betrayed a great deal of uncertainty about the party's social, political, and organizational integrity. [18]

In a curious way, the Bolshevik Party acquired substance through notoriety, with Lenin's seemingly over-ambitious calls for an immediate socialist revolution, most famously on his return to Petrograd in April 1917, outraging people from the entire political spectrum in post-February Russia. In June, the First All-Russian Congress of Soviets passed an overwhelming vote of confidence in the coalition government, with the governmental minister of posts and telegraphs, Iraklii Tsereteli, noting that no political party existed in Russia capable of wielding power.[19] "There is such a party," Lenin famously declared, "it is our party."[20] His Bolshevik comrades might not have been pleased at the mirth this boast aroused among some delegates. [21] The Bolshevik Party only belatedly picked up the gauntlet thrown down by restive workers and soldiers, who clashed bloodily with the police during the so-called July Days over the Provisional Government's political failures. As the popular demonstrations collapsed in disarray and disillusionment, the Menshevik and SR press stepped up its criticism of the Bolshevik Party as an organization lacking substance. The moderate socialist paper, *Den'*, insisted in late July that Bolshevik days were numbered, that the Bolsheviks "almost everywhere have liquidated their activity." The article cited a lack of "noise and emotion" at demonstrations, Bolshevik speakers being met with indifference or mockery by the audiences, and "sharp resolutions" against the Bolsheviks being adopted by various workers' committees in some areas.[22] Such articles persisted well into October, one arguing that four months of organizational work by the Bolsheviks since July had produced "almost no results." [23] The party was an illusion, an organization whose very formlessness and passe-partout program allowed its diverse supporters to see in it all manner of things at once. The mask it used to attract and deceive its members concealed endless political maneuverings by its small group of leaders in their pursuit of power. [24] This mask, and this mask only, set Bolshevism apart from anarchism: "Is it not better to call things by their names?" asked the Menshevik newspaper, *Rabochaia gazeta*, on October 19. [25]

Who were the party's best agitators, the Bolshevik daily *Rabochii put'* slyly asked at the beginning of October: "Trotsky, Kamenev, Kollontai? You are mistaken, it is Kerensky, Tsereteli, Avksent'ev!" In response to recent Bolshevik gains in the Moscow elections, the SRs and Mensheviks had felt a need to "cope with the 'Bolshevik' danger." But in persecuting and banning the Bolshevik Party, the article went on, the government succeeded only in increasing the "fascination with our party." [26] Lenin felt moved to quote the words of the poet Nikolai Nekrasov: "We hear the sounds of approbation, / Not in the sweet murmur of praise, / But in the savage cries of animosity!" [27]

1. A Group of Communists at the All-Russian Congress of Soviets in 1918 (Courtesy of the RGAKFD in Krasnogorsk)

As critics of all kinds assailed the flimsiness of the Bolshevik Party, social and political commentators critiqued its ideology and practices with a ferocity they clearly felt unnecessary for the other brands of socialism on the political scene in 1917. "Russian Bolshevism," wrote the symbolist poet Aleksandr Blok, to his mother in July 1917, "is to such a degree saturated and oversaturated in practice with [things that are] foreign to itself and, in general, to all politics, that it is impossible to speak of it as a political party." [28] In non-Bolshevik circles, the term "bolshevism" was frequently used as a general synonym for any form of extreme radicalism. [29] The Bolsheviks were now revealing themselves, the poet Zinaida Gippius wrote in her diary on October 26, and she saw "under them... by no means 'Bolsheviks,' but the whole unenlightened, stupid rabble and deserters, caught up mainly by the word 'peace.' But, then, the devil knows them, these 'parties,' chernovites [supporters of the PSR leader Viktor Chernov], for example, or *novozhiznentsy* (internationalists) [those grouped around the social democratic newspaper *Novaia zhizn'*]." [30] The lyricist M. M. Prishvin wrote in his diary on September 14, 1917:

Who are these Bolsheviks that real living Russia everywhere curses and nonetheless all around Russia life happens under pressure from them—what's their power [v chem ikh sila]? Many now—and this is the fashion nowadays—call them cowards, but this is completely wrong. Without doubt there is some ideological power [ideinaia sila] in them.[31]

By September and October 1917, the Bolshevik Party was engaged in an intensive campaign throughout Russia to convey the viability and vitality of its organization to its own members. A Viatka Province congress of the RSDRP on October 17 was addressed by a Bolshevik explaining "the essence of Bolshevism" to the assembled. [32] Letters to the Bolshevik Central Committee from the provinces in September and early October boasted of Bolshevik organizational successes at the local level, promising even greater success if only more party workers (rabotniki) could be found. They also told, however, of organizations of Bolsheviks only recently separated from the Menshevik "defensist" or internationalist organizations of the area, of still unified congresses and conferences of the RSDRP, and of fledgling and still poorly interlinked local organizations of Bolsheviks. [33] Vladimir Nevskii, a Bolshevik activist who would spend much of the next ten years helping to define his party and its ideology for the masses, referred in August 1917 to the popular confusion and misconceptions about the Bolsheviks: "They say of the Bolsheviks that they are bourgeois, rich people (and this is why they call themselves Bolsheviks), thieves, pogromists, cheats,… that… their most prominent warriors… Lenin, Zinoviev, Kamenev, Kollontai… are spies and traitors in the pay of the German tsar [sic] Wilhelm." Nevskii saw no paradox in repeatedly boasting of the party's growth to 250,000 members while noting at the same time the widespread ignorance in the population of what a Bolshevik was, what a Bolshevik wanted, or even what a political party was exactly. [34]

All of these concerns of Bolsheviks and opponents alike about the state of party culture in Russia, and about the Bolsheviks in particular, crystallized with the news that a meeting of Bolshevik Central Committee members on October 10 had, at Lenin's insistence, called for an uprising ten days hence to coincide with the planned Congress of Soviets. The advanced ranks, namely the proletariat, were at the height of revolutionary readiness, argued Lenin, while the enemy camp was at the height of vacillation. Together, these factors formed the necessary preconditions for revolution. It would be a "betrayal of Marxism and of the revolution," he continued, not to practice the "art" of insurrection now. [35]

Lenin's hectoring evoked opposition from elements in his own party who believed that the time was far from ripe for an insurrection and that at best the next Congress of Soviets or the Constituent Assembly might provide the Bolsheviks with a redoubt from which to block any further encroachments by the Provisional Government. Indeed, the Military Revolutionary Committee (MRC), the future coordinating body for the insurrection, was set up on October 12 by the executive committee of the Petrograd Soviet to evaluate and formulate the military defense of the capital against a feared attack from Germany or from counterrevolutionary elements. When rumors of a Bolshevik "action [*vystuplenie*]" were bruited in the popular press, Lenin's own supporters publicly denied that such a move was being planned, restricting themselves to assertions that they would be in the "first ranks of the insurgents" should the masses' "decisive struggle" occur.[36] The objections of two prominent members of the party's Central Committee, Grigorii Zinoviev and Lev Kamenev, to the plans for insurrection spoke to the seeming paradox of a party-led popular revolution. At a meeting of the Central Committee, Kamenev put this paradox into words: "Two tactics are contending here: the tactic of plot and the tactic of belief in the moving forces of the Russian Revolution." [37] Their arguments that the Russian population as a whole was not yet ready for revolution, that international worker support for the Bolshevik Party was both soft and limited, and that the workers and soldiers of Petrograd were by no means spoiling for a fight and might easily turn away from them in the event of a revolutionary war were implicit criticisms of the organizational coherence of the burgeoning party. Their insistence that the party still needed both to explain its program to the broad masses and unmask the policies of the Mensheviks and SRs addressed the weak party identity and soft party allegiances of the population at large. [38] Some of the same considerations were clearly at play in the urgings of Lenin's staunchest defenders, Trotsky among them, to put off any formal declaration of revolutionary power until such a declaration could receive the imprimatur of the Second Congress of Soviets in late October.

As Lenin's extended polemic with Zinoviev and Kamenev in the days before the insurrection showed, he was acutely aware that the battle of representation had to be won, both within his own party and on the broader stage. "This little pair of comrades," he said, "who have scattered their principles to the winds, might cause a certain confusion of mind." [39] In a defense in the Bolshevik newspaper *Pravda* of his dissident actions, which included a temporary walkout from the Central Committee, Zinoviev referred to the "divisive atmosphere in which we live and act." [40] Acts of faithlessness in the socialist cause could redound only to the bourgeois or petit bourgeois cause, and Lenin's apoplexy was undoubtedly a mixture of ideological and tactical outrage at these "strikebreakers." *Novaia zhizn'* trumpeted these disagreements as evidence of the disarray, conceit, and deceit of the Bolshevik leaders. [41] The press quoted copiously from Lenin's public pillorying of his comrades in the pages of *Rabochii put'*. "In whose hands is the Central Committee of the Bolsheviks?" *Rabochaia gazeta* asked sarcastically. Kamenev and Zinoviev, continued the article, had opposed the planned uprising because they believed that, given the "present correlation of social forces," it would be "ruinous for the proletariat and the revolution." "What is there to say," it concluded, "about a party that is headed by the most shameless adventurers or panic-stricken fanatics, against which even Zinoviev, 'Zinoviev the Dishonest' [*Zinov'ev 'Nechestnyi'*] has to protest? Surely the fate of many thousands of workers and soldiers is not in the hands of these people?" [42] The Party's deceit was only further revealed by its leaders' practice of evading public questions about the plans for an uprising or of denying them outright. [43]

People's fears of the Bolshevik Party were not primarily of the party per se, which, many believed, would simply be unable to hold power in the long term.[44] The collapse, a leading Menshevik, David Dalin, argued, would come not from without but from within: "Disillusionment, decay, internal disintegration of Bolshevism are inevitable in a very short time." [45] The party, *Rabochaia gazeta* predicted, would fall "like a house of cards." [46] Critics were concerned rather with the mercurial supporters who had flocked to the party in the course of 1917. Already on October 10, the SR daily, *Delo naroda*, wrote that the "Bolshevik mass" itself was disintegrating into the extremes of the political spectrum. [47] Even the much-touted support of the army was illusory, according to the moderate socialist press, the army being either against, or at best passive toward, the Bolshevik plan.[48] Other parties may well have dreamed about taking the same Bolshevik path, Gippius wrote in her diary on October 26.[49] Still, she implied, they were held back by their own sense of ideological and organizational unreadiness to wield the reins of power and by a belief that the people of Russia were not yet ready for socialist power. Who then would restrain what one newspaper called the "anarchist, syndicalist, naively mutinous mood" of the masses?[50] Fear of attracting such "dark forces," *Den'* argued, had even caused the Bolsheviks to delay their initial plans for action. [51]

OF COUPS D TAT AND REVOLUTIONS

The nonsocialist press, roundly dismissed by the Bolsheviks under the term "liberal bourgeois," quickly identified the Bolsheviks' threatened overthrow of the Provisional Government as the cause rather than the cure of Russia's ills. *Rech'*, the newspaper of the Kadet Party, rued the fact that "revolutionary democracy [*revoliutsionnaia demokratiia*]" did not appreciate the "mortal dangers" its actions represented both to the motherland and to the revolution that had already been achieved in February, and it singled out the Bolshevik role in fomenting "anarchist and criminal elements" in the capital. [52] When the Bolsheviks took power from the Provisional Government on October 25, 1917, these various fears and misgivings quickly translated into a fusillade of concentrated anger against the Bolsheviks and what their opponents saw as an illegitimate and reckless action.

The newspaper of the Progressists' Party, *Utro Rossii*, stressed how the coup by the "two emigrants [namely, Lenin and Trotsky]," out of touch with the Russian people (*narod*) and the soldiers at the front, was tantamount to a betrayal of Russia to the Germans, a betrayal that could be avoided only if the army supported the legitimate Provisional Government.[53] The newspaper "exposed" the class origins of Trotsky, this "landowner's lad [*pomeshchichii synok*]."[54] Its pages carried public condemnations of the Bolshevik actions from what it regarded as the legitimate pillars of a stable system: the Moscow city police, the state employees of Moscow's credit institutions, the State Bank, and the All-Russian Post and Telegraph Union (Vserossiiskii pochtovo-telegrafnyi soiuz).[55] Chronicling the deteriorating economic situation in Moscow, with its cumulative effects on transportation, food supply, employment, and housing, the newspaper gave the impression that it was most concerned about the economic effects of the Bolshevik takeover.[56] The paper rejected Bolshevik claims of revolution as mere illusions that blinded them to the inevitable economic pitfalls ahead. It referred to Bolshevik "fabrications," namely the terms they used, such as "counterrevolutionary" and "bourgeois," to besmirch their enemies, as little more than cynical devices to sustain this illusion. At the same time, however, the newspaper expressed fear of the seductive power of these revolutionary illusions over both the masses and the Bolsheviks themselves: "The flames of pure faith burn in their souls, and thanks to their religion the true among them are ready even to step onto the sacrificial pyre." They believed though that worsening economic privation would eventually dispel the masses' illusions.[57]

The Bolsheviks (and socialists in general for that matter) dismissed this kind of criticism from the nonsocialist press not only on ideological grounds but, in fact, saw it as confirmation of the need for revolution. *Rech'* was quickly closed by the Petrograd MRC on November 8, 1917. It stuttered through various renamings until its final end in August 1918, and its demise elicited little sorrow from socialists. Criticism of Bolshevik actions from within the socialist camp, however, could not be so easily dismissed. The Bolshevik Party would have to be in a far stronger political position before it could declare its socialist critics anathema. The first months after October 1917 saw the Bolsheviks mount a sustained ideological defense of their actions in response to its socialist critics in particular.

As the Bolshevik leaders insistently began to tell their tale of revolution at the Congress of Soviets, their socialist opponents countered them at every turn. "The uprising of the popular masses needs no justifying," Trotsky had told the congress. "What happened is not a coup [*zagovor*] but an uprising. We tempered the revolutionary energy of the Petrograd workers and soldiers; we openly forged the will of the masses for the uprising, and not for a coup." [58] Menshevik speakers at the congress offered a different reading: the Bolsheviks, isolated from opponents and supporters, had engineered a coup in Petrograd, nothing more. The coup was successful (at least for the time being), they argued, only because it had happened—they threw Trotsky's own words back at him—"in the silence of night when all ordinary citizens [*obyvateli*] were peacefully asleep." [59] At issue in this battle was not what constituted a revolution. At issue was whether the October events possessed the necessary elements to be legitimately so regarded.

Those who argued against the Bolshevik tale of revolution employed all of the rhetorical and oratorical methods at their command. Their ability to tell their story would ultimately founder on their lack of access to the machinery of government, the repressive arm of which the Bolsheviks would eventually employ without compunction. From the very outset, however, and before the Bolsheviks applied systematic censorship and repression, the socialist counternarrative was weakened by a number of factors. It was by definition a *counter*-argument, and thus it was defined in essential aspects by the component parts of the Bolshevik argument *for* October as a revolution.[60] Moreover, the reluctance among the most eloquent opponents, the Mensheviks, to countenance power themselves until the proletariat had reached maturity, while certainly guided by ideological principle, may well have seemed to the masses curiously out of touch with the current situation.[61] Finally, the long history of cooperation by all brands of socialists at the local level may have further undercut these sometimes intricate arguments among socialist leaders over the nature of revolution, leaders who were known for their long tradition of volatile, personal relationships with one another.[62]

The first significant actions of the Mensheviks and SRs at the Second Congress on October 25 did not bode well for their argument. They ceded significant positions of authority to the Bolsheviks in a demonstrative walkout, an action they saw as a principled refusal even to engage what they regarded as an illegitimate political seizure by an unprincipled minority.[63] Instead, it symbolized for many the reactive nature of their position. Their quitting of the congress ceded to the Bolsheviks powerful symbolic and physical sites of representation—the Second Congress of Soviets and Smolny. The decision by the invited stenographers to accompany the departing delegates was intended to deny the Bolsheviks the legitimation implied in the act of officially chronicling the meeting. It merely compounded the Mensheviks' and SRs' own lack of voice. In a resolution, the now Bolshevik-dominated Congress represented the Menshevik and SR walkout itself as an act of illegitimacy, an attack on the authority (*polnomochie)* of the "All-Russian representation of the workers' and soldiers' masses."[64]

In the days and weeks after October 25, 1917, the population of Petrograd, and ultimately the rest of the country, awoke to bold banner headlines on the front pages of their newspapers, proclaiming that significant events were underway. These banners ran the gamut of possible representations of the events, from "All Power to the Soviets of Workers, Soldiers, and Peasants—Peace! Bread! Land!" to "Seizure of Power by the Bolsheviks" to "Bolsheviks Give Up Russia to Wilhelm."[65] Every day, people saw armed Red Guards and soldiers on the streets of Petrograd and Moscow, in the railway stations, telephone exchanges, and post offices. They encountered roadblocks and were asked to present identification at strategic points around the cities.

The SRs and Mensheviks agreed with the Bolsheviks that mass will was the key to revolution. While conceding that the Bolshevik "action" was an accomplished fact, *Rabochaia gazeta* denied that it was either a revolution or even an uprising (*vosstanie*). It was, rather, a South American-style military junta, a "pronunciamento" by the Bolsheviks, in which the popular masses had taken no active part.[66] The new Bolshevik rulers could have no understanding of the masses' long-term needs, because they did not share a class background with them. In illustration of this, hostile articles drew parallels between the new dictatorship and the old autocracy, between Lenin and Nicholas II, between the Bolshevik leaders and "Caesar and Pompey or Augustus."[67]

Short announcements in the Menshevik newspaper chronicled the step-by-step military-style seizure by the Bolsheviks of the railroad stations, State Bank, bridges, Telegraph Agency, and the Admiralty.[68] The final move of this planned coup came when the "Bolsheviks of Petrograd" had "criminally arrested" the Provisional Government and declared power, "against the will of the revolutionary people [*narod*]."[69] *Delo naroda*, under the heading "The Revolution Has Triumphed," initially merely reproduced the laconic announcement that had appeared in the evening edition of the Bolshevik *Rabochii i soldat* for October 25 about the passing of power into the hands of the revolutionary committee of the Petrograd Soviet.[70] Two days later, however, it proclaimed that "on October 24–25 there has occurred no great workers' revolution, something which can be accomplished only after many years of organization of the toiling masses, but rather a seizure of power by a clique [*kuchka*] of dreamers." Unlike the February Revolution, the Bolshevik adventure in no way expressed the "hidden thoughts of the toiling masses."[71] The February Revolution, wrote *Rabochaia gazeta*, had been "historically necessary" because it was "irresistible, in as much as at a given place and at a given time no rational and social forces can stop or hold back the given movement." The "October events," on the other hand, were precisely the opposite, because the Bolsheviks "made the October 'revolution,' and it will suffer the fate of all those revolutions that are scheduled and made on a particular day at a par-

2.   Revolutionary Storytellers: Red Guards at Smolny, October 1917 (Courtesy of the RGAKFD in Krasnogorsk)

ticular hour." "Public opinion is correct," the article concluded hopefully. "It is only a senseless, political adventure, an adventure that has seized the hour, thanks to the beneficial soil in the country for military coups."[72] Some saw the cause of revolution itself as irreparably harmed by false Bolshevik claims for October. As one diarist put it in April 1918:

> The Bolsheviks have not only defiled the revolution, they have done more—perhaps, they have killed the religion of revolution forever. For more than a hundred years, revolution has been the religion of Europe; the revolutionary was sacred in the eyes of friends and enemies. Even more among enemies than friends.[73]

The Bolsheviks addressed their critics point by point. "Where is the conspiracy?" asked *Pravda* on October 31. Claims that they had staged a conspiracy, namely a "secret agreement of a few people," were unfounded. They had openly agitated at mass meetings and in the press, and the "overthrow [*perevorot*]" had been carried out by "tens, hundreds, thousands of workers and soldiers." The uprising was successful, the editorial concluded, "precisely because it was not an adventure of conspirators but a popular revolution."[74] Bolsheviks bristled at the term "clique." *Sotsial-demokrat,* the official organ of the Bolshevik party, ridiculed a telegram from a garrison head in the town of Rzhev that referred to the seizure of power in the town by a "clique of Bolsheviks" and adding, however, that he did not have enough forces to take back the city. "Power seized by a clique," the newspaper mocked, "yet the head of a garrison cannot take care of this 'insignificant clique'!"[75]

Such representations of the events of October 1917, *Pravda* pointed out repeatedly, were a colossal misunderstanding of the significance of the events: "So this is how history is being written. [SR-Menshevik newspapers] are calling one of the most grandiose events of recent times, the proletarian-peasant revolution,... a 'military plot,' a 'forcing of the will of a minority onto a majority.' " The article asked why the February overthrow was regarded as a revolution and the October Revolution as a military conspiracy. February, it suggested, had removed only one individual from power and was, therefore, more deserving of the designation "conspiracy." After all, the October Revolution, it continued, was smashing "the ruling social force to its roots" and placing power in the hands of genuine "democratic forces [*demokratiia*]." The revolution had indeed happened twenty-four hours before the "formally designated time," namely the opening of the All-Russian Congress of Soviets of Workers' and Soldiers' Deputies, "which no one can deny truly represents the majority of the people." Nonetheless, the article fudged, it still expressed the will of a majority of the Congress of Soviets, which had made no secret of their opinion of the need for a "break with the bourgeoisie."[76]

The Menshevik and SR press argued that the lack of mass support meant that another crucial element was missing from this "revolution," namely the popular passion and drama that were integral to popular uprisings. This was no small accusation, for the very legitimacy of revolution lay in its drama and passion. To deny these qualities was to deny the revolution. In criticizing the "Bolshevik conspiracy," *Rabochaia gazeta* wrote that "revolution brings freedom, a joyful feeling of liberation, celebration."[77] Not only were the popular masses not taking an active part, even the small detachments of soldiers that had helped the Bolshevik leaders related to it "without any kind of enthusiasm, with indifferent resignation."[78] The SR daily drew an unflattering contrast with the February Revolution: "Where are the crowds of many thousands who welcomed the February Revolution? Where are the worker mass meetings? Where are the demonstrations filing past with red flags and victorious songs on the streets of Petrograd?"[79]

Rather than riding the passion and drama of revolution, *Rabochaia gazeta* implied on November 1, the Bolsheviks were isolated by mass indifference and were "suffocating in the Petrograd atmosphere."[80] Despite Bolshevik efforts to persuade the workers and soldiers that the party enjoyed the support of the country and the front, it was already clear by the second week that "the entire country is not for but against the Bolsheviks," proof of this, the article offered, being Bolshevik silence about events inside Russia.[81] The Mensheviks had already questioned the meaning of Bolshevik support outside of the capital. "We keep reminding the Bolshevik adventurers that Petrograd is not Russia," wrote one commentator two days earlier. There may well be a Bolshevik soviet in every little town, he continued, but they are "islands in a sea of reactionary philistinism."[82] *Den'* wrote that the "manufactured" nature of this uprising was revealed by the fact that it possessed no "spontaneity [*stikhiia*], no passion, in general, no temperament." This "invented revolution" was empty because it had been created "not by proclamations, not by fiery appeals, but by articles and feuilletons."[83] The notion of the October Revolution as a paper revolution was addressed repeatedly by both sides. They drew upon a debate that preceded the change of power and that contrasted the dickering of indecisive bureaucrats against the action of resolute revolutionaries. On October 22, the Bolshevik *Rabochii put'* noted that the SRs responded to Bolshevik plans for an "action" on October 25 with calls for the reworking of preliminary directives in various subcommissions: "The Bolsheviks stand for decisive measures and the SRs promise to make quiet drafts of everything."[84]

After the change of power, the early issues of *Pravda* and *Sotsial-demokrat* were filled with the decrees and proclamations being issued by the new Bolshevik government and the Second Congress of Soviets, presented as vivid proof to the population that this new power was not the ineffectual power of the Provisional Government but was, rather, in a state of feverish activity. The decree on land was announced in a banner headline in *Pravda* on October 28. The paper pointed out that the decree was signed at two in the morning of October 26.[85] The Mensheviks drew analogies between this flood of Bolshevik activity and the earlier posturings of the Provisional Government. The Bolshevik lists of newly appointed ministers, according to *Rabochaia gazeta*, were "empty paper, for citizen 'ministers,' who have only recently appeared, cannot simply take state power. It slips from their hands because around them is emptiness, created by themselves, because they are isolated from everybody."[86] A poem in *Novaia zhizn'* attacked the emptiness of Bolshevik power, each stanza concluding: "On the suppression of the reaction, the factions [*fraktsiia*] are deliberating, / Do not fear the reaction, the factions are deliberating!"[87] These decrees were by no means "paper decrees, resolutions 'without force and meaning,' " the Bolsheviks responded, but would have their real effect "the more the force of revolutionary power grows."[88]

The socialist opponents of Bolshevism were hamstrung in their critiques by their essentially reactive postures. Indeed, as the PSR claimed that the Bolsheviks had stolen their land program, so the Mensheviks denied Bolshevik claims to be legitimate heirs to genuine Russian social democracy. They preferred, in these early days, to avoid a direct confrontation with the Bolshevik leaders and to allow the full impact of Bolshevik policies in practice to disillusion the workers. At the same time, though, Mensheviks continued to argue, as they had before October, that civil war was a probable outcome of any Bolshevik seizure of power. Their writings immediately after October implied that a wait-it-out stance might not be Russia's best option. The "Bolshevik conspiracy," wrote *Rabochaia gazeta*, "if it is not liquidated as soon as possible by the resources of the working class itself, threatens to plunge the country into the horror of a civil war, whose like in cruelty and bloodshed has never been known." [89] In fact, the Mensheviks, and other critics of Bolshevik power, argued that the coup itself amounted to nothing less than civil war. [90]

The upcoming Constituent Assembly, finally scheduled for January 5, 1918, after repeated delays, would have seemed to offer the ideal stage to confront the legitimacy of Bolshevik power head-on. Prominent liberals were unequivocal in their condemnation of the very notion of the Constituent Assembly as a legitimate venue in post-October Russia. Liberal historian, and member of the Central Committee of the Kadet Party, Petr Struve argued that the convocation of the Constituent Assembly was being forced by threats from "drunken 'revolutionaries' and soldiers who have lost their senses." [91] Socialists however were more reluctant to use the Assembly as an opportunity to delegitimate the Bolsheviks publicly, even though the PSR had polled six million more votes in the elections to it, and the Menshevik leaders, despite having won only a fraction of the vote, were well suited to the cut-and-thrust of open debate. [92] As Haimson has pointed out, the PSR leader Chernov adopted a conciliatory tone at the Assembly, and only Tsereteli, no longer the Mensheviks' chief spokesman, openly criticized the legit-imacy of the Bolshevik claims to revolutionary power.[93] They were perhaps reluct-ant to be seen joining the nonsocialists in any public criticism of the Bolshevik regime. Moreover, popular support for the Constituent Assembly seemed lackluster at best. Neither the shooting of demonstrators on the streets leading to the Tauride Palace on January 5, nor even the forced dispersal of the Constituent Assembly by the Bolsheviks a day later elicited mass protests from either the worker or peasant populations.[94] The Assembly, then, never became the cause célèbre of the opposition socialists. Indeed, most dropped it rather quickly after its dispersal.[95]

This contestation over the meaning of the events of October 1917 was not re-stricted to internecine quarrels among small groups of political activists at the heads of various political parties. It informed the words and actions of a broader array of activists, many of whom expressed their support or opposition in aesthetic terms. The inimitable style of Gippius's diary entry for October 27 betrayed a deep disquiet over the current situation and what was at stake:

It is very strange what I am about to say. But... it is *boring* for me to write. Yes, amid the red fog, amid these loathsome and unprecedented horrors, at the bottom of this senselessness is boredom. A whirlwind of events and—immobility. Everything is falling down, is flying to the devil and—there is no life. The essence of life is missing: the element of struggle. In human life there is always the element of voluntary struggle; it almost does not exist now. There is so little of it in the center of events.... And there is the smell of carrion.[96] (Gippius's emphasis)

Other literati, by no means Bolshevik by membership or even sympathy, embraced the whirlwind. Blok saw in it the exact opposite of what Gippius saw there:

What has been conceived? To change everything. To make everything so that everything becomes new, so that our deceitful, dirty, boring, ugly life becomes just, pure, happy, and wonderful. When such intentions, from time immemorial ensconced in the human soul, in the people's soul, break apart the chains shackling them and burst forth in a turbulent stream, bursting dams, washing away the superfluous parts of the banks—this is called revolution. Anything less, more moderate, more base, is called rebellion, riot. But this is called revolution. It is akin to Nature.[97]

For the poet, noted one literary critic in 1921, "revolution has two sides. Not only planning and calculation, not only reason, are in it. There is soul [*dusha*] in it."[98] Vladimir Mayakovsky, one of the most committed of the revolutionary poets, "enjoyed the Revolution physically," according to his friend, the literary critic Viktor Shklovsky. "He needed it very badly."[99] The proletarian poets, who would thrive in the first years of the Soviet state, attempted to capture the revolution in a series of aestheticized images and purple passages: Karl Marx as the guardian angel above the barricades; the proletarian as behemoth with the new world at his feet; the factories as iron flowers, harbingers of the new spring.[100] Blok evoked imagery of an apocalyptic scale, warning the West in his poem, "The Scythians," to ignore revolutionary Russia only at its peril:

You are millions. But we sweep an endless flood.
You'd stem our torrents? Ah, be wise.
For we are Scythians. Asia is our blood
And crowding hungers slant our eyes.[101]

Not all literati saw the symbolist Andrei Bely's "dawn-luminous" revolution.[102] Some saw, instead, the approaching darkness of an imminent hell on earth. The writer V. V. Rozanov decided in mid-November to publish biweekly or monthly writings under the general heading: "Apocalypse of Our Time."[103] In her diary entry for October 25, 1917, Gippius described the difference between the February Revolution and the Bolshevik seizure as that "between the bright sky of spring then and the dirty, dark gray, scummy [*sklizkie*] clouds now," metaphors of darkness being a common feature of writings at that time.[104] The Bolsheviks, in Prishvin's view, represented a "darkening [*pomrachenie*]," against which the "spirit of the land" had to be raised.[105] The dark, ignorant masses were abroad in the shadows, the "abominable crowd," as the publicist V. G. Korolenko called them in his diary entry on November 20, 1917. Bolshevik calls, he added, were "like a red flag to a bull," suggesting perhaps both the foolishness of the Bolsheviks for waving the flag and the bull's inherent uncontrollability and inevitable fate.[106] The prima ballerina, Matil'da Russian prim Kshesinskaia, confided to her journal her fear of the dark and the random acts of mob violence it brought.[107]

Few poems reflect the contested areas better or more succinctly than Blok's complex "The Twelve," written in January 1918 and drawing explicitly on the press headlines of the day. [108] In it twelve Red Guards march through the streets of Petrograd in the midst of a blinding snowstorm. The poem conveys confusion and elemental force. Most striking in this poem is the poet's ambivalence about the identities of these individuals and the political actors of the time. The twelve could as easily be convicts as revolutionaries ("Convict clothes the best would do"). The twelve are unsure of the identities of those in power, if anybody could be in power in such tumult ("Who waves a red flag through the din? / Damn the dark. I'm blind"). The Bolsheviks and their slogans are dismissed by a bent old woman who sees in their banners only wasted material that could be used to wrap children's bare feet: " 'Holy Mother, pray for us, pray / Those Bolsheviks will be the death of me.' " As religious scholar Sergei Hackel has pointed out, the "political profile" of the Red Guards is not clear from the text; Blok's embrace of certain Left SR attitudes hardly prepared him "for acceptance of a specifically Bolshevik Party organ as the harbinger, the agent, and the guarantor of revolution."[109] Nonetheless, Blok heard the music of revolution, and in January 1918 he called on his fellow artists to "listen to the revolution with the whole body, with the whole heart, with the whole consciousness."[110] Vladimir Kirillov, a proletarian poet, heard a less musical, more elemental revolution: "We're drunk with a rebellious, brutal passion; / Let them scream: "You are the hangmen of beauty.""[111]

Many Bolshevik leaders were as dissatisfied with these aesthetic arguments in favor of revolution, with their overblown and often obscure religious and apocalyptic imagery, as they were with the poetic and prosaic attacks on it.[112] Their sensitivity stemmed in part from the realization that, their statements to the contrary notwithstanding, their own reports of October seemed to lack color and passion. Terse announcements of the occupation of strategic points around Petrograd were enlivened to a certain extent by bold banner headlines and pithy and not-so-pithy slogans. Nonetheless, the Bolsheviks lacked a clear focus that could be used to distill for the public in emotive terms the revolutionary essence of the October Revolution that was so publicly deemed missing by the opposition press. The Bolsheviks needed a symbol of revolution as a dynamic and dramatic event. They needed a Bastille for their own tale of October. Their opponents did all they could to ensure that the Winter Palace would not become such a symbol for the Bolsheviks.

THE SEIZURE OF THE WINTER PALACE

Bolshevik newspapers made some early attempts to portray Smolny, the site of their declaration of revolution and the seat of the new government, as a focal point of the October Revolution. In this nerve center of the revolution, all were governed by the "spirit of strict proletarian discipline." In a paradigm of the future new society, the "lively, seething life" inside Smolny could be seen on the ground floor, in the post office, transport department, sentry rooms, and factory-planning committees that were located there. The "battle centers" of the revolution occupied the third floor.[113] Nonetheless, as a static, if lively, site of action, it still lacked the dynamic and dramatic possibilities of a Bastille. It also ran the risk of seeming to be too much a Bolshevik-centered and localized operation, a perception that the Bolsheviks were laboring hard to avoid.

Even before the Bolsheviks realized it, their opponents saw the potential symbolic power at stake in what was really the only concerted military action of the day in Petrograd. *Delo naroda* implied as much with its sarcastic praise of the Bolshevik seizure of the palace:

> They can be proud of their victory, which of course will quickly be inscribed in golden letters on the tableau of the history of the Russian Revolution. They just moved the guard and the Red Guards, the armored cars, the destroyers, cruisers... against a women's battalion and small groups of junkers. Is this not a shameful business?[114]

From the outset, socialist opponents cast the Winter Palace, the seat of the Provisional Government where Menshevik and SR representatives had served, at the center of their argument that a coup d'état had taken place. Early Menshevik reports contrasted the overwhelming superiority of the Bolshevik forces laying siege to the palace on October 25 with the resolute determination of those inside, the junkers in particular, to defend it. These stouthearted defenders were even reported to have successfully repelled attempts to take the palace by force late on October 25.[115] *Novaia zhizn'* chronicled the change in the mood of the Provisional Government from October 25 to 26. Its determination to "nip in the bud, using the most energetic methods" any attempt to seize power gave way to resignation in the face of superior forces.[116] *Rabochaia gazeta* noted the decision of the besieged Provisional Government on October 24 not to "submit to any illegal demand," and pointed out the small number of Bolsheviks involved in the planned coup and their isolation from the Central Executive Committee of the Soviets, the SRs, and the Mensheviks. Indeed, it added, Bolshevik pickets stationed at one of the roads leading to Palace Square had turned back a delegation from the city duma, accompanied by members of the Menshevik and SR factions of the Congress of Soviets, which was on its way to the Winter Palace in the evening of October 25 to protest Bolshevik actions. The paper also implied that the interest of the masses in this Bolshevik action was little more than curiosity aroused by the sound of gunfire at the palace late in the evening. Significantly, it further implied that the Bolsheviks kept inquisitive eyes away from their supposedly popular revolution: "From all streets, crowds of the curious came in the direction of the Winter Palace, but they were prevented from passing any farther by order of the troops of the soviet, since the pickets there allowed nobody through."[117]

Once the palace fell, the Mensheviks and SRs ceased depicting a brave-hearted, if quixotic, resistance of the legitimate government to the Bolsheviks. They began to portray the Winter Palace, instead, as a quite different site, one lacking any meaning as a locus of real power. They reported the Cossacks' unwillingness to fight to defend the palace, the growing anxiety and confusion on the defenders' faces, the Provisional Government in the palace engaged in endless talk. They used the Winter Palace to symbolize a "paralysis of power."[118] Why, poet and publicist Vladimir Amfiteatrov asked in his diary on October 25, should the Cossacks and junkers stay to defend a government that was socialist, leftist, and, in fact, different from the Bolsheviks only "quantitatively but not qualitatively?"[119] One volunteer who went to help defend the Winter Palace at midday on October 25 saw only "complete absence of management, despite the fact that there were quite a lot of military units."[120] The minister of justice, P. N. Maliantovich, entered the adjacent Army Headquarters (*Glavnyi shtab*) building unchallenged at this time: "Are all these 'our people'? How many here are Bolsheviks? There could be any number of them. They could just come in and... take the place. Later they did exactly that: came in and sat down and those who had been sitting there got up and left—the headquarters was taken." This had convinced Maliantovich that "defense [of the Winter Palace] was futile, sacrifices useless."[121] By no longer representing it as the final heroic stand of the Provisional Government, they attempted to divest it of any future potential symbolic significance for the Bolsheviks. The Winter Palace, wrote *Utro Rossii*, would simply survive the Bolsheviks, just as it had served and outlived the tsar.[122]

Opponents of the Bolsheviks contrasted this symbol of institutional powerlessness against the brute power of the unscrupulous and unprincipled mob, which, though inspired by the Bolsheviks in Smolny, was by no means controlled by them. Soldiers, "under the influence of drunks in the crowd," broke the windows to the wine cellars, allowing the mob to begin a "drunken orgy."[123] Amfiteatrov wrote in his diary on October 26 of hearing stories about the night's "carnage [*reznia*]" in the corridors of the palace and about the "abomination and baseness" of the treatment of the women's battalion, after the junkers had been shown mercy and were allowed to leave.[124] Soldiers, Red Guards, sailors took part in the night's drunken excesses, according to opposition press reports, and women came to the palace on the following day to steal and sell bottles of wine on the streets. A drunken orgy lasted all day, leaving Palace Square littered with the bodies of inebriated soldiers and sailors. The military units that were sent from Smolny to stop the looting and destruction ended up joining it. The Red Guards who arrested the members of the women's battalion, reported *Delo naroda*, so mistreated them during their detention at a military camp at Levashovo that three committed suicide. The dead and wounded that littered the square and Liteinyi Avenue came not from a revolutionary struggle but from petty drunken brawling by armed individuals. No revolutionary restraint, no high-minded revolutionary ideals, inspired these people. *Delo naroda* singled out Nikolai Podvoiskii, the leader of the MRC, to illustrate the absence of behavior worthy of the name revolutionary. Just before the February Revolution, it reported, he had pleaded in tears with a tsarist official in Petrograd not to exile him to a provincial town, assuring him that he would desist from political activity. The writer remembered with disgust "this 'revolutionary' who for a warm little spot in Petrograd disavowed everything he believed in." It was not surprising, therefore, that this "revolutionary," "while staying in the shadows, deceitfully ordered the soldiers to battle and conducted a war with a women's battalion."[125]

Notwithstanding opposition attempts to depict a "Rape of the Winter Palace," the Bolsheviks, at this stage, did not attempt to make the palace a major focus of their revolutionary narrative. Even though the image of the Bastille was perhaps the most potent symbol in the revolutionary arsenal, Lenin's call in 1905 for people to rise up and take the "Russian Bastilles" was a rare invocation of it.[126] Bolshevik newspapers reported the "taking [*vziatie*]" of the palace on the night of October 25–26 in laconic terms. The occupation had been highly organized, with few losses, the disciplined revolutionaries ever in control, and the town orderly.[127] G. Chudnovskii, who together with Podvoiskii and V. A. Antonov-Ovseenko had been charged by the MRC with coordinating the operation around the Winter Palace, stressed the absence of genuine support for the Provisional Government by its so-called defenders, citing a reluctance expressed by the Cossacks and junkers to serve as cannon fodder in the defense of the Winter Palace.[128] *Pravda* even noted the honorable qualities of the junkers who had invited Chudnovskii to the palace and then, when he had been arrested by Petr Pal'chinskii, a deputy minister, escorted him to freedom from the building.[129] The goal at this stage was to create the impression of an impotent Provisional Government, defending the empty husk of the old order as symbolized by the Winter Palace. The Bolsheviks did not want to do anything to help these defenders appear as helpless victims of the new order. Indeed, rather than seeking to represent the Winter Palace as a loathsome symbol of the old regime, the new Soviet government immediately set about preserving it by setting up the Artistic-Historical Commission of the Winter Palace (Khudozhestvenno-Istoricheskaia Komissiia Zimniago Dvortsa) to inventory the *objets* in it. It made sure to thank those who had undertaken the "selfless defense and preservation of national treasure [*narodnoe sokrovishche*]" on the night of October 25.[130]

This early representation of the taking of the Winter Palace as a virtual sideshow to the revolution, was the result, as James von Geldern has observed, of a reluctance by Bolsheviks and other revolutionaries to embrace the imagery of the French Revolution. They had, after all, long criticized it as a bourgeois revolution, and the Provisional Government had already used various positive images of it in the course of 1917.[131] Furthermore, the Bastille had been "prepared and instrumentalized by the media of the age" as a redoubtable fortress whose storming would symbolize an end to tyranny.[132] The Winter Palace had undergone no such process. The palace had never served as a prison per se, and no stormed liberation of the prisons of Petrograd had occurred during the October Days to evoke ready comparisons with the Bastille.[133] As we shall see, however, the imagery of a storming was too potent a symbol to resist, and it would eventually loom large in the evolving narrative of the October Revolution.

A LITTLE MORE FAITH

The story of October would emerge over time in the telling. In these first weeks and months, the vehement disputes among socialists and nonsocialists over the legitimacy of October hinged on their view of the Bolshevik leaders and the nature of their party. The party, they argued, really consisted of a small and shameless group of Bolshevik intellectuals, with few real ties to the people in whose name they claimed to act. Bolsheviks were therefore accorded center stage in the counternarrative. Many socialists, artists and intellectuals among them, had embraced the October Revolution without explicitly embracing the party. Contrasting his pleasure at the revolution with his disdain for Bolshevik cultural policy, the literary critic Osip Brik in December 1917 publicly called for people to "be wherever culture is at risk, steadfastly defending it from any, including Bolshevik, vandalism." [134]

For their part, Bolshevik leaders strove in these first months to create the impression of a party in the ascendant, but they did not explicitly link it to the October Revolution. They came closest to a direct link in the parallels drawn at the end of 1917 between the October Revolution and the Paris Commune, in which, *Pravda* wrote, "we are literally reading our own history, often coinciding in the smallest details." [135] The united actions of Russia's workers and peasants through their soviets were contrasted with the French peasantry's failure to support the Parisian proletariat, a betrayal that doomed the Paris Commune. Very soon, however, such analogies attributed the fall of the commune to the proletariat's lack of understanding of its own class interests and to the lack of a "powerful political party able to lead its movement," of the kind that had so benefited the October Revolution. [136]

Still, after October 1917, the periodic Bolshevik membership reregistrations, the establishment of degrees of membership (associate, candidate, "sympathizer"), and the publicly expressed doubts about the class and political origins of new members bespoke continuing anxiety among the leaders of the party about the revolutionary qualities of its membership. After October, the Bolshevik press carried numerous testimonials to functioning and vital Bolshevik organizations at the local level, although even the reports about older local committees gave an impression of mercurial support at best. [137] It reported frequently on the end of the recent formal and informal links between Bolshevik and Menshevik organizations. [138] Tales of personal conversions to the Bolshevik Party from other parties were also prominently featured. [139] At the same time, no secret was made of the dearth of personnel and resources in provincial Bolshevik organizations, which, as one local report put it, left "the Bolshevik mood of the masses completely unutilized." [140] In an article headed "There Are No Bolsheviks, There Are No Mensheviks," *Izvestiia*, the newspaper of the Petrograd Soviet, carried a pledge from a worker to vote for whoever would bring immediate peace, land, and workers' control of industry. [141] Menshevik newspapers peppered their columns with Bolshevik expressions of their own doubts, citing, for example, Lunacharsky's concerns that the party was accepting ever more "nonideological officials [*bez-ideinye chinovniki*]" into its ranks. [142] The announcement of newly established local Bolshevik organizations was usually accompanied by the fillip that, despite their still poor organizational state, they had already garnered much support from the local populace. [143]

In these first weeks, leading Bolsheviks spoke quite openly about how Bolsheviks were perceived in the country at large. In late December 1917, a Bolshevik of long standing, Emel'ian Iaroslavskii, cited the writer Maksim Gorky's depiction of the general attitude toward Bolsheviks in the countryside:

> The village does not know any ideological Bolsheviks, any pure socialists. For it, the Bolshevik is the rear soldier. This rear soldier Bolshevik is mainly a hooligan. This animally [*zoologicheski*] confused person calls himself "Bolshevik" because he is convinced that he is most like one. [144]

The problem was part of a generalized ignorance of many of the new terms of this new order. Many comrades in local regions, wrote *Izvestiia*, had not grasped the significance of the transfer of power into the hands of the workers, soldiers, and peasants and did not yet realize "what the October Revolution obliges us to do." [145] "What do the Bolsheviks want?" asked *Sotsial-demokrat*, unwittingly conveying with this title the sense of the Bolsheviks as "outsiders" or "unknowns." The man in the street (*obyvatel'*) wanted to know the answer to this question, it went on. Separating him from the workers and soldiers who "know perfectly well that the Bolsheviks are defending the interests of the poor," it defined the man in the street as the "small shopkeeper, the artisan, the female teacher, the middle postal official, the telephone operator." They believed the rumors flying around the capital that the " 'Bolsheviks are thieves.' 'Bolsheviks want to take everything.' 'Bolsheviks are German agents.' 'Bolsheviks are enemies of any order.' 'Bolsheviks are rapists.' " [146] At a meeting of teachers about a month after the takeover, Iaroslavskii was surprised at the question from one of those present as to who precisely was now in power in Russia. [147]

Despite assurances from the Bolshevik press that the "little people," being the "blind instruments of capital," were not in danger, Bolshevik attempts to define themselves in broad strokes of contrast did not bode well for the ranks of the uncommitted in the Age of Revolution. [148] "There is no need to doubt, brothers / in these hours of severe darkness," began a poem called "A Little More Faith" that appeared in *Pravda* in mid-November. [149] Such calls to faith relieved the Bolsheviks of the need to define themselves more explicitly. Instead, they began very quickly to limit the space within which one could define oneself as anything other than a Bolshevik. Their intended audience for their revolutionary tale was not the members of the other radical parties. Their calls to faith were directed mainly at the nonparty people (*bezpartiinye*) and the even more amorphous category of sympathizers (*sochuvstvuiushchie*), who, though "Bolshevik" in mood, they believed, still lacked the necessary commitment. In early October, an article in *Sotsial-demokrat* criticized those members of the soviets who called themselves nonparty but nonetheless voted for various parties. "In fact, they turn out to be party people," the article continued. The problem, it was implied here, lay in their failure to show faith and to commit to the revolutionary cause (as represented by the Bolsheviks). That this failure might not always be tolerated was hinted at in the concluding call to "comrade soldiers" to "size up the nonparty deputies and remove the splitters from the Soviet." [150] Whether these nonparty types were truly uncommitted, undecided, or secretly supporting the semilegal or underground parties and groups at this time, is in a sense irrelevant. The Bolshevik message, and the threat it held, was clear. Have faith, it said, faith meaning, of course, the correct understanding of the significance of the October Revolution. "The time in which we are living," Iaroslavskii had responded to the teacher's question about who was now in power, "demands from each person the complete realization of what has happened, especially as the teacher, to whom not only children but also adults are now turning, is presumed to have such an understanding of the events." [151] This applied not only to the rank and file or the as yet uncommitted but also to the party's own leaders. Any failure on their part to grasp the significance of the October Revolution was nothing less than heresy. The actions of Kamenev and Zinoviev on October 10, Kamenev's forced (and temporary) resignation from the Central Committee ten days later over these actions, and the decision of both to quit the committee on November 4 over its reluctance to share power with other socialist parties, represented fundamental acts of faithlessness. Their actions were treacherous because they had provided ammunition for their opponents' press campaign that was raising "a hue and cry about the 'disintegration of our party,' about the 'failure of the uprising.' " Such actions, *Pravda* wrote, were the actions of "all those of little faith, all vacillators, all doubters." [152] These calls to faith in a polarizing world did not augur well for the Mensheviks and SRs, whose reasoned and relentless criticisms attacked the Bolsheviks' argument of revolution in its core elements. Here was heresy not from within the party but from within the socialist movement, but it was heresy just the same.

There was still time for the masses of the nonparty people to see the light, as the Bolshevik focus on the various conferences of party people throughout the

Civil War period showed. A proletarian poem captured a personal conversion to Bolshevism in all its early ambivalence. The author conceded his initial indifference toward the Bolsheviks:

> I hurled no cries of hostility at you,
> Nor did I toss you a welcome.
> Now and then I lashed you with satire,
> at times with caricature.

He finally joined the Bolsheviks in response to an increasingly well-defined enemy:

> They shouted at you: Deception! Blackmail!!!
> I believed these evil words little…
> But… *bourgeois sabotage*
> pushed me under your banner…[153]

Threat and promise are integral to tales of revolution. As a tale of renewal, it included the destruction of the old. As a tale of epiphany, it excluded those who would not or could not see the light. "What is a Bolshevik?" asked one writer in December 1917. "It is a mortal faith in the people, a faith until the grave." [154]

TO DIE FOR OCTOBER

During these first three months after October, the Bolsheviks made their call to faith most poignantly perhaps in their revolutionary celebration of the most sublime of human experiences, death and loss. What better place was there for the storytellers of revolution than on the stage of death? Mourners gathered there in a shared and ritualized articulation of grief and imagining, primed to (re)consider the significance of the life lost and the place of that individual life in a changing world. "Death," Walter Benjamin has written, "is the sanction of everything that the storyteller can tell. He has borrowed his authority from death."[155] Historian Catherine Merridale observes that as early as 1870 radicals of various stripes had attempted with their graveside speeches to infuse the funerals of prominent artists with revolutionary meaning. [156] Like the later Bolsheviks, these elite revolutionaries saw the opportunities presented by the act of mourning. Their opponents, too, realized that the red funeral was a fundamental challenge to the old order, and that it had to be combated at every step. Where these secular funerals were tightly choreographed to convey a sense of the new traditions of Soviet Russia, the traditional, religious funerals that also took place in these months were equally designed to reassert older values.

Death was clearly too valuable a medium to be left by either side to manage itself. From the very first days after taking power, the new government sought to

3.   Red Funeral in Moscow, November 1917 (Courtesy of the State Central Museum of
Contemporary History of Russia)

inscribe the October Revolution in the ritualized commemoration of the revolutionary death. Red funerals, along with crowd scenes, street demonstrations, mass
meetings, and barricades, were regarded by filmmakers charged with producing
a multipart documentary of the October Revolution in early 1918 as among the
"main moments of the Russian Revolution." [157] On November 4, 1917, the *Sotsial-
demokrat* called on the population to "preserve the memory of the Moscow battle
days and of the fallen comrades," appealing for "lists of the killed and wounded,
of the episodes of fighting" to be sent to the editors of the newspaper. [158] The
scant, incomplete, and frequently incorrect information pieced together through
such appeals, together with obituaries from newspapers and journals of the period,
would eventually be published in book form, the martyrs achieving in death a
defined revolutionary purpose and a coherent Bolshevik Party identity that was
probably unknown to them in life. [159] Bolshevik newspapers carried lists of the
wounded and killed who now lay in the hospitals and infirmaries (*lazarety*) of
Petrograd and Moscow, identifying them by name and social status: worker,
sailor, junker, officer, and so on. [160] In stark contrast to such individual martyring,
some non-Bolshevik newspapers set up a committee of representatives from
various public organizations and political parties to organize a fund for the "victims of the dictatorship of the Bolsheviks." The "hundreds and thousands of...
victims of the Bolshevik terror" were too numerous to list, they implied, although
they regularly carried lists of those who contributed to the fund, the amounts

they donated, and their social position (for example, doctor, group of civil servants, accountant, joint-stock company). [161]

Deprived of the requisite martyrs by the relatively bloodless nature of the events in Petrograd, the Bolsheviks first drew upon the bloodier experience in Moscow in order to cast the revolutionary experience as personal sacrifice in the cause of collective redemption. In Moscow, the Commission for the Organization of Burials of Victims of the Revolution (Komissiia po organizatsii pokhoron zhertv revoliutsii) was set up to organize one of the first ceremonial burials on Friday, November 10. [162] The building committees (*domovye komitety*) were expected to ensure public support of the burials, and relatives of the slain who wished to attend had first to obtain an authorization (*udostoverenie*) from the Soviet of Workers' Deputies. All factories, plants, and trade enterprises, except those related to the food industry, had to close on the appointed day. On the morning of that day, individual delegations bearing red banners marched from the workers' quarters of the city along the Moscow streets through the Iverskii Gate and on to Red Square to the fraternal grave at the Kremlin wall. At 11 a.m., the procession appeared bearing the coffins, some open, some closed. The coffins of fallen Red Guards were borne on the shoulders of workers; the coffins of soldiers were carried on artillery gun carriages. The marchers carried wreaths and red and black banners, and a choir sang the song "Eternal Memory" ("Vechnaia pamiat'"). Huge red posters hung from the Kremlin walls, proclaiming: Long Live the Proletarian and Peasant Revolution! Long Live an Honorable Democratic Peace! Long Live the Brotherhood of Nations! One enormous embroidered red banner hung the length of the wall, proclaiming in white and gold letters: To the Victims, the Heralds of the World Social Revolution! [163] The orchestra played a funeral march and the "Marseillaise," despite a long-standing dislike of it by the Bolsheviks and many other socialists as the "bourgeois" anthem of the French Revolution and the Russian Provisional Government. [164] The burial procession presented a tableau of the new official hierarchization of Soviet society: the banner of the regional committee of the party (*raionnyi komitet*) held by a worker and peasant, at the head, followed by a choir, then the rows of borne coffins, then the relatives of the slain. The rear was brought up by an orchestra and by representatives of various state, party, and military organizations. At graveside, little girls sang "Eternal Memory" over the rows of coffins and speakers delivered speeches marking, as the popular daily *Gazeta dlia vsekh* noted sarcastically, "the 'victory' of the Bolsheviks." Finally, the coffins were lowered into the fraternal grave.

A local burial in the Vyborg District of Petrograd on November 19 followed much the same pattern. [165] The specially appointed Funeral Commission of the Vyborg Region (Komissiia po pokhoronam Vyborgskago raiona) laid out a route for the procession honoring the fourteen Red Guards, mostly from that region, who had fallen. At the Children's Hospital in the Vyborg District, pallbearers were to gather at 9 a.m. to begin the procession, a similarly hierarchized arrangement of representatives from the regional Soviet, various political organizations, the Red Guard, military units with music, and then representatives from the various factories of the district. Each row of the marchers would have six persons, and for every one hundred people an organizer (*rasporiaditel'*), distinguished by a red sash across the shoulder, was assigned. *Pravda* described the funeral procession as a paragon of group solidarity and shared emotion: "plant by plant, men, women, the young, with banners… singing 'Eternal Memory' " marched past the fraternal grave on the hill in orderly rows. "The harmony [*stroinost'*] of the procession and its grandioseness," it continued, were striking. [166]

These burials were described in quasi-religious terms, contrasting faith and brightness with indecision and gloom:

> Today we are burying those who, with burning faith in the right cause, bravely joined battle with the enemies of international brotherhood… today is the day of fallen warriors, irreconcilable, bright, who came to conceive a holy hatred of everything indecisive, cowardly, vacillating, of everything oppressive and gloomy…. Today, as from the Easter candle, from the light of these souls, we warm in our hearts new fires of strivings for proletarian ideals; with bright, unprecedented rapture we gather around the red banners of the world evangelium—Socialism. [167]

Present at the burial in Red Square of a young friend killed on the streets of Moscow on November 1, a young Komsomol (Communist Youth League) member wrote two weeks later of the district party banner that "beat and flapped in the wind, and at times it unfurled so triumphantly it sent a shiver down your back, with the band playing a march behind us." [168] "The sky pours autumn tears on the graves," went one poem, "Your courageous valor, we confirm with our struggle." [169] These new red funerals, *Izvestiia* implied, were fundamentally different from the earlier red funerals of the post-February days, being distinguished by the genuineness of the feeling they evoked. "Today," the paper noted of a procession on December 17, "there were none of the hypocritical tears, deep sighs, and lamentation with which in March the Rodziankos, Miliukovs, and Guchkovs [the leaders of the Kadet Party or the more conservative Octobrist Party] approached the graves of the fallen warriors [of the revolution]." [170]

Far from seeing these funerals as a collective and harmonious act capable of inspiring poetic flights or a revolutionary frisson in those present, opposition reports stressed the hollowness of these ceremonies. No priests, *Delo naroda* pointed out, were in attendance, although *Gazeta dlia vsekh* noted that "thousands of candles warm the raised hands of believers" at the Iverskii Chapel. [171] One observer placed the burials at the Kremlin wall in the context of ancient battles in Russia, stressing the age-old shedding of tears for the fallen, but noting that this time "no enemy had killed Russian sons on the open field [*v chistom pole*], they had destroyed one another." [172] The moderate socialist and nonsocialist press alike attempted to make martyrs of the victims of a coup d'état. The ceremonial burial of ten junkers in Smolensk cemetery in Petrograd in early November was funded by the Petrograd city duma, but it had neither the organizational nor financial resources to match the grandiose red funerals. The non-Bolshevik press told, though, its own tale, a tale of the new regime's illegitimacy. In contrast to the reports in the Bolshevik press of the highly structured red funerals, the opposition press offered the impression of funerals organized spontaneously by disparate groups, most often a vaguely defined "socialist student body." The presence of deputations at these funerals from, among others, the officer corps, the Committee for the Salvation of the Motherland and Revolution (Komitet spaseniia rodiny i revoliutsii), and the city self-administration (*gorodskoe samoupravlenie*), as well as the church rites and liturgy at the graves, offered their own tableau of the legitimate centers of power in this country. [173] A planned funeral for some forty junkers and students experienced several delays "due to the 'comrades,' the Bolsheviks," wrote *Gazeta dlia vsekh*. The funeral was finally permitted on November 13. The newspaper described a scene reminiscent of the paintings of nineteenth-century religious processions by Il'ia Repin or Vasilii Perov. At 10 a.m., marchers carried white catafalques from Moscow University, on which were placed thirty-three open and four closed coffins. These coffins were simple, wooden, undecorated, bearing no wreaths (the money collected for wreaths would be used instead to establish grants at the higher educational establishments). They were then carried in the rain to the Bratskoe Cemetery in the village of Vsekhsviatskii, accompanied by a host of people (not the serried ranks of the red funerals), including students, soldiers, officers, and "many simple people." The road of the procession filled up with a "mass of people [*massa naroda*]"; priests delivered the liturgy and students sang "Eternal Memory" and "Holy God ["Sviatyi Bozha"]" as they made their way slowly to the Bol'shoe Voznesenie Church. Along the route, as the procession moved from the university to the church, people watched, "they all cross themselves, tears in their eyes." At the church, a thousand people already waited, too many for the church to hold. "A little sun peeked out," the article noted. The final burial in the cemetery was accompanied by "speech after speech, one more powerful than the other," and a "deathly silence." [174]

Clearly, such funerals were intended to evoke much more traditional images of death than those intended by the organizers of the red funerals. Funeral ceremonies in the first weeks of the new regime presented starkly contrasting tableaux of the social structures and political expectations of the old and new regimes. These very different ceremonies offered two sets of martyrs, two sets of mourners, and two mutually exclusive representations of what had happened in October 1917. Despite the cultural and religious power embodied in the junker and student funerals, the limited political and financial power at the disposal of those who organized them ensured that they would not long continue. The grand scale and detailed organization of the red funerals bespoke the resources at the disposal of the new Bolshevik government. More than this, the serried ranks of marchers, many in uniform, the military bands, the imposing reds and blacks of the posters and enormous banners, the "long graveside speeches of revenge" that accompanied at least the state funerals of high officials contained more than a hint of violence.[175] Louise Bryant, an American socialist and journalist committed to the cause of the October Revolution, wrote of being deeply moved by the singing at a mass burial near Red Square in early November, which "rose and swelled, rich and resonant in the thin winter air—like a great organ in some fine old cathedral," musing at the same time how such a spectacle caused enemies to cower "behind drawn blinds." [176] Official reports of the funerals sometimes pointed out the absence of bystanders (*postoronnaia publika*), both describing the scene as they saw it, perhaps, and impressing on readers the need for a display of commitment at such events. [177]

These implicit threats revealed the fundamental inability of the red funerals to coexist with their more traditional counterparts. As their organizers clearly realized, both red and traditional funerals were seductive because of their ability to draw the mourners into their grand tales about their country's history—different and mutually incompatible tales. Both the narratives of revolution and of coup d'état were robust articulations of past events, internally coherent and eminently credible. The Bolshevik and non-Bolshevik press alike regularly denounced rumors that were deemed too outlandish. In response to a rumor in Moscow on October 26 that pitched street battles in Petrograd had razed the Winter Palace and left 75,000 people dead, Gorky noted that even the Russian, "a child of fairy tales who loves horrors and is capable of creating them," did not believe such nonsense. [178] In the Constituent Assembly elections in November 1917, the Bolshevik Party enjoined voters to choose the "Party of the Bolsheviks," and "never vote for the SRs, Mensheviks… for these parties gave their blessings to the shootings of workers and soldiers, directed the hand of the junkers against the people, or silently watched the struggle without taking part." Two days later, Iaroslavskii stated in *Sotsial-demokrat* that neither had ever supported the shooting of workers and soldiers, an implicit admission that the Bolsheviks had overstepped the bounds of narrative credibility. [179]

In short, each narrative fulfilled what anthropologist Michel-Rolph Trouillot has called the requisite "claim to knowledge," namely that "that which is said to have happened is said to be known to have happened." [180] The real threat of the counternarrative for the Bolsheviks lay in the fact that, in these early days, the events of October 1917 could still be experienced as either coup d'état or as revolution. For revolutionaries, whose entire adult lives had been devoted to enlightening the dark masses with the revolutionary message, this was wholly unacceptable. For them, this was not a mere description of events but an argument about their transcendent significance. This argument could only be blunted by representations of these events as sterile and meaningless. They could not allow the counternarrative to persist for long, and they had no reason to stint on their methods.

2

THE DRAMA OF POWER

Red dawn,
red sunrise.
Red speeches
at the red gates,
and the red,
on Red Square,
people.
—Nikolai Aseev, "Red Calico," 1920

Although the competing narratives were internally consistent and credible, the power to tell them was not distributed equally among the storytellers. Critics painted a picture of overwhelming Bolshevik power with which the Bolsheviks themselves might have been pleased: "The Bolsheviks have cannon, bullets, armored cars, battleships, cruisers, airplanes, the Red Guards, the police department.... It would seem that it is a huge and powerful apparatus of power, and at the same time popular, based on the trust of tens of millions of peasants, workers, and soldiers." Through such hyperbole they intended to highlight the absence of "moral force" in this power.[1] The Bolsheviks did not share their critics' notions of morality. They had long criticized the power of representation at the disposal of the prerevolutionary "bourgeois" culture as one of the most effective manifestations of political power. Even before the overthrow, the Military Revolutionary Committee had ordered the seizure of the printing press of the nonsocialist paper *Russkaia volia*, and most of the "bourgeois" newspapers were closed in late November 1917. [2] Decreeing a limited and temporary press ban two days after the takeover, the Bolsheviks noted that the press had been "one of the most powerful weapons of the bourgeoisie" and it could not be left in bourgeois hands to "poison minds and introduce chaos [*smuta*] into the consciousness of the masses."[3] The implications of this reasoning were immense, for it made the act of censorship not a matter of temporary tactical expediency but, rather, a philosophical argument that should logically entail, as Trotsky added at a session of the Central Executive Committee of Soviets on November 4, 1917, the physical confiscation of bourgeois printing presses and newsprint stocks. The ban on the bourgeois press, Trotsky noted in a resolution to the session, was "an essential transitional measure in establishing a new press regime in which public opinion will not be fabricated autocratically by the capitalists who own the newsprint and printing presses."[4]

SILENCING THE COUNTERNARRATIVE

Astute moderate socialists, equally aware of the power of representation, recognized that the Bolsheviks would inevitably turn this weapon against them as well. These "adventurers and conspirators," wrote *Rabochaia gazeta*, would be forced to resort to "brute force and terror" in order to "force their will on a great country and a free people." It would also ensure, it added hopefully, that the population would see through it: "And this is revolution? Think about it, comrade workers and soldiers!"[5] Menshevik predictions that the Bolsheviks would close meetings, ban demonstrations, disperse unions, and crush party organizations soon came to pass. Immediately after their takeover in October, the Bolsheviks demanded that all of the still legal private socialist presses carry all Bolshevik and Soviet decrees and resolutions on their front pages, as well as editorials from the Bolshevik organ. They accompanied these measures with denunciations of the moderate socialist press. They often reprinted "lies" that appeared in the Menshevik and SR newspapers about the razing of the Winter Palace, about Bolshevik snipers shooting from the rooftops at passersby in a destroyed Petrograd, and about the collapse of the "Bolshevik mutiny."[6] By pointing out wherever their critics in the press overstepped the limits of the narrative, the Bolsheviks were attempting to recast the issue of censorship in terms of truth versus lies rather than coercion versus freedom. The non-Bolshevik press chronicled the daily acts of censorship and repression. By summer 1918, the opposition press lay in ruins, its newspapers closed, its printing presses confiscated, its editors arrested or exiled.

Censorship, repression, and voluntary and forced emigration were undeniably effective means of silencing the counternarrative, and the formative importance of the question of legitimacy to the historiography of this period has ensured that these measures have been well documented and rightly so.[7] Yet the counternarrative itself had a fundamental weakness. Unlike the narrative of revolution, it embodied no transcendent meaning. It could invoke no Great Story in its service, and it could conjure no ready-made emotive symbols and images (there was no countericon to the Storming of the Bastille). Whereas the narrative of revolution was intended to be the bearer of drama, emotion, and passionate commitment, the narrative of coup was intended to convey sterility, adventurism, and senselessness. *At its most successful*, it could only make of the October Revolution a cynical grab for power on a par with the failed July Days and the Kornilov affair.

The Bolsheviks—and other revolutionaries—accompanied their silencing of the nonsocialists, Mensheviks, and SRs with a rich and varied telling of their tale of revolution. They tried to tell a clear and comprehensible tale, one that could be read in only one way, although at this early stage the narrative contours of the October Revolution were not yet set. [8] The major contestation over revolution or coup d'état would be revisited at key junctures in the coming decade. In the meantime, and even in the turbulent times of the Civil War, the Bolsheviks turned to more creative ways to convey the coherence and significance of their revolution. Their intended audience was not, of course, their socialist critics. The contestation over October had never been about the persuasion of opponents, whose very acts of criticism placed them beyond the revolutionary pale. The new leaders believed that the major obstacle to their argument for revolution was people's understandable failure to realize both the significance of the events of October and their own place in the Great Story. [9] In the chaos and fragmentation of the Civil War, Russia's revolutionaries would find significant obstacles to their efforts to convey their tale of order and coherence.

THE CHAOS OF WAR

Between the middle of 1918 and the middle of 1920, the Bolsheviks found themselves confined to Moscow, Petrograd, and the Russian heartland, fighting intermittent battles against counterrevolutionary forces: White armies led by former tsarist generals to the south, north and east, and various foreign forces, notably Germans, but also British, French, Japanese, Americans, Poles, and Czechs to the west, north and east. They had to contend with hostile governments on formerly Soviet soil, notably Admiral Aleksandr Kolchak's anti-Bolshevik government in Siberia and the SR-led Committee of Members of the Constituent Assembly, or Komuch, as it was called, in Samara, as well as with uprisings against both Whites and Reds in 1919 and 1920 by bands of peasant deserters from the Russian Army.[10] Nor was the threat only military, with the anti-Soviet movements being as concerned as the Bolsheviks to learn about and "enlighten" the population in their territories. The "Enlightenment state," as Peter Holquist puts it, was "not solely a Bolshevik ideal."[11] Even areas that remained under Bolshevik control throughout the Civil War exhibited what Donald Raleigh has called, with reference to Saratov Province, "patent separatist tendencies," although these localist tendencies amounted neither to a challenge to the center's revolutionary narrative nor, as he puts it, an "alternative to the establishment of a party autocracy."[12] The Mensheviks and SRs, so persecuted by the Bolsheviks in the months after October

1917, even enjoyed a brief political resurgence in spring 1918, and the Bolsheviks' own claimed constituency, the workers, frequently displayed their discontent in strikes and demonstrations.[13] Food and energy crises, disease, and the upheavals of repeated mobilizations for and frequent desertions from the Red Army reached epidemic proportions.[14]

Even as they fought this civil war militarily, the Bolsheviks continued to pursue their iconoclastic ideological agenda, attacking traditional religious, sexual, and social norms with initiatives that inevitably introduced even more disorder into individual lives and aroused the ire of at least some of the population.[15] Their renaming of cities, streets, and squares, and their replacement of old monuments with new revolutionary statuary, brought people face to face every day with the revolution. With the symbolic change from the Julian to the Gregorian calendar on February 1 (14 New Style), 1918, Russia joined the West, and by implication the promised revolutionary future there, in a thirteen-day leap out of the past.[16] They did all this with their own party in a parlous state, no small problem for Bolshevik leaders who had yet to resolve the vexing conundrum of a party-led revolution. While the Soviet press chronicled the steady growth in Bolshevik Party organizations across the country, and praised the movement of experienced Communist propagandists and educators into local communities, Bolshevik leaders subjected their party to intense critical scrutiny in both private communications and at official party gatherings.[17] Sometimes, Bolshevik insecurities were revealed unwittingly; for example, the Bolshevik propagandist V. A. Bystrianskii marveled in January 1918 that "one year ago Bloody Nicholas was in power..., one year ago we revolutionary Social-Democrat Bolsheviks were an insignificant clique [*nichtozhnaia kuchka*]."[18] At the Seventh Party Congress in March 1918, however, which saw deep disagreement over the Brest peace, the insecurities were on view. Speakers described a party overwhelmed by its pell-mell growth to three hundred thousand members during the previous year. Iakov Sverdlov, who, as secretary of the Central Committee of the party, knew its cadres better than anyone, pointed out that the party was stretched thin by the demands from the new local organizations for qualified workers and by the immediate need to conduct party agitation and propaganda among the peasantry, something the party had not been doing systematically long before October. The situation was exacerbated, he continued, by a lack of information on the size of individual party organizations, the complete disappearance of many, and the emergence of new ones.[19] In May, the Central Committee sent a circular letter to "all committees, all groups of the Russian Communist Party, all members of the party," describing the wretched state of the organization:

We are experiencing an extremely acute, critical period…. As a result of the departure of masses of responsible party workers [*rabotniki*] to Soviet [governmental] activity,… as a result of the influx into our party of broad masses, who have joined it only recently, the harmoniousness [*stroinost'*] and discipline of our organizations have been severely impaired. The emergence in the party of a special tendency, so-called "Left Communism," contributes to this trend. All members of the party must be aware of the severity of our crisis, must know the results of the disarray that has started in the party ranks…. The worker masses will not be able to hold on to the power won by them in the October Days, if there is no powerful will permeated by unity.[20]

Another Central Committee memo expressed concern over the quality of the membership, conflicts within the local organizations, weakened discipline, and a deterioration in party work. The party, it informed local organizations, should not be a place for "the idle, hooligans, adventurists, drunks, and thieves… vacillators and unsteady people" but should "become whole, forged from a unified group."[21] At stake was nothing less than posterity itself, with *Pravda* musing on the difficult task facing the "future historian" of a party whose central committee had little idea of the state of its local organizations, rarely receiving any of their publications, resolutions, proclamations, decrees, or minutes of meetings.[22]

At the Eighth Party Congress in March 1919, Bolshevik concerns about the internal state of the party and the perception of it in the broad population were even more acute than a year earlier. One after another, Bolshevik leaders recited a litany of ills. Most devastating in his criticism was N. Osinskii, an editor of *Pravda*, who decried the growing bureaucratism, the demise of party activity, and the absence of any links between the center and the lower ranks of the party. In the past year, he said, "our party has had no political line." In a final comment to which the party leaders would have been especially sensitive, given the earlier Menshevik and SR attacks on the "emptiness" of their "paper revolution," Osinskii said that "many of our good words remain on paper." Despite periodic attempts to restrict or even cut off debate on this subject, particularly when local representatives of the party were to be given the floor, the catalog of ills continued. V. P. Nogin, a member of a Central Committee commission investigating the state of the party organization, reported that the commission had received "such an endless number of horrifying facts about drunkenness, debauchery, bribe taking, robbery, and reckless acts by many party workers that it makes one's hair stand on end." Furthermore, he said, most of the people who had created the local organizations of the party had stopped working in the party. Even party activists who were most critical of such negative comments, such as L. S. Sosnovskii, N. A. Skrypnik, and V. A. Avanesov, agreed that there was a "colossal shortage of party workers... who can understand [party] decrees correctly and grasp correctly the meaning of the circular letters from the Central Committee and correctly interpret them in terms of party life." The party, argued another speaker at the congress, was full of people "with party cards but carrying nothing [*bez bagazha*] in their heads." [23]

Notwithstanding Lunacharsky's assertion that the first anniversary celebration of October 25 "was also the great celebration of our party," many leading Bolsheviks saw instead broad popular ignorance of what their party, or their revolution, signified. [24] Lenin had found himself in a "nasty position" at the Seventh Party Congress when asked by a Swedish socialist: "But what is the program of your party—is it the same as that of the Mensheviks?" Such a "monstrous contradiction," Lenin continued, could not be allowed to stand. [25] The inauguration at the congress of the term "Communist" into the official idiom had, some argued, only caused more confusion between Communist and Bolshevik. By changing the name of the RSDRP(b) to the VKP(b), argued Iurii Steklov, the editor of *Izvestiia*, the party was in effect ceding the long years of revolutionary prestige garnered under the name of the RSDRP to the Mensheviks and their kind. The word "Communist," he added, "will say something for... the leaders—for the masses it will be a minus."[26]

In 1918 and 1919, Bolshevik leaders directly addressed the most negative popular images. "Everywhere you hear only: 'Bolsheviks, Bolsheviks, who are these Bolsheviks'?" wrote Zinoviev in 1918. [27] He added elsewhere that the "male and female workers who have recently arrived from the village and did not participate in the first revolution in 1905" thought that the Communist Party had been in existence "for only a few days [*bez godu nedelia*]." He acknowledged that a widespread belief existed that Communists were greedy self-servers, but noted that in fact these so-called Communists were "not Communist at all.... They represent bourgeois spawn... which has wormed itself into our ranks." [28] Zinoviev stretched the Communist origins to their limits: "The Party of Communists, in the broad sense of the word, if you include the international workers' movement, has existed not for one year, not two, and not even two decades, but for seventy-two years," namely since the *Communist Manifesto* of Marx and Engels.[29] His thumbnail sketch of the history of the Bolshevik Party since 1903 quietly excised the Mensheviks: "The Bolsheviks are,... in short, the toiling people of the towns and villages. They joined together, formed one society—a *party*, which is called the Russian Social Democratic Labor Party." [30] (emphasis in original)

THE HARMONY OF RITUAL

Surrounded, as they saw it, by disarray, crisis, uncertainty, and popular ignorance of their cause, the Bolsheviks and other revolutionaries strove to convey the discipline, unity, commitment, and clarity of meaning of a committed revolutionary life. Of course, revolutionaries disagreed over how this clarity might be achieved. Their methods ranged from the obliteration of Russia's cultural heritage desired by Futurists, to the making of a new proletarian culture through such movements as Proletkult, dedicated to the creation of a specifically proletarian class literature.[31]

Inspired by, among other works, the Russian edition of Julien Tiersot's *Les fêtes et les chants de la révolution française*, first published in Paris in 1908, some revolutionary artists turned to ritualized and theatricalized performances of their tales of revolution, although Lunacharsky himself believed that Soviet efforts fell short of the creative genius of the French.[32] Through such performances they sought to transcend the linguistic and cultural barriers they saw separating the broad population from the revolutionary project. In the service of the revolutionary state, these rituals helped to demarcate the ideological, social, and political bounds and bonds of the new order, asserting new "definitions of significant social relations."[33] "The ultimate message is clear," writes Florencia Mallon in her study of the role of Cinco de Mayo parades in the creation of a "revolutionary" culture in Mexico, "only those who march to the right music and the right beat can participate."[34] Routine and ritualized celebrations of the October Revolution, explicitly on the anniversaries of October 25, but also on other dates under other guises (for example, May Day, Bloody Sunday on January 22, the February Revolution on March 12), provided opportunities for the new Soviet rulers to rededicate the revolution to changing circumstances and to draw specific sections of the population into an active relationship with it.[35]

The annual celebration of October represented what von Geldern has called in another context "a fixed point that prevents the onset of chaos and allows for meaning and hierarchy."[36] Throughout the next three years, the party provided significant resources and opportunities to present the "drama of power to the people."[37] Those who organized the celebrations sought to provide an easily read script of revolution by controlling both their "aesthetic form and ritual performance."[38] The English, French, and Russian cameramen who shot documentary footage of the funerals, parades, and processions were filming nothing less than the script of revolution in its form at that time, with the new technology of film adding its own imprimatur to that script.[39] The control over the Communist celebrations extended both to the *pre*-scripting and *post*-scripting of the celebrations, an effort by the party and its agents to mold a new social and political landscape for this society.[40] The Bolshevik press carefully explained the structure and significance of the celebrations in the days preceding them and their significance and popular reception after them. Given the repressive press conditions after the summer of 1918, these readings of the celebrations should not be confused with "popular" reactions to them. They are what they are, parts of the process of creating a foundation event.

HUNGRY OCTOBER

Through its form and content, the official anniversary celebration of October in November 1918 contrasted the present turmoil and chaos with the possibilities of an organized revolutionary state. First, by feeding into the established cultural practice of regularized celebrations of great events, the regime telegraphed the stature of the October Revolution to the population. Second, the celebrations provided the population with multiple means and sites at which to experience an October that would be tailored to changing needs over time. Third, they provided the new leaders with a focus for their continuing efforts to tell their tale of October. Finally, the form and content of the official celebrations in Moscow and Petrograd were reprised across Soviet Russia.[41] The organizers of the anniversary celebrations of the October Revolution in 1918 attempted to use them not only to convey a set of revolutionary virtues to the population but also to provide a symbolic representation of the class contours of the new revolutionary society and the major moments of the October Revolution. The meticulously choreographed celebrations also betrayed, perhaps, an uncertainty among the leaders as to the status of this new regime, in the provinces in particular; there was also a certain mistrust of the population at large and of the kind of activity it was capable of generating on its own. Generations of Russian revolutionaries of all kinds had long harbored ambivalent feelings about the independent activity (*samodeiatel'nost'*) of the masses.

A week before the anniversary celebrations, the regime set up an organizing committee (Komitet po organizatsii Oktiabr'skikh prazdnestv) under Kamenev and Vadim Podbel'skii, the head of the Post and Telegraph Service. This committee was subdivided into subcommittees dealing with various aspects of the celebrations: Theater, Music, and Fine Arts (Sektsiia teatral'no-muzykal'naia i izobrazitel'nykh iskusstv); Technical-management (Tekhnichesko-khoziaizstvennaia sektsiia); Route and Pyrotechnics (Marshrutno-pirotekhnicheskaia sektsiia); Communications and Information (Sviazi i Informatsii); Agitation (Agitatsionnaia sektsiia); Food Supply (Prodovol'stvennaia sektsiia); and Transport (Transportnaia sektsiia).[42] The strict hierarchy was intended to convey a sense that the workers themselves were responsible for this mass celebration of the new state. "Exemplary proletarian order," assured one article, "would reign during the celebrations, and

4. The *Krasnaia gazeta* Car in Petrograd at the First Anniversary of the October Revolution (Courtesy of the State Central Museum of Contemporary History of Russia)

only strict comradely discipline and restraint of the worker masses will create such order."[43]

The disbursement of revolutionary largesse in the form of food was a major part of the committee's planned activities in 1918. After all, for good reason in the extremely straitened conditions in the capitals, the 1918 celebration was known as the "hungry anniversary."[44] The mass feeding of the population of Moscow planned for the day of the celebration was meticulously organized. On October 23, an organizational meeting was held by representatives of the Soviet food supply organizations and the military authorities (*Voennoe Vedomstvo*) on this question. After an exchange of opinions, it was decided to choose a commission from these representatives to organize the public feeding on the day of celebration over the whole of Russia; it would communicate its directives to the provinces by newspaper and telegraph.[45] Although the commission voted down a proposal by some of its members to provide free dinners for the entire 1.4 million people of Moscow, it passed a proposal to raise food rations for all "categories" and to supplement them with fish, butter, and other "luxury" items. Official bodies, such as factory-plant committees, promised a hundred free cigarettes per person.[46] The newspapers carried repeated assurances that these new rations would indeed be forthcoming on the day.[47] Prisoners in Moscow jails were also slated to receive supplementary rations.[48] On October 23, 1918, the Soviet government officially communicated to the German government a request that Russian prisoners of war be permitted to celebrate the new national holiday of November 7 (moved from October because of the new calendar) with a day off work and distribution of parcels, and that they "be informed of this at the same time in an appropriate fashion." [49]

Izvestiia announced that children's rations would be raised according to age group (up to three years old, three to twelve, and so on).[50] Children were a special, and highly publicized, priority of the upcoming celebrations. From young people, one article noted, could be expected "complete understanding and fervent sympathy for the great overthrow."[51] *Izvestiia* called on students in late October 1918: "Every social group, every individual, had attentively to scrutinize the path they had traveled and in criticism of the past year build a program of future activity."[52] A special children's committee (Detskii komitet po ustroistvu Oktiabr'skikh torzhestv) planned a variety of instructive entertainments for November 7 for young people of all ages, including matinee shows in local cinemas, performances of children's ballets, puppet shows such as *David and Goliath* in the central theaters of Moscow; all were free, of course. On the day of the celebration, the older children were to go from their schools to the nearest squares to hear speakers explain the significance of the October Revolution, and later that day every school would be required to send a delegation to Red Square to attend the unveiling of memorial plaques and lay wreaths at the graves of the "victims of the October Revolution."[53]

The visible "fruits" of this new regime also came in the form of free concerts and shows (*spektakli*) arranged by the local organizing committees at the behest of the Moscow Organizing Committee. Directors of the state theaters, it was announced, had been brought in to stage plays and ballets, traditional and modern, for the workers of the regions of Moscow.[54] The choice of plays to perform sometimes presented a problem, there being few in the "old treasure house of mankind," as Lunacharsky put it, that met the new demands, although some, such as Romain Rolland's *The Taking of the Bastille* and Schiller's *William Tell* were "more or less in harmony with our mood."[55] Plans were also announced to send about seventy troupes of actors to the front to perform shows, plays, and ballets for the troops; they were designed to invoke "a spirit of heroism and a cheerful mood." [56] In honor of the day of celebration, an order was issued that "not a single shot" be fired. Presumably, as a proof of revolutionary righteousness and honor, the order also threatened with punishment any "scoundrel" who fired from behind a corner, from a window or a roof.[57]

The meticulous nature of these plans showed a desire by the new leaders to convey as clear and homogeneous a reading of the celebrations as possible to the population. Spectators and participants were often provided with direct explanations of what they were experiencing at the celebrations. The "political significance" of the communal feeding, it was stated in a typical sentiment, was obtained "by freeing the female from the preparation of dinner at home and creating a mood of freedom and solidarity of the proletarian masses, when everyone will realize that the government has taken care of all those who took part in the festivities."[58] *Pravda* printed a short primer for party organizations on what had to be discussed at mass meetings organized in honor of October. The article began with the usual caveat that the "depth" of the October Revolution could not, of course, be "appreciated at the present moment" and that, for this reason, it was not surprising that the regional committee of the party was receiving requests from local areas for instructions on how "to explain the meaning of the October Revolution to the broad toiling masses." Local agitators were instructed to "characterize the activity of the Provisional Government as purely bourgeois in composition (Miliukovian) and also as coalitionist (Kerenskian)" and to stress its unwillingness to accommodate the desires of the workers and peasants. In addition, the "treachery" of the Mensheviks and SRs after the February Revolution had to be contrasted with the "revolutionary consistency of the Bolshevik Party on all questions." The article outlined the major events to be focused upon, from the July Days of 1917 through the Kornilov plot, to the Preparliament, representing these events both as a crusade of the counterrevolution against the workers and peasants and as the "growth of the October Revolution." The major events of the October Revolution itself were deemed to be the formation in Petrograd of the MRC; the Second Congress of Soviets; the formation of Sovnarkom (the Council of People's Commissars) and the decrees on peace, land, and workers' control. The article dealt not only with the prescribed framework but also indicated that the events had to be conveyed "in such a spirit that the October Revolution in Russia is the greatest stimulus for all workers of all countries."[59] Leading Bolsheviks were often assigned to address such mass meetings in order to explain the "results of the October Revolution" to the assembled.[60] In the press, the entrance of these leaders into the halls or squares where they were addressing the crowds was always heralded by "colossal choirs and orchestras," and they became paragons of revolutionary heroism and asceticism: Sverdlov in his leather jacket "literally molded from steel"; Lenin "simple, clear with a mild smile on his face," who at a mass meeting in Red Square was raised aloft by those around him.[61]

The Bolshevik press physically framed its coverage of the celebrations with reports on the revolutionary situation in Germany and the rest of Europe, which had been "sparked" by October, usually in terms that related these events to the Russian experience.[62] Leading Bolsheviks stressed the historical uniqueness of October, contrasting the revolution's survival with the failures of earlier promising uprisings of the "working class," most notably in Paris in 1848 and 1871, and in Russia in 1905. They also stressed October's role as the spark that would ignite revolution throughout Europe and ultimately the world, evidence of which could already be seen in Bulgaria, Germany, and Austro-Hungary.[63] Of course, in many countries workers were "bound hand and foot by imperialist reaction" and were thus unable to "raise their voices," although in those countries where these bonds were not so tight, such as Switzerland and Germany, local organizations had undertaken to celebrate the anniversary of October.[64]

Celebratory exhibitions in the capitals presented visual depictions of October. A large exhibition in Moscow entitled "One Year of Proletarian Revolution [*God proletarskoi revoliutsii*]" filled several halls on Tverskaia Street with books, newspapers, photographs, and illustrations pertaining to the October Revolution. *Izvestiia* pointed out that many photographs and drawings were on display showing "various moments of the revolution," such as the "uprising of the proletariat, the Congress of the Committees of the Village Poor, barricades, firing on the streets, the graves of fallen fighters." The communal dining room in the building, the newspaper noted, undoubtedly helped bring people in to the exhibition.[65]

Meaning did not inhere in the artifacts and symbols invoked by the new regime. "The Bolsheviks," von Geldern points out, "came to power with few symbols of their own," instead sharing certain symbols with other radical parties.[66] They took pains to provide the necessary explanations for the symbols and signs of the new order. A decree on the "Monuments of the Republic," signed on April 13, 1918, ordered the removal from streets and squares of monuments erected in honor of the tsars that were interesting "neither from a historical nor artistic perspective." Broad artistic competitions were announced for designs for monuments that would "mark the great days of the Russian Socialist Revolution."[67] The monuments, statues, and emblems were always accompanied by an explanation of their significance, a significance that could be given different inflections over time.[68] The many new monuments and statues being planned for Moscow and Petrograd were fitted with explanatory plaques, or more ambitious ways of conveying their meaning. The publishing department of the Moscow Soviet, for example, announced its plans to publish in honor of October a series of popularly written and accessible biographies of "well-known activists" to whom monuments were being erected, including Marx, Engels, Robespierre, Rodin, Voltaire, Radishchev, Rimsky-Korsakov, Shevchenko, Hugo, Zola, and Beethoven. In these pamphlets, the "historical situation will be characterized... in which the activity of these public figures, writers, or artists took part."[69]

The meaning of symbolic manifestations of the celebrations was explained in detail beforehand in the press. In the fireworks display that lit up the skies of Moscow on November 6, for example, the exploding rockets "meant that the edifice of capitalism is collapsing, burying under its debris the exploiters and oppressors."[70] The ubiquitous hammer and sickle invariably shone "in the crown of light of the rising sun."[71] The Moscow Organizing Committee of the anniversary celebrations declared on November 1 that at nine o'clock in the evening of November 7 each region should hold a ritual burning of the "Old Imperialist Order" and the rising from the ashes of the "New System" at a centrally located square. An appropriate symbol, made of lightweight, combustible material, should embody all of the "elements of the Old Order: capitalists, priests, police," a central place among these emblems being occupied by the "contemporary pillar [stolb] of international imperialism."[72] On the ashes must be raised an appropriate emblem of the "New Socialist System," to be decided on by local regional comrades. The meaning of the celebrations was relayed in more oblique and creative ways too. The People's Commissariat of Enlightenment (Narodnyi Komissariat Prosveshcheniia, or Narkompros) planned to mark the celebrations with displays of modern technology, intending to illuminate the entire center and outskirts of Moscow with enormous batteries of floodlights projecting moving images on the sky. These celebrations would open with a flyover of fifteen airplanes and an aerial display from the Moscow Aviation School.[73]

The cities of Moscow and Petrograd were linguistically and physically landscaped as revolution, most obviously in the christening of streets and buildings with new revolutionary names.[74] In Moscow, Red Square was draped in black and red flags, the entire length of the Kremlin wall hung with posters. Red and black banners ran the length of the square from St. Basil's to the Iverskii Gate. The black banners carried slogans in honor of fallen comrades; the red banners bore revolutionary slogans. The Bolshoi and Malyi Theaters were also draped in flags and posters with edifying slogans.[75] Similar decorations adorned the buildings and squares of Petrograd, the organizing body there allocating over 160,000 yards of red material for the decoration of seventy-one key "points and buildings."[76] The still unformed nature of the narrative of October was well-served by its symbolic reduction to block colors and sharp contrasts, a corollary of the continuing attempts to define by contrast (Us/Them, Red/White) rather than by nuanced distinction.[77] Import, if not unequivocal meaning, was conveyed by the choice of triumphal music to mark the programs of evening entertainments. The program at the National Choral Academy (Narodnaia Khorovaia Akademiia) on November 8 consisted of Berlioz's *Triumphal Symphony*, Chesnokov's *Songs of Revolution*, and Beethoven's "Ode to Joy."[78] Emotive music, from a Chopin funeral march to the "Internationale," and solemn rituals were intended to heighten the impact of the designated sites on the marchers' route. At Mars Field, two delegates from a designated region were to ascend a special platform and, as a sign of allegiance, strike an anvil with a hammer at the same time as the orchestras and choir performed the "Internationale."[79]

In the 1918 celebrations, Smolny was presented as the focus of October. It became a "fairy-tale castle" in press reports: "The center of all festive celebrations of the Great October Revolution was Smolny which, as comrade Lunacharsky said in his speech, serves as the cradle of the social revolution of the entire world."[80] The "grandiose work" announced to prepare it for the celebration included a twenty-one–meter high, three-tiered triumphal arch in front of the "residence of the leaders of the October Revolution," bearing the slogan "Workers of the World Unite."[81] The semicircle of the adjacent square was artistically decorated, and the left and right sides of the entrance were topped by turrets that lent the gates an old-Russian style. Obelisks along the entire semicircle were draped in garlands of green and red material, and posters were hung between them with such slogans as "Long Live the International Congress of Soviets." All of the processions on November 7 marched to Smolny, and in the evening it was the venue of a ceremonial meeting of the Petrograd Soviet addressed by various high-ranking party and government officials.[82] The Winter Palace, by contrast, was apparently not even on the routes of the processions.[83] It had been decorated "in a severely reserved style," the grilles draped with red material and garlands of green, while huge red panels covered the yellow walls. The palace and Uritskii (formerly Palace) Square produced a "strictly harmonious, soft, soothing impression."[84]

The processions were microcosms of the new social order, illustrations of the new hierarchy of Soviet society. Tight control over participation and access signaled the new system of supervision, privilege, and exclusion. A special information office (Informatsionnoe Biuro) was set up to issue all instructions and permits for Moscow and the provinces.[85] In the city, it was announced that, in the interests of "an organized and planned execution of the celebrations," all central and regional bodies participating in the celebrations must act in constant communication with the representatives of the Organizing Committee. The committee introduced a system of passes intended to control access to various parts of the celebrations. The Organizing Committee members and their representatives were to receive round passes that gave them unfettered access to all venues, while special triangular passes were needed for automobile use on the days of the celebrations. All theaters, cinemas, and concert halls would be open only to those who possessed tickets obtained from appropriate distribution committees. All speakers at public functions could be summoned only via the Moscow Committee of the Russian Communist Party.[86] Every public and government body that wished to march in a procession had to inform the regional Route Commission (Marshrutnaia Komissiia) by November 3; failure to do so resulted in exclusion from the procession.[87] Automobiles or motorcycles could be used in the processions only with the explicit prior approval of the Transport Section.[88] Indeed, automobiles in general could be used on November 6 and 7 only if they displayed a special pass from the Organizing Committee.[89]

The processions that formed a major part of the two days of celebrations must have presented a stark contrast to the prerevolutionary tsarist processions of the elites of that society. On the first day of the celebrations in November 1918, each worker region (*raion*) was to send a procession on a predetermined route in the direction of Smolny, paying respects on the way at various memorials to the "victims of the October Revolution." The procession had to be composed of representatives, in columns of ten to twelve, of various organizations in that region: the standard-bearer carrying a banner was followed by an orchestra, after which came a member of the executive committee (*ispolkom*) of the regional soviet, then the regional committee of the Communist Party, representatives of the Red Army, Red Navy, and so on. The second day's processions would be divided up by membership in trade unions, eighteen in all, ranging from the Union of Metal-workers at the front to the Union of Railroad Workers bringing up the rear.

In early November, newspapers began carrying a list of recommended slogans for people to use on their banners during the processions. The suggestions did not include explicitly Bolshevik slogans. They proclaimed the harmony and self-discipline of the new order in typically polarized class terms, the self-sacrificing toilers versus the parasitic bourgeoisie, the revolutionary selflessness of workers versus the self-serving greed of allied capital.[90] Newspaper reports mentioned female workers only in their function of distributing badges to the marchers at the start of the procession and taking collections among them for gifts for Red Army soldiers. Peasants figured in the event only as "guests," occupying spectators' platforms on Mars Field and at Smolny, lumped together at the latter venue with "foreign guests" in a crowd of some two thousand invited spectators.[91] At a joint meeting of representatives of Communist organizations and soviets from Moscow's regions on October 20, Grigorii Belenkii, a member of the Moscow Committee of the party, impressed on them that the most important aspect of the celebration of the anniversary of the revolution was not its external features, the decorations, processions, and so on, but rather its internal manifestation, its "spiritual power [*dukhovnaia moshch'*]." This power, he implied, would be felt by all "genuine supporters of Soviet power" as they marched together in the demonstrations and processions.[92] The celebrations left no doubt as to who qualified as such.

OCTOBER BESIEGED

The anniversary celebrations of October one year later shared the general goals of the 1918 anniversary, although financial constraints cut them to fit the different needs of a country in the depths of the Civil War. Reports of the plans for the upcoming celebrations did not give an impression of ambitious and meticulous organization but rather of uncoordinated and hurried projects.[93] Many of these projects had an experimental flavor to them.[94] The Petrograd Provincial Department of Labor (Petrogradskii Gubernskii Otdel Truda) announced that the October Revolution would this year be celebrated only on one day, November 7.[95] The sumptuous decorations of the first anniversary contrasted with the far fewer adornments of the 1919 celebrations. Despite their modest scale, implied *Krasnaia gazeta*, their significance was even greater than in 1918, with gun emplacements and barbed-wire barricades being the city's primary decoration now: "Red Petrograd was clad in iron armor, under the blows, the final blows of the dying counterrevolution, and in iron armor it meets its great holiday." The insecurities of the besieged regime were evident in the article's raising of the specter of mass action: "What other power would risk constructing inside the town this formidable network of fortifications if it were not able to rely upon the greatest trust and the greatest support from the toiling masses?"[96] Gone were the ambitious plans of 1918 to feed great numbers of people in the capitals. In their place was the more modest goal of providing a "celebratory meal" for the children in the regions of Moscow, and additional rations in the form of meat, caviar, jam, white bread, chocolate, red wine, and cigarettes for wounded Red Army soldiers.[97] Free concerts and shows, to be accompanied by mass meetings, as well as plays stressing revolutionary content were announced for the day of the festivities, although not on the scale of 1918.[98] The processions of marchers once again filed from the local worker regions of Petrograd to congregate at Smolny, but this year Smolny seemed to bear mute witness to the revolutionary celebration: "And there, at the top, from one of Smolny's windows, the head of a child poked out. Wide-eyed, it watched the unprecedented spectacle. An unforgettable impression will remain with it of the procession of Petrograd workers."[99] This year the Winter Palace (by now renamed the Palace of Arts [Dvorets Iskusstv]) was to host a ceremonial meeting of the Petrograd Soviet at noon on November 6.[100] On the following day, the processions passed buildings decorated in red material and flying flags and banners. "Long Live Our Glorious Red Army," and other such slogans, proposed this year by the Moscow Committee of the RKP, reflected present concerns about the Civil War and the deprivations it had brought in its wake.[101]

The 1919 anniversary was written as a metaphor of revolution under siege, with commentators drawing explicit historical parallels with other such incidences.[102] October became an explanation for the personal daily vicissitudes suffered by the population as a result of Civil War conditions. Articles on the forthcoming celebrations were framed on newspaper pages by reports on the Civil War.[103] In Petrograd, Zinoviev linked the direness of everyday conditions (severe depopulation, hunger, disease, murder of worker leaders) to the critical place occupied by the city itself as the most sublime expression of the October Revolution: "Nowhere in Russia is the beating of the pulse of the proletarian struggle felt so vitally as it is in Petrograd…. Go out onto the streets and squares of Petrograd. There… every stone is a piece of the history of the Russian Revolution."[104] On November 7, 1919, Lenin, in a greeting to the workers of Petrograd on their holiday, wrote that the "banner of the proletarian revolution," raised by the workers and toiling peasantry, still waved, "despite the difficulties and torment of hunger, cold, destruction and ruin… despite the furious spite and opposition of the bourgeoisie, despite the military invasion of world imperialism."[105] As if to deflect comparison with the earlier privations of the war under the tsar, the press did its best to equate the people's tribulations with the just revolution they themselves had carried out: "Many and continuous are the sacrifices borne by the Russian workers, by all toilers of Russia in this struggle. They were the first ones who had to light this red torch themselves."[106] Speakers looked forward to the third year of revolution, which, they assured their audiences, would be a "year of victory."[107]

WRITING THE RECEPTION

As Raleigh points out, the party's strict control of these public festivals makes it very difficult to gauge "how they might have fired the imagination of their participants."[108] Press descriptions cannot be relied on to show that these early celebrations possessed a "fresh, spontaneous, improvised quality and an atmosphere of chaotic enthusiasm and communal feeling," in contrast to the routinized structure of later festivals. [109] Every aspect of the celebrations—form, content, and the description of their reception—was designed to convey harmony and clarity of meaning. The celebrations were popular, went the argument in the Communist press, *because* the populace understood what they signified. *Pravda* gushed: "What enthusiasm, what rejoicing" on the faces of the people in the streets, who "walk arm in arm and laugh, and sing free and proud songs." The symbolic burning of the Old Regime at 8 p.m. at the *Lobnoe mesto* (the prerevolutionary "place of proclamations" on Red Square) was watched by approving crowds, who "understand completely the significance of the great holiday of the October Revolution."[110] "The streets of Petrograd," wrote one observer in a special anniversary publication, "splendidly decorated and embellished, tell better than words and articles of the great force, the power of the state apparatus. A gray day became a holiday for the entire population,… the broadest circles, which were *only now* [emphasis added] being touched by the movement, took part in the processions and gatherings."[111]

The processions were always composed of festive workers, soldiers, and sailors; the slogans were revolutionary, the strains of the "Internationale" spontaneous and transcendent. "Exemplary order" reigned throughout, proof that the proletariat had "grown up" and "no longer needs nursemaids in the form of policemen."[112] The milling crowds were "literally overwhelmed by the beauty of the spectacle" of the illumination lights.[113] "In joyfully Red, revolutionary Petrograd," wrote the Old Bolshevik Vladimir Bonch-Bruevich, "the people celebrated victory over the dumbstruck class enemy."[114] Often the atmosphere was described as so infectious that it seized hold not only of the workers "but also of the broad masses of the petite bourgeoisie [*meshchanstvo*] and intelligentsia, who until then had reacted neutrally or even with hidden hostility to the festival of the revolution."[115] Even the "most inveterate enemies of the worker-peasant revolution," in spite of themselves, showed delight at the decorated buildings and squares.[116] The communal singing was often represented as a metaphor for the power inherent in common action: "From the look of them, each individually would in no way raise a voice, but here, together with the others, walking side by side, each wants to sing more loudly." Even the weather signified a positive response to the celebrations, frequently providing a metaphor for the promise of October, as the gray, rainy day invariably gave way to more auspicious skies: "The sky is bluer. The sun shines brightly. It wants to light up this November day because this day is great. It will be remembered eternally, this Red day."[117]

The imposition of strict press censorship by June–July 1918 ensured that there would be few alternative readings of these celebrations inside Soviet Russia. An article in a non-Bolshevik newspaper before censorship suggests how a public critique of these celebrations might have sounded. A report on a mass demonstration in late 1917 saw in the event nothing but an illustration of official coercion of and isolation from the population. "Official in character" (*kazennyi kharakter*), the report observed, the affair could muster fewer workers and soldiers than usual and, in this instance, fewer workers than soldiers. Plants had refused to take part, the article continued, in response to a call by the Union for the Defense of the Constituent Assembly (Soiuz zashchity Uchreditel'nogo Sobraniia) and, instead, held mass meetings in their factories. Most ominously, the article concluded, the procession route was unusual in that it filed past a German delegation. [118] After censorship, there remained only occasional oblique critiques of this kind. One article noted an earlier "bourgeois" criticism of these kinds of celebrations that had pointed out their "narrowly class content" and described the May Day parades of 1918 as a "military parade." [119]

Opposing readings of these celebrations were generally confined to personal diaries and private correspondence. The prominent historian Iurii Got'e wrote in his diary on November 5, 1918 that Moscow was preparing for the revolutionary anniversary with banners and decorations with "bloodthirsty slogans." The increased rations were but bribes to curry favor with the population. On November

7, he joined the crowds on Tverskaia: "Like any Russian crowd, it was somber and dull; the side streets were dark and quiet, and there were even few flags. There are no newspapers, nor news bulletins, even cut and distorted; some people are having a good time, others dissemble, yet others wait." [120] In foreign published reminiscences of his time in Russia, John Pollock, an Englishman doing relief work among war refugees from early 1915 until the middle of 1919, described the celebrations as shabby and forced affairs. Most of the thirty million rubles allotted for anniversary decorations in Petrograd, he wrote, was siphoned off into various pockets: "Never were decorations so skimpy.... Many were the old May Day banners, violent puzzles in crimson and black, now somewhat fly-blown. The new efforts were beneath contempt, and the illuminations at night unworthy of a seaside subscription dance." No harmony and purpose here; only coerced attendance could be seen in the faces of those in the processions, only indifference in the eyes of those watching them:

> On the first day of the jubilation, processions dragged along the main streets laboriously, eyes fixed on the ground. They were a sorry sight and of far less interest than the way they had been assembled.... At night crowds of the country "poor" and townspeople, curious to see if anything would happen, drifted about in silence; there was no enthusiasm, nor indeed emotion of any kind. For what was being celebrated?... Festivity, to be successful, must have some reason.[121]

A year later, the more muted celebrations evoked even deeper depression in Got'e at their hopelessness and emptiness. In his diary entry for November 8, 1919, they became a metaphor for his own unrelieved gloom at Russia's situation:

> That is how my view of the world of the last few days can be described. Unrelieved gloom. One can only await what happens, without making any kind of plans or calculations. Yesterday's festivities were much more modest than last year. No kind of handouts to the inhabitants except a half-pound of white bread to the children. The school lunches are much skimpier than last year. Everything that was left has been given to the Red Army men. I didn't see the demonstrations, but in places they were thin, and in other places people were herded into them by force. The crowds of demonstrators that together with troops made up an adequate number of people in the necessary places were collected by those means.[122]

The celebrations were certainly criticized inside Soviet Russia, but in terms that merely reinforced the integrity of the narrative of revolution. If the celebrations had failed, in the view of some critics, it was in their creators' technical or aesthetic inability to do justice to October. [123] It was regrettable, if understandable, according to an article in the journal of the Department of Fine Arts (Otdel Izobrazitel'nykh Iskusstv) of Narkompros, that, for lack of time and experience, barely a fifth of the plans for the celebrations had been realized. More disturbing, however, was that the festivities and decorations bore striking similarities to those of prerevolutionary "tsarist days." The problem lay not with any inadequately developed "proletarian taste" but with those artists in charge who "had pondered little over the idea of the celebration."[124] The artists, wrote the critic Lev Pumpianskii, "had still not 'immersed themselves in [*vchuvstvovalis' v*]' the revolution, had not nurtured in themselves the splendid, thunderous energy with which the contemporary air itself was saturated." They failed to capture the spirit of the October Revolution because they had not made themselves the "condensers and preservers of this energy."[125] The Futurists were particularly critical of the role here of the intelligentsia for failing to realize that the proletariat needed an art "born from the noise of factories, plants, streets," rather than from the "quiet, pitiful strains of guitars and violins that caressed the ears of the bourgeois ensconced in their cozy apartments."[126] Such critiques of the "silence of art" since October 1917 called for a fresh art cut to the changed times.[127] "All parties to the debate over style," in von Geldern's words, "agreed that artists should devote themselves to the Revolution. The real disagreement was over the nature of the duty and how it should be met."[128] Although the artistic dispute is often couched in terms of exuberant artists clamoring for artistic elbow room from an inherently conservative Bolshevik regime, the Bolshevik Party per se was not a decisive factor for these artists at this point. As Katerina Clark points out, Petrograd intellectuals worked largely unhampered by the Bolshevik authorities during the period of War Communism, and cultural bodies were run largely by nonparty intellectuals.[129] In these early years, it was still possible for intellectuals to support the revolution without explicitly supporting the Bolsheviks.

REDS AND WHITES

For those who created these red funerals, political demonstrations, and revolutionary festivals in 1918 and 1919, the legitimacy of October was beyond question. They consciously and unconsciously contrasted the order and meaning of revolutionary commitment with the disorder and emptiness of passivity and ambivalence. In the charged atmosphere of Civil War Russia, they contributed with their efforts to the inexorable polarization of political life that would ultimately demand commitment (both political and military) from more and more segments of the population in the form of increasingly stark choices in this new regime: worker versus bourgeois, Us versus Them, Red versus White.[130] The Civil War, in Bolshevik representations, was a war between revolution and counterrevolution, and not, as the conference of the Menshevik RSDRP at the end of December 1918 argued, a civil war *within* the various "democratic forces [*demokratiia*]."[131] The Bolsheviks saw no reason to draw any such "forces" together to fight the "real" counterrevolution of foreigners, Russian capitalists, and landowners as defined by the Mensheviks and SRs. Only through ever sharper social and political polarization, the Bolsheviks believed, could the revolution be secured for Russia's proletariat.

The poet and playwright Vladimir Mayakovsky captured this process of polarization strikingly in his 1918 drama, *Mystery Bouffe* (*Misteriia-Buff*). Praising it as the rare play that met the needs of the time, being "comprehensible to anyone," Lunacharsky expressed fears that the Futurists who were to stage it would make "a million mistakes," inserting into it "eccentricities" inherited from the "Old World." [132] The play was a paean to the October Revolution, intended by Mayakovsky to resonate with the times: "We glorify / the day of / uprisings, rebellions, revolutions." [133] Seven pairs of Clean (the bourgeois) and seven pairs of Unclean (the proletarians) survive the elemental Flood of Revolution in an ark. The play follows the protagonists from the reestablishment of the old order by the bourgeoisie to the reemergence of the workers from their banishment in the ark's hold to seize power and throw the bourgeoisie overboard. In the final scenes, they meet again in Hell, the bourgeoisie, unimproved by their recent experiences, destined to languish there in the Past, the proletariat, their spirits forged in revolution, to proceed to the Promised Land and enjoy the Future.[134] *Mystery Bouffe* was notable for the lack of shading and nuance in its characterizations and plot. Its world, in von Geldern's words, "was remarkable for its incapacity for compromise…. On the stage, no meeting of worlds was possible…. Conflict—the revolution—was a meeting of opposites that could not end in truce." [135] Mayakovsky was drawing on the general polarizing trend in post-October political and cultural life, and others, Gorky and Lunacharsky included, had argued against any "half tones" in the theater, in the interests of rendering plays more accessible to the audiences. [136]

At this stage, however, this polarizing trend did not involve a choice for or against the Bolsheviks per se. *Mystery Bouffe* contained no Bolsheviks, but not, as von Geldern implies, because it was conceived before October 1917. [137] After all, Mayakovsky wrote it for the most part in 1918, completing it shortly before the anniversary celebrations. It was, in fact, the norm at this time to write the

October Revolution without the Bolshevik Party. The ubiquitous worker figure that was featured in Soviet posters became explicitly *Bolshevik* only in the course of the 1920s. [138]

AND BOLSHEVIKS

The reluctance of Bolshevik leaders to write an unequivocal role for the Bolshevik Party in the October Revolution contrasted with the central place accorded it in the coup narrative by the opposition press. It also conflicted somewhat with the Bolsheviks' own efforts to create an international party profile with themselves as the rightful leaders of the new Communist International (Comintern), founded in March 1919. Zinoviev, much concerned about the weak popular recognition of Bolsheviks and the Bolshevik Party inside Russia, claimed apparently without irony that in international terms "it is true that now 'Bolshevism' has become an honorable word, for, when [the German Communist] Karl Liebknecht was released from prison, he sent his first telegram to the Bolsheviks, not the Mensheviks. Now everyone speaks of world Bolshevism." [139] Foreign recognition (and, it should be said, criticism) of Bolshevism was often invoked by the regime when it was trying to proclaim the viability of Bolshevism. [140]

Within the increasingly polarized world of Civil War Russia, however, the terms "Bolshevik" and "Communist" found greater definition as the new polity's calls for commitment became ever more uncompromising. The 1918 anniversary celebrations commemorated the "continuous struggle" of the past year "against the darkness in the rank and file [*nizy*] who did not understand their own advantage, against the indifference of comrades who were tired of three years of fighting and constant privations." [141] The targets of the calls to commitment were not, generally speaking, erstwhile revolutionary competitors like the Mensheviks or SRs. [142] Nonpartisan (*bespartiinye*) conferences were a major feature of mass political life until 1921, and desires were often expressed at them for all parties to come together in the interests of the working class. [143] Nonpartisans were regarded as possessing less tarnished revolutionary credentials than those individuals who had been committed at one time or another to one of the opposition radical parties. An editorial in the Petrograd Bolshevik organ in September 1918 identified the category of "sympathizers (*sochuvstvuiushchie*)" among the uncommitted. These people were not merely guided by the belief that it was "dangerous to go against us, and dangerous to be with us" but must in fact have supported the revolution, because otherwise "the October Revolution would have been an adventure." [144] Poems in the Bolshevik press in 1918 called upon the population not to doubt, not to be weak of will: "Oh, I know! Grave doubt like a black snake your heart torments." [145] The time had come to choose, another poem addressed the "vacillators": "There can be no nonpartisans in the midst of battle, / Where host struggles with host in mortal combat." [146]

A year later, Bolshevik Party leaders, perhaps somewhat surprised by their survival in power and emboldened by their successes in the Civil War, began to push their ideological agenda more publicly, now referring explicitly to the *Bolshevik* victories of the war. Bolshevik newspapers often excerpted hostile foreign press reports on the inability of the Entente powers to stop Bolshevism, whose influence was "spreading like an epidemic." [147] The "Day of the Wounded Red Army Soldier," announced to coincide with the October celebrations, involved the explicit identification of Red Army soldiers as Communists. [148] The achievements in the country by the network of soviets over the past two years were now linked explicitly to the RKP. The steadily increasing percentage of Bolsheviks at the congresses of soviets since October 1917, *Izvestiia* argued, showed that "the Soviet government was *the entire time* under the leadership of the RKP" [149] (emphasis added). To be "nonparty" ceased to mean merely to be uncommitted. It was increasingly represented as a threat to the October Revolution. "In the Soviet press," wrote an eyewitness, A. Terne, in a memoir of the period, "one constantly encounters the assertion that the lack of political convictions is absurd. The Communists want to draw every citizen of Soviet Russia into the business of politics." [150] Terne was making the point that by far the largest majority of people did not, in fact, number themselves in any of the political groupings during these years. Still, during the Civil War nonpartisanship came to signify commitment to the enemy. "'Be nonparty!' our enemies tell the workers," wrote Zinoviev. " 'Be nonparty, stand to one side, do not try to understand the battle that has now divided the entire world into Whites and Reds. Do not support the Communists.... Be neither hot nor cold.'" [151] Announcing the start of a weeklong recruiting drive on November 7, 1919, the "organization of Communist-Bolsheviks" of the city of Ekaterinburg appealed to all the "nonparty toiling masses" to think "seriously and deeply about what the Communist Party is, what it is fighting for," adding a special such appeal to the Red Army soldiers, who have "many, many times, if only in passing" thought about these questions. [152] The decision before the ranks of the uncommitted was no longer whether to show faith in the revolution but whether to commit to the Communist Party: "Petrograd workers know that in the event of victory, the enemy [that is, the Whites] will make no distinction between workers and Communists, they understand that it will hang everyone who has calloused hands, and they are rushing into the ranks of their party." [153] In November 1919, the press showcased the reminiscences of newly committed female workers. [154] Similarly, the "primitive and semiliterate poems" in the press at this time were offered as evidence of the workers' spontaneous, if still poorly articulated, desire to commit. [155] By the last weeks of 1919, the space for the un- committed was shrinking: "You must know for certain, / With whom you wish to stand." [156]

3

APOTHEOSIS OF OCTOBER

And tyranny s ancient stronghold overthrown.
Freedom is gained! The exultant paeans rise,
Noise of great ruining, and a sudden glare,
As fire victorious storms the trembling skies.
—Rupert Brooke, "The Bastille," 1905

In the winter of 1919–20, the Red Army had won significant victories against major White armies, and the Civil War seemed to be drawing to a close with the onset of spring in Russia. If the immediate peril to October from White troops and White propaganda seemed to have waned, however, the challenge presented by the appalling social privations and suffering in Soviet Russia seemed more acute than ever to many Bolsheviks. Such concerns helped fuel the threat to the integrity of the Bolshevik Party and Bolshevik identity itself from within the party.

THERE IS SUCH A PARTY

Of course, disagreement and even organized dissent were not unknown at the highest levels of the Bolshevik Party. In 1918, the Left Communist group, which numbered leading Bolsheviks such as Nikolai Bukharin, Andrei Bubnov, Alexandra Kollontai, and Evgenii Preobrazhensky, had criticized the party's decision to make peace with Germany at Brest-Litovsk in March instead of conducting a revolutionary war. The Military Opposition, including some of these Left Communists, had arisen and coalesced around dissatisfaction with the use of military specialists in the Red Army, among other military issues. [1] This kind of dissent waned as the specific rallying point lost its relevance and the group lost its support within the party. In the course of 1920, though, the criticism leveled by the Democratic Centralists and the Workers' Opposition went to the legitimate role of the party in the revolution and the party's attitude toward the workers in whose name it claimed to act. At the Ninth Party Congress in March 1920, they defended independent trade unions as the best defense of the economic rights of the workers in the Soviet state. For Lenin, among others, the very idea of the separation of political power from economic power was an absurdity left over from the tsarist system. It also implied a profound mistrust of the party's ability to train the workers to run the economy in the long term, and to oversee its management in the short term. This mistrust, combined with the Democratic Centralists' outright criticism of the party's bureaucratized and autocratic leadership style (and its flouting of local democratic practices) created a picture of the party that was desperately at odds with the aspirations of its leaders. [2] Several months later, at the Ninth Party Conference, the Central Committee devoted special attention to the conflicts and friction caused by the perception of inadequate communication between the leading heights (*verkhi*) and the party rank and file (*nizy*). Leading Communists were deeply concerned that the party possessed no substantive, reliable, or properly trained base of support at the local level. [3]

By 1920, most of the leadership had become convinced of the *urgent* need to define the party more sharply, particularly its historical credentials and its revolutionary genealogy. Up to this point, such explicit calls had been sporadic. With the zeal of the recent convert to Bolshevism, perhaps, Trotsky published a brochure in 1918, *October Revolution* (*Oktiabr'skaia revoliutsiia*), in which he did not shy away from identifying the pivotal role of a coherent Bolshevik Party in the October Revolution. He wrote it for fear that "the internal connections" of the events would be forgotten by the participants and because, prior to October 1917, the entire apparatus of the bourgeois press was motivated by a single idea, "to make the Bolsheviks impossible as a political party."[4] Old Bolsheviks must have been galled to read about the prerevolutionary activities of "our party" and the frequent references to "we Bolsheviks" from a parvenu who had joined their party only shortly before October 1917, and after a political career in which he had most often set himself above all political parties and factions.[5] Nor would they have been won over by his criticism of what he called the "wait-and-see mood" among the "leaders of our party" on the eve of October.[6] Trotsky, instead, traced a process of self-realization by the Bolshevik Party in the latter part of 1917. The workers' demonstrations of June that embraced Bolshevik slogans, he pointed out, showed "not only our enemies but also ourselves as well that we were much stronger in Petrograd than was generally supposed."[7] The Bolshevik Party, he implied, compared well with the "formlessness" of the Socialist Revolutionary Party and the politically astute but organizationally weak Mensheviks prior to October.[8]

The ABC of Communism (*Azbuka kommunizma*), written by Bukharin and Preobrazhensky in 1919 represented a more mainstream and widely distributed effort within the party to define itself as a historically pivotal force. Written as a commentary on the new program adopted by the Communist Party at the Eighth Party Congress in March 1919, the tract identified a coherent party: "Our party was the first to formulate and the first to realize the demand for Soviet power."[9] The reader found little evidence here, though, of a coherent and discrete prerevolutionary evolution of the Bolshevik Party. The authors opened their volume, instead, with a potted history that noted the absence of a "precise program, written on paper," and commented instead on the common roots of the Bolsheviks and Mensheviks until their split in 1903 at the Second Party Congress. They may have even seemed to the astute reader a little defensive in the face of Menshevik accusations that their new program constituted a repudiation of their old program.[10]

The single and most unequivocal representation of the Bolshevik Party (and Bolshevism) as the theoretical and organizational engineer of the October Revolution came from Lenin's pen in 1920. In his *"Left-Wing" Communism, an Infantile Disorder*, distributed at the Second Congress of the Comintern in July 1920, Lenin painted a protomythic picture of the Civil War Bolshevik Party as a model organization, marked by close links between the leaders and the masses, and guided by a political vanguard with a consistent and clear vision of its political strategy and tactics. The sine qua non of this organization was that the "broadest masses" had been convinced "*by their own experiences*" (Lenin's emphasis) of the correctness of the political leadership. Commitment, then, involved both comprehension of and identification with the correct cause. Lenin dated Bolshevism "as a trend of political thought and as a political party" from 1903, but observed that the party's experience drew upon the "granite theoretical basis" of Marxist revolutionary theory as it had developed from the 1840s to the 1890s. He retold the Russian revolutionary experience as a tale of Bolshevism's "merciless struggle against petit bourgeois, semi-anarchist... revolutionariness, the tradition [sic] that has always existed in revolutionary social democracy"[11] He retold the European revolutionary experience in terms of the absence of such a struggle. The once hallowed German social democratic movement—Trotsky would still refer to it later as the "mother, teacher, and living example" for Russian Social Democrats in the emigration[12] —now drew criticism for its failure to generate the kind of "party that the revolutionary proletariat required to enable it to gain victory."[13] Thus did Lenin begin in earnest the process of rewriting the narrative of Russia's revolutionary past, in which both European and Russian social democracy finally found their fulfillment in Bolshevism.[14] His uncontested political status in Soviet Russia, and the process of his mythologization that had begun with the failed assassination attempt on him on August 30, 1918, ensured that his voice would have particular resonance.[15]

For the present, however, these fragmentary and explicitly *Bolshevik* aspirations did not yet define the October narrative. The party was still concerned about the negative images of Communists and Bolsheviks in what a 1920 pamphlet described as "dark and poorly conscious worker or peasant." "Where must the nonparty person go?" asked the pamphlet, and replied, "between [the nonparty people] and the Communists there is no difference."[16] Parables of conversion of male and female workers to the party became a feature of the official press.[17] So, too, did assurances that the Bolsheviks could no longer be overthrown by force of arms.[18]

TOWARD A BASTILLE FOR OCTOBER

In late 1920, then, *revolutionary* imagination, rather than specifically Bolshevik aspirations, continued to inform the narrative. The third anniversary of October provided authorities with an opportunity to gild their military victories and to stress the imminence of the bright Communist future, rather than to dwell on the hardships of the years of the Civil War. The press noted the gains made in the areas of the economy (notably food supply and transport), health care, and education, even the waning of former hostility from some social groups.[19] This "sacred holiday [*sviatyi prazdnik*]" was dedicated to "our Red martyrs" of the revolution and the Civil War.[20] October Besieged gave way to October Triumphant.

Revolutionary artists brought the holiday to life on the streets of Petrograd on a scale and grandness never seen before. Mass spectacles had already been performed in the city a year earlier, a product of the experimentation of Red Army and Proletkult theater workshops.[21] In 1920, the third anniversary celebrations profited from the unlikely union of unparalleled state sponsorship and funding and the unbridled creative instincts of prominent figures from the prerevolutionary world of Russian arts. The mass spectacles were revolutionary—not Bolshevik—festivals, and the organizers were not required to show party credentials. Indeed, some artists regarded the poorly defined Bolshevism of 1917–1919 as but a preliminary stage on the path to the "revolution of the spirit."[22] All, however, were inspired by the drama and passion of revolution. Iurii Annenkov, Nikolai Evreinov, Sergei Radlov, Vladimir Solov'ev, Adrian Piotrovskii, Aleksandr Kugel', S. D. Maslovskaia, Vladimir Shchuko, Hugo Varlikh, Nikolai Petrov, and L. N. Urvantsov brought to the service of the Soviet state their considerable artistic talent and experience from prerevolutionary work in experimental theater, cabaret, and music. With their program of "Theatrical October," radical artists (Vsevolod Meyerhold and the Proletkultists among them) declared traditional theater to be a new front in the Civil War and strove to invent new dramatic forms to replace the old. While not all radical artists hewed to a single approach, they shared a broad goal of radically transforming social consciousness through a new theater.[23] They used theater not to depict or reflect the revolutionary events of the day but rather as an active agent in the construction of October. Like the red funerals and earlier anniversary demonstrations, the mass spectacles were an effort not only to capture the essence of a broader revolutionary narrative in a single emblematic performance but also to present a revolution that was, as Clark puts it, "in sync with a revolution in the consciousness of the participants themselves, a revolution both aesthetic and political-cum-social." Their organizers' goal was nothing less than that of "making citizens."[24]

These mass productions were informed by theorists like Platon Kerzhentsev, a prominent figure in Proletkult, whose aim was to explode traditional theatrical spaces and practices and to infuse politics with drama. He literally took the performance to the streets and replaced the traditional troupes of professional actors with trained amateurs. He was not attempting to reproduce the events of October 1917 in a literal sense but rather to provide his revolutionary interpretation of the tumult going on around him. By breaking down the traditional boundaries between performer and spectator, Kerzhentsev intended to unsettle the spectators' traditionally passive role and open them up to an intimate experience of October. Inspired by Romain Rolland's work in constructing a "People's Theater," artists like Kerzhentsev believed that this new theater was most important for the shared emotions it could evoke in its audience.[25] Such artists attempted to convey the possibilities of collective, revolutionary action and a sense of the dynamism, dramatic action, and increasing commitment that this new revolutionary polity demanded of the population. As such, their aims coincided with the state's aims as identified by Lunacharsky in October 1920, namely "to diffuse the revolutionary image of ideas, sensations, and actions throughout the country."[26]

Even when they dealt with episodes of distant history, the mass spectacles were always about the October Revolution.[27] Three in particular, however, helped to advance the narrative of the October Revolution, as their organizers sought to aestheticize the revolutionary experience. Two took place on the site of the former Stock Exchange building on Vasilevsky Island in Petrograd.[28] On May Day, two thousand participants, watched by some thirty-five thousand people in the square in front of the exchange, took part in the *Hymn to the Liberation of Labor—a Mystery* (*Gimn osvobozhdeniiu truda,—misteriia*), directed by Annenkov, Kugel', and Maslovskaia. On July 19, twice as many took part in the more ambitious *Toward a World Commune* (*K mirovoi kommune*), which coincided with the Second Congress of the Comintern. The piece, directed by Petrov, Radlov, Solov'ev, and Piotrovskii, and with forty-five thousand spectators in the audience, placed the upper classes—the oppressors—on the columned upper platform of the exchange, while the lower classes—the oppressed—occupied the square below it. The steps separating them represented the site of mass action, as the masses stormed up them in a spontaneous act of revolution.

As their scenarios show, the spectacles were designed to produce a historical genealogy for the October Revolution. *Mystery* generated a sense of revolutionary inexorability with its sequence of historical scenes, depicting first the Roman slave revolt under Spartacus, then the peasant uprisings under Stepan Razin, and finally the October Revolution.[29] *Commune* presented the Russian Commune as the ultimate realization of the promise of the Paris Commune. The small segment of Parisian workers who had set up the doomed Paris Commune had failed because of their lack of support from the workers of other countries. *Commune* was an allegory of awakening by the world's workers to their own interests, an awakening slowed by the actions of the leaders of the Second International who supported the World War and in doing so split the world proletariat. In the Russian Commune of 1917, the now conscious workers saw through the dissembling of the old socialist leaders and established the Third International, one that reflected their true interests and paved the way for the "World Commune."

The major motif of these spectacles was the storming, that most potent symbol from the iconographic repertoire of the storytellers of the French Revolution. Up to that point, artists and propagandists had most often used the imagery of the revolutionary storming to symbolize Russia besieged, the workers and peasants safe *within* the fortress.[30] With the mass spectacles of the 1920s, the storming became a major feature of the process of constructing October, a single, focused event that could convey the passion and drama of collective revolutionary action. Indeed, as one contemporary pointed out, the Stock Exchange building was chosen as the site for *Mystery* precisely because of the possibilities afforded by the "broad steps that freely accommodated the crowds of the oppressed and insurgent slaves."[31] Roman slaves, Russian peasants, and Parisian communards all stormed the steps, but only the workers and soldiers of the October Revolution were successful as they charged up them to the Kingdom of Peace, Freedom, and Joyful Labor and the World Commune. These stormings were perhaps the most effective way of conveying the communal message of these spectacles. The individual actor was largely invisible, subordinated to the broad social categories (rulers, oppressors, and bourgeoisie opposed by slaves, workers, and soldiers) that advanced the action.

STORMING THE WINTER PALACE

The most concerted effort to create a Russian Bastille, however, came in a spectacle that dwarfed these earlier efforts and which the press vaunted as "an apotheosis, a ceremonial crowning of three years of Soviet power." [32] The organizers intended the ambitious *Storming of the Winter Palace* (*Vziatie Zimnego dvortsa*) on November 8, 1920 to be October's "total event," the reduction of the entire revolutionary narrative to an emotive and transparent symbol. [33] They staged the spectacle in and around the palace with up to eight thousand participants and one hundred thousand spectators. [34] With a collective of directors (including Evreinov, Kugel', Petrov, and Konstantin Derzhavin), with set designs and costumes by the artist Annenkov, and music by Varlikh and a five hundred–piece orchestra, the event proclaimed the fruitful possibilities of communal action.

The directors declared at the outset that it was "not the nature of theater to make a protocol of history." [35] Rather, *Storming* was to produce a greater truth, the distillation in a single emblematic event of the October Revolution's essential qualities. Evreinov felt a "joyous need to remind the entire population in distinct and persuasively graphic forms" of this portentous event, an event that "signifies the fall of the old revolutionary power... and the start of a new power." [36] He placed newspaper advertisements to attract "as far as possible, actual participants in the October storming [*Oktiabr'skii shturm*]" to take part in the storming scenes, as well as disabled soldiers from the World War. He pledged to reproduce the "remembered event," as far as possible, and to stage the past "to the point of complete illusion." His pledges notwithstanding, Evreinov's "theater of memory [*teatr vospominanii*]" was very much the translation of his own mnemonic vision of October for the audience. His goal was to make the audience experience *his* vision as part of *their* memory. "Nothing can die in the confines of memory," he wrote, "in the confines of the memory of my transforming spirit." [37] For the first time in the telling of October, the Winter Palace became the primary spatial and thematic focus or, as Petrov called it, a "gigantic actor" in this drama:

> The director has to make the stones talk, the spectator feel what is happening there inside and behind these cold, red walls. And we have solved this problem in an original way by employing a cinematographic method—each of the fifty windows on the second floor... will show one or another moment of the development of the internal struggle. [38]

The spectacle was accompanied by various pieces of emotive music, with Derzhavin noting that "in mass theater the semantic significance of the word is equal to zero. Mass theater is known only from the sound of speech and the noise content of its effects." [39] An announcement of the performance "demanded" of the spectators that they join in the communal singing of the "Internationale" at the conclusion of the storming. [40]

The action took place on Uritskii Square (the former Palace Square) and partially inside the palace itself late in the evening of November 8. Opposite the palace within the semicircle formed by the military General Staff buildings, two huge platforms, a Red and a White, were erected. The spectators occupied two areas in the center of the square. The Red platform bore the proletariat, the White platform the Provisional Government. The two platforms were connected by an arched bridge on which the two camps would join battle at various moments throughout the spectacle. The White stage was under the direction of Kugel' and Derzhavin, the Red was under Petrov, while the third "stage," the Winter Palace with its sixty-two gigantic second-floor windows, was under Evreinov. [41] The action began with the July Days and ended with the symbolic storming of the palace. As with the earlier mass spectacles, the Bolsheviks were largely absent, identified here only for their failure to lead the masses against the government in July, whereupon the workers "organized themselves" and led the charge to the Winter Palace in October. [42]

The theme of collective action was reprised at every stage and in every manifestation of the spectacle. The tale of the *Storming* was related not only through the content and structure of the performance itself but it was also prefigured in the announcements about the upcoming show and retold in descriptions of it after the fact. *Zhizn' iskusstva* reported that a "collective author" of ten individuals from Petrograd had come together to create the spectacle, and they "were working extremely unanimously and enthusiastically. No friction was observed, no kind of struggle over pride. One comrade's idea was taken up by another, who urged on another's idea, developed and embellished it. As a result, a grandiose work has appeared." [43] One short announcement reported Evreinov telling the participants in the rehearsals that were conducted day and night at the Winter Palace that they were "parts of a collective actor." [44]

Most important, the spectacle was designed to provide "the masses" with the notion that they were not an inchoate mob. The movements of the mass groups of participants in the performance were intended, wrote Derzhavin, to create "in the spectator the impression of a powerful organism." [45] Prior to the *Storming*, Lunacharsky had also judged these mass spectacles by their success in allowing spectators to conceive of themselves as something other than bystanders to history: "In order to experience themselves, the masses must manifest themselves externally, and this is possible only when... they themselves are their own spectacle." Lunacharsky hoped that the "organized masses" that took part in such large-scale functions would draw in the "remaining unorganized masses" watching from the sidelines, so that the "entire people demonstrates its own soul before itself." [46] Reports duly observed the desired effect in the audience: "The spectators are electrified, another moment and it seems the crowd will tear itself away from the fence and together with the automobiles and crowds of soldiers and workers rush to storm the last stronghold of the hated Kerensky regime [the Provisional Gov-

5. Set Design for Evreinov s Storming of the Winter Palace, November 7, 1920 (Courtesy of the State Central Museum of Contemporary History of Russia)

ernment]." [47] The scenes of mass action on the Red stage contrasted sharply with the much more individualized scenes on the White stage. Most notably, Kerensky was one of the few identifiable individuals, occupying the highest platform on stage and, some reports suggested, controlling the Provisional Government members like puppets on strings. [48] He epitomized the isolated and elite nature of Provisional Government rule, the histrionic gesturing of his speeches conveying the desperate impotence of his position. Fleeing the palace while disguised in women's clothing, represented his final emasculation.

At the beginning of the performance, the Provisional Government, "at the peak of its glory" in early 1917, was contrasted with the "complete lack of organization" of the Reds. As the worker masses began to organize, however, fear and indecision took over the Provisional Government, which eventually fled to hide within the walls of the Winter Palace. [49] In the early part of the spectacle, the brightly illuminated White platform was a picture of decisive organization; the "Marseillaise," the Provisional Government anthem, rang out loud and clear. On the Red platform, the disarray of soldiers and workers was paramount, their weary way home accompanied by the hesitant strains of the "Internationale," the song of the Paris Commune: "The still unorganized proletariat tensely listens to the hundred thousand spectators, waiting for... the call to final action from the people [*narod*]. But the *narod* is still timid and the necessary word is not heard from its

6. *Storming of the Winter Palace,* November 7, 1920 (Courtesy of the State Central Museum of Contemporary History of Russia)

mouth!" [50] As the performance progressed, the "hearts and minds" of the masses were won over by communist ideas and vaguely defined "agitators," and the masses crossed over to join the workers. [51] From that point, the White platform became a study in chaotic, confused movement to the slightly off-key playing of the "Marseillaise," whereas the Red platform became a model of coherent and revolutionary action as workers and soldiers converged on a large red flag to join in a communal rendition of the "Internationale." Evreinov's own description of the dramatic final storming has proven enormously influential on the tone of later representations of the *Storming*:

> From under the arch of the General Staff darted armored cars and the entire Red Guard of then Petrograd! From the Moika came the Pavlovtsy! [a military regiment] From the Admiralty Passage came armed sailors—"the beauty and pride of the revolution," as Trotsky called them then. Their common striving, their single purpose—the Winter Palace! From beneath the gates of this besieged fortress can now be heard the clamor of armaments on the move! The junkers disguise them with a huge pile of logs, and the historic battle begins, in which the Red cruiser *Aurora,* visible in the distance, takes part. In the lit windows of the Winter

Palace the silhouettes of those doing battle!... These Reds in a rapid charge have penetrated into the palace and they are disarming, after a battle, the defenders.... The rat-a-tat of machine guns, the rifle shots, the rumble of artillery—everything merged into a deafening symphony of decisive battle. Two, three minutes of total thunder already seem like an eternity to nerves that are too taut.[52]

Evreinov's effort to create a Bastille for October was clearly a conscious one. He had already drawn upon imagery of the French Revolution in his earlier works celebrating the February Revolution, and he boasted that this *Storming* was on a scale "that could only have been dreamt of in Paris on July 14, 1790 on the Festival of the Federation." [53] Yet, as Rolf Reichardt and Hans-Jürgen Lüsebrink have shown, the "basically banal, almost militarily insignificant event of 14 July 1789" in Paris became the symbolic Storming of the Bastille and the dominant image in the popular imaginings of the French Revolution, because philosophers and writers had long prepared it as such. As a "prophesied, 'expected' event," then, the storming had been prepared as the "precondition for a new era of freedom." "The symbol justified," they write, "even provoked, the symbolic act." After the destruction of the prison on July 14, 1789, a wide range of graphic, sculptural, theatrical, argumentative, and narrative methods would be employed to fulfill the prophecy. [54]

The taking of the Winter Palace was not the prophesied, expected event of the October Revolution. The Winter Palace did not occupy a place in the Russian popular imagination in 1917 as a symbol of oppression in the same way as the Bastille had in France. It had never served as a prison either literally or figuratively.[55] It had undergone no such demonization in the radical press in the previous twenty or so years. After February 1917, the Provisional Government had taken it as its seat, and in January 1918 the new Bolshevik government had quickly established the Commission for the Preservation of Relics of Art and Antiquity (Komissiia po okhrane pamiatnikov iskusstva i stariny) there to preserve Old Russia's treasures. Although the concentrated military operations in and around the Winter Palace on October 25 and 26, 1917, offered those writers in search of a Bastille perhaps the best material, this material was not ideal. After the takeover in October, the Winter Palace had been cast by all sides as a symbol of political impotence. Even when it became the stage for Evreinov's spectacle, press reports remained ambivalent, continuing to cast it as a symbol of the impotence of both the Old Regime and its successor "bourgeois" government. Over the next three or four years, its symbolic malleability persisted, its halls housing at various times prisoners of war from the old army, congress delegates from a committee of the poor from northern Russia, delegates from a congress of female workers, young children of preschool age, the organizers of May Day celebrations, and so on. [56]

While reports of the *Storming* told of the final scene in which the "insurgent people [*narod*] begins the attack against the last bastion of an already overthrown power,"[57] Evreinov described the silhouetted battle scenes in the brightly lit windows of the palace being fought against defenders of the "phantom power [*prizrachnaia vlast'*]." The defenders of the government were, he had noted derisively, an "operetta women's battalion" and "a group of unfortunate cripples [that is, war-wounded]." [58] The *Storming*'s structure and performance also betrayed a certain mistrust of the popular masses and of their propensity for coherent action. While reports routinely boasted that the *Storming* was done "with the participation of the popular masses," this was not strictly true. [59] The production was as exclusionary as it was inclusionary, from the symbolic social polarization of the Red and White stages to the equating of the active, committed masses with proletarians; "Two sides, two camps, two classes," as *Petrogradskaia pravda* put it. Spectators had "free" access, but special tickets were required for access to the stages, and it was forbidden to move around the square during the performance. Fearing widespread panic, the press published warnings about the gunfire, factory sirens, and movements of armed soldiers that would be involved in the performance. [60] Lunacharsky had advocated seeding the crowds of spectators with professional actors and amateurs as a way of raising the mood at key points during these mass performances, even adding that wine could also be useful in this regard, although it could have "uncultured consequences." [61]

Lunacharsky, in fact, doubted that the masses who were acting in these spectacles were even capable of creativity: "In no way must one wait until the crowd on its own is able to create something, other than happy noise and the colorful movements of festively attired people." [62] Indeed, articles on the spectacles chronicled the enormous degree of organization, control, and timing they demanded. Radlov expressed undisguised glee at the degree of control he exercised over the actors in one of the spectacles at the Stock Exchange. [63] Annenkov recalled the "almost insuperable" technical difficulties presented by the lighting and decorative requirements of the *Storming.* [64] Piotrovskii, in fact, thought that this excessive organization undermined the primary goal of the spectacles:

> The whole question is the extent to which the masses organized for the festival are acting *consciously*. And here the festivals of 1920 were, without doubt, off track. To mobilize completely untrained worker clubs, to take military units under command, and in the course of a week prepare them for action, this can indeed lead only to a mechanical performance

[*mekhanichestvo*], to *Platzparad*, [a parade ground drill] to the death of the living spirit of the festivals." [65] (Piotrovskii's emphasis)

This was harsh criticism indeed. What were these festivals for, if not to convey the "living spirit" of revolution?

ACTS OF MEMORY, ACTS OF MEANING

The dramatic enactments of the October Revolution during these first three years provided a revolutionary script, however incomplete, that gave individuals opportunities to see themselves as members of October's cast. By calling for eyewitness testimony to the foundation event of the new regime, the authorities invoked established conventions about the inherent value of eyewitnesses as an immediate source and reassured the eyewitnesses themselves of their importance to the event they had witnessed. Regardless of concerns about the objectivity of the eyewitness, notes Andrew Lass, "an individual's narration is valued because it authenticates what it provides: the what and how of past events. The witness's eye is also the eye of memory." [66] As Nikolai Sukhanov pointed out in 1919, his reminiscences of 1917 were "*personal reminiscences*, nothing more. I write only what I remember, only in the way I remember it. These notes are the fruit not of reflection and even less of *study*: they are the fruit of *memory*." [67] (Sukhanov's emphasis)

Within the first days of the October takeover, *Sotsial-demokrat* asked people to send lists of those killed or wounded in the fighting in Moscow, as well as any leaflets and bulletins or information about the course of fighting there. [68] In November 1918, a notice on the front page of *Izvestiia* called on all "comrade participants of the October overthrow" to send articles, reminiscences, poems, and "materials related to the October Revolution" for a special jubilee issue. [69] The authorities announced plans to publish collections of reminiscences on the October Days in large print runs and at considerable cost.[70] By calling on individuals to engage in acts of memory about October, the authorities made them locate themselves as contemporaries or, better yet, as participants in the event, and sustained October in what Paul Connerton has called "the tense of a metaphysical present."[71]

The recording of recollections was clearly initiated by the new authorities in the capitals, but, as individual acts of meaning, these recollections were no less valid or sincere for that fact. In that most dramatic theater of memory, the *Storming of the Winter Palace* in November 1920, some of those involved in the original taking of the Winter Palace now had the opportunity to revisit and re-present their past actions as actors in a coherent and comprehensible narrative of historical significance. The dramatic enactments of power imparted the message, at every turn, that great things were afoot. In Petrograd at this time, wrote one contemporary, Vladimir Vasilevskii, "there was the feeling that something was happening, something big, great, something tangible and at the same time unexpected."[72] Press reports evoked the revolution as an implacable but cleansing force of nature, a storm, or sometimes an avalanche or earthquake. A revolutionary whirlwind, wrote Gorky in June 1918, "will cure us, make us healthy, revitalize us for work and creativity."[73] With the headlong rush of events impressed upon them, reminiscers wore their efforts to discern the meaning of these events as a badge of authenticity for their memories. At the same time, they believed that these events could acquire their true and full meaning only with the passage of time. Nevskii, who helped organize the military preparations for the uprising and who would figure prominently in efforts to collect reminiscences in the 1920s, concluded his reminiscences thus: "The preceding lines are not history but simple recollections for the great anniversary—incomplete, fragmentary recollections, and probably colored by a good share of subjectivism, but the time has not yet come for a history."[74]

Nevskii's sentiments notwithstanding, anyone who agreed to or indeed embraced the call to compose their memories on the occasion of the anniversaries did so in an act of recollection in which meaning pursued experience into memory. They strove to make *revolutionary* sense of their past experiences, as they told their tales of October. By far the most ambitious and coherent of these attempts was John Reed's *Ten Days That Shook the World*, conceived in 1918 as part of the "battle of the printing-press" that "raged" from October 26, 1917, over the meaning of the events in Russia.[75] Written by a committed American radical explicitly to advance the cause of revolution, *Ten Days* turned on the events of October 25 that Reed had witnessed. Reed apparently derived the narrative structure of his work from Trotsky's earlier pamphlet, *October Revolution*, which had been the first to situate October in a broader political context stretching from the July Days of 1917 to the Brest peace in March 1918.[76] As Reed pointed out, he supplemented his "chronicle" of the events he had himself observed and experienced with other "reliable evidence" from the radical press, as well as information obtained while he worked in the Communist Department of International Revolutionary Propaganda (later the Department of Foreign Political Literature).[77] *Ten Days* was widely distributed abroad in foreign-language editions, most notably English and German. It received its most famous endorsement from Lenin, who in 1919 called it a "true and unusually vivid account of the events."[78] Reed's (and Trotsky's) narrative sweeps were the exception at this time, for the majority of reminiscences came in response to the authorities' appeals for personal recollections of specified events.

Nonetheless, these acts of meaning all shared certain features. Personal reminiscences of past events by definition write the author into these events, at the very least as an observer and quite often as a participant, broadly defined. Some placed their authors in local gatherings defending Bolshevik ideas in the face of hostility from ill-informed crowds. In the end, the author invariably won over the assembled in a fiery act of suasion.[79] Others emphasized the individual part they played at key points in the eventual decision to launch the uprising:

> I asked for the floor, as a representative of the "*dvintsy*" [soldiers sent to Dvinsk military prison in June 1917 for antigovernment activity]; my soul caught fire, together with the soul of the auditorium, having met one another with applause, with cries: "Long Live the Proletarian Revolution," I took the podium, and with my heart ablaze with the joy of the struggle, I told the workers who the *dvintsy* were…. And the hearts of the workers burned with the vengeance of arbitrariness [*proizvol*], and the hymn of the "Internationale" washed over the gray head of the chairman of this meeting.[80]

Not a few reminiscences hinged on moments of personal transfiguration at a mass meeting or in the heat of the battle. Individuals might recall being intensely moved by the spontaneous and communal singing of the "Internationale," or by the "shining eyes of the proletarians, the knit brows of the soldiers." [81] Increasingly by late 1919, these might be explicitly *Bolshevik* moments. One agitator, sent in late 1917 by the Moscow Soviet to the small town of Iukhnov in Smolensk Province, recalled telling the assembled workers that the Bolsheviks were the only party that deserved to head the state. [82] In other reminiscences, the man in the street listened to the bourgeoisie, many factory workers were "Menshevik-minded," but the "organized proletariat" heeded the Bolsheviks. [83]

The Bolshevik press began to carry accounts of personal epiphanies by "common workers," which dramatized their reasons for committing to the Bolshevik Party. [84] Such personal identifications with the October story put a face on the social groups that moved history and peopled the October narrative with mythic characters who advanced the narrative at crucial junctures. In Reed's *Ten Days*, the protracted debates at the Second Congress of Soviets were resolved not by any of the intellectuals present but by the "common man" whose native wisdom cut through their endless talk:

> A young, lean-faced soldier, with flashing eyes, leaped to the platform, and dramatically lifted his hand: "Comrades!" he cried, and there was a

hush.... "You have heard the statements of two representatives of the Army committees; these statements would have some value *if their authors had been representatives of the Army*—" Wild applause. "*But they do not represent the soldiers!*" Shaking his fist.... "I tell you now, the Lettish soldiers have many times said, 'No more resolutions! No more talk! We want deeds—the Power must be in our hands!' Let these impostor delegates [the Mensheviks and SRs] leave the Congress! The Army is not with them!" The hall rocked with cheering. [85]

Such individual moments of clarity were intended to signify an epiphanic comprehension of the significance of the events. In the polarized political landscape of the Civil War years, those who recalled the events of 1917 did so in equally polarized terms. In 1919, a female worker recalled Petrograd in October 1917 as a city divided into opposed and immediately identifiable areas, some containing soldiers and Red Guards ("the proletariat"), others the junkers, students, and so on (the "bourgeoisie and conciliators"). [86] Mikhail Ol'minskii, the founding father of these efforts to gather recollections of October, recalled the "unprecedently sharp, graphic [*nagliadnoe*] separation in these days into lines separating the bourgeois and semibourgeois strata from the proletariat and peasants (soldiers); the October Days in Moscow explained class consciousness in a way that ten years of propaganda and agitation had been unable to do." [87]

In the first reminiscences from 1918, the sharp definition of social groups contrasted with murkier representations of the political leaders and organizations that had burst onto the revolutionary stage with October. At no point in Reed's tale, James White notes, did the Bolsheviks take the initiative; rather they came to power through the MRC in response to the threat of force from their opponents. The initiative for the insurrection came from the workers, not the party. [88] Reed noted popular confusion about the precise identities and allegiances of the various groups of actors abroad in Petrograd during the October Days. On the day before the takeover, at the corner of Morskaya and Nevsky, Reed recalled seeing squads of soldiers with fixed bayonets stopping all private automobiles and turning out the occupants, but "nobody knew whether the soldiers belonged to the Government or the Military Revolutionary Committee." [89] In a piquant anecdote, Reed told of Trotsky being refused entry to Smolny on October 25 by a guard who challenged him for his lack of identification papers: " 'Trotsky?... I've heard the name somewhere.' " [90] In Moscow, reminiscers described a picture of the Central Committee of the party out of step with even its own party workers (*rabotniki*), talking but not acting, and prevaricating in the face of the "mass [that] was spoiling for battle." [91] Ol'minskii recalled "few organized forces" in Moscow on the eve of the revolution, a "counterrevolutionary" Soviet of Soldiers' Deputies, and a "disorganized and unarmed" body of soldiers. As for the MRC, it was compromised by "conciliationist" tendencies. After the pitched battles on the streets of Moscow in late October, the MRC had the embattled junkers in the Kremlin at its mercy, but chose to accept their surrender, and released them, as Ol'minskii pointed out, to fight again:

> The incomplete victory in Moscow happened exclusively thanks to the actions of the Military Revolutionary Committee. And if there was victory nevertheless, then we are obliged for it entirely to the spontaneous up-surge of the masses, and also the steadfastness and energy of the district [*raionnyi*] leaders, who were the entire time with the masses and marching in lockstep with them. [92]

The reticence of the MRC was contrasted sharply with the resoluteness of the masses to take the Kremlin from the "White Guards" and junkers: "The artillery roared, noise… rumbling…. 'Hurrah!,' the first victory, the inspirers of which were the *dvintsy*. Still more clearly shone our eyes, still more joyfully beat our hearts." [93] The Moscow artillery, with cannon trained on the Kremlin, exercised revolutionary restraint, shelling the Kremlin only when the choice was between "people as victims and Kremlin buildings as victims." [94]

Reminiscers often focused on certain moments or sites of the revolution, which allowed them to tell a coherent "piece" of the still elusive revolutionary tale. Sometimes the *absence* of a site performed this function. Beneath the seeming calm on the streets of Petrograd on October 25 and 26, for example, Reed saw signs of the "vitality of the social organism":

> Day broke on a city in the wildest excitement and confusion, a whole nation heaving up in long hissing swells of storm. Superficially all was quiet…. In Petrograd the streetcars were running, the stores and restaur-ants open, theatres going…. All the complex routine of common life—humdrum even in war-time—proceeded as usual. [95]

Most often, reminiscers structured their tales around one or more dramatic crescendos to convey a sense of revolutionary inexorability, if not inevitability. Trotsky hinged his recollections on an event on October 22 in Petrograd, three days before the Bolshevik takeover, when critical organizational steps were taken toward insurrection:

October 22 became the day to review the forces of the proletarian army. It went off splendidly in all respects. Despite the warnings coming from the Right that a river of blood would flow in the streets of Petrograd, the masses of the people flooded the streets to attend the mass meetings of the Petrograd Soviet. All our oratorical force was mobilized. All public places were packed. Mass meetings went on without interruption for hours. They were addressed by speakers from our party, by delegates to the Soviet Congress, by representatives from the front, by Left SRs, and anarchists. Public buildings were flooded by waves of workers, soldiers, and sailors. There had been few such gatherings in Petrograd even during the revolution.... Tens of thousands of people [*narod*] washed over the building of the People's House in waves, rolled through the corridors, packed the halls. On the iron columns, huge garlands of human heads, feet, and hands, hung like bunches of grapes. The air was charged with the electric tension that signals the most critical moments of revolution. "Down with Kerensky's government!" "Down with the war!" "All Power to the Soviets!" Nobody from the ranks of the former soviet parties dared to address these colossal crowds with a word of objection. The Petrograd Soviet held undivided sway. In reality, the campaign was already won. It remained only to deal the final military blow to this phantom power.[96]

In this emblematic moment, the masses, guided by revolutionary restraint and purpose, drove the revolution before them in an inexorable wave, with the Bolsheviks, at best, riding the wave.

In a rare exception, Zinoviev identified the Winter Palace as one of the main sites of the revolution in his recollections of 1919, in which he described how it was "stormed" on October 25, 1917 by "tens of thousands of the noblest proletarians of Petrograd." [97] Smolny, the seat of the new polity and the operations center for both the Bolshevik Party and the MRC, more often figured prominently in the early reminiscences. Reed, for example, referred to "great Smolny, bright with lights... like a gigantic hive." [98] On November 7, 1918, Zinoviev addressed the ceremonial meeting of the Petrograd Soviet, singling out the central place of Smolny in October and its emergence onto the "proscenium of history": "Barely a year ago, few knew this building, few were interested in it. But now there is not one honest proletarian in the whole world who does not know that Smolny exists."[99] Kamenev and others recalled the meeting in Petrograd at which a disguised Lenin came out of hiding to harangue the party into staging the overthrow. Fifteen or twenty people attended, he noted, who became the "main actors of the October overthrow." Furthermore, the meeting handed the "political leadership" of the overthrow to a group of five people (*piaterka*): Lenin, Trotsky, Joseph Stalin, Feliks Dzerzhinskii, and Kamenev. This group met at various secret locations around Petrograd, although these reminiscences also singled out Lenin's foresight and strength of will as the decisive factor in the organization of the overthrow. [100] Trotsky depicted Smolny, this "center of government" turned "fortress," as an information center coordinating the various military and political operations in Petrograd during these days. [101]

The leaders always tempered their focus on the narrowly military operations of Smolny and the MRC with discussion of the underlying motive forces of the revolution. Podvoiskii invoked the tense mood of the "revolutionary soldiers," who were "all consumed by one thought," namely to bring down the government and declare: "All Power to the Soviets." [102] Trotsky recalled the uncertainty in the MRC about the forces they could muster, and the reluctance of the command staff in Smolny to take responsibility for the operations. [103] Kamenev was more certain, noting that "for us it was completely clear that not only the worker population of Petrograd but the entire Petrograd garrison stood behind us," as did the overwhelming majority of the delegates arriving for the Congress of Soviets. [104] Nevskii, too, depicted the organizers' role as a response to the popular demands of the workers and soldiers, who in the course of 1917 had convinced the peasantry of the "commonality of interests of all toilers." He traced the history from early March 1917 of the Military Organization (*Voennaia organizatsiia or Voenka*), set up by several comrades (including himself) under the aegis of the Petrograd Committee of the RSDRP(b), in an effort to prepare the soldiers for an uprising. Nevskii portrayed the organization as an initially small group of organizers that very quickly found itself following rather than leading the soldiers' calls for revolutionary action. It was shaken from its indecision by the impatience of the "popular masses" and by Lenin's resolute and prescient calls in September and October for immediate uprising. During the October takeover, the workers and soldiers ("under the influence of our party") were the spontaneous movers of the events, and, *in response to* the rising mood of the masses, the Bolsheviks formed the MRC, which became the "main guiding force of all subsequent events." [105] Stalin represented the Bolshevik actions as a "swift and strictly organized uprising" forced upon the party by growing economic disintegration and the reluctance at the front to continue the war in spite of efforts to do so by the Provisional Government. [106]

In these early reminiscences, the "gigantic actor" of the theatricalized spectacle of 1920 was still a sideshow to the main events. [107] Trotsky remembered how during the night of October 25 "all of the most important points of the city" had been taken "almost without opposition, without a fight, without victims." The Winter Palace housed a government that, as Trotsky put it, "had already become a shadow of itself. Politically it had already ceased to exist." [108] Reed found little dramatic material there when, on the afternoon of October 25, he visited it along with fellow journalists Bryant and Albert Rhys Williams. Walking through dark, empty corridors, he saw a room full of soldiers lounging about, drinking and smoking, and female soldiers billeted in a back room "out of harm's way."[109] Such reports hardly prepared the Winter Palace as a hated symbol of tyranny that merited a revolutionary storming. Reed offered a cursory report of the taking of the palace, citing the following Red Guard account:

> Along about eleven o'clock we found out there weren't any more *yunkers* on the Neva side. So we broke in the doors and filtered up different stairways one by one or in little bunches. When we got to the top of the stairs the *yunkers* held us up and took away our guns. Still our fellows kept coming up, little by little until we had a majority. Then we turned around and took away the *yunkers'* guns.[110]

Reed's recollection of the masses as a "black river, filling all the street, without song or cheer," hardly conveyed their revolutionary élan. [111]

Others remembered the taking of the palace in more detail, but did not portray it as a revolutionary storming. Antonov-Ovseenko, who had helped to coordinate the attack, recalled that the "entire attack on the palace had, at this time, a completely disorderly character." The various defenders of the palace quickly dwindled, as the Cossack unit (*sotnia*) left, and the junkers and the women's battalion began surrendering when the artillery fire began. Attempts by small groups of attackers to penetrate the palace were repelled; some were even captured by the junkers in the process. Antonov-Ovseenko said that only when he and Chudnovskii were sure that few junkers were left did they order the attackers into the palace, entering it without resistance. [112] Podvoiskii, also charged with organizing the taking of the palace, concluded his short recollection in 1918 in anticlimactic fashion:

> As soon as… shells began to fall on the palace, the final vacillations ended. The junkers ran out from behind the barricades and shouted that they were surrendering. Then huge masses of our troops poured into the palace. A search was carried out, and the Provisional Government was found in one of the rooms and arrested. [113]

The Winter Palace would be stormed in memory, as it had been on stage, only as individuals began to draw on the powerful images and symbols furnished by the anniversary celebrations. Even though the palace would continue to play an ambivalent role in published recollections of October in 1920, it also began to acquire more dramatic form. In contrast to his earlier recollections in 1918, Podvoiskii began in 1920 to refer to the "storming [*shturm*]" of the palace. He still represented it as a symbol of the impotence of the Provisional Government; the "class struggle" had so undermined support for the government that the Winter Palace's defenders had melted away without firing a shot. Now, however, Podvoiskii's recollection of the taking of the palace acquired a dramatic climax, though still triggered by the revolutionary desires of the soldiers and Red Guards rather than the measured intentions of the Bolsheviks:

> Several grenades exploded in the corridors of the Winter Palace. This put an end to the vacillations. Sailors, Red Guards, soldiers, accompanied by the crackle of machine gun crossfire, flew over the barricades of the palace, crushed the defenders, and poured through the gates of the palace.... The palace is taken.... They fly up the stairs.... On the steps they grapple with the junkers.... They overrun them.... They rush to the second floor.... They scatter the defenders of the government.... They crumble.... They proceed to the third floor, everywhere in their path overrunning junkers and defeating them.... The junkers throw down their weapons.... In a flood, the soldiers, Red Guards, sailors surge forward.... They search for the guilty parties of the disaster. [114] [ellipses in original]

By the end of 1920, the October narrative was acquiring sharper definition and urgency, just as social identities and the choices they represented became clearer during the quickened times of the Civil War. Spurred, perhaps, by the quite different tale about the meaning of October being told by anti-Soviet movements to those populations under their control, [115] the Bolsheviks began to see the need for an increasingly clear and (they hoped) accessible story of their revolution. As the structure and performance of the funerals, demonstrations, and spectacles revealed, October was cast overwhelmingly as a masculine, workers' revolution, if spearheaded at critical junctures by the Red Army. The peasantry and women were marginalized symbolically and physically as politically unconscious and, thus, inherently unreliable. October, in its 1920 version, was best captured by the male worker who, staring in these uncertain times with clarity and certainty into the future, dominated so many of the posters. [116] Its essential meaning was now conveyed by its own, flawed, Bastille. This Bastille could be a physical spectacle like Evreinov's, or a recast recollection like Podvoiskii's.

FROM THEATERS OF MEMORY TO INSTITUTIONS OF MEMORY

For many Bolshevik leaders, however, the power of the anniversary celebrations concealed a fundamental weakness. The theatricalized representations of the October Revolution in the first three anniversary celebrations sought to produce a primarily sensory experience in the individual. The Red motif of the processions, mass meetings, and ceremonial burials, the literal and figurative spotlighting of significant moments in the evening performance of the *Storming of the Winter Palace*, and the ever-present strains of the "Internationale" were intended to limn the personal experience of these celebrations as part of a collective experience. They would all help furnish the individual with visual and auditory cues to revisit these memories. This experience depended to a large extent on personal presence at these communal gatherings. Press reports inevitably fell short in their attempts to convey to those who had not been present at the spectacles the immediacy and vividness of the experience of these theaters of memory. Commentators on Evreinov's *Storming* rued the fact that "such a grandiose enterprise" was being undertaken for a "one-hour spectacle that cannot be repeated tomorrow," although they welcomed the intention to "immortalize" it on film. [117] The spectacles were expensive, their effects ephemeral, and many planned shows went unrealized. [118]

While leading Bolsheviks clearly believed that theatricalizations of October contained intriguing and powerful storytelling possibilities, the message and its accessibility were always their paramount concern. The abstraction, symbolism, and mysticism of many revolutionary theatricalizations in 1919 and 1920 were often seen as an impediment to a clear message and, in some cases, a potential subversion of it. The Bolsheviks were not always at ease with the mercurial and unpredictable talents of the Futurist and Proletkult artists, who celebrated their revolutionary intentions with such defiant pride.[119] Moreover, they seemed troubled by the spontaneous participation that some artists demanded from their audiences in an attempt to break down the traditional theatrical barrier between performer and spectator. The meaning of October in these performances seemed to depend too much on the whim of artist and audience alike.[120] By 1920, Lunacharsky began to raise doubts about the credentials of these artists as *legitimate* arbiters of the revolution: "This artistic judgment on the ideal aspirations of the revolution can emerge only when the artist himself is... really imbued with revolutionary consciousness and is full of revolutionary feeling." His comment that these "votaries of art" should themselves be the "urgent" object of Communist propaganda foreshadowed the Soviet regime's move toward greater centralization and institutionalization.[121] Inspired by the same desire to distill and convey the essential revolutionary experience of this new life, artists would continue their work toward a new theater in the 1920s, although they would be forced to do so with diminishing resources and increasing attacks from the Bolshevik authorities.[122]

This official mistrust ensured that the days of the mass spectacle were numbered, although their spirit would be resurrected several years later on film.[123] Evreinov's *Storming of the Winter Palace* did not spawn a host of local Bastilles. Even in Moscow, which had seen pitched battles in the streets in October 1917, it had proved difficult to find a focal moment around which to build the October narrative. In 1920, reminiscences generally paid homage to the overthrow in Petrograd as the spark for the uprising in Moscow, and the mass festivals planned for Moscow went unrealized.[124] Petrograd, as the "place of origin for the Revolution," seemed to have a greater claim to the resources needed to stage such spectacles.[125] For the anniversary in 1920, Moscow, and other cities around Soviet Russia, decorated their streets only with posters and red flags and held mass meetings and lectures instead of the more ambitious and expensive processions and festivals.[126] Often, jubilee issues of local newspapers and published collections of speeches by the "leaders of Soviet power" marked October in the provinces.[127] The Bolsheviks were vocal in their fears that October would come to be identified solely with Petrograd, without resonance in the provinces. This was an untenable proposition, given Bolshevik sensitivity to criticisms about the isolated nature of their revolution. They realized that the local areas could not come to understand the significance of the revolution on their own. At an evening of reminiscences, Trotsky recalled that Lenin

> did not fear an uprising and even insisted on it, but he linked the fate of this uprising not only with the cause of the conflict in Piter [Petrograd] alone…. We had a Petrograd point of view… but Lenin started from the viewpoint of an uprising not only in Piter but *all over the country*, and he did not assign such a great place and significance exclusively to the uprising of the Petrograd garrison.[128] (Trotsky's emphasis)

The Bolsheviks were also deeply concerned about the difficulties of sustaining the revolutionary enthusiasm of the early period. Their faith in the passion and drama of October was balanced by their conviction, drawn from the lessons of Europe's revolutions in the previous century, that these qualities could not be sustained for long. Revolutionary resolve could be shaken, in the words of a newspaper article from 1919, when the "initial revolutionary festive upsurge" gave way to the "revolutionary quotidian."[129] "The soul of the revolution," literary critic P. S. Kogan wrote in 1921, "is losing its magical light…. Those who have been martyrs have against their own will become masters, those who have been destroyers have become officials. Their passion has begun to burn slowly and evenly, their inspiration is becoming settled, their enthusiasm—latent."[130]

In the 1920s, the poetry of the revolutionary performance of October would give way to the prose of its institutionalization, although, as Michael David-Fox notes, the "ritualistic, scripted, and even theatrical quality of Bolshevik political culture" would continue to mark life in the 1920s.[131] At a plenum of the Moscow Soviet on the day before the third anniversary celebrations, Lenin spoke of the change that was needed for the "harder part of our task," namely that of building the new society: "The enthusiasm that infects us now can last another year, another five years. But we must remember that the struggle we must undertake now is about little matters [*melochi*]."[132] The annual celebrations of October would continue, their form and structure tailored by the Soviet authorities to the regime's perceived economic, social, political, or cultural requirements for a given year.[133] Gone were the grandiose and dramatic theaters of memory of 1920, with their vivid but ephemeral images. They made way for the "institutions of memory," to which every new regime must eventually turn if it is to provide a material foundation for the ideology it claims as its own. As the Civil War wound down, the Bolshevik regime established academies and societies, with branches throughout Soviet Russia, to train a new generation of Marxist scholars and to systematize the publication of the canon of works by the founding fathers, Marx, Engels, and, especially, Lenin.[134] Other bodies were formed to chart the historic role of the trade union movement and the Communist youth movement in the revolutionary struggle, and to honor the Old Bolsheviks and political prisoners and exiles who had suffered under the tsarist regime.[135] Each institution required its own personnel and publications; and new archives, libraries, and museums were set up to organize, store—and sanctify—the materials they generated. Through the steady and continuous accretion of "evidence" of many kinds, this new system bore insistent testimony to October as its foundation event. It laid the cornerstone of a project to build a socialist workers' state, replete with its own economic, political, cultural, and ideological institutions capable of producing a repository of knowledge—a new socialist science. Although this project was implicit in the revolution from the very beginning, as argued by the Bolsheviks, it was rendered urgent by the upheavals of the first months of 1921, as workers, peasants, and sailors offered the most direct challenge yet to Bolshevik power and to the Bolshevik claims for October.

Part 2
THE MEMORY
OF OCTOBER

ISTPART AND THE INSTITUTIONALIZATION OF MEMORY

Our attitude to the documents of the revolution must be as active as our attitude to the events of the revolution.
—Istpart, 1920

Widespread unrest among workers and peasants throughout provincial Russia had been steadily increasing throughout 1920. In early 1921, it reached flashpoint. The series of "peasant wars," as Orlando Figes calls them, were considered by Lenin to be "far more dangerous than all the Denikins, Yudeniches, and Kolchaks [leaders of White forces] put together." [1] The epidemic of strikes and unrest that spread through most of the industrial areas of the country at the same time represented far more than an economic challenge to the government. To a revolutionary polity obsessively engaged in surveilling its population as a means of transforming it, the gulf in communication between center and periphery revealed by this unrest represented a serious threat. [2] Worse yet, as the demands of the strikers in several Petrograd plants in late February escalated from economic demands, such as regular rations, shoes, and warm clothing, to explicitly political demands, including political and civil rights, it seemed to the Bolshevik leaders that October itself was under attack. [3]

THE CHALLENGE OF KRONSTADT

One month later, a group of sailors from the Baltic Fleet stationed at the fortified city of Kronstadt in the Gulf of Finland mutinied in sympathy with the demonstrating workers in Petrograd, and demanded both economic and political reforms. Notwithstanding Lenin's dismissal of Kronstadt in *Petrogradskaia pravda* as "a completely insignificant incident," [4] these sailors articulated a direct, political challenge to the party and its representations of October that echoed the earlier efforts of the Mensheviks and SRs. Kronstadt had long been praised by the Bolsheviks as an ideological stronghold of the October Revolution. In early March 1921, however, the sailors' Revolutionary Committee declared that it stood for "the power of the soviets and not of the parties," and publicly accused the Communist Party of being "deaf to [the workers', peasants', and Red Army soldiers'] justified demands that emanate from the depths of their souls." [5] Just as the Bolshevik Party had figured prominently in the earlier Menshevik and SR contestations of the October Revolution, so the Communist Party now loomed large as an oppressive force in the committee's representations of its own revolution. The Bolshevik authorities found themselves in a battle with veterans of October, among them Red sailors from the *Petropavlovsk* and *Sevastopol* battleships, over ownership of the terms of revolution. Trotsky denied these sailors their revolutionary credentials, arguing that the real October veterans had long since been deployed elsewhere and replaced by "accidental [*sluchainye*]" elements. [6]

A measure of the severity of this ideological challenge was both the ferocity and brutality of the Communist response to it, and the party's decision at the Tenth Party Congress in March to launch the New Economic Policy (NEP), abandoning many of its most unpopular policies from the Civil War years, notably grain requisitioning. The Bolsheviks cast their suppression of the "Kronstadt crime" as an act of revolutionary necessity, which came only after a long display of revolutionary restraint (reminiscent of their earlier storming of the Winter Palace), as they made all efforts to persuade the sailors to lay down their arms and avoid bloodshed. Rather than attack the Kronstadt insurgents' representations of revolution directly, they cast the "mutiny" as the product of the "provocationist work of the SRs, Mensheviks, anarchists, and the White Guards." [7] Trotsky accused "centers of counterrevolutionary plots" abroad, namely Russian émigré circles and foreign imperialists, of instigating the events in order to scuttle Soviet efforts to conclude peace with Poland and a trade agreement with England. [8] The old argument was reversed: in foreign exile, the Mensheviks cried revolution; in Russia, the Bolsheviks cried conspiracy. The Martov-led Menshevik Internationalists in the emigration denied these charges and stressed the spontaneity of the uprising, the result of the economic hardships and excessive bureaucratism of the Soviet regime. [9] From Berlin, Martov stressed that the initiative for the Kronstadt uprising had "come from those very masses that up until now have been the bastion of Bolshevism." [10] He drew pointed analogies with the earlier fate of the Paris Commune, referring to the "proletarian revolution... drowning in blood."[11] On the Bolshevik side, Zinoviev stressed the hollowness of the Kronstadt events, arguing that the Paris Commune had failed precisely because it had lacked the firm base of a party with a long history and strong traditions behind it.[12] On March 18, the day after the uprising was put down, Petrograd newspapers celebrated the fiftieth anniversary of the Paris Commune. The Bolsheviks, with a flair for irony, later renamed the *Sevastopol'* the *Paris Commune.*[13]

Kronstadt was also directly linked by its contestors to the question of the party's legitimacy. Martov cited the struggle in the Communist Party, which he had predicted would occur once the Civil War was over and which would create the "political and psychological preconditions" for the proletariat to move against the Bolshevik regime, Kronstadt being the climactic manifestation of this crisis.[14] The Mensheviks' leading journal abroad made much of the "disintegration of the ruling party" due to economic and political pressures and the swamping of the party's old guard by individuals motivated only by their own selfish interests.[15] The shaky compromise Lenin had engineered at the Ninth Party Congress in March 1920 to preserve party unity among competing factions was in shreds a year later. The sharpest intraparty critics, the Workers' Opposition and the Democratic Centralists, lacked an independent organizational base but continued to air their dissent at all levels of the party and government, as well as in the press.[16] This dissent hinged on the old, but fundamental, issue of whether the workers' state was born of a spontaneous, mass revolution or was a top-down imposition by the party.

In January 1921, Lenin had referred publicly to a crisis in the party, calling the organization "sick."[17] A little later, the party gave itself a bleak report card. The military exigencies of the Civil War had merely masked the intraparty "illnesses," and a "well-known rift" had occurred between the party and the broad masses of the average workers. The impoverishment of the entire country and the government's inability to satisfy new economic demands were aggravated by the influx into the party of opportunistic people "alien to revolutionary Communism." "In the stormy October Days," these people had taken up provincial (*guberniia*) and county (*uezd*) posts, for which they were ill-suited and which they were now reluctant to relinquish. These "elements of decay" had become "almost the leaders of the rank and file." Even worse, the hermetic conditions of the development of local party organizations had fostered "official elites," which were reluctant to accept new blood from the center, and jealously guarded their prerogatives. They had become an obstacle to growth and initiative in the organization, as revealed by the recent drop in new party members and the decline in the authority of party organizations. The report recommended that broad circles of the party be brought into the decision-making process and that the focus of party activity be shifted from the committees and circles to plants and factories. The party center, it concluded, had to provide concrete instructions to local areas in all matters.[18]

THE SOCIAL FRAMEWORKS OF ISTPART

The events of the first months of 1921 served to galvanize Bolshevik efforts to institutionalize October. Keenly sensitive to perennial criticism from within their own party that they were isolated from their supporters, the Bolshevik leaders did not want to confirm this sense of dislocation with fragmented histories of the revolution and of their party. The new socialist institutions, many of them conceived soon after October 1917, became viable entities only after 1921, as the state began to allocate resources to them with increased urgency. One organization in particular was charged with writing a coherent history of the revolution and the party as a means of providing the sense of cohesion and history that the party members seemed to lack so desperately. The Commission on the History of the October Revolution and the Russian Communist Party (Komissiia po istorii Oktiabr'skoi revoliutsii i Rossiiskoi Kommunisticheskoi Partii, hereinafter Istpart), was set up under the Commissariat of Enlightenment (Narkompros) by a Sovnarkom decree on September 25, 1920. Its original members harbored no illusions about the enormity of their charge. In late 1921, Nevskii provided Istpart with a wretched picture of the situation in Petrograd: factories and homes without fuel, perennially oppositional workers, skilled workers quitting the city, and women fleeing from economic hardships to prostitution. "I am by the way a pessimist!" he noted.[19] The task of writing October was now in very different hands. It would no longer be guided by eclectic artists and scholars loosely bound together by their faith in revolution, but by a quite small band of men and women who had shared life experiences and a worldview for many years.[20]

In his studies of the social frameworks of memory, Maurice Halbwachs stresses that any group reconstruction of past events must originate in the shared conceptions of members of that group, and that only those experiences that are "of concern to the greatest number of members" will be articulated as part of that group memory.[21] Indeed, shared experiences and conceptions are critical to the internal coherence and vitality of recollections of events, affording them the credibility and authenticity of mutual reinforcement, as individuals in this like-minded group strive to harmonize their interpretations of past events. In doing so, as Halbwachs put it, they "drop those details that, it seems to them, do not interest their community."[22] These individuals draw upon multiple mutually reinforcing factors to determine what interests them or what is relevant. Their own ideological, political, and cultural conceptions operate in a close relationship with the ideological, political, and cultural goals of the system in which they live.

Sovnarkom initially appointed nine individuals to Istpart's board (*kollegiia*): Ol'minskii as chair, and V. V. Adoratskii, N. N. Baturin, Bubnov, Bystrianskii, Nevskii, S. A. Piontkovskii, M. N. Pokrovskii, and D. B. Riazanov. A decree from the Organizational Bureau (Orgbiuro) of the Central Committee of the party on December 2, 1921 moved Istpart under the jurisdiction of the Central Committee and supplemented the board with other prominent party activists, including A. Ia. Arosev, N. N. Avdeev, Ts. S. Bobrovskaia (Zelikson), A. I. Elizarova, P. N. Lepeshinskii, M. N. Liadov, S. I. Mitskevich, Podvoiskii, M. A. Savel'ev, and O. A. Varentsova. Its chair, Ol'minskii, was its driving force during the first years of the 1920s. An unwavering Marxist then in his late fifties, who had joined the RSDRP in 1898, he had been a long-time ally of Lenin both inside Russia and in the emigration, and together with other Marxists like Baturin and Lepeshchinskii, regarded himself as the much-needed guardian of Bolshevik party history. The conceptual and ideological world of all of these men and women, though, was shaped by a number of common experiences. They shared an explicitly revolutionary worldview, but a worldview bounded by a party framework. With the exception of the relatively young Piontkovskii, who was twenty-nine years old in 1920 and joined the Communist Party only in 1919, all had enjoyed long careers as professional revolutionaries, having joined the RSDRP around the turn of the century. Their world was one of local party groupings or committees (Adoratskii and Arosev in Kazan', Bubnov in Ivanovo-Voznesensk, Bobrovskaia and Liadov in Baku, and Varentsova and Baturin in a series of different local party organizations) and of periods spent at the central party organizations in Moscow and Petrograd.

For the vast majority of these people, periods of intense party work inside Russia had been interspersed with periods of equally intense, but isolated, internal or foreign exile. They were accustomed to hammering out ideas in the often intimate and closed political circles of Russian Social Democracy in Europe. The intense conditions of the "circle milieu [*kruzhkovshchina*]" of the emigration would later be called by Fedor Dan a "sad inheritance from a sad past." [23] Indeed, in 1891 Friedrich Engels had already feared that doctrinal disputes in the Russian émigré colonies would undercut the forces opposing tsarism:

> Everybody knows everybody else and consequently every step forward is inevitably accompanied by splits, by polemics, which take on an extremely personal character. This is typical of every political "emigration."... I was always convinced that the party with sufficient moral strength to rise above this atmosphere of personal scores and to refuse to be influenced by squabbles would gain a great advantage over the other parties. [24]

This *kruzhkovshchina* provided solace, friendship, and intellectual stimulation. It also fostered, as Haimson has noted, "elitism, sectarianism, and intolerance."[25]

7.   M. S. Ol'minskii (Courtesy of the RGAKFD in Krasnogorsk)

The "stifling air of the narrow circles and conventicles... [in] Russian Social Democracy," wrote Dan, allowed the Bolsheviks' splitting tactics so effectively to "poison" the factional battle in Russian social democracy. [26] These same conditions also fostered in the members a sense of posterity, a belief in the seminal historical importance of their own revolutionary past. Indeed, several, including Pokrovskii, Baturin, Riazanov, Liadov, and the young Piontkovskii, had been brought into Istpart for their academic training or experience in historical studies. [27]

There was also much of the *kruzhkovshchina* in the local party groupings inside Russia prior to 1917, the predominant image of an organic network of interlinked and functioning committees being in reality a product of the later mythopoesis of the October Revolution. Although individuals often worked in these groups across factional lines, they were still very much defined by their party experience. This party framework also defined Arosev, who had first worked in SR organizations in Kazan', Petrograd, and Moscow; Riazanov, who had left the Bolshevik Party over disagreements with Lenin, to rejoin only in 1917; Bubnov, who joined the Left Communists in 1918; Avdeev, who joined the Menshevik Internationalists

8.   P. N. Lepeshinskii (Courtesy of the RGAKFD in Krasnogorsk)

after February 1917; and Liadov, who was readmitted to the Communist Party only in 1920 after flirting with Menshevik positions.

Many of the men and women in charge of Istpart had cut their political teeth in various editorial roles in the social democratic or Bolshevik press in the pre-1917 period. Indeed, the radical press was the most, and at times the only, tangible, physical manifestation of party life inside Russia. These central organs of the local radical parties and groups provided a sense of continuity and unity of purpose in a time of overlapping and amorphous political allegiances and identities. Few people understood the state of the radical parties prior to 1917, or the state of knowledge about their revolutionary movement, better than those who had worked on the editorial boards of the beleaguered radical press. Finally, several of these individuals had been physically involved in the military preparations for the Bolshevik takeover in October, and in various events around the cities of Moscow and Petrograd at that time. Podvoiskii, Nevskii, and Bubnov had been members of the MRC in Petrograd in October and had been involved in the occupation of the Winter Palace. Arosev and Varentsova had been involved in the

9. Pokrovskii, Khodorovskii, and Lunacharsky at the Fifteenth Congress of the RKP(b), 1927 (Courtesy of the RGAKFD in Krasnogorsk)

MRC in Moscow that had commanded troops of the Moscow Military District. Their historical experience to that point would ensure that the events of October would become *the* seminal event of their individual revolutionary biographies.

These individuals were the officially sanctioned arbiters of October's memory, in particular, and of the memory of the revolutionary movement, in general. Their shared life experiences and worldviews ensured that they would regard their charge not merely as an important one but as one vital to the revolutionary cause itself, to their own autobiographies, and to the new Soviet state. They might argue over the specifics or logistics of the task of recording the history of the October Revolution, but the need for the task itself was beyond question for them. Istpart represented a physical meeting place at which these individuals' concerns could be articulated and formulated in more coherent form, and a coordinated strategy devised to meet these concerns. From this larger group of Istpart activists a subset formed, as infirmity, absence, reticence, or unsuitability reduced active membership in the group to a handful of individuals and severely curtailed its activities for the first three years of its existence. [28] These limitations notwithstanding, the Istpart board's regular attendees (namely Ol'minskii, Adoratskii, Lepeshinskii, Nevskii, Baturin, Mitskevich, Varentsova, and Elizarova) helped shape the structure and content of the materials on October over the next few years, in the process constituting the October Revolution as an insistent archival presence. [29]

THE NATURE OF THE EVIDENCE

All of the Istpart board were acutely concerned about the quantity and quality of the materials available on both the revolution and the party. "Almost no sources" existed, Ol'minskii bluntly informed the Ninth Party Conference in September 1920.[30] Since October 1917, the Bolshevik press had regularly carried general appeals to collect any and every piece of information. Articles referred vaguely to "the enormous quantity of historically valuable materials" that existed, citing as examples unpublished reports on revolutionary activity, revolutionary songs, personal impressions about events, reminiscences, posters, leaflets, banners, and so on. They called for people to seek out new sources that might yield "revolutionary material" on October and the RKP.[31] One of its main tasks, Istpart noted, was to gather documents "that depict the day-to-day side of the revolutionary age—correspondence, diaries, notes."[32]

In the case of the party, the dearth of information was critical, and the Central Committee appealed in mid-1918 to all party organizations to send it "every newspaper, every proclamation of the smallest organization for the future historian of the Great Russian Revolution."[33] In some ways, this dearth was thought to be understandable. Individuals could not be expected to comprehend the significance of a great event like October without the necessary perspective that only time could bring. Moreover, the long years of conspiratorial existence of the revolutionary parties had hardly been conducive to the physical preservation of material evidence of their activities. As Pokrovskii wrote, at that time archives were "carried in the pockets of secretaries and destroyed tens of times over." [34] Little wonder then, according to *Pravda* in early 1919, that "among comrades very few know the history of the party," and especially the "first founding congress" of the party. [35]

At stake here, as all these revolutionaries well understood, was the past itself. Their battle with their enemies over the representation of the past was a timeless one, and one that had been fought earlier for the French Revolution. The "bourgeoisie" had adapted the French Revolution "to its needs," Istpart's founding address noted. It had done so by selecting only those "events that were important from the viewpoint of the class interests of the bourgeoisie, [and] heroes that the bourgeois heart found pleasant to remember." By choosing to write about the Storming of the Bastille, for example, and to ignore the rise of the Left Jacobins, and by choosing to canonize Georges Danton and ignore Maximilien Robespierre, the bourgeoisie "made the past serve the present." [36]

Because information had to be "made to mean," those in charge of producing, selecting, and compiling the information were of critical importance. In instructions to the party faithful about the kinds of information to gather, Istpart warned that "[our enemies] will try with all their power and are trying to reinterpret the Proletarian Revolution in their own class interests." [37] At the Ninth Party Conference, Ol'minskii decried the "pathetic state" of knowledge about the party, adding that the few archives that existed were "to a great degree in the hands of Mensheviks," and that documents being collected now were falling into "alien hands." As far as the history of the party was concerned, he asked rhetorically, "can the correctness of Martov and [Aleksandr] Potresov be counted upon?" [38] "This archival matter," he concluded,

> should in no way be entrusted to our political enemies in this area. In other areas of archival business, that is another matter, but in the field of purely party history and the history of the revolution, of the relations between these and those parties, it is highly desirable that all this not be entrusted to outsiders, to those hostile to our political tendencies. [39]

Nonparty people who were well known and had shown complete loyalty to the party could have access, if they obtained special permission from the "appropriate organ." Only RKP members were "absolutely reliable" and should be placed in charge of these materials.[40] And even they, it was pointed out elsewhere, might not be up to the task, because of their inexperience in archival matters or their "incorrect views about the significance of documents." They had to be made to realize that "archival holdings are the property of the republic."[41] Within a few years, access to them would be ever more tightly controlled.[42]

The Bolsheviks were certainly aware of the representations of the October events being disseminated by the Kadets, SRs, and Mensheviks they had forced into emigration. Pokrovskii was unhappy that the Kadet Pavel Miliukov was publishing "volume after volume on the history of the revolution," while "we have nothing yet in this area."[43] Forced emigration certainly denied the critics of the Bolshevik regime the means with which to articulate and disseminate their representations of events on any meaningful scale inside Soviet Russia. The Bolshevik leaders, though, clearly underestimated the power at these exiles' disposal to establish the counternarrative as a dominant representation of the events of October 1917 in the West.[44] At the time, Pokrovskii was far more concerned with efforts under way *inside* Soviet Russia to chronicle October. He singled out for criticism the Society for the Study of the History of the Revolutionary Liberation Movement in Russia (Obshchestvo izucheniia istorii osvoboditel'nogo dvizheniia v Rossii), which had been set up in Petrograd at the end of 1919 under such "not quite counterrevolutionaries" as Vera Figner and N. A. Rozhkov, as well as M. K. Lemke, P. E. Shchegolev, and the renowned prerevolutionary historian E. V. Tarle. Despite their "desire to write this history objectively," Pokrovskii implied that, they would be unable to do so, because they lacked a Communist perspective and would "gather materials and elucidate them from their own point of view."[45] He described the collection of revolutionary materials as a "battle," which, if lost, would mean that "our children must learn the history of the revolution from White Guard pamphlets."[46]

This recognition of the power of representation guided later warnings about the pitfalls of researching "counterrevolutionary" events on the basis of tsarist documents. In a memorandum to the central Istpart, the Moscow bureau advised that such documents should be used only moderately and with extreme care, and should never be simply reprinted, even if furnished with explanatory notes. The problem, the bureau added, was deciding from which viewpoint to consider the counterrevolutionary events, and a "bare account of the events is not appropriate."[47] In a similar vein, an article from Tula warned readers not to take the categories used in "counterrevolutionary" writings at face value. It criticized documents from the Tula gendarme administration archive for the way the authorities at the time had "tried to represent the behavior of the Black Hundreds... as 'nationalists' ('patriots') in extremely soft colors and, on the other hand, exaggerate the colors when representing the actions of the opposing side." The article observed that this representation, combined with the probable failure of local investigators to record eyewitness accounts of Black Hundred excesses, whipped up a "hatred of 'revolutionaries,' 'students,' 'orators'... among the wealthy and petit bourgeois circles of the Tula population."[48]

This same mind-set produced the sometimes obsessive "rules of secrecy" governing the deliberations of high-level party bodies during and beyond the Civil War years.[49] It informed the detailed instructions about how collected documents should be classified and archived, how they should be preserved and stored, and which institutions had jurisdiction over which sources.[50] At the Tenth Party Congress in spring 1921, Ol'minskii imagined a dark possibility, a time in the not-too-distant future when young Communists, fourteen or fifteen years old at the time of the February Revolution, would be asking: "And what is the February Revolution? And what is the October Revolution?" Ol'minskii recalled how in 1912, when the labor movement was reviving and the Central Committee of the party called for a strike for January 9 (the anniversary of the 1905 massacre of workers in Petrograd), the editors of *Pravda* were visited by young workers expressing their readiness to strike but asking what January 9 signified.[51] Little wonder then that the Istpart project was launched as a call to arms, with Baturin demanding a:

> comprehensive elucidation of the history of the October overthrow and

its inspirer and creator—the RKP.... The history of the development of this party, its victories and defeats must be written as soon as possible. It must appear not for the edification of posterity; it is needed as a weapon in the ceaseless struggle, as an accompanying thread to the final victory.[52]

Given the insecurities expressed by Bolshevik leaders about the general population's perception of their party, and their perennial efforts to provide sharper contours to Bolshevik identity, it is hardly surprising that the state of party history appeared especially urgent to them. "Almost nothing has been done for the history of our party," Bystrianskii wrote in *Petrogradskaia pravda* in October 1920:

> There are no popular primers [*posobii*] or serious works at all. This is understandable. Only members of the Communist Party would be able to give the true history of its past, to give a true picture of the unification of the proletariat and its class party, a picture undistorted by the distorting mirror of bourgeois prejudices.... But there were no Communists to write the history, because their energies were directed at the creation of the historical process, at the active participation in it.[53]

Initially, Istpart was a response to these concerns about the party. In August 1920, the party had set up the Commission on the History of the RKP(b) (Komissiia po istorii RKP(b)), headed by Ol'minskii, and including Bubnov, Baturin, Nevskii, Adoratskii, and Pokrovskii. For the next month, it occupied itself almost exclusively with the question of how best to approach the study of the history of the party. Individuals or small groups were assigned to investigate local libraries and archives for relevant materials, to contact local party committees to learn what work had already been completed on party history, to draw up a notice about the urgent need for party members to write their memoirs, and to compile an appropriate questionnaire to be sent to older party members.[54]

The first plans they had drawn up by early September failed to define the precise relationship between the history of the Bolshevik Party and the history of the October Revolution: four subcommissions were set up covering the period up until 1903 (Baturin, Riazanov, Ol'minskii), 1903–1917 (Baturin, Ol'minskii, Nevskii, Riazanov), the history of the RKP from October 1917 (Baturin, Bubnov, Nevskii), and the history of the revolution from October 1917 (Adoratskii, Piontkovskii, Pokrovskii).[55] Pokrovskii suggested that a separate commission be formed to study October.[56] Although pursued under one roof, the histories of the party and of the revolution were not at first integrated into a single subject, each initially being pursued separately by two subcommissions of Istpart.[57] Interestingly, this derived in part from a belief held by these Bolsheviks that the histories were intended for quite distinct audiences, with general histories of October for the general population and primers and readers on the history of the RKP for party members and agitators. Indeed, the first plan of work drawn up in September 1920 by Nevskii for the party subcommission was aimed at the "lecturers, propagandists, and party workers, in general, [who] lack not only a collection of materials to prepare their lectures but cannot indicate to the audience the most basic features of the daily experiences of the party, the October overthrow, and the history of the RKP in particular."[58] Istpart leaders were disturbed by the first plans of work they saw from local Istpart bodies such as the Urals regional bureau, which appeared to want to reproduce the uncomfortable bifurcation of party and revolutionary history. As early as November 1920, the local leaders had already assigned individuals to head up separate sections (*sektsii*) to study the history of the party and the history of the workers' movement up to 1917. The central Istpart quickly warned them against any such division of tasks and asked, "How is it possible to elucidate the history of Soviet construction, the Civil War, and so on separately from [*vne*] the history of the party?"[59] With the first issue of the *Istpart Bulletin* in 1921, Ol'minskii officially reintegrated them:

> Not only the history of the Great Russian Revolution but also the history of the RKP (at least from the moment of the birth of social democracy in Russia)—the genesis and growth of that motive force that unflinchingly pushed forward the spontaneous element [*stikhiia*] of the Russian Revolution, beginning on the eve of 1905 to the October Days of 1917, cannot fail to be at the center of attention of the historian of our contemporary social storms.[60]

Of critical concern in this battle over representation was the nature of the evidence. Because materials were so scarce, what constituted legitimate materials and where might they be found? Ol'minskii identified three kinds of potential sources: party literature, decrees and protocols of congresses and conferences, and police archives. The police archives, he warned, were a problematic source, as they provided a distorted reflection of the history of the party.[61] Moreover, Baturin noted that the gendarme and police archives, which many revolutionaries had believed would hold much valuable information on the underground parties, had quickly proven to be disappointing, drab, and nowhere near as abundant as expected.[62] Nor were the first two sources mentioned by Ol'minskii beyond reproach. As Ol'minskii told the Tenth Party Congress, the need for the party to hide itself from the police for so long meant that the materials it produced in the past had of necessity been dry and unrevealing of the "behind-the-scenes life and activity" of the party, and of the "motivations" behind the resolutions. These sources also left many gaps in the history of the party. They began with the sundry tiny groups that agitated among the workers at the start of the 1880s and jumped straight to the appearance of the Union for the Struggle of the Liberation of the Working Class (Soiuz bor'by za osvobozhdenie rabochego klassa) in 1895. "And in these ten years," Ol'minskii asked rhetorically, "what? Was the proletariat asleep? Was there no development of the Social Democratic Party?"[63]

Ol'minskii's, and the Istpart board's, misgivings about these sources went to their conception of the genuine nature and location of their revolution. They believed that the history of the revolution and party came together most tangibly and vitally at the local level. Failure to preserve provincial documentation could leave incomplete newspaper runs as the sole source on the revolutionary movement:

> And, by the way, it was at the local level that the revolution was realized in fact—in the centers, its planning and slogans were mainly worked out.... If we lose the provincial material, we will be unable to show how the revolution occurred and what was, in fact, accomplished by it.[64]

The party had to be sought at the local level. "Without materials on the history of the party collected in the provinces," Nevskii wrote the Central Committee in December 1922, "there is no doubt that the history of the party cannot be revealed."[65] Not only should the history of October and of the party not be left to the party's leaders, it could *only* be written from the ground up. Revolutionaries of various stripes expressed this same conviction. "The time has not yet come for the history of Soviet power," Lenin told the Ninth Party Congress in March 1920. "Were it to come, we—I am speaking for myself and, I think, for the Central Committee—do not intend to be historians."[66] Just before the Bolshevik takeover, the Menshevik Boris Nikolaevskii had noted that the central press, despite the more open conditions of 1917, had produced almost no materials on the history of the party (by which he meant the RSDRP in general). "With such a dearth of information at our disposal about our party's past," he wrote, "with the almost completely unelaborated status of our party's history, especially with regard to facts," the provincial press was the only place to find the necessary historical documentation. Here would be found the local activists who "built our party, placing stone on top of stone, brick on top of brick, remaining the entire time in the shadows, then departing into obscurity, but leaving behind heirs and successors."[67] Only the democratic provincial press, wrote another commentator in 1919, "summoned from the underground" by the February Revolution, could provide the necessary "everyday context" for the "memoirs that will be written (and, in part, have already been written) by 'party leaders.' " The author singled out Sukhanov's recently published memoirs as an example of the kind of work that revealed nothing about revolutionary life or the "mood of the masses" that was so essential to an understanding of the post-February 1917 period.[68] Such views were heard in the Istpart board too. "It is necessary to resurrect the daily experience [*byt*], to reconstruct how they lived then," Ol'minskii told the Tenth Congress of the Party in March 1921:

> We will understand nothing in the revolutionary labor movement if we do not know the conditions of life of the workers at the time—not only the level of their wage, but the entire circumstances of their life: apartment, everyday life, factory conditions, how we dealt with them in the factories.[69]

CRUMBS OF TRUTH

Istpart was born of a need for stability and coherence in these unstable and inconstant times. An internally consistent history of the revolution and party would help provide a stable past to anchor the Soviet regime. "Through corroboration, the truth can be revealed," Ol'minskii told the Ninth Party Conference. "Everywhere there are mistakes, everywhere there are also crumbs of truth."[70] Istpart not only had to gather the pieces, it had to fashion from them a whole revolutionary narrative. The production of a narrative flexible enough for all manner of groups and individuals to locate their own role in it was aided immeasurably by Ol'minskii's exploding of the temporal boundaries of October and the Bolshevik Party:

> With regard to the "October Revolution," this revolution is not limited to the October Days of 1917: it is still continuing, and it is impossible even to predict when it might be said that this revolutionary period will be over; with regard to the history of the Russian Communist Party (Bolshevik) it would be wrong to limit the task to the period when the word "Bolshevik" appeared (1903), and its history must be taken from the time of the first independent political act of the proletariat in Russia.[71]

His statement made of the October Days a pivotal moment in a much broader, amorphous process of revolution, and subsumed the RSDRP in the Bolshevik Party rather than treat the Bolshevik party as a faction of the RSDRP.

Every step taken by the Istpart framers was toward narrative coherence. Their organization's very administrative structure was just such a step. Istpart was conceived as a grid of local bureaus, centered on the Istpart bureau at the provincial level (*gubistpartotdel*), which would be set up under the provincial committee of the party. This network grew from the center outward to the provinces, although one organization in Novgorod claimed to have been engaged in this kind of activity before the creation of Istpart.[72] By October 1921, Istpart had twenty-one active local bureaus, growing to seventy-two a year later (fourteen at the regional level and fifty-eight at the provincial level).[73] Each was to have its own board of at least three people, including at least one member of the local committee of the party, which vetted the committee members according to length of party membership, social status, and scholarly qualifications. These local bureaus were to collect and systematize any materials on the history of the local labor movement, the local party organizations, and "the October overthrow" in a given region. This was all to be done in close contact with Moscow and "in accordance with its wishes and instructions."[74] The bureaus had the right to demand from all institutions and private individuals any materials they might have and appealed to all "organs of Soviet power" for assistance in procuring them. They were also charged with organizing libraries, museums, and exhibitions; publishing their work in local journals and in book form; arranging public lectures and meetings on the history of October and the RKP; and organizing evenings of reminiscences. The aim of all this activity was "both the theoretical study of history and the unification of veterans of the labor movement." The provincial bureaus had to make monthly detailed reports of their activities to the respective provincial committee of the party, to the Istpart bureau of the party committee above it, and even to the central Istpart.[75] From this grid, the central Istpart would be able to build up a complete picture of the revolutionary movement from its individual parts, literally mapping the revolution.

Although conceived as a centrally directed network, the local Istparts' work had to be infused with local participation. Istpart called for short popular histories of the revolution at the local level and for young people from party schools to be involved in putting them together.[76] From the very beginning, grassroots' circles (*kruzhki sodeistvii*) were planned in order to assist the local Istpart branches. These circles were to draw in the oldest members of the party and "direct participants in the revolutionary events, from various localities if possible."[77] Local bureaus were also instructed to collect materials on the activities of members of local organizations or participants in the local labor movement by finding and questioning their relatives and acquaintances and by obtaining photographs and correspondence from them.[78] If only the right questions could be asked of the right people in the right places, it was believed, the revolutionary movement would yield up its past and the party's role in that past. Ol'minskii expressed this fervent belief best:

> I think that ultimately in every city there can be found a sympathizer or a member of the party, some little old chap [*starikashka*] or other, who is not doing important political work, who is not being moved from city to city, and who can undertake this work with love.[79]

Even in late 1921, while reviewing the slow growth and results of the organization at the local level, Ol'minskii still found it unnecessary to send "special people" to the local areas to guide work and believed that the work would automatically improve "when interest arises at the local level, when there are individuals who will get to grips with this matter."[80]

They received plenty of guidance and direction from Moscow, as well as from local party centers. Moving the Istpart network from the jurisdiction of the Commissariat of Enlightenment to that of the party made the existing party network across Soviet Russia accessible to them, at least in principle. Local Istpart bureaus were ordered by the central Istpart in 1922 to subordinate themselves to the local provincial or regional committees of the party.[81] The first circulars from Istpart to the local party organizations made clear that the local Istpart bureau had to relate the local area to the revolutionary movement as a whole. In 1921, Istpart informed the local bureaus that they had to explain the work of the local labor movement, reveal the work of the party in its interrelations with other parties, establish the role of the local organizations of the party in the revolutionary movement up to February 1917 and from February to October 1917, as well as highlight the role of the party in socialist construction. Furthermore, each bureau was to invite five or six comrades to work in it and collect and order chronologically all materials on the history of the local labor movement, local party organizations, and the October overthrow, to form the basis of a revolutionary archive.[82]

ARCHIVAL COHERENCE

Archival coherence was particularly coveted by revolutionary leaders, who contrasted their own quite coherent party identities with the more general perception of political parties as entities fragmented both spatially and temporally. "Archives assemble," Trouillot points out. "Their assembly work is not limited to a more or less passive act of collecting. Rather, it is an active act of production that prepares facts for historical intelligibility. Archives set up both the substantive and formal elements of the narrative."[83] Early in 1919, *Pravda* had called for a party archive to be set up as a repository of sources for future study.[84] Still, until the end of the Civil War, plans for a centralized network of such archives existed largely only in the form of unenacted legislation.[85] These desires received a boost with the establishment of Istpart. In its first address to party members, Istpart observed that "an archive does not simply mean a heap of documents stuffed into a cupboard. An archive is a mass of documents, sorted out and put into order, classified [klassifitsirovannyi], distributed either according to their content or... chronologically."[86] It instructed its bureaus to search for local police archives and for any archives of local party organizations, assigning to the latter task their own members to work under the local party committees.[87] It also immediately issued detailed instructions on how to store documents to protect them from loss, theft, or damage.[88]

Gathering together under one thematic (and physical) roof the scant documents about the scattered and often short-lived organizations of the pre-October RSDRP produced a sense of continuity never actually known by the local organizations. This could be seen in practice in the work of the Petrograd bureau, which set up a historical commission of thirty people under Shchegolev. In November 1920, this body began to examine all available materials and divide them according to periods corresponding to the "more or less completed moments in the history of the RSDRP." This activity had already yielded some 723 proclamations of the RSDRP, mostly from 1903 to 1912.[89] These proclamations were brought together and organized chronologically to produce an impression of a coherent and inex-orable development of the RSDRP.

In one of its first acts, Istpart sent representatives abroad to locate and, if possible, bring back with them the "foreign archives" of the party. These referred not only to official records of the foreign delegations of the RSDRP but also to holdings of individual revolutionaries from their periods of emigration, and even materials from former Russian prisoners of war.[90] One such trip in 1923 retrieved a large amount of material from Paris, representing about a fifth of the library and archive "founded in Geneva by the Bolsheviks at the end of 1903." These materials included "almost all émigré publications published abroad," as well as manuscripts, documents, and illegal publications. The individual who reported to Istpart noted that "most" of the books in these materials were "Menshevik."[91] In February 1924, Ol'minskii proposed to the Central Committee of the party that an archive of Istpart be established to house all of these materials and to or-ganize them chronologically as a basis for future research. The leaders of both wings of the RSDRP had long fought the perception inside Russia that their long years in the emigration alienated them from the masses in Russia. In this central archive, the emigration became physically and symbolically integrated as part of the revolutionary movement in Russia.[92]

10. Delegates to the Second All-Russian Congress of Archival Workers, 1929 (Courtesy of the RGAKFD in Krasnogorsk)

Far less successful were Istpart's efforts to gather the archives of party bodies inside Russia for the period after 1917 and into 1918. Istpart reported to the secretariat of the Central Committee of the RKP in late 1924 that the archives of the Central Committee itself, of the Moscow Committee of the party, and of the Council of the National Economy (VSNKh), the Commissariat of Justice (Narkomiust), and the Commissariat of Enlightenment for that period had been lost.[93] Nonetheless, throughout the 1920s a unified, institutionalized party archive remained a major goal and continued to be regarded by Istpart leaders as a more concrete alternative to the "personal reminiscences and subjective experiences" being gathered so energetically.[94]

LITERARY COHERENCE

Ambitious publication plans by Istpart also accommodated the twin goals of narrative coherence and flexibility. Assigned to the Petrograd bureau, Nevskii, in late 1921, called for a "completely rational plan" of work and proposed a structured plan of publications for his bureau carried out "under the constant guidance of the chairman [of the bureau]." The plan included works on the history of the Petrograd organization of the RSDRP, the compilation of lists of "Social Democratic revolutionaries [sic]" who took part in it, monographs on individual periods of the Petersburg workers' and social democratic movement, and the production of a "pragmatic, preparatory condensed sketch" of the Petersburg Social Democratic Party organization.[95]

Individual bureaus of Istpart divided their work according to various periodizations of the revolutionary movement. The Moscow bureau used the following chronological breakdown: the circles of the 1890s; the fight against populism; 1900–1903 (*Iskra*); 1903–1904 up to January 2 (the Zubatovshchina); 1905—January 9; the First and Second Dumas, to June 3, 1907; the reaction, 1907–1912; the revival (*pod"em*) of 1912–1914; the war; the February Revolution; October 1917; after October.[96] Although individual periodizations might break down a little differently from region to region, they all told a teleological tale of revolutionary inevitability, and all local bureaus collected and organized their materials according to this tale.[97] Like Ol'minskii's broad definition of the October Revolution and the party, the template was flexible enough to incorporate local events into the grand narrative.[98] It allowed local bureaus to work on any period of the last two decades and still reinforce the general narrative.[99] Anniversaries provided Istpart with a convenient stimulus to set up yet one more subcommission or department to tell one more part of the revolutionary story. In 1923, for example, in light of the forthcoming centenary anniversary of the Decembrist uprising of 1825, a specially established subcommission planned a series of monographs on the history of the revolutionary movement beginning with that uprising.[100] By the end of 1923, Istpart was already preparing for the twentieth anniversary of the 1905 Revolution, having charged Ol'minskii to come up with plans for collections of articles and poetry, as well as lists of cinematic representations and revolutionary belles lettres in honor of 1905.[101]

VISUAL COHERENCE

This attempt to achieve literary coherence was matched in Istpart's plans by an effort for visual coherence. In late 1918, the organizing committee of the October anniversary for that year had appealed to all involved to send it one example of every publication produced in honor of the occasion for a planned Museum of the October Revolution (Muzei Oktiabr'skoi revoliutsii).[102]

A year later, artists involved in designing artifacts for the October celebrations of 1919 were asked to hand over all drafts of emblems, posters, and other artifacts for a planned Museum of People's Celebrations (Muzei narodnykh torzhestv).[103] By 1920, the Museum of the Revolution in Petrograd was organizing a countrywide expedition to gather historical materials on the revolutionary movement. The

11. Iaroslavskii and Savel'ev at the Museum of the October Revolution, Moscow, 1928 (Courtesy of the RGAKFD in Krasnogorsk)

Soviet authorities even invited prominent political figures from abroad such as the anarchists Alexander Berkman and Emma Goldman to join it, although Berkman thought that his inclusion in such "nonpolitical" work signaled his exclusion from "more vital work" by an increasingly hostile Communist regime.[104]

One of the major tasks for all Istpart bureaus in the 1920s was the construction of exhibitions and museums devoted to the October Revolution and the party. As the Novgorod bureau put it, its museum's task was to collect, store, and organize materials on revolutionary history as a precondition for the "dissemination of a correct understanding [*pravil'nye poniatiia*] of the revolution and the spreading of revolutionary ideas."[105] Savel'ev told the Istpart board in June 1923 that Moscow's Museum of the Revolution was aimed at a different audience than its own *Exhibition of Istpart* (*Vystavka Istparta*), which was on display in the hallways of the Kremlin. Where the former was a "museum of relics" aimed at a mass audience, the latter had a "clearly pedagogical aim" as a "party seminar" aimed at the "more prepared party comrades."[106] Indeed, the *Exhibition of Istpart* had been set up in the summer of 1921 in the House of Unions (*Dom soiuzov*) specifically to acquaint party members with the history of the party and was timed to coincide with the Tenth Congress of the party that would focus on the need for party unity.[107]

Whatever the intended audience, and despite Berkman's and Goldman's misgivings, these museums and exhibitions, by concentrating and organizing (usually chronologically) under one roof all available materials on a particular theme, imparted a strong and coherent visual impact to scattered documentation. Photographic materials were considered of special value. On orders from the Moscow bureau, small groups from local plants took photographs of buildings that were "noteworthy in terms of the history of the revolution."[108] The Podol'sk bureau typically combed its local gendarme archives for photographs and files on RSDRP and PSR members, arranging them in an exhibition of the revolutionary movement in Podol'ia.[109] In 1922, Istpart petitioned the Central Committee for fifty million rubles for photographs for an exhibition, with the money supposedly to be recovered from the sale of these photographs.[110] Temporary exhibitions on discrete themes often formed the basis of future, permanent museums of the revolution in local areas.[111]

As early as 1921, the Ekaterinoslav bureau organized an exhibition on the "history of the party and the revolution," which was visited by, on average, 150 people a day, mostly groups brought in from local schools and military units in Ekaterinoslav.[112] The museums and exhibitions varied widely from area to area. They could be as small as the museum set up by the Vitebsk bureau, which contained "several photographs" and some local and central newspapers from the post-1917 period, or the exhibition opened in a workers' club in Simbirsk, containing a few photographs of local party workers taken from tsarist police (Okhrana) files, several copies of the newspaper *Iskra*, and a charter from the local party organization of Ardatovskii County, which, "for a long time after the February Revolution, received no information from the center.[113] They could be as large as the Museum of the Revolution set up by the Novgorod bureau, which by 1923 contained 215 proclamations, 318 photographs, 500 examples of illegal literature, and 210 posters. A two-part exhibition was organized in the museum on the *History of the October Revolution and the Party* and the *March of the Great October Revolution*, comprising almost 2,000 exhibits and visited by over 17,000 people over a year and a half.[114] Local bureaus invariably boasted of the high attendance figures at their museums and exhibitions, and, like the Novgorod bureau, stressed that they were "eagerly visited by Red Army men, workers, and peasants."[115] These museums and exhibitions were not conceived as sites of passive viewing but as sites of active propaganda. They very often supplemented the displayed items with public lectures on relevant themes or courses on the history of the party, which helped contextualize the exhibits.[116] As the Novgorod bureau noted, the "colossal" number of visitors to its exhibit was a result of the fact that the museum was in a discussion club (*diskussionyi klub*) where local conferences regularly took place.[117] The high attendance figures were also, of course, a product of group excursions organized by local committees, organizations, and factories.

TOWARD A LITERATURE OF WHOLE MEMORIES

Despite their goal of producing a coherent revolutionary narrative, the Istpart leaders still feared that all of their efforts would inevitably fall short of conveying the inherent vividness and drama of the *lived* revolutionary experience. Only the personal reminiscences of contemporaries could provide this. "Surely we [Russian Communists] just *know* about our revolution?" Istpart asked with a hint of exasperation. "Everybody remembers what they saw around themselves in that corner of Russia where fate tossed them for the past three years.[118] Of course, this statement was directed at party members. In the highly ideologized atmosphere of early Soviet Russia, not all eyewitnesses were equal, nor were their memoirs. Indeed, a large part of Soviet revolutionary culture up until that time had been about separating the legitimate from the illegitimate voices in the new society. But even the voice of the party intelligentsia, which had played such a role in October, could not be heard at the expense of the voice of "worker social democracy.[119] While maintaining that Istpart drew "no distinction between the workers and the intelligentsia" in its work, Ol'minskii warned that the

> intelligentsia, especially in the prerevolutionary period, lived one life, and the worker another life…. Therefore, if our history is written only from the reminiscences of the worker, then this will be one history, and from the reminiscences of the intellectual, this will be another history. There will be two different histories.[120]

Still, as the Moscow bureau implied, the more legitimate of the two histories in this proletarian dictatorship was that of "the workers… who have a revolutionary past, and even nonparty workers."[121] Their social status alone did not guarantee the unimpeachability of their reminiscences. A Vitebsk bureau leader told an Istpart conference in 1923 that "the mass worker for the most part knows only his own corner of work and therefore cannot provide a complete picture in his reminiscences."[122] Even the worker, then, had to be restricted to discrete revolutionary episodes or epochs, or to certain themes, such as the activities of local party organizations (especially those in individual plants). The collective reminiscence was deemed the most reliable memoir. Bringing together "groups of comrades who took part in the party organizations at the same time and in the same plant, or at various periods in one plant," would help produce a "complete picture of the party organization at the plant."[123]

Istpart's task was not merely to gather materials but, as Ol'minskii put it, to "create [*sozdat'*] the literature of memoirs (reminiscences)."[124] He might have added that it included the creation of the legitimate reminiscer as well. Only personal reminiscences by the right people would add flesh to the dry bones of the past provided by the published materials. "The conditions of everyday life," wrote one author, "must frame those memoirs that will be written."[125] Ol'minskii urged party members to reminisce in as much richness and detail as possible:

> It is desirable, comrades, that you not take a pro forma attitude to this... but, on the contrary, that each time you recall in as much detail as possible not only the content of the resolutions, decrees, and leaflets but also the psychological, daily peculiarities of the moment.[126]

At the same time, the Istpart board was acutely aware that the vagaries of memory made the very act of recollection problematic. The short-term nature of personal memory, wrote *Petrogradskaia pravda*, threatened the very existence of October.[127] Without the necessary perspective of time and context, individuals could not be expected to realize the broader, revolutionary significance of their recollections. Ol'minskii drew an analogy with legal cases, in which "all witnesses talk nonsense [*vrut*], willy-nilly, and so the perspective is distorted."[128] Furthermore, when they did remember, they often had a tendency to augment their own role in the events. Most valuable among the manuscripts, diaries, and notes that constituted revolutionary documents, Istpart pointed out, were those "compiled for current life and not intentionally for the sake of posterity." [129] These problems were exacerbated by the sheer logistics of eliciting information from large numbers of often illiterate people.

The desire to compensate for the inherent, natural shortcomings of memory contributed to the coherence of the memories so elicited. Local bureaus were instructed by the center to register and question old party activists, who had been either Bolshevik or Menshevik up to 1917, and urge them to write their reminiscences. These reminiscences were to be reviewed by the bureau members, with gaps filled in by supplementary questioning of the author. A further layer of potential mediation was added when local bureau workers were authorized to write down reminiscences for those who were unable to write.[130] Istpart further instructed that the inherent fragility of personal memory rendered it quite acceptable when writing one's reminiscences to consult documents, newspaper articles, or books.[131] Istpart requested that any documents used by the respondents to "supplement, corroborate, or reinforce" their information be sent to the commission.[132] This was thought to be especially necessary when making use of Okhrana or gendarme materials, which had to be verified against the memories of "old party comrades."[133]

The explicit goal here of Baturin and the other Istpart leaders was a set of whole memories of the revolution from the right people. The past had to be reconstructed piece by piece, noted *Petrogradskaia pravda*: "Scattered and fragmentary when taken separately, they [that is, personal reminiscences], in their totality, must supplement one another and make possible a complete compendium of information and an illustration of party life at different times and in various regions."[134] Istpart drew up lists of prominent fallen comrades, for whom biographical material had to be collected, and published their names in revolutionary journals.[135] High-ranking party members were among the first targeted by letters from the central Istpart urging them to write down their reminiscences. Old Bolsheviks were to be found, registered, and invited to compile their memoirs, or else have their oral reminiscences written down for them.[136]

STRUCTURING MEMORY

Clearly, the quest for coherent memories and legitimate voices made this project far more than the "simple" recording of reminiscences by participants or contemporaries (if such an act is ever simple). The very process of elicitation of these reminiscences structured their form and content in fundamental ways. Most often, individuals articulated their memories of October first as responses to questionnaires (*ankety*) from central or local authorities.[137] Form was conferred by the context in which these questionnaires were completed. They were often distributed at party or state gatherings, or at specially convened evenings of reminiscences, as had happened on the third anniversary of the October Revolution. Party officials, often sent from the Istpart central bureau, were generally on hand to assist in their completion. Local activists were sometimes in Moscow and Petrograd by the time they filled out the questionnaires, having moved there to take up one or another party or state position, and, perhaps, they already viewed their earlier local experiences from the telos of the October Revolution.[138]

The questionnaires distributed by the Bolshevik Party to its committees throughout Russia in 1918 revealed the party leaders' deep ignorance about the state of their own party organization, as they scratched for the barest details about local organizations and their communications with central party bodies during and after October.[139] At the same time, these questionnaires told the tale of October in a quite complex process of elicitation and exhortation. Asking for the name of the respective local party organization, the number of its members (whether they were locals or "imports" from outside the area), when it was first set up, whether it had its own press, party school, or library, and whether other socialist parties were working in the same region structured individual recollections as a function of a party culture. Asking for the names of individual party members, their age, level of education, length of party service, and any punishment they had suffered as a result of their party activity conveyed a sense of the party as a life-long cause. Asking whether the local organization had sent delegates to the Seventh Party Congress in March 1918 in Petrograd—and "If not, why not?"—raised the specter of accountability. [140] A short fourteen-question survey of the major events of the Civil War years in villages and settlements pointed out which events were deemed relevant ("unrest, disorder, uprisings, plots, battles") and which moment was pivotal (the organization of the "Soviet institutions" in the village). [141]

By 1920, the highly detailed questionnaires drawn up by Istpart offered a richer and more insistent script of an inexorable revolutionary movement *as a function* of a coherent party organization. The entire script hinged, of course, on the October Revolution as the culmination of that movement. Respondents were asked how much they knew of the broader revolutionary events in other parts of the country, such questions providing the possibility of imagining one's own actions as part of a broader and internally connected revolutionary movement. [142] Whether they responded positively or negatively to such questions, the respondents, by definition, articulated themselves and their activities as part of that revolutionary narrative.

The inexorability of the revolutionary narrative was conveyed by a series of chronological questionnaires dealing with each stage of the revolution in turn. Moreover, within each questionnaire, chronological progression was conveyed through the sequence of questions. The prologue to October was dealt with in an extremely detailed questionnaire covering the "First Period" leading up to the February Revolution. The questions led the respondents sequentially through main moments of the revolutionary narrative up to February 1917: war with Japan, the massacre of workers in Petrograd on January 9, 1905, the strikes of October, the period of the reaction [*reaktsiia*], the Lena events, the war. They also identified for the respondents the most important events in their local area ("strikes, clashes with troops and police, expropriations, terrorist acts") and asked them to describe the role played by them and their party organizations in these events. [143] The story was picked up in a separate questionnaire relating to February 1917, its questions leading the respondents through the major moments of that period (the February Days, the retreat in Galicia, the July Days, the Kornilov affair). The final prompt completed the teleology: "The order to withdraw revolutionary troops from Petrograd. Slogans. Agitation among troops and workers. Plan of action and preparatory work. Links with the center. The fight for power. Victory." [144]

In questionnaires about October, the questions provided strong cues to respondents about the commitment required of genuine revolutionaries. They were asked to describe their own and their comrades' actions at crucial junctures during the October Days and to describe the path by which "worker-peasant power" was organized in their locality. Their opinions were requested about other organizations in their area, such as trade unions, and the degree to which their opinions differed from the majority opinions. They were asked for their recollections of the attitudes of the "peasant and worker masses" to certain events or organizations. Similarly, they were asked to describe the "struggle with SRs, Mensheviks, and other counterrevolutionary parties" at crucial stages. The battle lines in the new society took on the sharpest contours in those questions relating to the aftermath of October. Questions provided a social script that could have left little doubt in the respondents' minds about legitimate and illegitimate voices in this society. Questionnaires asked respondents to break down their evaluation of the Committees of the Poor (*kombedy*) after October according to "poor peasants, middle peasants, prosperous peasants." They also invited respondents specifically to identify which of the following groups were engaged in "counterrevolutionary incidents in your locality": former landowners, former bourgeoisie, former officers of the tsarist army, former tsarist officials, the clergy, intelligentsia, students, kulaks, deserters, groups of workers and peasants, the Kadets, SRs, or Mensheviks. The groups that had supported Soviet power were to be identified by name. A final question asked the respondents to identify any "remnants of the Old Regime," a tidy catch-all for the outlived past. [145]

These early questionnaires did not script an explicitly Bolshevik October, asking, for example, "Which parties, besides the RKP, took part in the overthrow [*perevorot*]?" They did, however, privilege the RKP, by asking about relations between local organizations and the central party institutions, about the foreign centers of the party, and about the Ninth and Tenth Party Congresses. Questions about the pre-October period asked about the "attitude of the population to the RSDRP (Bolshevik)? The work of the party after the July Days? The Sixth Congress of the party? The growth of the party?" The questions told a tale of the party's steady emergence onto the political stage in spite of considerable trials. Respondents were asked to recall episodes of the tsarist authorities' repression of their organizations and of personal victimization at the hands of the tsarist police. They were also asked to recall episodes of joint work with other parties and factions, although the questions were also intended to make them think about the probity of these earlier collaborations. "What questions (organizational, tactical, programmatic, philosophical)," asked a questionnaire, "most of all separated the organizations in which you were a member from Menshevik organizations?" A similar question asked about contacts between the local party organization and "public [*obshchestvennye*] organizations… institutions, official figures, prominent public nonparty workers [*rabotniki*], and representatives of the bourgeoisie" and asked the respondent to justify these contacts by describing who had been responsible for maintaining them and how they had benefited the party organization. The language of the questions invited respondents to recall their past activities in far more polarized terms than they would probably have conceived them at the time, the amorphous social enemy (the "authorities [*vlasti*]," "rightist elements," "monarchists," "bourgeoisie") giving way to a body politic of sharpening party political contours (Mensheviks, SRs, anarchists, even the "Menshevik-minded elements [*men'shevistski mysliashchie elementy*]."

In these questionnaires, the Bolshevik Party was the unmistakable yardstick of revolutionary commitment and clarity. The questions about the actions of the individual party organization *and of the individual* at crucial junctures were nothing less than a call for organizational *and personal* accountability to the revolutionary cause and the Bolshevik Party. Respondents were repeatedly asked to identify by name those party members who had actively engaged in party business, those who had "stood out at the conferences and meetings," and those who had led local organizations. A final question in one of the questionnaires was heavy with implications: "If you were a member of *another* party, then which one, for how long, what kind of work did you conduct and where, when did you leave it, for what reasons and under what political circumstances?" [146]

Many of these elements were echoed in questionnaires drawn up by local bureaus and tailored to local conditions. One questionnaire identified Samara's major events in the revolutionary movement, namely the attack by "the anarchists, maximalists, and Left SRs" on Soviet power in May 1918, and the fighting with the Czechs in the area. The questions traced a narrative of ultimately hollow counterrevolution, as the "petit bourgeois" Samara Constituent Assembly disintegrated from within, ending in a final flight in panic before the victorious Red Army. The questionnaire was important for the way it was intended to throw into sharp relief the contours of the body politic in Samara at this time. Respondents were asked to identify which strata were for or against Soviet power during the attack and how they had reacted to the "petit bourgeois" government of the Samara Constituent Assembly that took power in the middle of 1918. They were further asked about the part played in the arrests and shootings during the period of the Constituent Assembly by "SRs, Mensheviks, the intelligentsia, and the clergy", as well as about the role of the respondent's own local party organization and the respondent's *personal role* at these moments. A special set of questions asked about the role of local "Bolshevik-Communists" under the Czechs, respondents being asked to identify them, to describe their activities, their disagreements over questions of principle, and any instances of the "basic party line" being rejected. [147]

The form and function of these questionnaires derived from the same urge for narrative coherence that informed all other efforts to write about, celebrate, or remember the story of October from the moment of the Bolshevik takeover in October 1917. From 1920, Istpart brought to this process a set of storytellers who differed from earlier storytellers in terms of their shared life experiences. Most of them viewed the world through the prism of revolutionary activity and the party, and they saw the October Revolution through that same prism. For these men and women, the party's role in the revolutionary movement was self-evident, and their aim was that it would be recognized as such by the broader population as the story of October was told piece by piece across Soviet Russia. They were convinced that this story should, indeed could, only be told from the localities. Still, they underestimated the scale of the political, administrative, financial, and personal obstacles they would face. Although they did not have to contend with a potent counternarrative inside Soviet Russia, their efforts to tell the story of October would be sorely tested over the next three or four years, as local areas failed to produce the story these leaders were expecting.

5

HOW NOT TO WRITE THE HISTORY OF OCTOBER

It was through October that the pre-October party itself was able for the first time to recognize its real worth.
—Lev Trotsky, 1924

The local regions' responses to October have generally been studied for what they reveal about the varied or delayed routes to revolution.[1] Only rarely have these local stories been examined as a function of this broader state project to construct October as a foundation event for Soviet Russia.[2] It was an article of faith among the framers of the Istpart project that the revolutionary tale had to be told in every locality of Soviet Russia, with the guidance of the center but by locals themselves. Out of the disarray and disintegration of the Civil War period and its immediate aftermath, the leaders of Istpart imagined a coherent tale of revolution, replete with genealogies and seminal events, heroes great and small, and clearly defined foes. As their efforts in the first years of the 1920s revealed, however, the revolutionary imaginations of *local* activists were curbed by a formidable array of financial, organizational, and political factors.[3] Created and shaped by the central organization, local Istpart bureaus certainly produced dramatic tales of revolution. The center found these tales wanting, though, in key respects.

ISTPART IN PRACTICE

The central Istpart's insistence on an integrated history of revolution and party, after its initial flirtation with separate histories, was tempered by an acute awareness of the palpably woeful state of the party at this time. Reports by the Agitation and Propaganda Department of the Central Committee of the party (*Otdel agitatsii i propagandy TsK VKP(b)* or Agitprop) on the state of the local party organizations in 1922 must have deepened the doubts of Istpart members about the possibility of finding the materials they needed. The poor political literacy of many party members weakened party agitation among the nonparty mass of workers and peasants. The party organizations of the Urals (covering Ekaterinburg, Cheliabinsk, Ufa, Tiumen', and Perm' Provinces), a major industrial center, provided a devastating picture of famine, poverty, crime, unemployment, and hostility among the workers. The local party organizations were marked by rampant drunkenness, nonattendance at meetings, parochialism (*mestnichestvo*), and a "departure from party interests." Members were even leaving the larger local party organizations (such as Ekaterinburg) at an alarming rate as a result of material need, isolation from the top party committees, a lack of party literature, and "the unexplained nature of the contemporary course of the party." All over the region, party members were moving to other provinces without informing their local committee, or were using any pretext possible to be called or recalled to the center. Expulsions were increasing for "party crimes" (*partprestupleniia*), party discipline was weak, and in many areas the provincial committees were moribund. In some areas, members were not paying their party dues or were forced to neglect their party work because their very survival depended on securing paid work outside of the party. Ties to the local nonparty population were often weak, and local party bodies often acted as closed cliques engaging in personal reprisals based on individual or local interests.[4] The weakness of party identity and the poor state of the party organization were chronic problems. At the height of the crisis in 1921, Nevskii captured the confused mood of the population: " 'Yes, we know what happened in October,' the workers and peasants say, 'but that was in October and there were still Bolsheviks then and it was okay, and now there are only Communists left, and this is why, people say, things are very bad.' " For some people, he observed, the word "Communist" signified only "violence, and coercion, and cold, and hunger."[5]

When Istpart was transferred by a Central Committee decree of December 2, 1921 from the Commissariat of Enlightenment to the Central Committee of the RKP, all existing local bureaus were ordered to transfer to the jurisdiction of provincial and regional committees of the party.[6] Local Istpart bureaus received direct orders to subordinate themselves to the provincial bureaus of the party, which would provide "all guiding instructions and individual assignments."[7] Far from producing the network of guided articulation hoped for by Istpart, this action merely exposed the Istpart bureaus to the many problems plaguing the local party organizations. For their part, these latter organizations by no means embraced the Istpart bureaus, even displaying a cavalier attitude toward the Istpart project itself. Often, local party committees simply ignored central Istpart directives to set up Istpart bureaus in their regions, or carried them out in only the most perfunctory fashion. At times, local party organizations summarily closed local Istpart bureaus and confiscated their resources.[8]

Some bureaus existed in name only for the first two years; others existed but lacked physical premises or material resources. Istpart members were often overloaded with other party duties or were assigned the Istpart position because they were too old or infirm to perform other duties.[9] In some cases, the local bureaus were reorganized in late 1922 and early 1923, in effect establishing completely new bureaus.[10] Local bureaus complained about what the Kazan' bureau euphemistically called the existence of "freedom of action," namely the absence of instructions from either the provincial committee of the party or the central Istpart.[11] As late as September 1925, the head of the Orenburg bureau, Markovskii, referred to the difficulty of working "without decrees and instructions, even without local orientation." A month later, he asked the central Istpart to help his "young organization... map out a path in its work." He requested publications (special jubilee issues of *Rabochaia Moskva*) as well as instructions on how to organize exhibitions and other such events. Finally, in view of the deficient historical expertise of those engaged in Istpart work, he expressed an "urgent need to attend even a small course" on how to approach Istpart work.[12]

The Istpart project had no other choice than to rely on individual initiative at the central and local level. This was not, after all, at odds with the belief of leaders like Ol'minskii that the history of party and revolution should be sought not only among Communists but among "all citizens of Russia."[13] The Tver' bureau believed that without public interest (*obshchestvennost'*) in their work "nothing can be produced."[14] Some bureaus looked to the recently established local affiliates of the Society of Old Bolsheviks (Obshchestvo Starykh Bol'shevikov) in the early 1920s to energize their work, and the local affiliates in turn looked to the Istpart bureaus for collaboration in their work.[15] As the Moscow bureau reported, the work relied on individual plenipotentiaries (*upolnomochennye*) who, in turn, "gather around themselves circles of people who obtain materials for us." The bureau complained, though, that, when ordered by the center to examine a particular epoch, it had "literally to catch people on the street" and order articles from them. "Some wrote them," it noted, "many did not."[16] It also forced the local bureaus to use any available local networks to try to combat the general indifference to their efforts, opening them up to all kinds of potential institutional rivalries.[17]

Istpart's difficulties were not only local. The Moscow and Petrograd bureaus, and even the central Istpart bureau, encountered the same problems of overburdened Communist officials and institutional confusions and rivalries. In late 1921, Nevskii reported that his Petrograd bureau's work depended on the interest of one person, Praskov'ia Kudelli, who was overloaded with other work. The other members were similarly overburdened, absent, or forced into other work in an effort to obtain a measure of material security for themselves in these difficult times. He complained of the lack of archival guidance from the Historical-Revolutionary Archive, since Shchegolev had been removed from his post as director. Nevskii complained that Kudelli had brought in ten or twelve young people to work on the history of the Petrograd SD organization, but their work had been held up by the lack of any concrete plan or instructions. One inexperienced comrade had been working on the *Rabochaia mysl'* period of the RSDRP and had failed to see the inherent biases in the materials: "The main activists of this movement, in his opinion, turned out to be completely unknown second-rank personalities who had received too much emphasis in the first place in the Okhrana sources."[18]

By 1923, the bureau had accomplished almost no organizational work in the local areas of Petrograd, and various commissions set up to work on specific themes and periods had produced nothing.[19] When work was accomplished, it was generally when members of other organizations, such as the Historical-Revolutionary Archive or lower-level Istparts, were brought in to help on specific projects.[20] In April 1923, these difficulties sparked a complete reorganization of the Petrograd bureau, which brought in a new staff from the provincial committee of the VKP. In the following six months, until September, the Petrograd bureau listed impressive accomplishments. The staff set up a rudimentary Istpart network at the district level of Petrograd. Several of these district Istparts reported some success in sending plenipotentiaries into enterprises and institutions to collect materials on the October Days of 1917, with the Vyborg and Volodarskii District bureaus even organizing subcommissions in several of their local enterprises. Even county bureaus were established in some areas, and they sent out plans of work to rural districts and plants. The Troitskii County bureau boasted no less than twenty-four comrades gathering materials on underground party work in 1917–18 in their county.[21]

The Moscow bureau quickly established a five-member staff and a network of seven district and twenty county bureaus in Moscow Province. In reality, though, only the head of the central bureau was active. Those working in the local bureaus of Moscow had few opportunities to meet and coordinate their activities, and they received no coherent guidance in their work.[22] No systematic work had been done by early 1922, mainly because the local bureaus in Moscow were staffed by overburdened individuals. Frequently, work depended on a single committed individual. The Moscow bureau complained that the Moscow committee of the party was indifferent to it; the bureau tried to circumvent this apathy by assigning plenipotentiaries at the county level to create commissions for collective work on the history of the party organization. It also attempted to draw in members from organizations such as the Institute of Red Professors and the Communist Academy to collaborate on specific projects.[23] The Moscow bureau was reorganized in late 1924, just as its Petrograd counterpart had been in April 1923.[24]

Neither the Moscow nor the Petrograd bureau enjoyed especially close or consistent links with the central Istpart. In October 1922, the central Istpart ordered three members of the Moscow bureau, Elizarova (Lenin's sister), S. I. Chernomordik, and Bobrovskaia, to draw up a constitution of mutual relations between itself and the Moscow bureau.[25] Even the leaders of the central Istpart complained that the leading party bodies ignored them—or worse. The Twelfth Party Congress in April 1923 saw no problem in extending a formal greeting to Ol'minskii as a dedicated party member, while pointedly ignoring his work in Istpart.[26] The Thirteenth Congress a year later could manage only a passing endorsement of Istpart, calling on party organizations to devote "the most serious attention" to it. [27] At an Istpart conference in 1923, Lepeshinskii complained that the party was sending only sick people to work in the central Istpart.[28] In January 1924, Ol'minskii wrote to the Central Committee complaining that it only tolerated Istpart. He had received almost no directives or material resources from the Central Committee; personal communications with members of the Central Committee had been limited to cursory consideration of purely administrative questions; and other key organizations, including the State Publishing House (Gosizdat), had provided no publishing support whatsoever. The personal efforts of a few Central Committee members were the exception.[29] Istpart viewed the decision to reorganize the Petrograd bureau in early 1923 as a unilateral decision of the Petrograd committee of the party and an encroachment on its prerogative. It asked the Secretariat of the Central Committee to confirm Nevskii as the head of the Petrograd bureau, although it also recommended that several of those appointed by the party committee remain on the bureau staff.[30] The daily, material situation of the central Istpart's staff was not as acute as of those in the localities, but it was troubling enough for Istpart to impress on the Central Committee the urgent need to improve the situation.[31] Only thirty-nine of the one hundred local bureaus, Istpart complained in August 1923, were capable of conducting work.[32]

Clearly, the horrendous political and infrastructural problems plaguing the Istpart network threatened the evidentiary foundation it was trying to lay for October. The central Istpart had certainly intended the widest possible distribution throughout Soviet Russia of any local Istpart publications, and repeatedly (and in vain) it instructed all local bureaus to send it a copy of all of their publications forthwith.[33] In practice, it quickly realized that the local bureaus could not be relied on to sell or distribute them on their own initiative, and it tried to set up a formal arrangement with Gosizdat to supply various local shops with them.[34] In response to a local request in early 1922 for more literature on the history of the party and the revolutionary movement, the central Istpart was forced to respond that such works were still a "bibliographical rarity."[35] Local and central bureaus alike expressed deep concern about the quality of the evidence of October they were able to gather, and of the credentials of the guardians of that evidence. The Ekaterinoslav bureau, for example, complained in 1923 that archival materials had been lost and that documents in general were treated in the "most barbaric fashion."[36] Archival materials were often being stored in damp, mice-infested sheds or were not gathered together in a secure place.[37] They could be bought in open markets and had even been used by the Main Committee on Paper (Glavbum) as a source of clean paper.[38]

When trying to procure tsarist archives, local Istparts often ran up against the very different worldviews of those who had headed the Old Regime's archives before October 1917. The Novgorod bureau, for example, complained of "old bourgeois specialists [who did] not want to work with us and would not provide materials," while the Podol'sk bureau complained of the "Petliura [leader of a nationalist Ukrainian government during the Civil War] professors" of Podol'sk University who would not relinquish the local gendarme archive. The Novgorod bureau enlisted the help of the provincial committee of the party and the provincial executive committee of the Soviet to "[destroy] the old class apparatus of the provincial archive and [build] our own Red provincial archive from party workers."[39] Finding enough suitably trained Communists to place in charge of archival work was a perennial problem.[40] Representatives were sent from the central Istpart to local areas to conduct three- or four-month training courses for the new Red archivists, although they also encountered obstacles from the old archival staff of the provincial archive (*Gubarkhiv*) who regarded them as lacking the proper education or training for such work.[41] Nor was Istpart the only competitor for these archives. Without the knowledge of the central Istpart, individuals on mandates from the Commissariat of Enlightenment and the Central Archive (*Tsentral'nyi Arkhiv*) toured several provinces, commandeering archives of local landowners and taking them back to Moscow. [42]

LOCAL OCTOBERS

By early 1923, the Istpart bureaus had published some thirty-three booklets (*knizhki*) about the October Revolution, many of them filled with reminiscences and accounts of local experiences.[43] These early publications represent a moment at which central aspirations encountered local exigencies. In 1924, the central

Istpart complained about several deviations (*ukloneniia*) from direct Istpart work. In particular, the Istpart of Kirgiziia was preparing to celebrate 150 years of the Pugachev movement; the Kiev bureau was organizing an exhibition devoted to the 110th birthday of the Ukrainian poet Shevchenko; and the Far Eastern bureau was preparing a special collection of articles commemorating one hundred years since the Decembrists. "Are all these jubilees revolutionary jubilees?" asked Istpart. Although these all had their place in history, it continued, they had no direct link with the history of the party and the history of the proletarian revolution.[44] None of these jubilees, however, represented a conceptual challenge to the revolutionary narrative. Examination of the terms and categories, the literary mechanisms, and narrative conventions used by these local tellers of revolution reveals an urge on their part to make sense of their local experiences *as part of* the October Revolution. The entire structure of the project to write the history of the October Revolution ensured that a coherent tale would emerge, even if it could not guarantee its precise contours.

In a sense, the October Revolution took its most tangible and coherent form in these booklets and journals that constituted the local Octobers. The local Istpart bureau in Rybinsk, a town on the Volga near Iaroslavl', for example, by bringing together the previously unarticulated and unconnected experiences of railroad, factory, and plant workers in scattered towns such as Uglich, Myshkin, and Rybinsk, gave them symbolic coherence as the manifestation of the October Revolution in Rybinsk Province.[45] The steady accretion of compilations of accounts from Kungur, Izhevsk, and Ufa produced a picture of October in the Urals region that was larger than the sum of its parts.[46] The editors of *Sibirskie ogni* (*Siberian Fires*) sought to draw together the "hitherto scattered forces of Siberia into this unified creative enterprise."[47] Just as the journals *Krasnaia byl'* (*Red Fact*) and *Revoliutsionnoe proshloe* (*Revolutionary Past*) gathered the fragments of disparate experiences together into Samara's and Ufa's Octobers, so too did *Revoliutsionnoe byloe* (*Revolutionary Past*), *Puti revoliutsii* (*Paths of Revolution*), and *Proletarskaia revoliutsiia na Donu* (*Proletarian Revolution on the Don*) for the Tula, Kazan', and Rostov regions.

Central directives and instructions, questionnaires, and evenings of reminiscences were all intended to provide the framework for local organizations to understand the significance of their local events as constituent parts of a larger revolutionary context. The local revolutionaries involved in these publications displayed much of the same urge toward coherence already seen in these central efforts. In their journals and newspapers, they often supplemented the gathered reminiscences with reprinted official documents or chronicles of events drawn up by the bureaus to authenticate the local tales. The editors of *Krot (Mole)*, the local journal of the Kungur bureau in Perm' Province, for example, supplied explanatory notes to point out any "inconsistencies." Such supplements, they added, were intended to "aid comrades in the work of remembering the past."[48]

In these local Istpart journals, the past became prerevolutionary, namely a chronology of seminal events that charted the path to October (not, of course, to February). The 1905 Revolution became enshrined as the "dress rehearsal," the World War as the postponement, and February 1917 as the necessary first step to October. *Proletarskaia revoliutsiia na Donu* devoted an issue to the October Days and subsequent issues to its long prologue, beginning with the 1902 strike in Rostov, "which played such an enormous role in the history of the revolutionary movement in Russia."[49] The Samara bureau of Istpart told the readers of its *Krasnaia byl'*: "You will see how closely linked is the proletarian movement of Samara Province with the movement all over Russia."[50] It illustrated Samara's revolutionary pedigree in a table comparing the course of the labor movement in Russia and Samara from 1902 to 1916 with the concurrent development of the Social Democratic Party in Russia and Samara.[51]

The articles and reminiscences that filled the pages of these local journals were gathered explicitly according to this new periodization. They all reflected the sharp break from the old world to the new, symbolized by the date of the Bolshevik takeover in Petrograd. "October 25, 1917 fell... like snow on the head of the man in the street [*obyvatel'*]," wrote N. Krasil'nikov of the town of Krasnokhol'm, although its "liberal" town administration "did not attribute it any special significance... and peacefully continued to rule the destinies of the town."[52] The fault of the town administration, he implied, lay in its failure to register the imminence of October. If the break between the old and the new was not immediately evident in the transfer of power to the local soviet, reminiscers might register October's arrival in other ways: "It is true that externally Myshkin changed little in comparison with its earlier appearance, but the psychological breach [*treshchina*] in the ideological mood of the population is evident."[53]

In areas slow to embrace October, local accounts identified both the individuals and social groups responsible for this delay, and those who ultimately overcame it. An article in *Krot* described the local transfer of power to the soviets there as a "power vacuum [*bezvlastie*]" in which "the unorganized strata of society" gave their instincts free rein, raiding the wine cellars and launching an anti-Jewish pogrom. Only when the local revolutionary committee organized local forces—"around a nucleus of Bolsheviks"—could the unrest be quelled. Significantly, the reminiscence ended with the lesson learned about the true revolutionary meaning of the violent actions: "As the soldiers themselves said later, they were ignorant [*temnye*], uneducated soldiers, who saw in the destruction of shops the struggle with the bourgeoisie and in the destruction of the wine cellars the legitimate compensation for the deprivations experienced during the war years."[54]

Local Octobers often articulated a symbolic break with the past through a physical clash with the old, if not a climactic storming. Workers in Tula recalled how they heroically took to the streets as one with red flags, singing the "Marseillaise," and joining bloody battle with the Black Hundreds and their police and gendarme accomplices.[55] Drama could also be found elsewhere, October's quiet arrival in Izhevsk in the Urals being juxtaposed against the battles fought by the "force of agitation even before October, and this was the service performed by the Izhevsk organization of the RKP of Bolsheviks."[56] The introduction to a collection of reminiscences from Rybinsk conveyed well this urge to find the intrinsic drama of revolution in local events:

> Those who know Rybinsk Province, and those who do not know it but have read this collection, may ask: "What kind of revolution is this?" "Indeed, was it possible for there to have been a revolution here in the sense in which we understand revolution, namely a revolution accompanied by fighting on the barricades, heroic skirmishes with the hostile classes?" These are the questions that might occur to some readers on reading this collection.... When we came to publish the present collection we considered the colorlessness of the revolutionary events in the province.... Here there were none of those roars of the revolutionary storm, those heroic deeds and sacrifices that could be seen in our proletarian capitals and other industrial centers. And yet what happened here represents, in the context of the conditions of Rybinsk, the greatest drama, whose depth and meaning not everyone has recognized yet.[57]

The point of these local Octobers was not that October arrived there months after the Bolshevik takeover in Petrograd, but that *October* arrived. They identified their own Octobers most prosaically as the bare transfer of power to the local soviet in which local Bolsheviks had gained or were gaining the upper hand. In these local reminiscences, though, October served as shorthand for a grander process, a symbol of far more than a simple transfer of power. It was the yardstick against which all else was defined in conceptual terms. Without the inscription of October as a defining event, the occupation of Rostov by ataman Kaledin and his Cossack soldiers in December 1917, which toppled the month-old Soviet Republic of the Don, could not have been articulated as the "bourgeois counterrevolution," "the hated counterrevolution of Kaledin," or even conceptualized as part of a coherent "White Guard movement [*belogvardeishchina*]" by reminiscers several years later.[58] The Reds could not exist conceptually without the Whites. Similarly, without October, the Rybinsk Communists would have been unable to conceive of or articulate their past experiences in terms of "soviet power" pitted against "bourgeois institutions dedicated to stifling the revolution." Under this vaguely defined catchall, reminiscers could variously condemn the "Committee of the State Duma" in March 1917, the "bourgeois-liberal Committee of Public Organizations" in mid-1917, the "yellow trade unions" and "Committees to Save the Motherland and the Revolution" after October, and the "SR-Uchredilka illusions" that informed the Iaroslavl' uprising in July 1918. In short, without soviet power, there could be no bourgeois power, without the "huge giant—the proletariat," there could be no "philistine, petit bourgeois [*meshchanskii*] bog."[59]

THE VIEW OF THE PARTY FROM THE PERIPHERY

The structure of the Istpart project ensured that it would be impossible to talk about the October Revolution without also talking about the Bolshevik Party, although the precise form of the party and its relationship to the revolution remained unclear. As late as 1922, the Society of Former Political Prisoners and Exiles (Obshchestvo byvshikh politicheskikh ssyl'nykh i katorzhan) could still inform the central Istpart, apparently without reproach, that it intended to subordinate itself to Istpart but wished to remain "in formal terms an extraparty body." It pledged to draw in all individuals, "regardless of political direction," who were able to contribute valuable materials, and resolved to focus on that "period when our party was just one trend in one common Marxist movement."[60] In the earliest publications of the Soviet regime, emphasis on worker initiative as an agent of change contrasted sharply with the roles ascribed to any party organizations, the Bolshevik Party included. [61] While these works certainly contrasted the spontaneous and unprepared nature of the February Revolution with the planned and organized nature of October, they nonetheless introduced an organized Bolshevik Party only well into 1917. [62] Istpart's official journal, *Proletarskaia revoliutsiia (Proletarian Revolution)*, referred in 1921 to the actions of the "relatively small group of Bolsheviks, relying on the mood of the masses and on the disorganization and ideological emptiness of the coalition government to seize power in its own hands."[63] Such ambivalence could also be seen in Ol'minskii's efforts to create a linked revolutionary pedigree for October and the party. In 1921, he identified a "gap in our history," namely the absence for the decade from 1885 to 1895 of "either a labor movement or the growth of elements for forming a proletarian party." The reminiscences gathered to fill that gap, he noted, showed that the ranks of workers "displayed immeasurably greater independence and initiative than has been attributed to them to date."[64]

Not surprisingly, perhaps, the local Istpart bureaus reproduced these ambivalences in their treatments of local party organizations before and during October. The Samara Istpart devoted the second issue of its journal in 1923 to the twenty-fifth jubilee of the "RSDRP, the leader of the revolution," but praised the efforts of "worker Samara, as the serried, disciplined unity of members of the RKP, one of the most stable columns on which the entire edifice of the RKP rests." It added ominously that very few party workers who remembered the "Samara past" were left in Samara.[65] For this same jubilee, other local Istpart bureaus collapsed the RSDRP awkwardly into the RKP(b). The Saratov bureau reported in early 1923 on its success in gathering reminiscences about the history of the "Saratov organization of the RKP (RSDRP)" and made sure that special issues of local newspapers, as well as evenings of reminiscences, were devoted to celebrations of the anniversary of the party.[66] Even the large Moscow provincial bureau abandoned its efforts in 1923 to produce a monograph for the thirtieth anniversary of the Moscow party organization because it would be "too superficial," and produced instead a more modest reader.[67]

At times, the intentions of the local bureaus, expressed in the introductory remarks to their journals, were at odds with the actual contents of the materials they featured. *Krot* reprinted a proclamation by the RSDRP from 1907 affirming that 1905 had taught the working class the need for unity and organization and that the RSDRP had been at the forefront.[68] The reminiscences and articles in this very journal, however, suggested that early organizational activity in the area was generally not reducible to party labels and that an illegal, hectographed party newspaper published in the area from 1906 had been a cooperative venture of Socialist Revolutionaries and Social Democrats.[69] Similarly, the reminiscences in the pages of the Tula bureau journal on the theme of "party organizations in 1905" offered a picture of weak, circle-based groups whose fortunes seemed to depend on the actions of a single influential individual at crucial junctures. These groups had almost no ties to the striking workers in the Tula plants in 1905 and were able to render them no support or encouragement. Local Social Democrats and Socialist Revolutionaries were often portrayed as lagging behind the revolutionary workers, or even vainly trying at mass meetings to keep the spontaneous speeches of the workers "within certain limits."[70]

In late 1923, an Istpart representative from Volokolamsk in Moscow Province explained why it would be so difficult to produce anything on the local party organization in 1905: "Our organization was one circle under the leadership of Katanska [Matrasevich]. This circle in 1905 had no ties with anyone. There was no time for work."[71] "Until February 1917," reported another local bureau, "there was no kind of organization at all in Podol'ia."[72] Nor did reminiscences about the immediate revolutionary period improve the picture. Some local bureaus complained that their party organization had received no information from the center at all after the February Revolution.[73] Recollections (in response to questionnaires) about the "Rybinsk organization of the RSDRP(b) [sic]" variously dated it from June 1917, and legally only from the end of 1917. They noted that "Bolshevik influence was not felt" before 1918, and that Mensheviks and SRs had been the "masters of the situation everywhere."[74] An observer at an SR meeting just prior to October 1917 saw "a multicolored meeting, not an SR meeting." He recalled there being a "popular Bolshevik organization" there at the time, but added that the general population of Rybinsk "had scarcely examined the political parties, and viewed the Bolsheviks with hostility." Indeed, his depiction of the "October Revolution" there gave the impression of a Bolshevik accession to power by default, the Mensheviks and SRs having lost credibility in the eyes of the Rybinsk proletariat.[75]

The Communists who reminisced in a Moscow military hospital on October 25, 1921 about their experiences of Rostov's October described a rather improvised and threadbare affair. One individual recalled how their small Bolshevik organization set up a military revolutionary committee in Rostov in late October 1917 on hearing of the "worker-peasant revolution" in Petrograd, although, he added, the MRC was largely isolated from any "information from outside." As a young, inexperienced Bolshevik, he found himself appointed the reluctant editor of the organ of the local soviet, with a "former-anarchist comrade" being assigned to teach "the novice." He wrote orders and decrees, and articles for the newspaper, although they were difficult to publish because of the absence of Bolsheviks among the typesetters. The newspaper was distributed around Rostov by ten Red Guards.[76] A Red Guard's recollections of the mechanics of the takeover in Rostov were no more reassuring about the role of planning and intent in this revolution: "The armed struggle was like a regular, working eight-hour day: we ate lunch and then went to fight again. In short, we were a bunch of workers who went about this matter in a disorganized fashion, who looked at this matter as if it were a necessity, and on the other hand as if it were a game."[77]

This hardly gave the impression of the well-oiled revolutionary machinery required by Bolshevik revolutionary lore. Yet these tellers of tales of fragmented party organizations, weak party identities, and erstwhile political failures were by no means blind to the script of revolution and the cues to it emanating from the center. Indeed, in their local Octobers, these revolutionaries wore their earlier political inadequacies as a badge of their political maturation since then. "We left Rostov with bitter hearts," one local Communist wrote of his small group's decision to flee the advancing Cossacks, "but with the firm resolve to continue the struggle and win out or die."[78] The workers had lived too long in "blind twilight," a Rybinsk activist recalled, until "the falling spark of the bright torch lit up the dark, working folk."[79] In 1922, 1923, and 1924, these workers-become-Bolsheviks described their earlier difficulties as steps on the path to their present state of consciousness. A worker's recollections of his time in Kazan' in 1917 charted his path from the beginnings of political maturity in the "underground student circles" in February to his becoming a worker at Plant No. 40, the "citadel of Bolshevism."[80] A worker from the Don region pointed out that he (and other present RKP members named by him) had been Mensheviks at the time of the revolution, although he stressed the primacy of his class credentials throughout: "When events unfolded, every worker, whether Menshevik or something else, was above all a worker."[81] Sometimes editors indicated the suspect political pasts of their authors.[82] Such personal confessions, and even the official identifications, of earlier political allegiances were not intended to invite reprisal but to plot the length and difficulty of the road traveled to political enlightenment. In the early 1920s, it seems, it was still possible to offer that one's road to Bolshevism at the local level could have led through Menshevism. In some local Octobers, individuals contrasted their confusion or ignorance about the early political organizations with the certainty of their commitment to a vital and coherent Bolshevik Party *in their present lives.* The party had established a House of the People *(Narodnyi dom)* in Rybinsk, noted one person, in an effort to bring cultural enlightenment to the workers and their families there. Now, he added, an "RKP cell" enjoyed "absolute" authority among the mass of the population.[83]

Many reminiscers invoked the vagaries of memory in their recollections of the early political organizations. In part, they claimed, the endemic secrecy forced on the revolutionary parties by the conditions of oppression meant that they might well have been unaware of Bolsheviks in their local areas. As a member of the Tula party organization noted, "It was even difficult to know individual members of the committee."[84] Still, this suggested that individual members could be found, given the right circumstances and effort. [85] In October 1925, the central Istpart, apparently without irony, asked Kudelli, the head of Istpart in Leningrad (as Petrograd had been renamed in 1924), to write her reminiscences about the "Tula party organization" in 1905, as it had "become apparent that you were the leader."[86] Other reminiscers marked their journey toward consciousness by acknowledging their failure to comprehend the significance of the party or the magnitude of the developing revolution *at the time.* People joined whatever local organizations existed, one person explained, because "at that time we were still nonparty, we had scarcely looked into the parties, there was no workers' party in Kungur."[87] The Kungur bureau observed a "weak understanding of the ideas of the social revolution among the Iasyl'sk comrades" in 1918, as well as a "parochial [*mestnicheskii*] approach to the class struggle." In mitigation, the bureau pointed out that compared to today "we were still political naïfs in 1918."[88] "If in 1917," noted the Rybinsk Istpart, "we were weak, had no experience, did not know where to start our work, now, having behind us five years of tense struggle and work, we proudly can look into the future."[89] Thus did their past ignorance become the measure of their present political maturity.

Notwithstanding these caveats, the centrally inspired and centrally driven project to write the history of the October Revolution was still fundamentally about the construction of a prerevolutionary political culture as a function of the Bolshevik Party. Reminiscers articulated their experiences of October using the hardening categories of class and party that had become the currency of Soviet Russia in the early twenties. A description of Rybinsk in 1917 epitomized the vivid social polarizations of the new regime and was heavy with both the threat and promise of the revolution:

> The merchants went to the Stock Exchange, to the hotels, church, and the baths. Their wives and daughters, decked out in the latest fashion, promenaded along the boulevard and Krestovaia Street. The petite bourgeoisie [*meshchanstvo*] spent their time in the bars and taverns. The workers, shop assistants, and stevedores [*kriuchniki*], cursing their forced thirteen- to fourteen-hour working day, drowned their sorrows with vodka.... The young people spent their time flirting, visiting clubs, parties, and dances.... Busy, commercial Rybinsk lived contentedly, drunkenly, gaily.[90]

As they responded to the ubiquitous questioning of this new regime, individuals unavoidably identified themselves in relation to distinctions of class and party. Reminiscers frequently read back concrete party identities onto the local "non-party" organizations in their areas by identifying individual members as "*later*—Kadets" or "*subsequently*—Bolshevik" (emphasis added).[91] A short collection of reminiscences on peasant uprisings in Kungur County framed them as clashes between those of revolutionary mood and those of mutinous mood, party identity being assigned retroactively by the passing observation that "we were followers of the Bolsheviks."[92] Four or five local activists in Kungur gathered at an evening of reminiscences in late 1922 to remember the "history of the Kungur organization of the RKP(b)" for various periods from 1910 to 1918. A recurrent theme in the evening was that both ordinary workers and party members in Kungur were searching for explanations of the disagreements between the Bolsheviks and Mensheviks. The Kungur "party" organization was rudimentary at best, barely existing between 1905 and 1910, contained one "Bolshevik" (who published in the local "Menshevik" newspaper) and one undecided, and the "social democratic circle" they set up in 1910 "was not a party cell."[93] Although ignorant of the Central Committee's position on the war, the members of the circle came out decisively against the war because of their "class instinct and the

Bolshevik ferment [*zakvaska*]" of recent years. Even with Lenin's theses, delivered from Moscow at Christmas 1914, however, the circle "still did not reach the correct understanding of these questions." In the absence of Bolshevik newspapers, the circle relied on a Menshevik-Internationalist newspaper, which during these years "played a large role in revolutionizing the workers. If by the end of 1916 the entire depot was Bolshevik, this must be attributed not only to the propaganda of the circle but also to the influence of *Golos* [*Voice*] (how strange that a Menshevik newspaper Bolshevized the workers)."[94] At the end of 1916, the circle received instructions from Ekaterinburg on how to establish party work, and apparently it was ready for the first time to send representatives to a regional party conference, which never took place. On the eve of the revolution, the mood of the workers of the depot was "definitely Bolshevik (the influence of the circle and *Golos*)." At the start of 1917, the circle had fifteen permanent members, and it had the support of several reliable nonparty sympathizers.[95] A group of young people who organized a small "cell of sympathizers with the RKP" under Kolchak rule also came under the rubric of the Kungur organization of the RKP.[96] Even the obituaries of local activists that had been collected in an effort to reconstruct the party invariably identified them as "nonparty" or "not Bolshevik."[97] The term "sympathizer [*sochuvstvuiushchii*]" of the Bolsheviks became a common device in these local materials to convey Bolshevik support and individual bravery in the absence of a coherent local party organization.[98] Similarly, authors often assigned prerevolutionary party identity by describing the deceased as having "been close to members of the Social Democratic circle… and having subscribed to *Pravda*," or having conducted "agitation for the Bolsheviks." Sometimes, it was noted that the "Whites made a Bolshevik" out of this or that individual.[99] In such ways could a coherent and distinct Bolshevik identity within a polarized party political culture ultimately emerge from the fragments of prerevolutionary political organization.

A BOLSHEVIK LIFE

The personal Bolshevik journey can be followed in the autobiography of A. Martsinovskii from Saratov, the retroactive explanation of a nonparty life in party terms. Using narrative conventions and literary devices common in the memoirs of the period, Martsinovskii dedicated his own memoir in 1923 "to the twenty-fifth anniversary of the RKP(b), in whose ranks I have worked for many years." Martsinovskii's self-designation as a "worker-Bolshevik" had very little to do with formal party affiliation but was the product of an effort to reconstruct his life as one of organizational continuity and evolving political (specifically, Bolshevik) awareness. This poor uneducated Jewish man from Kiev Province did not know in 1900 "what parties existed (let alone their names)." He remembered joining the RSDRP in 1904 but understanding little and mainly posting leaflets, although "I don't remember what about." In 1906, he was a member of a local fighting squad (*druzhina*) in the town of Uman' in Kiev Province, although he remembered his section of the squad being Socialist Revolutionary rather than Social Democratic. Arrested and exiled to Siberia, he joined a "nonparty union of exiles." In Odessa from 1910, he worked in trade unions, because no party work was being conducted at all. Indeed, Martsinovskii referred to the "party idea" gaining ground only from the start of 1912. Moving to Ekaterinoslav in March 1913, he again encountered weak party work and had little success organizing circles in plants. His peripatetics eventually took him to Saratov where, he recalled, he "sensed" the coming revolution in February 1917: "The approach of decisive events was somehow felt, and only the leading directives were awaited." Thinking back over his political past, he recalled that the local party committees in which he had worked had consisted "almost everywhere" of workers: "We officials had to work in the underground without the intellectuals... and then they appeared after February with little red bows in their buttonholes, beat their breasts and cried: 'We are revolutionaries.' "[100] In Martsinovskii's memoir, 1917 became an inexorable, party-led march to October, but with an inflection that allowed him to represent himself as a lifelong Bolshevik in spirit, although with few organizational links to the national Bolshevik organization he had, understandably he believed, failed to recognize at the local level at the time.

THE VIEW FROM THE CENTER

Such tales of personal epiphany and political maturation, a mainstay of the party press since the October Days, should have been gratifying to many of the Soviet leaders. What was the role of the revolutionary teacher and guide, after all, if not to lead people like Martsinovskii to the path of consciousness? When they began to read these local Octobers, however, the Istpart leaders saw their inadequacies rather than the journeys of epiphany they charted. Lepeshinskii had already informed the All-Russian Conference of Istpart Workers in 1923 that although most of Istpart's attention had been devoted to drawing up "a chronicle of the October Revolution" and giving "a complete picture of the Russian Revolution," the publications produced so far had not "justified our hopes." They had shown "no definite viewpoint, no definite plan." His concerns were echoed at the conference by the head of the Kiev bureau, who complained that while the bureau had "very rich" materials from the 1890s to the revolution, almost no archives existed from 1917 on, and the frequent evacuations of Soviet power during the Civil War years had left few party materials.[101]

Reviewing the Istpart literature in 1923, Nevskii observed that "the majority of reminiscences of provincial collections of articles either speak of trifling matters and generally known facts or in a short space cover such long periods that they become a simple and uninteresting list of all well-known events." Worse yet, they were often published in journals without notes or explanations, and even valuable articles thereby "lose their significance" and even "give a false representation."[102] The provision of context or perspective was, of course, crucial to the goals of the entire history-writing project. The desired goal of a coherent history of party and revolution was not helped, in the view of the Istpart leaders, by the clearly centrifugal tendencies of certain local efforts. A letter from the central Istpart to the head of the Perm' bureau complained specifically that the Kungur journal *Krot* was made up of "fragmentary, subjective, disconnected, unverified reminiscences with a dash of SR-ism."[103] Such criticisms were not appreciated by some local bureaus. Members of the Kungur bureau responded that they had never intended to produce articles "written on the basis of scientific research of archives" but were merely moles "digging in the historical documents and in the memories left in people's heads."[104] As late as 1925, local bureaus still complained about the difficulties of finding basic documents on the history of the October Revolution and the party for their areas.[105]

The Istpart leaders were most distressed, though, by the singular failure of these local Octobers to integrate the twin goals of the project. At the Istpart conference in 1923, Lepeshinskii noted that, while work on the history of the Bolshevik Party was going better, "of course, our past is still none too clear." He added that "almost nothing" had been done by Istpart to "systematically elucidate the history of the party," mainly due to the failure of either personal reminiscences or published archival materials to shed light on significant periods of the party's history.[106] In late 1924, the central Istpart complained about the Briansk bureau's lack of production, and asked with some exasperation: "Surely, the Briansk [party] organization has a revolutionary past?"[107] Nevskii's review of the literature singled out specific journals (in Saratov, Tver', Gomel', Novgorod, and Tula) for their failure to devote the requisite attention to the history of local party organizations there, or, worse yet, for their assertions that such organizations had not existed in the formative years of social democracy. While generally praising the work of the Tula bureau on the revolutionary movement in 1905, for example, he criticized the complete absence of the party organization in it, in particular the lack of information on its leaders, the mutual relations of Bolsheviks and Mensheviks, the party press, and the kinds of work it had carried out.[108] In a similar vein, an Istpart official in 1925 criticized a work on Moscow in 1917 for the author's overuse of documents from "Black Hundred and counterrevolutionary groups," the most egregious example being her exclusive reliance for her treatment of the events of

January 9, 1905 on Socialist Revolutionary proclamations, completely eschewing Bolshevik proclamations, "although there was one [sic]." It was well known, the official added, that from 1914 to 1917 the "Moscow organization" was distributing leaflets, arranging meetings, and conducting more and more work, and yet the monograph in question displayed a

> lack (almost throughout the entire work) of information about the work of the party. [The author] limits herself to mentions throughout. This is not enough. This is especially noticeable in the introduction… [where] the work of the party is completely absent, indeed the author states that the party was not there at all.[109]

The official reception of these local Octobers was a symptom of a much larger problem for the party in these years, namely a renewed crisis in the party over questions of history and past political acts. In November 1924, the Moscow Istpart met with plenipotentiaries from the districts and counties of Moscow province and stressed the renewed urgency for a cogent history of the RKP and its role in October. Referring to the significance of collecting materials on the uprising of 1917, one speaker observed that "the basic principles of the organization of 1917 have still not been revealed…. Now it is important, more than ever before, because some people maintain that the October uprising was not prepared by our party."[110]

TROTSKY S CHALLENGE

The all-important context that lent renewed urgency to these concerns was the so-called "literary discussion" that had been going on at the highest levels of the party since the publication in 1924 of Trotsky's *Lessons of October* (*Uroki Oktiabria*), as well as several of his other works.[111] Coming from the pen of one of the revolutionary pantheon who had been lionized in the previous year for his military contributions to the revolution,[112] this work sparked an unprecedented argument in the party. On one level, *Lessons of October* was a blatant attempt by Trotsky to downplay his many past differences with Lenin, stressing instead how his and Lenin's political and ideological views had coincided at the critical junctures of the revolutionary movement. In December 1921, Trotsky had written to Ol'minskii asking him not to publish certain letters critical of the Bolsheviks that he had earlier written to Nikolai Chkheidze, a longtime member of the Menshevik faction, and head in 1917 of the Petrograd Soviet. There could scarcely be two old émigrés in the party, he wrote, "who did not call each other names when writing to each other under the influence of an ideological dispute, momentary exasperation, etc." Trotsky argued that publishing correspondence "from all those who took part in the 'squabble' " in the emigration would only rehash all the old disagreements, especially if, as Ol'minskii had apparently requested, the correspondents added "explanations" of their letters.[113] Trotsky was reluctant in his *Lessons of October* to define publicly his past disagreements with leading Bolsheviks. He did not shy though from cataloguing their past political vacillations as a way of highlighting Lenin's (and by implication his own) consistent and steadfast position in the run-up to the October overthrow. He noted the reluctance of Kamenev and Zinoviev, in particular, to support Lenin's calls to take power in October, because they "overestimated the enemy and underestimated the forces of revolution, denying that the masses were in a mood for battle."[114] The underlying assumption of *Lessons of October* was, as James White suggests, that the representation of one's role during the October Days or the revolutionary movement was deeply connected to one's present political status, as Kamenev and Zinoviev had found out at the hands of Trotsky, and as Trotsky would later find out at the hands of erstwhile comrades.[115]

Lessons of October was more than a mere settling of personal scores or a cynical jockeying for political position. It offered the most systematic representation yet of an unequivocally *Bolshevik* revolution, namely October as a function of the Bolshevik Party. Trotsky attributed the failure of the world revolution to materialize after October 1917, and more recently the defeats in Bulgaria and Germany, to those countries' failure to draw the necessary lesson from the October Revolution in Russia. "Without a party capable of leading the proletarian overthrow," he wrote, "the overthrow itself becomes impossible. The proletariat cannot seize power by a spontaneous uprising." The leading Communist parties of the West, he added, "had not only failed to internalize our October experience but were quite ignorant of the facts of it." Nor, he implied, should apparent disarray in the party be understood as anything other than a measure of the difficulty of the journey already traversed by the party, for "crises arise in the party at every serious turn in the party's course."[116] In this context, and with this lesson in mind, Trotsky made an urgent call for the comprehensive picture of the October overthrow that had so far been lacking in Soviet Russia.

Leading Bolsheviks unleashed a veritable campaign against Trotsky's representations of October and the party. They had little disagreement with Trotsky's assertion that October had found poor representation in print. But just as Sukhanov's early work had been an early stimulus to the Bolshevik leaders to attempt their own representation of events, Trotsky's works threatened to fill the vacuum with, for many leading Bolsheviks, an equally unpalatable version. "Trotsky intends to fill this gap [in the history of October] by publishing his own collected works," argued Piontkovskii. "Of course, given such an approach to the subject, the question of what the works of comrade Trotsky will contain... acquires huge historical interest."[117] Others were concerned about the effect of such representations on the young in the party who lacked "the most elementary knowledge... about how the history of our party developed, and some of whom, for lack of indigenous sources, drew their facts from works published abroad by leading Mensheviks, notably Iulii Martov."[118]

Trotsky represented Lenin as the major bulwark against the vacillation of those party leaders who had opposed any takeover without first getting the sanction of the Second Congress of Soviets. He also, however, depicted Lenin as prepared to pay lip service to such a sanctioned overthrow, constructing a "trap of Soviet legality" that ensnared opponents outside and inside of the party. As Trotsky bluntly put it, we fulfilled their desire "to be deceived."[119] The responses were equally blunt. Emmanuil Kviring wrote that this "accusation of conspiracy, Blanquism" against Lenin had been one of the "constant accusations by the Mensheviks over the long years of cruel struggle." He was particularly outraged by Trotsky's implication that only because of his (Trotsky's) steadfast advice did Lenin finally on October 25 accept the need to take power not "by a conspiratorial plot."[120] Trotsky's biographical sketch of Lenin, About Lenin (O Lenine), also published in 1924, gave the impression, Dmitrii Lebed' argued, that the October Revolution had not been the "revolutionary mass organized uprising" required by Leninist ideology, but that "Bolshevism came to the October overthrow with an incorrect tactic in the matter of the mass uprising and found the correct tactic only just before October itself."[121]

Ironically, while Trotsky's writings of this period privileged the Bolshevik Party as *the* major actor in the Russian Revolution, his very representation of that party brought him the severest criticisms, ultimately rendering him anathema to the Communist regime. He described the party in its early years as an organization completely unknown to "millions of workers and peasants... [who] have not yet realized it to be the champion of their endeavors." The guidance it received through Lenin's insight, foresight, and political genius came not from Russia, Trotsky implied, but from Lenin's fifteen years in the emigration, where he perfected his political views. He had "arrived in Petersburg with completed revolutionary generalizations," which were then put to the test on the working masses of Russia. Lenin's revolutionary clarity prior to October contrasted with the myopia of "our party... [which] did not yet understand all of its potential power and was, in consequence, a 'hundred times' more rightist than the workers and peasants."[122] Even after October, he wrote, the party was full of "workers with little consciousness" and "elements plainly alien to its spirit," who had been held together only by the "internal dictatorship of the Old Guard." Trotsky saw two floors in the house of the post-October party: "On the upper floor, people make decisions, and on the lower floor, people find out about them."[123]

Worse still, Trotsky represented the party largely as the expression of its internal disagreements, rather than as the product of steady political maturation over time. *Lessons of October* singled out Kamenev and Zinoviev repeatedly for their transgressions. Trotsky criticized far more than these two individuals, though, attacking not only leading Bolsheviks but also the party's newspaper *Pravda* and the broader rank and file for their revolutionary inconstancy. In his representation, the Bolshevik Party seemed to limp from internal crisis to internal crisis, held together only by Lenin's clear-sightedness. It was hardly an organization capable of revolutionary insurrection. At a time when many of Soviet Russia's leaders were attempting to locate the meaning of October in a coherent revolutionary heritage of ideological consistency and organizational maturation, Trotsky, instead, located the meaning of the latter in the former: "It was through October that the pre-October party itself was able for the first time to recognize its real worth."[124]

Grigorii Sokol'nikov dismissed Trotsky's work as little more than a chronicle of disagreements in the leadership of the Bolsheviks in 1917 and attacked his prosecutorial tone.[125] Kamenev even cited Trotsky's own comments in 1911 that "Leninists are a clique of intellectuals, who, under the leadership of Lenin, do not shrink from any methods, [and] hold in their hands by dark means the movement of the Russian proletariat.... The proletariat of Russia must be freed from the coercion of this clique."[126] A primary target of Trotsky's criticisms, Zinoviev, argued that Trotsky's *New Course (Novyi kurs)*, published in 1924, preached a "live and let live" attitude to "groups and trends" that had been part of the party in the past. He identified the dangers *for the present* of this kind of representation of the Bolshevik Party: "The party cannot be transformed into Noah's Ark, where all the creatures march in two by two; the party cannot be transformed into a conglomerate of individual groups and 'trends'; the party working in the conditions of NEP, a varied enough context, must be a unified Bolshevik Party, with the old Leninist steel [*zakalka*]. Otherwise we will perish."[127] Nikolai Bukharin was most uncompromising in his criticisms in an article titled "How Not to Write the History of October":

> Above all, in comrade Trotsky's work, the party disappears. It is not there, its mood cannot be felt, it has disappeared. There is Trotsky; Lenin is visible in the distance; there is a kind of dull-witted anonymous Central Committee. The Petrograd organization, the actual collective organizer of the workers' uprising, is entirely absent. The entire historiography of comrade Trotsky floats along on the "top floor" of the party building. As for the entire party skeleton... Where is the party?[128]

He further criticized Trotsky for making the period of party history before October "a completely secondary concern," and, he implied, for underestimating the steady growth of Bolshevism as a distinct ideology and of the Bolshevik Party as a coherent and continuous countrywide organization: "Comrade Trotsky... believes that in essence the party of Bolsheviks begins to exist 'in reality' only from the October Days."[129] The problem, Trotsky's critics argued, lay not with the party, but rather with Trotsky's own early political activities and his late arrival in the party. These kinds of histories of October, Ivan Stepanov argued, in which victory had taken place "despite the Bolshevik organization, in defiance of it," came from the pens of historians who, while they took an energetic part in its final battles, "had not joined all the crusades of the Bolshevik Party and had not experienced all its history with it and in it." Trotsky's misreading of the October Revolution had not been a momentary lapse of judgment but an abiding lack of appreciation of the significance of the revolutionary process and the coherence of the Bolshevik Party and its role in it. October was completed by the worker and peasant masses, and they won because their "fighting actions" were guided by Lenin and the Leninist party. Trotsky's failure to grasp this, Stepanov continued, had led to his "greatest distortion of reality," namely his failure to depict the broad and strong party organization Lenin had encountered on his return at the Finland Station in April 1917:

> Not two or three centers of *Pravda* people [*Pravdisty*], about which he had dreamt in 1915, but tens and hundreds of such centers, in all industrial and provincial towns and in many counties. These revolutionary people around *Pravda* were the living embodiment of the continuous chain of development, the living embodiment of that historical continuity that links December 1905 with October 1917 and which, preserved in the party organization, made it possible to transform the December defeat into an October victory.[130]

The arguments that flared up around Trotsky's incendiary analyses of the October Revolution, as well as Bolshevik evaluations of Istpart's early efforts, threw into sharp relief the perennial concerns over the history of October and the party. In the minds of many top party officials, not only the Bolshevik Party but Bolshevism itself yet lacked a sufficiently robust definition and presence in revolutionary history. Istpart leaders had long complained about the party's lack of attention to, and even respect for, their efforts. In January 1924, Ol'minskii wrote to the Central Committee expressing his hopes for "a fundamental change of the Central Committee's attitude to the work of Istpart."[131] The upcoming twentieth anniversary of 1905, "the first Russian Revolution," he noted, presented the party with the ideal opportunity to jump-start the project to write the history of October. As 1905 was a "prelude to the October overthrow," and as the interest of "the broad worker masses" in the Revolution of 1905 was so great today, Ol'minskii told the secretary of the Central Committee of the party, it would be a mistake not to use the jubilee "as an agitational-propagandist means of strengthening Soviet power."[132] So far, 1905 had not received, it was pointed out elsewhere, an "adequately Bolshevik depiction."[133] I. Gelis observed that the three years from 1925 to 1927 would be marked "by two noteworthy jubilees: the twenty-year 'prologue' and the ten-year 'apotheosis' of the proletarian revolution in Russia."[134] His choice of terms spoke volumes.

The man who had been the driving force of the Istpart project would not see in this new era. Comrades on the Istpart council accused Ol'minskii of being too dictatorial in his conduct, of not paying the council enough heed. He complained in vain to Stalin and other Bolshevik leaders, but eventually he resigned his post in October over the stress to his health caused by what he called the present period of "decline or disintegration" in Istpart.[135] His successor would bring a very different approach to the work of telling the story of October.

THE LESSONS OF OCTOBER
The Twentieth Anniversary of 1905

> **The revolution made progress, forged ahead, not by its immediate tragi-comic achievements but, on the contrary, by the creation of a powerful, united counterrevolution, by the creation of an opponent in combat with whom the party of overthrow ripened into a really revolutionary party.**
>
> —Karl Marx, *The Class Struggles in France*, 1848–50

Despite Istpart's best efforts, the coherent, integrated story of revolution and party had not materialized. To many inside the party, Ol'minskii's "crumbs of truth" of October seemed wholly inadequate for the spiritual sustenance of the Soviet population. Moreover, Trotsky's challenging interpretation of the meaning of October raised the question once more of who exactly were the legitimate arbiters of its history and raised the stakes of the entire project to write the history of the October Revolution. The years spanning the jubilees of 1905 and October proved critical in the effort to produce a seamless Bolshevik Party and revolution. Not since 1920 had the Soviet authorities assigned so many financial and material resources to their effort to tell the story of October and the party as an integrated whole, and they took their tale, and their search for its "artifacts," to every corner of the Soviet Union.[1] In addition to the usual range of publications, the central Istpart planned for the jubilee albums of photographs, books of poetry, as well as belletristic, visual, and cinematic representations of 1905.[2] It recommended that the 1905 celebrations in the villages include not only the elicitation of reminiscences from "participants, eyewitnesses, and contemporaries" to the events of 1905 and the staging in peasant reading rooms (*izba-chital'nia*) of living newspapers (*zhivaia gazeta*), illustrative reports (*illiustrativnyi doklad*), readings of satirical verses and folk verse (*chastushka*), but also, on the day of celebration, marches and excursions to the "area where revolutionary events occurred in the given region."[3] Through such methods might the individual experience of October be suffused with an aesthetic experience of poetic romance, visual drama, and an

immediate physical connection with a "site" of revolution. These ambitious jubilees would certainly represent a stride forward in the party's efforts to construct
a foundation event for the Soviet Union. They also inevitably triggered moments
of intense introspection by the regime.

KANATCHIKOV AND THE STRUGGLE FOR THE PARTY

When Semen Kanatchikov took the helm of Istpart in January 1925, he had already
been involved in both the "literary discussion" and the critical reviews of Istpart's
work. Like Ol'minskii, Kanatchikov was a party man in the most committed sense.
Unlike Ol'minskii, though, his long-standing dislike of the old émigré intelligentsia
in the party made him especially intolerant of the intelligentsia opposition at this
time. He saw himself as one of the new breed of worker-intelligentsia born exclusively of the Russian experience. A member of the RSDRP since 1900, and of the
Bolshevik faction since 1905, he had seen party service in Moscow, the Urals,
Petersburg, and Kazan', and paid for this service with Siberian exile. His local
experience and his role in workers' education after October left him in no doubt
as to where the arbiters of the history of the revolution should be sought.[4]

Kanatchikov announced his tenure at Istpart with a salvo in the "literary discussion," published in *Proletarskaia revoliutsiia* in January 1925. He called on
Istpart to fight for the party, and condemned those who were trying to "distort
our Bolshevik theory." He cited Lenin's remark that the working class could assert
its leadership only if the "best and most loyal representatives of this class were
organized in a centralized, disciplined party." Noting that the Bolsheviks' struggle
for just such a party had begun before 1905, Kanatchikov added his voice to the
general condemnation of Trotsky. This condemnation showed, he wrote, that
"the basic principles of Leninism have penetrated and been internalized not only
by the leadership of our party but have also been mastered in their basic elements
by the overwhelming majority of the rank-and-file cells of our party."[5]

In a secret memorandum to the local Istpart bureaus in March 1925,
Kanatchikov made his concerns and demands patently clear. He complained
about the variety of ways they interpreted their work. Some bureaus, he wrote,
understood their work to mean that the history of the RKP should never be conceived separately from the general revolutionary movement. Others believed that
it was impossible to write about the history of the party and at the same time
disregard the role of the other socialist parties. Still others thought that the local
peculiarities of the regions involved in the revolutionary struggle had first to be
studied by Istpart before the desired "complete history of our party and the entire
revolutionary movement" could even be broached. Linking his remarks explicitly
to the present discussion in the party about Trotsky's work, Kanatchikov made

clear to the local bureaus that they had one task: "to collect and study materials for a history of the party of the *Bolsheviks*, starting from the birth of Bolshevism and ending with our party's yesterday"[6] (Kanatchikov's emphasis).

Soon after he became chair of Istpart, Kanatchikov ordered all local bureaus to abandon any other jubilees they might be working on and focus solely on the upcoming twentieth anniversary of 1905.[7] Plans for the jubilee had been under way since February 1924 under Ol'minskii, when Istpart took the initiative to create the All-Union Commission for the Celebration of the Twentieth Anniversary of 1905 (Vsesoiuznaia Komissiia po prazdnovaniiu 20–i godovshchiny 1905 g.).[8] The commission had drawn up plans to produce screenplays for films depicting the 1905 Revolution as well as a series of brochures for popular consumption. It further charged Mitskevich to work out a plan for a jubilee exhibition both in the centers and at the local level, and named January 22 and December 21 as the days on which speeches, processions, and demonstrations should be held in 1925.[9] Istpart also planned a collection of general articles on the peasant experience of 1905 and stressed the need to explain to peasants the significance of celebrating the 1905 Revolution and their role in it. These articles should carefully delineate the disagreement between Bolsheviks and Mensheviks on the peasant question "as a central moment determining the outcome of the struggle" and explain the work of the party in preparing and organizing the armed uprising. [10]

By October, Ol'minskii's plans for 1905 were more modest, a result perhaps of fast-approaching deadlines and of the fact that the All-Union Commission was now chaired by Mikhail Kalinin, the head of the central executive committee of the All-Russian Congress of Soviets (Vserossiiskii Tsentral'nyi Ispolnitel'nyi Komitet Sovetov, or VTsIK) and the formal head of state. The commission had been divided into separate literary and organizational-spectacle subcommissions, and was charged by a decree of the Organizational Bureau of the Central Committee "to show the fighting alliance [*smychka*] of workers and peasants." The task for Istpart now, Ol'minskii informed the local bureaus, was to provide a picture of local events only, drawing on all available materials and "Bolshevik and Social Democratic literature (correspondence in émigré publications and leaflets) in general," with a view to producing a collection of articles for the region, "for example '1905 in Kiev,' '1905 in Nizhnii Novgorod,' etc." The literature should be published by August 1925, "in no event later than that."[11]

Kanatchikov quickly introduced tighter administrative control over the jubilee by setting up a council (*sovet*) under his leadership that was to meet every three weeks. It was to oversee Istpart's work in general and to work on individual campaigns "linked with questions of the moment." As for the current campaign on 1905, the new council stated flatly that "Istpart is dealing mainly with questions of the internal history of the party."[12] *Proletarskaia revoliutsiia* printed editorials outlining the priorities and tasks for the upcoming jubilee. Avdeev pointed out to all who would write on the history of the RKP and the October Revolution that they must explain "from a Marxist viewpoint, the causal logic" of the events they were describing, namely the "permanent connection between phenomena." Without a proper understanding of this causal logic, he continued, it was impossible to write a complete history of the RKP and the October Revolution. Avdeev offered the following example of how this methodology should be applied to sources. In July 1914, a proclamation was distributed in the name of the Petersburg Committee of the RSDRP calling for a three-day strike protesting the shooting and beating of Putilov workers by the police on July 16. At the same time, another proclamation with the same signature called on workers to storm the arsenal, seize weapons, and begin an armed uprising. By applying his methodology, Avdeev wrote, the former proclamation was clearly revealed as genuine, because it was in keeping with the tactics of the Petersburg Committee at the time, while the latter was not. [13] Significantly, Avdeev's own logic assumed the existence of the kind of ideologically consistent party organization that was presently under construction. Once the materials had been properly evaluated, continued Avdeev, the historian had to be sure to use them for the "correct" description of events. The historian's goal was a coherent picture of the events, and he would frequently have to "restore missing links in the chains [of facts] by resorting to hypotheses or analogies." He would be guided in this by application of the "Marxist method of the materialistic conception of history," which, unlike the idealist conception, stressed neither divine intervention nor a few "great individuals" but rather the role of mass actions, ideals, and institutions. Significantly again, Avdeev offered Lenin's *State and Revolution* as the best guide in this regard because it showed that "the dictatorship of the proletariat, as the form of state power, explains and elucidates the history of the Paris Commune."[14]

Proletarskaia revoliutsiia also printed a new set of instructions on how to write memoirs and reminiscences about the history of the party and October. In keeping with the mood of the time, these instructions now cautioned that reminiscences were coming not only from workers but also from intellectuals of "the most diverse political origins," and that the task of "improving the quality of sources" was now an urgent one. Acknowledging that individual personal memories were not always independent of the individual's observations of "social-historical phenomena" going on around him, the author implied that the correct perspective was needed if the individual was to account for the various distortions and subjectivities inherent in personal reminiscences. At no time, he added, should individual reminiscers equate the work of an organization with their own personal participation in it, "because this will inevitably lead to the substitution of the role of the party and the masses by their personal role as a 'hero' of their own time." [15]

The objective needs of the revolution in the present clearly outweighed the subjective vanities of the individuals who recalled it. At the height of the "literary discussion," the Istpart board had pointed out that any works produced on the subject of October, broadly conceived, belonged to Istpart, and Istpart could revise them, with or without the author's consent or participation. [16] In October 1925, Kanatchikov informed the head of the Istpart bureau of the Urals regional committee that all materials produced for the jubilee of 1905 had to be vetted by the Literary Subcommission in Moscow, even if this meant delaying publication. [17] In a series of secret memos to the Central Committee of the party in the course of 1925, he also requested information on prospective authors, including their present party affiliation and their affiliation in 1905. Kanatchikov evaluated, and often proscribed, articles about 1905 on the basis of the past Menshevik or Socialist Revolutionary affiliations or sentiments of their authors. [18] He made similar inquiries of local Istpart bureaus. [19] On at least one occasion, Kanatchikov found himself at odds with the Moscow Istpart and the deputy head of the 1905 jubilee commission over the inclusion in a Moscow Istpart publication of articles by two individuals he called "odious" and undeserving of publication at all, regardless of the content of their writings. [20] As Kanatchikov pointed out in another case in May 1925, even though the "former Right SR" writing on 1905 was not now "an enemy of Soviet power," all his work was "inevitably saturated with SR ideology."[21]

This kind of direct political vetting was not unknown under Ol'minskii. The issue of past political allegiances and the extent to which they tainted individuals' recollections was a perennial one. Not all sources were deemed of equal value, and Istpart had expended much effort deciding which sources carried revolutionary legitimacy. Istpart was especially suspicious of one of the most common sources on 1905, namely local police archives. Savel'ev, Istpart's deputy director, warned local bureaus in late 1924 that such sources could be used to produce "a history of the police, but not of the revolution." [22] A review of a collection of articles on 1905 that drew heavily from police documents declared it in need of political and stylistic revision, because it reproduced the "language of the police-gendarme report." [23] Similarly, "White Guard materials" were deemed important only insofar as they contained information "about our organizations." [24]

But Kanatchikov's zealous focus on the Bolshevik Party as the sole *legitimate* measure of past political activity sharpened the political polarization inherent in the Istpart project from the outset. Under his stewardship, Istpart (and other organizations, such as the 1905 jubilee commission) would boost efforts that had been under way since October 1917 to provide the Bolshevik Party with the aura of organizational coherence and revolutionary continuity.

CONSTRUCTING THE PARTY

These early efforts had been piecemeal, and, as we have seen, poorly integrated into the general task of "telling October." In Istpart's very first bulletin, Bubnov had proposed a plan of study of the party that began with the years 1917 to 1920.[25] Two years later, Istpart came up with a detailed publication plan for the post-October history of the party, proposing a series of monographs covering party history in relation to the Brest peace, the trade union movement, economic construction under War Communism, the countryside, national relations, the petite bourgeoisie and the "intelligentsia after October," women workers, the young, and so on.[26]

A history of the Bolshevik Party for the pre-October period proved more difficult to plan and realize, in part because the years from 1922 through 1927 saw often sharp disagreements among leading Communist historians about the party's genealogy, disputes that the Central Committee refused at the time to adjudicate one way or the other.[27] One of the first publications about the party's prerevolutionary past was compiled from the ever-suspect documents of tsarist police archives.[28] For a planned "biographical library" of revolutionaries, Istpart asked comrades to send it the names of those who belonged in the library, or to search old issues of provincial newspapers for obituaries of departed comrades.[29] Undoubtedly, many of these dead comrades would scarcely have recognized the organization they were now helping to constitute. Furthermore, Lepeshinskii reported that the "great" demand for a "systematic course on the history of the party" would be met in part by the publication of a reader (khrestomatiia).[30] The central Istpart had called repeatedly in 1922 for a "generally accessible historical reader" and also a primer (uchebnik) on the history of the RKP, and a commission composed of Baturin, Mitskevich, and Lepeshinskii had been set up in September to draw up a concrete plan for them, apparently without much success.[31] The Central Committee of the party had also set up its own commission to compile such a primer, and Istpart contacted it in an effort to avoid duplication of work.[32] Materials like the reader were intended, as Lepeshinskii aptly put it at the 1923 Istpart conference, to "substitute for the history of the party," to create a "surrogate history of the party."[33] This surrogate would replace both the fractured history of the Bolshevik organization and the weak Bolshevik identity at the local level through October 1917.

In these early years, the Bolshevik Party acquired its most concrete form in the publication of its congresses and conferences, the irregular gatherings providing the leaders with a line of continuity of party history that they had not otherwise been able to achieve yet. In 1922, Istpart compiled a collection of resolutions adopted at the congresses and conferences of the "RKP from 1898 to 1921."

In so doing, it revealed the principles of selection that went into such documentary compilations. This volume, Kamenev pointed out in his introduction, was a response to an earlier such volume published in Petrograd in 1921, which was unsatisfactory because it contained resolutions not only from Bolshevik "but *also Menshevik* congresses" and therefore "gives an *incomplete* and *incorrect* picture of the development of Bolshevik Party thought [Kamenev's emphasis]."[34] The present volume "had to present the development of *Bolshevik* thinking and organization" and contained only Bolshevik proposals or drafts of resolutions. It only included officially adopted resolutions if these were the same as the Bolshevik drafts.[35] The Central Istpart used a similar presentist approach in deciding which issues to emphasize in the protocols of the Central Committee of the Bolshevik Party for 1917 and 1918 that it was preparing for publication.[36]

The protocols of the Third Congress of the RSDRP in 1905, published in 1924, were framed by an extensive introduction by the Old Bolshevik and historian Liadov. He first identified the "revolutionary labor movement" as the force that was arousing all social strata to political activity, but then he predicated the success of its initiative on its ability to "distinguish [*vydelit'*]" its own class party to lead the developing revolution. The RSDRP was clearly that party, Liadov continued, although, after the split at the Second Congress in 1903, "everywhere Bolshevik and Menshevik organizations were competing with each other. And each spoke in the name of the unified Social Democratic Party but proposed to the masses completely different tactics, gave differing evaluations of the current moment." The worker mass "was unable to make sense of this chaos of tactical disagreements and nuances of opinion."[37] Ignoring the large degree of cooperation between the factions at the local level, Liadov reduced this diffuse organization to a battleground of two clearly defined and ideologically coherent adversaries, the "decisive slogans" of the Bolsheviks contrasting with the "vague, opportunistic, slippery resolutions" of the Mensheviks.[38] The Third Congress, attended by "Bolsheviks alone," had literally made the RSDRP Bolshevik, he implied, while the Mensheviks, by attending their own conference in Geneva, had placed themselves physically and ideologically outside of the RSDRP.[39]

Many of these efforts were given a boost by a flurry of jubilee celebrations in 1923. For the twentieth anniversary of the Second Congress of the RSDRP of 1903, Lepeshinskii was charged with preparing for publication the protocols of the congress, as well as complete runs of the newspapers *Proletarii* and *Vpered*.[40] At the same time, the twenty-fifth anniversary of the "workers' party" in Russia (1898–March 1923) became a further focus of Istpart activity. In keeping with the rising tendency at this time to fold the history of the RSDRP into the history of the RKP, Istpart leaders decreed that the twentieth anniversary of the "Bolshevik faction" be celebrated at the same time as the twenty-fifth anniversary of the RSDRP. They further proposed to the Central Committee that an All-Russian party holiday (*Vserossiiskii partiinyi prazdnik*) be declared. They planned to publish an illustrated collection of articles and a special issue of the Istpart organ devoted to it, and to stage an exhibition in Moscow called *Twenty-five Years of the Party* (*25 let partii*). They proposed that the house in Minsk where the First Congress of the RSDRP took place be made into a museum of party history.[41] Individual members of Istpart were commissioned to write specific articles, Elizarova, for example, being told to write on the participation of the Moscow organization at the First Congress of the RSDRP for a planned collection for the jubilee of that congress.[42] In its annual report in April 1924, Istpart listed the works it had produced so far, chronicling the "major stages" and "individual episodes" in the life of the party.[43]

These jubilees appear to have found some resonance in the local Istpart bureaus. In Moscow, a special commission was set up under the county committee of the RKP to handle the celebrations of the twenty-fifth anniversary of the RSDRP.[44] The commission launched a broad agitation campaign about the history of the party among party members and convened a countywide meeting of its members to discuss the history of the RKP, the Twelfth Party Congress, the role of the party in the labor movement and in the struggle for Soviet power, among other things.[45] It proposed a "campaign of accounting [*otchetnost'*] of the party to the working class," in order to explain to the masses the significance of the RKP for the recent past, and convened general meetings of workers at the enterprise level to this end.[46] A meeting of the Istpart board in late 1923, attended by individuals carrying out Istpart work at the grassroots level, pointed out that the aim of collecting materials relating to the local party organizations was "not only to provide material for the historian but also *to delineate* [*obrisovat'*] *the contours* of the organization." (emphasis added). [47]

Lenin's death in January 1924 ensured that the party would acquire a specifically Leninist shape, finally inheriting the mantle of *What Is to Be Done?*[48] From early 1924, the party was represented increasingly as a function of Lenin the man and of Leninist ideology, a more energetic continuation of the cult of Lenin that had begun earlier.[49] In March, Istpart drew up a plan of work on Leninism that essentially reconceived the entire revolutionary movement in terms of Lenin's theoretical and practical contributions. The plan covered Lenin's prescient consideration of the theoretical intricacies of the major questions of Russia's prerevolutionary history: the problem of taking power, the nature of imperialism, the lessons of the state, the agrarian question, and the national question. The plan also proposed to examine Lenin in relation to the centralist design of the party of professional revolutionaries, the gathering of the party (*sobiranie Partii*), the split in the party,

12. Demonstration in Petrograd on the Twenty-fifth Anniversary of the RKP(b), 1923 (Courtesy of the RGAKFD in Krasnogorsk)

the crisis of the Second International and the birth of the Third.[50] The recently launched Institute of Lenin and the Institute of Marx-Engels were discussed extensively at the Thirteenth Party Congress in 1924.[51] The relentless publication of Lenin's works by the Institute of Lenin provided the Bolshevik Party with ideological cohesion. Lenin's oeuvre was, as Kamenev put it, "the wealth at the disposal of the party."[52]

In general, Istpart work at the local level grew livelier and more focused around the time of the 1905 jubilee. The Moscow bureau in late 1924 proposed to its local bureaus that they do more to collect materials on the history of the party and suggested that they appoint plenipotentiaries, particularly at the enterprise level, to this end, or, where they already existed, to heed them.[53] In November 1925, with a new secretary in place, the Orenburg bureau declared its intent with the 1905 jubilee to "start everything over, from the smallest to the largest matter."[54] Even the largely moribund Urals bureau of Istpart, desperately short of active collaborators in 1925 and largely ignored by central party bodies, managed to set up a special commission to deal with the 1905 jubilee and to publish a limited amount of literature.[55]

Some local bureaus found their own ways of engaging in what one bureau called the "construction of the whole [*postroenie tselogo*]." The Leningrad bureau put into "systematic order" the disorganized protocols of the first legal Bolshevik Petrograd Committee for 1917, compiled revolutionary collections of biographies of fallen party workers, and elicited collections of reminiscences on "worker moods, experiences, and struggle" and on Lenin in 1905.[56] Similarly, the Orenburg bureau, virtually defunct until the 1905 jubilee, spent the lion's share of its new-found energy and resources putting the party archive in order, numbering all the files of all the departments of the provincial committee of the party, as well as its county and district organizations, and classifying the archives according to personal files of party members, protocols of party meetings, congresses, conferences, and so on. The bureau's leader, Markovskii, outlined his bureau's future plans, leaving no doubt that the examination of the role of the party in 1905, required by the jubilee, was part of a broader redefinition of Russia's revolutionary history as a function of the Bolshevik Party. The bureau, he noted, would study the growth and development of the local party organization, its relations with other social groupings, including other parties, the emergence of "class self-consciousness and its ideological formulation," the actions of the parties during the war and up to the February Revolution, and the role of the local party organization in the October Revolution. Although Markovskii emphasized the need to "accumulate diverse sources" in order to be able to "compare various points of view," his approach, if successful, could produce *only* a steadily cohering Bolshevik Party as *the* formative element of the revolutionary past.[57] The Iaroslavl' Istpart organized all materials on the history of the Iaroslavl' party organization by year in individual folders (*papki*), drew up lists of the contents (*opisi*), and even displayed them under glass at the Istpart building, "so that party members who are interested in the history of the Iaroslavl' organization might in a short period acquaint themselves with them and have an idea what is there and what is missing."[58] The Orenburg bureau started work on a scenario for a cinematic film about 1905 and asked the Spectacle Subcommission (Zrelischnaia podkomissiia) of the Jubilee Commission to send directives on how to organize exhibitions, grants to help fund them, as well as objects to exhibit (if possible at no charge).[59]

Such local actions were a reassertion of the conviction, made urgent by the recent bickering in the party leadership over personal roles in October, that the genuine history of October and the party could be found only at the local level. Identifying the "hidden and serious political intentions" in Trotsky's works, Lebed' criticized the kinds of reminiscences that "have been extremely reworked over a period of time in the consciousness of the authors more in their desired direction than in the direction of reality."[60] Clearly, the personal vanities and political ambitions of self-indulgent political leaders had to be counterbalanced by the raw memories of local participants in October, elicited in a guided, collective context that helped mitigate their subjective tendencies. The principle of "public interest [*obshchestvennost'*]" became the watchword for the preparations for both jubilees. A network of "groups of assistance to Istpart [*gruppy sodeistviia Istpartu*]," "circles of Istpart [*kruzhki Istparta*]," and "plenipotentiaries [*upolnomochennye*]" emerged. The groups were to be organized mainly from party people, although, in the course of their work, they were permitted to draw in nonparty people as well. Istpart and party authorities made it abundantly clear to these groups that they were responsible for reconstructing the course of development of the Revolutions of 1905 and of 1917, in particular, and revealing "the role and participation of local party organizations in them."[61] They had to gather reminiscences from their members, collectively review them and thereby render memoir material into a "good-quality source" for the researcher. They relied for funds and support on the local Istpart bureaus.[62] The groups were also instructed to compile lists of party officials in a given region and to review materials relating to party organizations there.[63] A report by Istpart noted a "definite breakthrough" in drawing into Istpart work party comrades through these kinds of groups.[64]

Local bureaus took up the call. Reaffirming the importance of its work to the county and district party committees in its area, the Iaroslavl' bureau stressed the need for party circles in clubs and cells and in schools of political literacy to involve themselves in the renewed work on the history of the party, and to ensure that all involved "have clearly understood and recognized the entire importance of studying the past experience of the revolutionary struggle *in the interests of the present*" (emphasis added). They could achieve this, the bureau added, by explaining the significance at every opportunity, by collecting all relevant historical documents, and by organizing exhibitions, museums, and libraries from documents selected by them. They should also assign special representatives to organize cells to assist in Istpart work and set up circles to study the "history of the revolutionary movement and the history of the RKP(b)."[65]

During these years, the evenings of reminiscences (*vechera vospominanii*), which brought together participants or contemporaries to reminisce about predetermined topics or events, came into their own as major forums for the articulation of memory.[66] "We considered the evenings of reminiscences we held highly successful," remarked the Istpart of the Ukraine, "because entire plants took part in their organization."[67] The Kazan' bureau noted that the bright spot in its early activities was the organization of evenings of reminiscences "that are automatically forcing even the hopelessly reticent to tell their stories."[68] Elsewhere, the evenings of reminiscences were not always deemed so successful, the head of the Samara bureau complaining, for example, that they were organized very badly and produced little.[69]

CONSTRUCTING THE OPPOSITION

Notwithstanding all of these efforts to define both the Bolshevik Party and Bolshevism, the party was also being defined very effectively in terms of what it was not. The scripting of party and class categories so central to the Istpart project entailed the creation of an opposition between, on the one hand, the Bolshevik Party and the working class (or more broadly defined "toilers" [*trudiashchikhsiia*]) and, on the other, all other political or class groupings. Terne, a foreign observer in Soviet Russia in 1922, decried what he saw as the Communist regime's forced imposition of party categories on a population, the vast majority of whom had little sympathy with any party. It represented, he argued, a campaign of caricaturization against the banned political parties that was far out of proportion to their actual threat:

> Communist artists have even come up with distinct templates [*shablony*] for these caricatures: if it is necessary to portray a Black Hundred, Soviet caricaturists draw a gallant general or pot-bellied *muzhik-kulak*; a Kadet—*de rigueur* an individual in a morning coat with top hat and fat belly, with a massive fob watch on a gold chain (sometimes the same figure represents capitalists in general); the Social Democrat is a gaunt, tall intellectual with disheveled hair, with a carelessly knotted tie, dark spectacles, and with a bundle of papers under the arm; the same variant, but with a smoking bomb in his hands instead of the bundle represents the SR; sometimes the caricaturists depict anarchists in the same way, although usually the anarchist for them is a red-haired young fellow, in high boots and a cap, open mouthed, with bared teeth, ready to jump arm outstretched, holding a smoking bomb. [70]

The Soviet state's physical suppression of the opposition parties in the first few months after October 1917 had eviscerated the Menshevik and Socialist Revolutionary Party organizations inside Soviet Russia, although they persisted as an organizational threat in the short term in a few local regions. Well into the 1920s, however, the new regime sought tight control over Menshevik and Socialist Revolutionary accounts of past events. At key junctures, the publication abroad of SR or Menshevik representations of recent history spurred efforts inside Soviet Russia to write the history of October and the party. The party's Politburo set up a number of commissions to examine certain aspects of nefarious prerevolutionary Menshevik activity. In May 1920, one such commission, stacked with leading Bolsheviks, was set up to examine the "provocationist role of Mensheviks in the matter of inciting strikes during the war."[71] The trial against the SRs in 1922 was part of this process of self-definition.[72] Decisions on whether to publish various works by SRs or Mensheviks inside Soviet Russia were taken at the very highest levels of the party.[73] While the *Sotsialisticheskii vestnik,* published by the Menshevik Internationalists in the emigration as a sustained critique of Soviet Russia, may well have been prescribed reading matter for the party's leaders, its minimal distribution inside the country—even allowing for its being passed hand to hand—symbolized the absence of an organized base there from which to launch any kind of sustained ideological challenge to the Bolsheviks.[74]

These assaults, then, were directed not so much at existing or putative Menshevik or Socialist Revolutionary organizations but at Menshevik and SR institutional memory. It was, after all, precisely in this realm that the Bolshevik Party was haltingly acquiring its most coherent form. The "literary discussion" ensured that Menshevism, too, would find hitherto unknown definition and solidity as part of a broader "opposition," a foil to Bolshevism's inexorable historical evolution. Although "by no means everyone knows [it]," Kamenev wrote in 1924, "the thirty-year history of Bolshevism is the thirty-year history of its struggle with Menshevism." He contrasted this with Trotsky's declaration in 1911 that the idea that Menshevism and Bolshevism had put down deep roots in the proletariat was "an illusion." Most ominously for Trotsky personally, Kamenev added that Leninism had not only been forged in a struggle with Menshevism but in a "constant, systematic struggle with Trotskyism," or "masked Menshevism," as he called it. It was his "duty," he believed, to show that Trotskyism appeared in the Bolshevik Party not "in response to a particular problem but... systematically over long years at every turn of party history."[75]

In early 1924, the then head of Istpart, Ol'minskii, informed the Central Committee of the party that he had decided to "make a high priority of the study of the history of the RKP and above all the basic facts of the struggle of Bolshevism with Menshevism."[76] A year later, Istpart published a collection of articles and letters from the 1903–1904 period to explore "the essence of the struggle of Bolshevism with Menshevism (between the second and third congresses of the party)." The collection was a carefully selective representation of Russia's prerevolutionary political culture as one defined by coherent and competing political parties, and of the Bolshevik Party as *the* defining element of that party culture. In his introduction, Liadov divided the protagonists in the struggle for power inside the editorial board of *Iskra* into the "resolute [*tverdokamennye*]" and the "spineless [*miagkotelye*]." If Lenin's resoluteness at times appeared to isolate him from both the party organ and the Central Committee—Liadov pointed out that there were " 'no literary Bolshevik forces' at all" in Geneva at the time—he derived his authority from the support of the "Bolshevik delegates" of the Second Congress and the "Bolshevik organizations at the local level" inside Russia. This authority, Liadov implied, was undermined at every turn by "petit

bourgeois (SR) parties" as well as "future Mensheviks" and others who "overestimated the significance of the émigré culture [*emigrantshchina*]." It was further
undermined, in Liadov's estimation, by those less resolute Bolsheviks within the
Central Committee who chose to compromise with the Mensheviks in the party.
Gathering in Geneva to "take the revolutionary path," twenty-two Bolsheviks set
up the Bureau of the Committees of the Majority (Biuro Komitetov Bol'shinstva)
to replace the Central Committee and used the journal *Vpered* (*Forward*) as the
"ideological center of Bolshevism." Thus was the Bolshevik Party redefined in
terms of a group of individuals whose legitimacy was measured not by any organizational majority in the old RSDRP but by the true revolutionary path they had
followed. Liadov concluded his introduction:

> Only because it was saturated in this party mentality [*partiinost'*] in 1905
> was Bolshevism able to win in October 1917. At that time both Menshev-
> ism, and the Trotskyism that broke off from it, were reared in the spirit
> of anarchic-intelligentsia individualism. They underestimated the party
> at that time and thus were defeated over the entire twenty years of the
> future history of the party. [77]

During the Civil War years, the Bolsheviks had routinely yoked together the
various critics of its regime who shared little theoretical or practical ground and
were appalled at being mentioned in the same breath. In the course of the mid-
1920s, however, these critics found themselves assigned to an "opposition" with
its own coherent historical roots, an opposition *movement* of long standing, the
enduring rival of an equally coherent Bolshevik Party of long standing. The term
became a catchall for all manner of present and past disagreements inside the
party, with the July plenum of the Central Committee and Central Control
Commission (TsKK) in 1926 identifying the "unification of the Trotskyists, 'new
opposition,' and the Shliapnikov-Medvedev [members of the Workers' Opposi-
tion] trend in a general bloc against the party."[78] In October, a *Pravda* editorial
referred to the "United Opposition" that was leading the present charge against
the Bolshevik Party:

> In 1921 under Lenin's leadership the anarcho-syndicalist deviation, the
> so-called *Workers' Opposition*, was overcome, the Shliapnikov-Medvedev
> trend that had degenerated subsequently into pure Menshevism was
> censured, as were also the mistakes of comrade *Trotsky*. In 1923–24 the
> party carried the day over *Trotskyism*, which was recognized as a petit
> bourgeois trend that was revising Leninism. At the Fourteenth Congress

of the party the *New Opposition* was defeated and censured. Now victory has been won *over the oppositional bloc as a whole*, over all these groupings, which together were a closed front moving against the Central Committee.[79] (emphasis in original)

At the same time, the Central Committee and the Central Control Commission of the Ukrainian Communist Party jointly endorsed the Fourteenth Party Congress stand on the Opposition:

> The so-called New Opposition has not only shown not the slightest inclination to correct its ideological errors but has sought to deepen them further, having created an antiparty, anti-Leninist bloc, on the example of the liquidationist, petit bourgeois "August" bloc, with the remnants of the old factions [*fraktsiia*] and groupings that have already been condemned by preceding decrees of the party.[80]

The folding of a range of oppositionist critiques into an antiparty bloc was profoundly disturbing to the disaffected Bolsheviks. Trotsky fought it vehemently, arguing even into his exile that his was a criticism from within the proletarian party, not from without. In the declaration of penitence and fealty that he, along with Zinoviev, Kamenev, Piatakov, Sokol'nikov, and Evdokimov made in October 1926, admitting infractions of party discipline and abjuring future factional activity, Trotsky still placed the term "opposition" in quotation marks, even as he called for all groupings that had gathered around it to disperse.[81] Eventually, the term "opposition" would more often be called the "Trotskyite opposition," or just "Trotskyism."[82]

This is not, of course, to deny the very real expressions of criticism engaged in at the time by, among others, Trotsky, Zinoviev, and Kamenev. In the course of 1926 and 1927, Zinoviev was ousted from the Politburo, Kamenev demoted from his position as commissar of trade, and Trotsky removed from the Central Committee of the party as a result of their political stances and actions. Yet many Bolsheviks shared their concerns about the increasing bureaucratism in the party, their criticisms of the present government's foreign policy failures, and their advocacy of a more accelerated planned industrial development for the USSR. Something far greater was at stake here than individual acts of opposition. A coherent "opposition" was one of the requirements for a coherent Bolshevik Party. Zinoviev conceded as much, when he implied that his, Kamenev's, and Stalin's political battle against Trotsky in 1923–24 had been part of a battle for the integrity of the party. It had required a campaign against "Trotskyism": "There was a struggle for power. The whole art consisted in linking old disagreements with new questions. For this 'Trotskyism' was put forth."[83] In a letter to several comrades shortly before his exile to Alma-Ata in Central Asia in January 1928, Trotsky accused Zinoviev and others of using his article "Lessons of October" as a "formal pretext" for creating the "legend of 'Trotskyism.' " This was a particularly egregious crime against the party, he later wrote from exile in Turkey, because when they admitted this in 1926–27 it upset many oppositionists in the party who had truly believed the legend.[84]

WHERE DID LENIN S PARTY GO?

Istpart's sharper and more urgent focus did not remove its chronic infrastructural and financial problems. Throughout 1925 local bureaus continued to complain about the lack of material resources, the poverty of archival or printed sources, the chaotic nature of those sources that did exist, the overburdening of local Istpart officials with too much work, and the cavalier attitude from the party Central Committee vis-à-vis Istpart work in general.[85] The central Istpart made similar complaints about the state of source materials at the local level, and repeatedly urged the administration of the Central Archive (*Tsentroarkhiv*), in vain it noted, to review the backgrounds of those running local archives and purge the politically unreliable.[86] Such an important jubilee required an institutional effort on a nation-wide scale, and Istpart's good-faith efforts inevitably fell short, as Ol'minskii had been quick to point out to the Central Committee of the party in 1924.[87] The party allocated more resources to the local bureaus, but specified that these be used only for narrowly defined tasks relating to the 1905 jubilee.[88] In general, the jubilee literature arrived late, often after 1925, and not without criticism. Istpart even criticized the slogans for the 1905 jubilee proposed by Agitprop. Its use of terms like "masses" and "nation" was too vague to be easily understood by the masses, Istpart noted, and while Lenin was mentioned in some of them, "Where did his party go?"[89]

The focus on the history of the revolution as a function of the Bolshevik Party did not present the local Istpart bureaus with any ideological misgivings. The Leningrad Istpart bureau, staffed by a too small group of individuals, the party credentials of most of whom went back to 1903 and before, identified its basic task in mid-1925 as being to "give as full a picture as possible of the development of Bolshevism in Leningrad, to illuminate the work of its party districts." It complained, however, that this task could not yet be addressed, as it had not finished the difficult preparatory work of first finding, and then reviewing, all the necessary archival materials, and of studying the individual periods of the party's existence.[90]

Perusing the day-by-day chronicle of events from January 1905 through March 1906, published in 1926, the astute reader might have been surprised to find only an occasional mention of any party's presence amid the action, the rare mention of this or that Social Democratic Party conference or congress seeming perhaps quite distant from the workers' activities. Here was a chronicle of a worker-peasant revolution. Mensheviks and Bolsheviks were defined by the lesson they drew from the abortive events of 1905, the former advising the working class, as the introduction put it, to "forget their revolutionary dreams" and support the constitution, the latter drawing the conclusion "worthy of a proletarian party," namely that the defeat of 1905 did not mean the defeat of revolution in general. [91]

Although the central Istpart congratulated itself in early 1924 for the work that had appeared in its journal on the early history of the party, and especially for the large amount of materials on Lenin, it added that the provinces had produced far less.[92] Forced to draw from an extremely small pool of personal reminiscences or extant published sources, and lacking the long institutional memory that might have been afforded by a continuous and clearly defined Bolshevik Party presence in their regions, local bureaus strove for narrative coherence for their local area's revolutionary tales in ways that the center, and infrequently their own local leaders, found unacceptable. Reviewing the chronicles produced by several Istpart bureaus in the mid-1920s, the central Istpart rejected many for their failure to draw upon "party material" and their too heavy reliance on sources from "hostile organs." These factors, it noted, had produced chronicles "not of the revolution, but of the counterrevolution, where the role of the party was distorted or poorly explained."[93]

Moreover, these kinds of official surveys of both published and draft works questioned the very ability of the individual reminiscences, which figured so prominently in local treatments of 1905, even to grasp, let alone convey, the sense of a broader institutional coherence or of a revolutionary *movement* per se. The secretary of the publishing house Doloi negramotnosti (Down with Illiteracy) asked Istpart to edit the manuscript of a brochure on the history of the party written for a peasant audience. The brochure was criticized for missing "a number of moments" in the history of the party. It "completely ignored" certain disagreements between the Bolsheviks and Mensheviks at the Second Congress of the RSDRP in 1903, "inadequately explained" the two tactics in the Social Democratic Party in 1905, and said nothing about the struggle with "recallism, ultimatism, and conciliationism" in the years of the reaction from 1907 to 1912. Finally, it provided no information on "Trotskyism in 1905."[94]

Similarly, another proposed work dealing with Lenin's role in the revolutionary movement was criticized for using the term "*movement* of the RSDRP of Bolsheviks," for dating the beginning of Menshevism at 1896–97, for using the "incorrect" term "worker-peasant" movement, and for failing to mention the Bolshevik press. In a most telling criticism, the reviewer noted that the "*line of revolutionary Social Democracy* (Bolshevism)" portrayed diagrammatically in the work "takes turns that do not correspond at all to the turns in the line of the labor movement," and "it is unclear which events the author means by 'basic moments of the revolutionary movement': the congresses [of the party] or the upsurges of this movement."[95] A reviewer noted that a collection of reminiscences on Tula workers had successfully conveyed the "state of class antagonism [*klassovaia protivopolozhnost'*]" at the time, as well as the way in which the Tula workers had turned themselves from a "class in themselves" into a "class for themselves." Nonetheless, he continued, the work suffered from a "too individualistic and autobiographical approach," exemplified by a reminiscence that described the author's part in an "underground circle" up to 1905 while providing no information on the circle itself or its broader propagandistic influence over Tula workers in general.[96] A review of a manuscript on the experiences of 1905 at a plant in the Urals was even blunter: the author had completely ignored the "growth of the Bolshevik organization among the workers and its leading, organizing role." The work, it added, presented the entire movement as one of "unfolding spontaneity."[97] Although individual Social Democrats figured in the events of another plant in the Urals region in 1905, went a third review, there was no sign of "an organization as such."[98] Indeed, a work put together by the Bashkir Istpart on the revolutionary events of 1905 in the Urals expressed the ideological conundrums facing its compilers in 1925. The first third dealt with the workers' movement in 1905 in the plants and towns of the southern Urals, the minimal party involvement being identified as Socialist Revolutionary or Social Democrat. A subsequent section on Bolshevik Party organizations in Zlatoust had the unfortunate effect in print of distancing the local Bolshevik organization from the labor movement it was supposed to be guiding. Furthermore, the handful of reminiscences featured in this section gave the impression of piecemeal and minimal party organization, marked by the small number of people involved, ad hoc meetings often attended by SRs and Mensheviks, and periods of halting activity regularly stymied by tsarist repression and often by a lone agent provocateur. The picture of Gania Khrushcheva, a leading light in the tiny Zlatoust Bolshevik organization from 1906 until her exile in 1913, as "stocky, a well-formed figure—even today she gives the impression of being as hard as stone" may well have been an idealized image of a proto-Bolshevik, but it hardly conveyed the sense of the vital, coherent, regionwide and party-led movement desired by the center. [99] At the same time, such works might find themselves criticized for *failing* to mention a key figure in the local area. A review by the Urals Istpart of a work on the activities of a plant in Zlatoust in 1905 singled out its failure to include the significance and role of "the most important organizer of the labor movement in Zlatoust," Andrei Stepanovich Tiutev, the "generally recognized leader [*vozhd*]" of the region, or of his mother, who was active during the underground phase of the labor movement. The reviewer even suggested renaming Zlatoust Tiutevsk in their honor. The unresolved nature of the relationship between party and revolution was perhaps best captured by a poem that opened the former collection, and which assigned 1905 itself the role as prime historical actor in the revolutionary movement:

> It awoke the workers' quarters,
> and its trumpet-call penetrated into the cellar,
> when to the barricades, to the scarlet banners,
> it masterfully called the proletarians. [100]

The "belletristic shades" of the reminiscences, the Orenburg bureau implied in 1925, undermined the factual aspect of the material evidence of 1905, and it criticized a local publication for being a "set of reminiscences rather than a narrative [*povest'*]." Only by furnishing the correct contextualization, it argued, might such shortcomings be addressed. [101] One reviewer demanded that Istpart supply an introduction for these draft works, so that the reader might know whether the events described in the works were the "fruits of the author's imagination, or whether they really happened." If the latter, the reviewer added, then the reader should know what kinds of documents could substantiate the truth of the events and whether these documents were themselves sufficiently reliable. [102] A collection of articles on the events of 1905 in the Urals provided readers with an unmistakable contextualization:

> For the Bolsheviks it is obvious that revolution is the cause of the proletariat, that they, Bolsheviks, are obliged to participate in it and lead it, take on themselves the role of organizers and leaders. The platform of the Mensheviks is completely different: "Revolutions are not made," they declare, "revolutions are a spontaneous phenomenon, not dependent on the will of these or those leaders or political parties."[103]

Fundamental concerns over the nature of the evidence had accompanied the project to write October since its very inception. The concerns expressed in the reviews of the literature of 1905 were not new, merely more sharply articulated in the context of the 1905 jubilee and the broader context of dissension within the party. In August 1924, Dmitrii Sverchkov, a member of the jubilee commission under the Central Executive Committee of the USSR [TsIK SSSR], reiterated a call for personal memoirs that was reminiscent of the earliest and broadest calls put out by the Istpart organization. If the younger generation, which was only just now coming to political maturity, he wrote, were to have any idea of the 1905 Revolution, any and all experiences had to be recorded, from those of the "old activists of the revolutionary movement of 1905" to the "old party workers [rabotniki]" in the plants, factories, party organizations, circles, meetings, strikes, protests, demonstrations, and so on. Only then would the complete memory of 1905 be saved from "irretrievable loss." [104] Noting Sverchkov's appeal, however, Pokrovskii wrote a month later that "we cannot just amateurishly [kustarnym obrazom] remember 'what happened.' " Pokrovskii agreed that a complete picture of 1905 was sorely needed, adding that the present state of knowledge made it look like a "muddle of happenstances [kucha sluchainostei]." Yet, to "know the history of the events," he added, "means to know their causes and consequences, their interconnectedness," and this could not be achieved by a mere accumulation of information. Pokrovskii cautioned against a "fetishism of the document," because although the memoirs of Count Witte, a prominent official in the Ministry of Finance in 1905, had, like police or gendarme archives, raised "a corner of the curtain" on 1905, there simply could be "by definition... no revolutionary archives." Materials had to be found and sorted through "in which our own past was reflected, the past of our yesterday." Referring to the inevitable recourse to reminiscences, Pokrovskii captured the major misgivings about the nature of this kind of evidence:

> We have made use of them by an exclusively individual method, namely, we have told individual participants in past events to tell us what they saw and heard. But firstly not everybody is able to tell their tales without embellishing, and no one is able to leave their own personal viewpoint out of the event, for everyone is always the center. This is why all reminiscences, not only Goethe's autobiography, are interlaced with "poetry and truth"; and secondly, each individual reminiscence provides only one little corner of the historical picture. In order to produce a complete picture and take out the "poetry"—inevitable in all memoirs—it is necessary to collect reminiscences on a mass scale from many people. Only then will we obtain a balanced picture, close to the historical truth, so that... we get not "poetry" but "truth." [105]

The past, implied Pokrovskii, did not simply rise up from the sources, its meaning had to be revealed. Of crucial importance here was, of course, the revealer of that meaning. Earlier collections on 1905, Pokrovskii argued, had been put together from material that was "twenty years out of date and written by nonrevolutionaries, already completely primed to become counterrevolutionaries." The new multivolume collection on 1905 he put together would draw from more recent archival materials that were the product of a "Bolshevik, genuinely revolutionary treatment [*osveshchenie*]." Even this collection, he noted, suffered from the fact that "an entire important section, 'classes and parties,' " which should have been spread throughout each volume, had in fact been treated separately in a final, fourth volume.[106]

The poetry of the subjective reminiscence was thought to be incompatible with the truth required by the revolutionary movement. These sentiments ran up against an earlier belief among some Istpart leaders that had inspired the wide use of reminiscences, namely that a romantic, if not poetic, aspect to individual reminiscences of the "old underground activists" in some way was more seductive in conveying the truth of the revolutionary experience. From the pens of these activists, Istpart noted in its annual report in April 1924, "emerges in bright tableaux the thrilling revolutionary romanticism in which our young generation will be raised for a long time to come."[107] Of course, the entire Istpart project had been in some ways an extended exploration of this boundary between poetry and truth, an exploration that had been significantly influenced by the "literary discussion" of these years. In its report of April 1925, the central Istpart catalogued the "clear deviations" in the work of the local areas on 1905: a "passion for regionalism [*uvlechenie kraevedeniem*]", for the era of populism, for various jubilees (Shevchenko, the Decembrists, the Pugachevshchina), and too much attention to the history of the Menshevik faction in the RSDRP to the detriment of the Bolsheviks, including even the publication of articles about the Socialist Revolutionaries *compiled by the latter*.[108]

THE MAKING OF THE BOLSHEVIK REVOLUTION

The specter of the tenth anniversary of the October Revolution loomed large in the Bolshevik leaders' reviews of the experiences from the 1905 jubilee. At a meeting of the Istpart council in April 1926, Pokrovskii argued that the important anniversary of October had to be handled far more consistently than the 1905 jubilee. It had to be provided with real organizational authority and financial muscle if the lateness and poor quality of literature produced for the earlier jubilee were to be avoided. Mitskevich noted the lack of cinematic films, posters, or plays that had so far emanated from the October jubilee commission. Many at the meeting made special criticism of *Proletarskaia revoliutsiia*'s tendency to feature reminiscences in its pages, and called on it to start publishing "scientific-research articles" instead.[109] Sergei Gusev was more circumspect in *Pravda* in February 1927, decrying the cost of publishing so much material that would languish unread on shelves. He looked askance at early projected plans from Istpart to produce three times the amount of literature for the tenth anniversary than was produced for the earlier jubilee. He was even more deeply disturbed, though, by the nature of the publications than by their scale. Despite calls from the Department of Press (Otdel pechati) of the Central Committee that all publishers inform it of the kinds of literature to be published for the anniversary, few had done so. Moreover, works were appearing that were not on any of the lists or plans of state or party organizations involved in the jubilee.[110]

Inside Istpart, M. M. Essen echoed Gusev's concerns. The "flood of paper" being prepared for the tenth anniversary, she implied, merely increased the lack of individual accountability for the tales produced about October: "The richer the organization, the more independently it behaves, the broader its plans, the more ill considered its endeavors [*poryvy*]." For the tenth anniversary of October, every reader needed "one general book that tells the tale of the greatest battles and victories" rather than the forty or fifty publications being planned on the subject of a particular town. Essen's comments about what this one book should *not* look like showed how far the process of institutionalizing October had come since the earliest impulses toward dramatization and sacralization of the October narrative. The continuing veneration of the "fallen heroes" of the revolution, as she put it, no longer required the publication of "long boring collections… that almost no one reads, and no one buys." Similarly, the chronicles of local revolutionary events that were thought to be so essential to the project had turned out to be unsatisfactory, being composed of "materials of newspapers hostile to us, where the role of the party is ignored and sometimes distorted… and neither the class nor party struggle is reflected." The local areas needed detailed instructions to guide them in compiling their chronicles of events, she added. In the absence of such guidelines, local areas should not be producing generalizing works (*itogovye sborniki*) but should leave it to the center to draw general conclusions about the "entire USSR" from the materials collected.[111]

Some of these concerns stemmed from the realization that the Commission on the Organization and Execution of the Celebration of the Tenth Anniversary of the October Revolution (Komissiia po organizatsii i provedeniiu prazdnovaniia 10–letiia Oktiabr'skoi revoliutsii) had indeed come into the picture rather late, having been put together only in late 1925 under the Central Executive Committee of the USSR. Stalin and Viacheslav Molotov had been involved in putting the commission together, in consultation with Kanatchikov from Istpart, and delegates from Istpart were far outnumbered by leading party officials, even including Trotsky, Kamenev, and Zinoviev, at least for a while. The preponderance of party dignitaries was presumably a sign of the higher priority the party was giving this campaign than any other to date, although the Istpart network was still one of the commission's major beneficiaries of funds to produce the required works.[112] By the middle of 1926 the chairmanship of the commission had already shifted from Bukharin to Kalinin. Only by November 1926 would the commission finalize the compositions of the various subcommissions necessary for its functioning and send orders for the various Central Executive Committees of the Union Republics to form their own local commissions to organize the jubilee celebrations.[113]

Savel'ev expressed his concerns in a report to the Secretariat of the Central Committee of the party that the leadership and supervision of the publishing activity on the jubilee was "not completely guaranteed." He identified the "independent principles [*nachinaniia*]" of central and local publishing houses, public organizations, and universities as being "inadequately defined" and not under any specific supervision. Although works produced in the center generally met the standard intended for the jubilee, he added, local works contained "significant deviations" from recommended tasks.[114]

The jubilee commission bulletin set out clearly the priorities of the jubilee, however. It announced a grand exhibition "to explain the significance of the leading proletarian vanguard—the VKP, its major leaders and, especially V. I. Lenin…. The masses and the party must be represented in a process of ceaseless struggle, in a situation of sharp class antagonisms."[115] For their part, Istpart's leaders tried to make this explicitly party focus clear to the bureaus. In a series of guidelines on how to treat the materials on the history of October, Istpart linked an individual's ability to understand a process or event to his or her position "on one side or the other of the fighting classes." Istpart's main task was not only the gathering of facts, and their critical evaluation, but making "broad, scientific generalizations linking the revolutionary past with the revolutionary tasks of the present." For the history of October, Istpart had not only to use the "greatest consistency [*posledovatel'nost'*]" in its critical evaluation of the materials, and to link the events under study in a given region with the course of events in the entire country, but especially to work carefully on the "*chronology* of events of a given region," which must serve "as a canvas for all future scientific work in the area of the history of the party in the post-October period and of the October Revolution in general"[116] (emphasis in original). Work on the "history of the VKP(b) and the revolution, starting in the 1870s," Istpart noted in a directive to its local organizations, had to focus on the "direct history of the party. The history of the labor movement, the trade unions, peasant movement, the International, and other specific questions were of concern to Istpart only insofar as party life is reflected in them, or insofar as they are directly linked with the mass revolutionary movement."[117]

The jubilee celebrations should ideally penetrate every aspect of daily life.[118] A stream of memoranda and instructions from the central Istpart to the localities both reinforced this aim and attempted to address actual or potential transgressions by local Istpart works. In May 1926, E. Shteinman sent a note to Kanatchikov, pointing out that in connection with the preparations for the tenth anniversary of October, "the question has arisen in the localities about how to write the history of October and the Civil War, what can be written, what must not be written, what must not be printed." Shteinman had earlier attended a Ukraine-wide meeting of Istpart workers that had been unable to decide how or who should write the "history of our struggle in the Ukraine with hostile groupings, the *borot'bisty* [members of the non-Bolshevik Ukrainian Communist Party formed in 1919], and others," as some former *borot'bisty* were now party members.[119] Responding to queries from the Belorussian bureau of Istpart about which kinds of documents could and could not be published about October, Deputy Director F. N. Samoilov stressed that the jubilee had to produce a history of the October Revolution that "fully and completely corresponded to its historical reality." Materials pertaining to the "struggle of our party with other parties, or groupings," he added, had a rightful place in that history. Works by individuals who had earlier fought against the party but had now paid for their earlier sins and were working within the party had to be handled very carefully, reviewed and discussed with the Secretariat of the Central Committee of the Communist Party of Belorussia.[120] At stake here in the jubilee literature, as a secret memorandum from Samoilov in early 1927 put it, was the "explication of *our* understanding of historical reality" (emphasis added). Appropriate commentaries were required for local publications that "do not bear a clearly Bolshevik character and that are not put together in a politically literate enough fashion."[121] In April, the Briansk Istpart bureau was sharply criticized for its intention to invite nonparty groups to help it study the local revolutionary movement. Such groups, Samoilov pointed out, particularly in former Menshevik districts or "kulak rural districts," could "degenerate into cells hostile to us."[122]

Still, the jubilee commission did not want to see the jubilee project at the local level degenerate into a "squabble and a settling of personal accounts."[123] Local Istparts frequently asked the central Istpart to make decisions about whether to publish individual manuscripts written by former opponents of Soviet power. In the past, Istpart had, indeed, politically vetted such authors and rejected their proposed works.[124] It was not that the central Istpart wanted the local histories of October to be mere caricatures. The groups of assistance so key to the tenth jubilee of October, while made up of vetted Communists, were criticized by the center for lacking the courage to "recognize [past] mistakes, with the result that

in the past everyone and everything was Bolshevik and it was impossible to understand who the Bolsheviks were fighting against and why."[125]

The concern shown in the stream of instructions from the center to the local
Istpart bureaus was undoubtedly related to the scale of the plans for the tenth
anniversary celebrations. To offset the perceived failures of the 1905 jubilee, the
tenth anniversary of October had to be an emphatic success. Some local reports
complained in early September 1927 that preparatory work for the anniversary
was already taking on the "rote forms of the usual campaigns": the responsible
committees and commissions were marked by "narrowness" of membership or
duplication of duties, and their work was hampered by a lack of clear instructions
and by a general ignorance among the younger generation about the seminal
events of the October Days of 1917 and their significance.[126] Indeed, *Pravda* argued
that local newspapers were unable to lay out a "systematic explanation of the
events of 1917."[127] Nevskii argued that past anniversary celebrations of October
paled beside the spectacles and other mass agitation methods of the final months
of 1920. The staple mass meetings (*miting*) had become fruitless, moribund
gatherings that provoked little open discussion or liveliness. Obfuscatory language
had replaced the simple popular idiom, touchy issues such as religion were avoided
rather than met head-on, and praise of Soviet achievements had all but replaced
any criticism, even though "criticism is the business of the revolution," he wrote.[128]
A primer of instructions on how to organize these celebrations similarly criticized
the "empty ceremony" of organized meetings (*zasedaniia*) and other such gatherings. The red cloth that covered the table, the slogans, the portraits and busts of
the leaders, and the playing of the "Internationale" at the start of the meeting,
the primer implied, robbed those present of any active sense of participation.[129]
As Sergei Tret'iakov, a poet and playwright associated with the radical artistic
movement Lef, put it, the tenth anniversary should evoke "an unprecedented
stirring of the emotions of all strata of the population."[130]

Indeed, Nevskii seemed to be arguing for a grander effort in the anniversary
celebrations in the mid-1920s, something that awakened the independent activity
of the masses and recalled the mass productions of 1920. The Theatrical-Musical
Section of the Agitational-Spectacle Subcommission of the organizing commission
was charged with providing scenarios for open-air mass festivals during the upcoming anniversary.[131] This led to a conscious effort to reprise the successes of
the *Storming of the Winter Palace* in November 1920 in the mass spectacles seven
years later, this time on the Neva and at the Petropavlovsk Fortress.[132] A similar
impulse fueled the commissioning by Soviet cinematic organizations of a range
of films about October. [133] Mass forms such as demonstrations (*demonstratsii*),
mass stagings (*instsenirovki*), mass worker outings (*gul'ian'ia*), club evenings
(*klubnye vechera*), and agitation processions (*agit-protsessii*), *Pravda* pointed out,

would avoid the "old rote [*shablonye*] forms" and help the masses "work out and master the meaning and significance of October and the post-October path." [134] Nevskii also criticized the early mass spectacles, however, for their often "superficial treatment of the subject." He added that the museums and exhibitions that accompanied these celebrations had in the past been poorly systematized and had lacked adequate oral or written explanations of the exhibits.[135] The grandiose plans for no less than ten anniversary exhibitions in Leningrad, including an exhibition of the "commanding heights" of the economy, an exhibition of the Soviet press, and new sections for the Museum of the Revolution would presumably try to avoid these mistakes. [136] Podvoiskii was unequivocal about the goal of these tenth anniversary celebrations:

> With a thought-out, programmatic, planned use of these days, they will be transformed into a systematic course of self-formation and self-education of the masses. Worker outings and mass actions are designed so that, besides the elements of play and entertainment (or through these elements), they reflect the political tasks of the present day; they can be made into a tool of the political, trade union, and cooperative propaganda and agitation and a way of displaying the activeness and creativity of the masses, which were aroused and shaped in the class struggle and the revolution. [137]

Clearly, despite the myriad problems that beset their efforts at every turn in the first half of the 1920s, Communists at various levels of the party clearly believed that a well-told tale of the October Revolution was an essential step on the path to the new Soviet society. Major disagreements still existed among many Communists, however, as to what precisely constituted a well-told tale. Notwithstanding Pokrovskii's misgivings about the incompatibility of "truth" and "poetry," the tenth jubilee of October revealed a trend towards a more poetic telling of October, and a return to the more aestheticized October of the Civil War years.

TRUTH AND POETRY
The Tenth Anniversary of October

For ten years we have been making October,
For ten years October has been making us.
—From a poem for the tenth jubilee, 1927

The subject was revolution, the form was a cinema poem.
—Grigorii Aleksandrov on the film *October*

The ambitious scope of the tenth anniversary celebrations produced some of the most evocative tellings of October to date, rivaled only by the early mass spectacles. Indeed, for the first time since 1920, the Communist authorities devoted significant resources of manpower, money, and time to shaping the contours of the October narrative. This was perhaps their best effort to tell a transparent tale of October and the Bolshevik Party that was accessible to the masses, and it advanced the narrative in significant ways. More individuals than ever before articulated their past experiences as memories of the October Revolution. Vetted Communist officials, activists, and artists committed themselves to telling a clear and coherent tale of revolution. This did not automatically render the tales these people told acceptable to the Communist authorities, who felt barely in control of their ambitious efforts and worried constantly about the effects they were having on the population. This was especially true for the potent but unsettling art form of the cinema, which the state had just begun to draft into its service in a concerted way with these two jubilees. The tenth anniversary presents a case study in both the possibilities and limits of telling the story of October.

THE HARMONY OF OCTOBER

The tenth jubilee was intended to put the Soviet Union on display. Its achievements had to be actively witnessed both at home and abroad in a kind of World's Fair of socialism, attended by invited dignitaries from abroad. [1] The October Revolution was the main exhibit in this fair, and the jubilee told a more focused tale than ever before.

The structure and organization of the decorations, processions, and celebrations in Moscow and Leningrad were intended to convey the internal harmony of the revolutionary tale and its actors. The plans to decorate the city of Moscow for the anniversary had to be based on the "principle of maximum unity of the decorations of the entire city." All the central points of the city had to be decorated according to the "single general idea of the festival." The square in front of the former Kshesinskii Palace, for example, had to symbolize the transition from the Russian Empire to the Civil War; the Field of the Victims of the Revolution had to be dedicated to the memory of fallen warriors; the Narva Gates, to the Red Guard; the Moscow Gates, to the Red Army. A monument to Lenin in front of the Finland Station was decorated as the "apotheosis of October." [2] The Agitprop Department of the Central Committee recommended to its departments at the local level that they deliver lectures to all workers and peasant gatherings on "October: Its Preparation and Significance," "October and the General Results of the Past Ten Years," and so on. [3] Agitprop stressed the need in such lectures and in the press to discuss the "most important historical facts that took place in September-October 1917, examining also local revolutionary events." [4] Press reports boasted of the "gigantic dimensions" of the demonstrations for the anniversary, and noted the "enthusiasm, unity, and solidarity of the worker masses" marching in the processions and attending the meetings. The processions incorporated the "revolutionary activeness of the broadest masses of the proletariat and nonproletarian toiling masses of the USSR," and this could be seen, the report continued, not only in the major cities but also in the smallest towns and villages. [5] In Leningrad, eight hundred thousand people streamed along the streets to Uritskii Square in front of the Winter Palace, a display of the "unanimity, cohesion, courage, and certainty of the victorious proletariat." [6] Red Square, on the day of the celebrations, was a model of "natural order," with everyone in their places. The ranks of soldiers were, one observer wrote, "an affirmation of calm and comradely intimacy." In this parade, he saw the USSR reflected, "the tools of production in one hand and weapons in the other... a country of belief and unselfishness." [7]

The earlier dissension at the highest levels of the party, however, threatened to disrupt the harmony these celebrations were designed to convey. It certainly informed the preparations for the tenth anniversary celebrations. "Those who violate the unity of the VKP(b)," warned one of the Central Committee slogans for the anniversary, "betray October." [8] The campaign against the Opposition gathered steam in the run-up to the celebrations, as the Bolshevik press denounced it for serving as a banner for "all counterrevolutionary forces" and for harboring Menshevik and bourgeois views of the proletarian dictatorship. [9] The press regu-

larly featured declarations from individuals and groups affirming their decision
to leave the Opposition, apologizing for past oppositionist activity, and stating
their desire not to allow the Opposition to become a second party within the
party. [10]

Apparently for the first time, however, these jubilee celebrations were accompanied by counterdemonstrations by oppositionists. In 1929, Trotsky recalled
oppositionists marching in processions in Moscow and Leningrad on the day of
the tenth anniversary celebrations; they were carrying placards that called for
unity in the party. Trotsky's automobile was fired on, the placards were torn from
the marchers' hands, and the bearers were beaten, not by the masses, Trotsky was
quick to point out, but by "specially organized units."[11] Foreign observers reported
increased police activity and arrests of oppositionists even before the anniversary.[12]
Still, a German correspondent in Moscow at the time remembered seeing only
muted opposition during the celebrations. [13] Notwithstanding a press report
dismissing the "trivial attempts by several 'leaders' of the Opposition to disrupt
the harmony" of the official celebrations, [14]*Pravda* kept up a barrage of criticism
against these counterdemonstrations in the days after the anniversary. It reported
that oppositionists in Leningrad had been busily trying to organize their counterdemonstrations, opening underground printing presses, stealing typeface from
the offices of the *Leningradskaia pravda* newspaper, and encouraging one another
to bring their wives and children along to swell their numbers. These oppositionists, it added, were always shouted down by assembled workers whenever they
tried to address them. [15] It also excerpted reports from the foreign Communist
press condemning these demonstrations as "antiparty," and from the bourgeois
press chronicling their failure. [16]

Official reports and eyewitness accounts represented the counterdemonstrations
in farcical terms, the last quixotic act of a small group of prominent individuals
blinded by their own vanity. A witness noted that the opposition portraits in
Moscow windows hung not from workers' rooms but from the opposition leaders'
own apartments and were unfurled to "cries of indignation" from the masses. In
a scene worthy of the "kings of cinema, Chaplin and Lloyd," wrote the witness,
an individual on the roof of a building where such banners were displayed tried
to snag with a line and hook a red banner bearing portraits of Zinoviev and
Trotsky. From inside the apartment, Zinoviev and Trotsky endeavored to keep
his line from their banner with the aid of brooms thrust out of the window. [17]
Others described how Trotsky was heckled as a "traitor" during a public appearance, and how any "oppositionists" who stood on balconies overlooking the
processions and marches of the official November 7 celebrations were pelted with
apples, boots, or anything else that came to hand. Such reports invariably included
verbatim quotes from the crowds: "After October [Trotsky] sat with us... but

now, look, he 'corrects' our party!" While reports would concede that some workers greeted those on the balconies by raising their hands in salute, they did so only because they thought they were foreign dignitaries. In a familiar motif, an "old worker," suddenly recognizing those on the balcony, dropped his arm and turned his back to it. [18] Expressions of outrage by central and local party organizations at these actions by the oppositionists filled *Pravda*. [19] The "party as a whole," the Central Committee informed the party organizations on November 10, had "clearly and decisively marked itself off from the Opposition." [20] Thus did the Communist authorities attempt to transform the potential disharmony of the counternarrative into a source of harmony for the revolutionary narrative.

THE INEXORABILITY OF OCTOBER

Careful preparation and planning also helped to convey the inexorable unfolding of the revolutionary story. "The route of the demonstrating masses," Podvoiskii wrote, "must present a series of vignettes, illustrating the ten stages of the revolutionary path." He provided detailed instructions on the organization of the columns of marchers, the bearing of red flags, and the sounding of drums, trumpets, and bells at key moments in the vignettes of revolution. Flags were to be waved, and shouts uttered in unison, when two columns of marchers converged at a predetermined point in the procession toward Red Square. The route would take the marchers past "living pictures," platforms with spectacles and plays that enacted seminal moments: 1905, the "dress rehearsal for the October Revolution"; 1914; 1917; the Civil War. The final platform in the central square would be occupied by official representatives of government, unions, and party, who would greet the demonstrators. Podvoiskii did not envisage the demonstrators passively filing past these platforms. The columns had to display the "organized nature" of the masses, and the activities on the platforms were intended to provoke a "lively, bold" response in the marchers that would transform them into an "active, demonstrating mass." [21] These instructions seemed to herald a return to some of the earlier attempts by radical artists to break down the barriers between the watchers and the watched and to change the concept of spectator (*zritel'*) in this revolutionary society. The "spectator of the mass festival" had very little in common with the more traditional spectator of the theater or circus. The former "quite often, joining the ranks of demonstrators, taking part in their games and entertainments, joining in a song, beating time, speaking and exchanging jokes with the actors on the mobile stages, erases the boundary between spectator and actor and is transformed directly into an active participant in the procession." [22]

THE COHERENCE OF OCTOBER

The renewed focus of these celebrations on Leningrad and Moscow also provided a powerful narrative center for October. The mass spectacle finally returned to Leningrad, this time to the Petropavlovsk Fortress and the Neva River, "the stronghold of autocracy." The spectacle announced the February Revolution to the strains of the "Marseillaise" and a circle of burning torches around the fortress. It announced October by the illumination of factory chimneys, the gallows, the casemates of the fortress, and a single shot from the *Aurora*. The Civil War was signaled by machine gun fire and howling sirens and factory whistles; Lenin's death, by a "funereal, plaintive symphony of sirens." The apotheosis of the spectacle came as a tight circle of torch fires surrounding the Petropavlovsk Fortress gradually merged into a "continuous red glow," while a "majestic fountain" shot up from a barge on the Neva, the geyser lit in all colors, and hundreds of fireworks were fired into the skies. In a final scene, the illuminated profiles of the ships on the Neva stood out against the Leningrad night. [23]

A "Calendar of October" in *Pravda* in the days leading up to November 7 told a tale of clear-sighted actions by clearly defined proponents and opponents of revolution in the capitals. The first installment was devoted to October 10, 1917, as Lenin persuaded the Central Committee to adopt his call for immediate armed uprising (Zinoviev and Kamenev were identified as the sole dissenters), all against a backdrop of the "growth of revolution," as peasants rose up in various provinces and workers went on strike. Subsequent days of the calendar chronicled growing expressions of support for the Bolsheviks and their slogans from soviets, large plants, and factories, set against the continuing acts of treachery against the party line by Zinoviev and Kamenev. The calendar for October 25, 1917 noted the near unanimous endorsement by the Executive Committee of the Petrograd Soviet of the decision to set up the MRC, while the Mensheviks and Socialist Revolutionaries spoke of a "crisis of the soviet organization" at this time. The calendar carefully framed the technical steps taken by the Bolsheviks in preparation for their uprising, within the context of the growing strike movement, peasant unrest, nationalist movements, and the growing mobilization of the reaction against them. As the Bolsheviks took their clear-sighted and well-prepared measures, so too did the "counterrevolution" in the form of the Mensheviks and SRs. This gathering of the counterrevolution almost forced the hand of the revolution as it "went on to the attack" on October 24, 1917 when the Provisional Government undertook last-minute measures to crush the preparations for revolution, underestimating the will of the working class to take part in it. In response, the MRC "went over to a decisive open attack." [24]

The Bolshevik press further identified a literary focus for the October narrative, in a list of suitable readings. It showcased Lenin's published writings from the

February to October 1917 period, identifying in particular those works that displayed his decisive preparations for the uprising in September and October. In this connection, readers were pointed specifically to Lenin's writings on the internal state of the party at this time. The writings on October by other leading figures, including Stalin, Bukharin, Ol'minskii, and Pokrovskii, were also recommended, as were collections of documents and other works that gave a "successive, day-by-day chronicle" of the Revolution of 1917. Recommended works treated the major actors in the revolution in the following order: the party, the workers' movement and the soviets, the peasantry, and the army and navy. Few pro-Bolshevik memoirs were included in the list, John Reed's being a notable exception, although the memoirs of several "White Guardists" were listed. Most significant in this listing, perhaps, was its inclusion of very little that had been published prior to 1925 and absolutely none of the local studies from the early 1920s. [25] The earlier literature, as *Izvestiia* put it, "basically falls in the realm of... belles-lettres."[26]

The sharper focus on the October Days was used to elicit recollections from individuals in Moscow and Petrograd, producing some of the most vivid and romanticized published accounts since the earliest representations of October during the Civil War years. These recollections had a lyrical, vivid, quality to them. One woman recalled how a blazing house in Moscow lit up a nearby street "like a gigantic projector":

> Slowly, slowly the balconies fell... pieces of iron writhed, wrapped up in cigarette paper, coiling like snake tails around the remains of the roof.... The walls fell, transformed into the finest lace. In the fiery dance the open-work stairs howled, whistled; they rose up high like flakes and fell headlong, drawn by the force of the earth.

This destruction of the fragile and insubstantial contrasted with the constructive potential of the "wave of energy" unleashed in the people by October, the "wave of awareness that they are alive" at the beginning of a "*new* era [emphasis in original]." "It is necessary to burn with life," she wrote, "to feel its rhythm, its contemporaneity." [27]

Mikhail Vladimirskii stressed the eight days and nights of "tenacious... armed struggle" that constituted "October in Moscow." His recollections revolved around the role of the Moscow organization of the Bolshevik Party that since the February Days had prepared the revolutionary struggle through its work among the worker and soldier masses, work that made it "in fact the leader of these masses." The steady growth of party influence in the Moscow Soviet, the elections to the district dumas and other organizations led to the formation of a MRC in Moscow and the launch of the military takeover beginning on October 25. Despite his acknowledgment of the important preparatory role of the party, he also noted how each critical stage of the fighting was decided by the "insurgent workers," "revolutionary detachments," and "revolutionary troops." [28]

The tale of Moscow's October was certainly told as part of the broader October Revolution, although not as ancillary to events in Petrograd. Moscow's October was born of the revolutionary conditions specific to Moscow, with the news of events in Petrograd providing a fillip, but not the inspiration, for the revolutionaries in Moscow. A member of the Moscow MRC recalled how "scant and fragmentary" the information was about events in Petrograd, much of it coming to them from local Mensheviks and SRs. The "attempt to rise up in Leningrad [sic]," he recalled, "was depicted as a comical adventure, without any kind of firm foundation." Even Lenin himself was rumored not to be taking "his own adventure" seriously. On the eighth or ninth day of the uprising in Moscow, the Moscow MRC learned from emissaries from Petrograd that power had been taken there without the kind of serious street fighting seen in Moscow. The news spurred the Moscow MRC to go all out for an armed uprising in support of the Leningrad overthrow, notwithstanding uncertainty over Moscow's readiness for an uprising within Bolshevik ranks, among prominent Mensheviks, and even in military circles. The author of this account contrasted the uncertainty of these leaders with the "healthy instincts of the masses [that] demanded categorically the resolute and urgent completion of the struggle."[29] In his own account, Pokrovskii even seemed to imply that Moscow's experience of October was somehow more deeply felt, perhaps more genuine, than Petrograd's, precisely because of the tribulations of protracted battle: "The masses here were more deeply drawn into the cause, and their voice resounded more resolutely.... The rank and file were firm; the leaders felt their pressure and were easily and quickly straightened out."[30]

The immediate military and political events leading up to the overthrow of October 25 featured in many recollections and lent them the coherence of a tight narrative focus. Pavel Dybenko offered a day-by-day account of the Baltic Fleet's preparations to ready itself for the coming revolution, noting in particular the refusal of the *Aurora* to obey the orders of the Provisional Government; instead, "the faithful sentry remained at its post."[31] Podvoiskii recalled once again in even more detail the military preparations leading up to the storming of the Winter Palace, describing the MRC's plans for positioning various battalions and regiments at strategic positions around the city in late October. He took care, though, to trace these actions back to the Bolshevik Central Committee's realization that the urgent task after the Kornilov mutiny was "to prepare the masses for uprising."[32] His understanding of the Bolshevism of this period transcended mere party manifestations: "In October it was a rare soldier who was not Bolshevik, although, of course, the attitude to Bolshevism itself as a doctrine [*ucheniie*] was not a conscious one; he was simply a Bolshevik by mood [*po nastroeniiu*]."[33] Others stressed Lenin's revolutionary prescience and single-mindedness, all the more commendable given his long periods of physical isolation from events in Petrograd, and contrasted it with the absence of these qualities in Zinoviev and Kamenev, a fact that condemned them to commit their "fundamental mistake" about an immediate uprising.[34]

As in the anniversary celebrations of 1920, the choice of the Winter Palace as the centerpiece of many accounts provided a cohering moment of considerable rhetorical and narrative power. In *Izvestiia*, Podvoiskii's recollections of the taking of the palace were accompanied by a photograph of himself, Antonov-Ovseenko, and Chudnovskii, the troika in charge of the operation. Below it was a still photograph (unattributed, from Sergei Eisenstein's film *October*) with the caption "The Storming of the Winter Palace," and noting the time of the storming as midnight on October 25, 1917. Podvoiskii recalled the poor communications and improvised troop deployments that delayed the troika's decision to launch the assault on the palace during the night of October 25 until around 6 or 7 a.m. the next day. Despite the revolutionary aspirations of the troops besieging the palace, the leaders decided to show restraint and first demand the surrender of the palace: "The revolution wanted to avoid by all measures the shedding of blood." Repeated rebuffs from the ministers caused the troops to lose all patience and "on their own initiative, they advanced closer to Palace Square," exchanging fire with the defenders. Podvoiskii recalled the Winter Palace being in disarray at the time, the defenders inside deceived by their leaders into thinking that Kerensky had gone to muster reinforcements. As the blank shells from the *Aurora* rang out, the women's battalion was the first to surrender, the prelude to the storming. Although this version of Podvoiskii's recollections did not differ greatly *in its details* from his reminiscences of several years earlier, his vivid and dramatically embellished "storming of the Winter Palace" now drew upon ten years of cultural inscription of October, and incorporated all of the elements of harmony, inexorability, and drama that were the markers of that process:

> This was the heroic moment of the revolution, terrible, bloody, but wonderful and unforgettable. In the dark of night, in the fog and smoke, lines of Red Guards, sailors, soldiers, lit up by pale, smoke-shrouded light and the bloody bursts of shells, rushed from all adjacent streets and from nearby corners, like threatening, ominous shadows, stumbling, falling, and rising up again, but not for a second interrupting their headlong, hurricane-like flow. When the savage howling and roaring of three-inchers and six-inchers from the Petropavlovsk Fortress fell silent,

there remained in the air, muffling the ceaseless dry roll of machine guns and rifles, a continuous, victorious "hurrah," awe-inspiring, thrilling, uniting the entire heterogeneous mass. For an instant, the barricades themselves, their defenders, and those attacking them merged into a single dark, continuous mass, seething like a volcano, and in the next instant a victorious cry had already come from the other side of the barricades. The flood of people inundates the gateway, the entrances, stairways of the palace. Along the sides, corpses are strewn about, destroyed barricades are piled up, and crowds of people are standing without hats, with pale faces, quivering jaws, with arms raised upward as in a cry for mercy. The Palace was taken. The only piece of territory in the hands of the "Provisional Government of all Rus'" had been wrested from it by the hands of the people. [35]

FRAMING OCTOBER

Given his assistance in the production of Sergei Eisenstein's forthcoming film *October* (*Oktiabr'*), and by some accounts a role in the film itself, it was perhaps not surprising that Podvoiskii's recollections had acquired an almost cinematographic flourish. [36] Cinema presented the organizers of the jubilee celebrations of 1925 and 1927 with a radically new form of storytelling, one that used a powerful language of *enduring* visual imagery. Since the February Days, revolutionaries had explored this new art form's power to bring the revolution to the masses. Cinematographers rushed to produce films for the new regime, often reediting old films "in the spirit of the times, adding revolutionary titles, slogans, symbolic little endings." [37] After October, the MRC immediately tried to control the medium, authorizing only a few leading filmmakers to shoot in Petrograd "for the purpose of fixing [*zafiksirovanie*] the most prominent moments of the revolution." [38] Regular state and city decrees restricted access still further during the Civil War years. [39] Even authorized film committees had to beg for access to buildings and meetings, and their cameramen were sometimes arrested for unauthorized filming during parades and celebrations. [40] The Bolshevik authorities understood that film footage was always intended to "evoke feelings in the population and loyalty to the existing system," which was why the tsarist system had chronicled only "dazzling parades of victorious generals, meetings of tsarist dignitaries." [41] They had to be sure that they chronicled their own regime appropriately.

Bolshevik leaders had certainly discussed the potential of cinema, although Trotsky in 1923 publicly criticized the regime for failing to harness a medium that could create an "inexhaustible fount of impressions and emotions" and that "cuts into the memory." [42] What made the medium so pregnant with possibilities in the mid-1920s, however, was the application of the principle of montage. In the hands of the Soviet Union's talented young filmmakers, this technique added a transcendence to the art of telling October to which the Reeds, Podvoiskiis, and Antonov-Ovseenkos could only aspire—even in their most poetic flights of imagination. Rather like the act of remembering, the techniques of montage, which were being applied in many artistic fields at this time, slipped the bonds of linear storytelling by assembling and juxtaposing fragments so as to create what film scholar David Bordwell calls "a radically new relation among parts of a whole."[43] Like montage, memories are always more than the sum of the events recalled. Eisenstein created an essential *revolutionary* truth by editing together scenes that often jarred. Criticized at the time for inventing historical events in his films, he responded with a quote from Goethe: "For the sake of truthfulness one can afford to defy the truth." [44] He, and the small cohort of directors who produced films for the jubilee celebrations of 1905 and 1917, was completely committed to creating a "socially useful emotional and psychological effect on the audience." [45]

The Soviet state enlisted the cinematic talents of Boris Barnet, Eisenstein, Vsevolod Pudovkin, and Esfir Shub in the service of these important jubilees. Pudovkin's *Mother* (*Mat'*) and Eisenstein's *Strike* (*Stachka*) and *Battleship Potemkin* (*Bronenosets Potemkin*) were made for the 1905 anniversary. Shub produced her *Fall of the Romanov Dynasty* (*Padenie dinastii Romanovykh*) for the tenth anniversary of the February Revolution. Barnet's *Moscow in October* (*Moskva v Oktiabre*), Pudovkin's *End of St. Petersburg* (*Konets S.-Peterburga*), Shub's *The Great Way* (*Velikii put'*), and, most famously, Eisenstein's and Grigorii Aleksandrov's *October* were commissioned specifically for the October anniversary in 1927. [46] *October*, though, was the implicit or explicit telos in all of these films. They were all told as parts of the tale of October. All were mythic artifacts of the broad cultural process of creating this foundation event and should be analyzed as a function of that process.[47]

All of these directors, as tellers of revolution, strove to convey the coherence, inexorability, and drama of October, a task that they believed, as the original production plans revealed, required appropriately epic effort.[48] Through *Strike*, *Potemkin*, and *October* Eisenstein told a tale of October as a chronicle of the steadily rising coherence and purpose of the labor movement, of the emergent possibilities of armed insurrection as the only real outcome for the growing proletarian consciousness, and of the ultimate realization of those possibilities in the "storming of the Winter Palace." Through his adaptation of Gorky's novel

Mother, and through *End of St. Petersburg*, Pudovkin narrated the revolutionary odyssey through a portrait of generational conflict within a single family in 1905, and through the intensely personal experience of a peasant from Penza Province forced to Petersburg in search of work and who finds, instead, revolution. Through her careful juxtaposition of images culled from an enormous amount of original film footage in *Fall of the Romanov Dynasty*, Shub offered a critique of the tsarist regime in terms of the new Communist social and political categories.

In these films, prerevolutionary Russia was a starkly polarized country with clearly defined protagonists and with no organic links between rulers and ruled. The masses encountered the state through its obdurate and often brutal agents, not only policemen, soldiers, and prison officers but also railwaymen, factory supervisors, and foremen. The entire structure of Shub's *Fall of the Romanov Dynasty* illustrated this gulf—lengthy shots of the closed castes of educated society were juxtaposed to sequences of the equally closed castes of the oppressed masses. Against newsreel footage of ornately costumed military officers and nobles from Russia, Germany, Austria, and England marching in seemingly endless parades, she contrasted footage of plainly dressed workers and peasants engaged in various forms of manual labor. In Eisenstein's films, double-chinned officers towered over emaciated commoners, or the camera cut from overdressed representatives of the ruling classes enjoying undeserved leisure to robust workers, stripped to their shorts and engaged in honest leisure or labor. As film scholar James Goodwin points out, it was a contrast "between naked authenticity in the working class and elaborate cunning in the dominant class."[49] For Shub, the gulf was not merely Russian but universal. In the lengthy battle scenes from the World War, the identities of the soldiers are unclear, obliterated in this generalized slaughter of the world's working masses (scenes in *October* of Russian and German soldiers fraternizing in the trenches after the February Revolution similarly argued that the working classes of individual nations were all in it together). The war's toll was documented in terms of humanity's losses, unidentified by nationality, the intertitles announcing: "Killed, wounded, maimed, 35-million people," "The Faces of War," "The Prisoners," "The Wounded," The Refugees." The scenes that followed identified the tsar and various military generals as the guilty parties in this slaughter. *Mother* conveyed the social gulf between the privileged and the victims through shots of the courthouse (the "Pillars of Law and Justice," as the intertitle ironically put it) and through low-angle shots of a policeman and a mounted soldier. Inside the courthouse, her son stands accused of sedition, in the absence of any evidence. Court officials preen, doodle, clock-watch, and daydream their way through the juryless trial, callously indifferent to the fate of the man in the dock. The predictable sentence of hard labor cuts to a scene of a bust of Nicholas II. Here was tsarist authority, justice, and honor in practice.

These directors did not, however, romanticize the relationships in the lower classes in the tsarist period. Their films were, after all, intended to emphasize the significance of the revolutionary rite of passage. In *End of St. Petersburg*, the arrival of a newborn child in a poor village is no occasion for joy but rather the cause of the death of the mother in childbirth and the end of that peasant family. The newborn represents one more hungry mouth to feed and precipitates the father's flight to the city in search of food and work. The young peasant and his mother, arriving in Petersburg on the doorstep of a relative (a common path from the village to the city), encounter only mistrust, hostility, and selfishness in the city, with the suspicious and poverty-stricken wife of the relative failing to offer food to these starving newcomers as her own daughter eats. The mother answers her child's tears with a blow of her hand. The vignettes of violence and drunkenness in the home and the tavern with which Pudovkin opened *Mother* was a relentless condemnation of the self-defeating ignorance of the old ways. The conniving members of the reactionary and anti-Semitic Black Hundreds in the tavern draw their support precisely from this well of frustration and brutality, the simmering violence of the physically abusive, drunken father Vlasov being their reason for "luring him in," as the intertitle put it, to their strikebreaking activities. They buy him for a glass of vodka and barely notice his death in their service. It was the wretched social conditions, these films implied, that created such Vlasovs. They also created the police informants and agents who figured so prominently in these films, though never more dramatically than in *Strike*'s gallery of police agents operating under such designations as Monkey, Bulldog, Fox, Owl, each in turn exhibiting the physical traits of the animal chosen to represent them.

Each director also conveyed revolutionary coherence and inexorability through portrayals of *evolving* social relationships and attitudes among the masses. In *Mother*, the ignorance and violence of the reactionary father is leavened by the consciousness and tenderness of the revolutionary son. The mother undergoes her own revolutionary conversion in the course of the film, first handing over her son's hidden weapons to the police in a misguided attempt to save him, but later redeeming herself by passing him a secret message in prison and joining a mass procession to the prison to free the prisoners. Liberated from the coarsening effects of their exhausting labor by their work stoppage in *Strike*, workers are depicted in playful scenes of parental tenderness, a father playing with his young daughter after being woken by her as he (unusually) slept late, or, together with his wife, leisurely bathing his daughter. However, as the hunger and privation of a protracted strike sets in, these scenes of familial bliss are replaced by scenes of husband and wife at loggerheads, angry and frustrated with each other, while the scenes of workers joined together in solidarity are replaced by scenes of fighting and gambling. Without the liberating power of work and revolution, Eisenstein cautioned, the old social relationships among the workers would return. In *End of St. Petersburg* the revolutionary journeys of the peasant newcomer and his relative's wife are intertwined. The peasant is first frozen out by his own kin, but is then drawn into the friendship of strikebreakers through a friendly kinsman. His denunciation of the leader of the strikes to the factory owners brings him a promise of work, and only the arrest of a kinsman (not the strike organizer) makes him realize his "mistake," whereupon he attacks the factory owners and ends up in prison. Pressed into military service from prison, his revolutionary baptism comes in the wartime trenches, and he eventually joins the side of revolution after February 1917. At the same time, the wife in this tale makes her own journey of self-discovery, merely tolerating her husband's radical activities in the beginning of the film, actively aiding her husband's escape from police in the middle, and finally coming to the aid of the peasant, injured during the night of the storming of the Winter Palace. Both journeys come together in the final scenes of the film, the wife cradling the wounded man in her arms, now offering him and his revolutionary comrades the food she had failed to offer at the start of the film. Thus did the revolution awaken in the masses the feelings of brotherhood, generosity, and selflessness required to breach old attitudes.

The inexorability of the revolution, implied these directors, meant that these changes were irreversible, deep transformations in the hearts and minds of those individuals who had seen the light. In the course of their films, these transformations sometimes came gradually, sometimes in moments of epiphany. Under the old order, police fire on the dissatisfied masses—on the Odessa steps in 1905 in *Potemkin* and on Nevskii Prospekt in July 1917 in *October*. Under the new order, brothers refuse to fire on brothers, soldiers in *End of St. Petersburg* suddenly firing on their officer rather than on the radical haranguing them. The sailors in *Potemkin* turn their guns away from their comrades awaiting execution to the officer ordering it; the squadron sent to quell the revolt on the battleship refuses to fire on it.[50] The sailors' moment of epiphany is revealed in close-ups of individual firing squad members, their eyes displaying a new awareness of the significance of this order to shoot their own comrades. The moment is triggered by the sailor Vakulinchuk's call: "Brothers! Who are you shooting at?" Eisenstein also used graphically brutal images—the bloody massacre of workers in *Strike*, ghostly images of dead sailors hanging from the yardarms of the *Potemkin*, and the wounded child on the Odessa steps being trampled by people fleeing the soldiers—to capture the practices of the Old Regime and, thus, prepare his audiences for the personal epiphanies of his actors.[51]

Between the films made for the 1905 jubilee and those made for the October jubilee, another focal point of narrative coherence emerged in the form of the Bolshevik Party and Lenin. Pudovkin's drama of strike action in 1905, *Mother*,

centered on a group of workers of indeterminate revolutionary identity. The revolutionary activity of Eisenstein's *Strike*, filmed in 1924, was carried out by
"strikers," an "active group [*aktivnaia gruppa*]," or "circles [*kruzhki*]." Their strike
action was provoked by external pressures ("They've driven us into a corner
[*priperli*], so we have to strike") rather than by party agitation. Nor were the
workers agreed on their course of action. "It would be better if the people did not
strike!" argued one through an intertitle. The workers eventually go on strike
because one worker has been falsely accused of theft and commits suicide. The
role of the party in this strike is vague at best, the film opening with a quotation
from Lenin from 1907 emphasizing organization as the primary requirement for
a workers' revolution and intertitles informing the audience that the *calls* to strike
came from "the underground" and from a leaflet from the "Committee of the
RSDRP of the Bolsheviks." In *Potemkin*, the revolutionary actions of the sailors
are also the product of external pressures, with the sailors forced into a corner by
the officers' and doctor's callous indifference to their complaints about the mag-
got-infested meat they were expected to eat. Two rabble-rousing sailors,
Matushenko and Vakulinchuk, of unidentified political affiliation, help articulate
and channel the sailors' anger, although one disgruntled sailor is also moved to
violence by a line from the Lord's Prayer ("Give us this day our daily bread")
printed on the rim of one of the plates he is washing. Vakulinchuk sparks the
mutiny aboard the battleship, and outrage over his murder ("for a spoonful of
borsch") during the mutiny becomes the flashpoint for the conflict on the Odessa
steps.

The Bolshevik Party emerged more clearly in the films made for the tenth anniversary of October. Shub ended her *Fall of the Romanov Dynasty* before October,
but on a note of future hope, as the chaotic, milling masses on the streets of Petrograd are transformed into orderly and organized lines by calls to action from
Pravda's pages (through intertitles).[52] The radical action in Pudovkin's *End of St.
Petersburg* is identified only once as in the hands of a character called "The
Bolshevik"—and from the contemptuous lips of an army officer at that. The
moment is however pivotal for the shape of the revolutionary narrative, as the
Bolshevik worker ("One Man to Sway Them to the People") persuades the troops,
who had been brought in to defend the Provisional Government, to join the revolution instead and fire on their own commander. Lenin figures prominently
at the end of Shub's *Fall of the Romanov Dynasty*, first addressing the masses and
then in close conversation with a worker. *The Great Way* was wholly constructed
around the "cinematic myth of Lenin."[53]

In Eisenstein's *October*, the Bolshevik Party and Lenin were intrinsic to the
narrative. At the Finland Station scene the frame is repeatedly filled by a banner
clearly displaying the name of the Petersburg Committee of the RSDRP

13.   The Revolution Begins: Lenin at the Finland Station (from Eisenstein s *October*)

(Bol'shevik). It was the first time in all of these films that the party icon figured explicitly as part of the scenario and directed action. More usually, the intertitle "Bolshevik!" or "Bolsheviks!" (without, as scholars have pointed out, the ironic quotation marks that Eisenstein sometimes employed) advanced the narrative at key points, for example, the brutal murder of the Bolshevik during the July Days, the ransacked building of the "Petrograd Committee of the Party of Bolsheviks," the defense of Petrograd against Kornilov, and the dissuasion of the Cossack "Savage Division" from attacking the city.[54] "The Bolsheviks Must Seize Power!" cried the intertitle after the defeat of Kornilov. From the July Days, the film tells a tale of the inexorable organization and direction of the revolutionary process by the Bolsheviks, in the form of the Petrograd Committee of the Bolsheviks, the Sixth Party Congress, Smolny, the Bolshevik Central Committee meeting of October 10, the MRC, and the Winter Palace. At the same time, the revolutionary narrative unfolds in direct relation to Lenin's movements. He arrives in April at the Finland Station to the frenzied excitement of the waiting troops and workers. The "Ul'ianov" of one intertitle gives way to the "Lenin" of another, the man become revolutionary.

After the July Days, Lenin directs from the underground the Sixth Party Congress "that set the course for the armed uprising," pressing at the October 10 meeting of the Central Committee for an immediate uprising, slipping back into

14.   Phantom Power : The Empty Jackets of the Provisional Government Ministers (from Eisenstein s *October*)

Smolny in disguise at the crucial hour on October 24, and proclaiming the new revolutionary state at the Second Congress of Soviets. On the eve of October 25, Lenin himself takes over the direction of the uprising, circling in pencil the Winter Palace and Palace Square on a map. In counterpoint to this ideal Bolshevik image, the film offered a portrait of a less steadfast and prescient Bolshevik, a speaker advocating caution to the restive during the July Days ("An uprising is premature!"), Trotsky openly vacillating over Lenin's call to immediate action on October 10. "Mensheviks" later watch the busy, purposeful military preparations in Smolny as silent spectators from their offices.

Many of these films' most enduring images emerged from the directors' efforts to convey the inherent drama of the October Revolution. They prepared their audiences with scenes symbolizing the passivity and inertia of the tsarist regime. Pudovkin lingered on ornate, classical statues atop the buildings of Petersburg and on tsarist officials and factory owners sitting self-consciously immobile before the camera.[55] Eisenstein paused on a towering statue of Alexander III, the orb and scepter of imperial power in his hand, and on the empty jackets left at a conference table by Provisional Government ministers shortly before the Bolsheviks arrived.

Eisenstein's Kerensky was perhaps the most complete portrait of political impotence, throwing himself on a divan as Kornilov advanced on Petrograd and burying his head in plush pillows to shut out the news. Intercutting scenes of Kerensky with images of a mechanical peacock allowed Eisenstein to suggest the empty vanity of both the Provisional Government leader and the system that could produce such an ornate, technically sophisticated automaton. The mechanical aspect of the peacock, Bordwell points out, served as a metaphor for the lack of any genuine, human motivation in Kerensky's (and the government's) actions, beyond a clockwork, inertia-driven mechanism.[56] In similar fashion, Pudovkin's Kerensky in *End of St. Petersburg* is an operatic performer, overemoting his phrases on freedom, and being rewarded with flowers for his performance.

The passivity of the Old Regime in these films contrasted with the steadily accumulating scenes of dynamism of the masses. Sailors mutinied on their battleship in *Potemkin*, prisoners scaled the prison walls in *Mother*, young workers took their factory from the older, less conscious generation in *Strike*, and workers toppled the statue of Alexander III in *October*. In their films about the failed revolution (namely 1905), the directors used these acts of dynamism to suggest the pent-up revolutionary energies of the masses and, despite (perhaps because of) its failure, the inexorability of the future revolution. *Mother* ended with the bloody slaughter of the defenseless prisoners by the police, the mother the last to fall as Russia's own Marianne into Battle. *Strike* closed with scenes of slaughter on an open field. *Potemkin*'s Odessa steps were littered with corpses from the soldiers' advance.

The films made for the October jubilee culminated in a heroic storming of the Winter Palace. They prepared the palace for the storming by focusing on the superficial opulence of this building, its decor and furnishings, a metaphor of the hollowness and privilege of the Old Regime. As Tret'iakov implied, Eisenstein's lingering shots in *October* of the plush carpets, delicate porcelain, fine paintings, and classical statues of the Winter Palace set up an "aesthetic storming" of the privileges and vanities of the old order.[57] The many shots of the city's architecture and statues in Pudovkin's *End of St. Petersburg* were also offered as evidence of its "Shameless Grandeur," as the intertitle put it, contrasted at every step with the poverty and suffering of most of its inhabitants.

In *End of St. Petersburg*, Pudovkin conveyed the storming of the Winter Palace in an intense scene of charging workers and soldiers, machine gun fire, flames, and smoke. He did not show the workers and soldiers penetrating the palace, ending his film instead on vignettes of personal sacrifice and survival: the peasant newcomer lying dying on the street, the revolutionary husband emerging alive after the storming.

15. Marianne into Battle: The Final Stand of the Mother (from Pudovkin s *Mother*)

16. A Failed Storming: Massacred Strikers (from Eisenstein s *Strike*)

17. Revolutionary Restraint: Soldiers Patiently Await the Order for the Storming (from Pudovkin s *End of St. Petersburg*)

In *October*, Eisenstein signaled the final storming with a series of smaller stormings, or mass actions: the destruction of the statue of Alexander III at the opening of the film, the chaotic flight of demonstrators from police guns during the July Days, the liberation from the prisons of the "turncoats" and "traitors" (ironicized in quotation marks in the intertitles) during the Kornilov attack and of the weapons from the arsenal for the defense of Petrograd. The repeated shots of workers and soldiers streaming across Palace Square created a sense of relentlessness and inevitability. They had been on the move since 1905, Eisenstein's triptych of films suggested, from Odessa to Petrograd, as strikers to the factory forecourt, as mourners to a sailor's corpse, as martyrs on a flight of stone steps. The repetition of key scenes of mass movement in the storming in *October*, as one film scholar notes, "at the same time discontinuous and progressive, takes on little by little an incantatory power; didacticism is achieved in poetry."[58] In the film's final repetitive scenes, workers and soldiers storm up the stairs of the Winter Palace, a looped film of permanent revolution.

18. The Storming of the Winter Palace (from Pudovkin s *End of St. Petersburg*)

19. The Women s Battalion of Death Defends the Winter Palace (from Eisenstein s *October*)

20.   The Storming of the Winter Palace (from Eisenstein s *October*)

THE STORY SO FAR

Eisenstein, Pudovkin, and Shub all strove for clarity and transparency with their revolutionary films. Critics of the time, though, read them in a variety of ways. Shklovsky argued that Eisenstein's methods sometimes undercut his narrative argument, the raising of the bridge over the Neva, for example, "left him nothing with which to storm the Winter Palace."[59] At least one critic at the time understood Eisenstein's treatment of the women's battalion in *October* as a "general satire on women who take up arms for any cause at all."[60] Mayakovsky regarded Eisenstein's decision to use an actor to play Lenin as insulting, and promised to pelt the screen with rotten eggs when the "fake Lenin" appeared.[61]

Eisenstein became the lightning rod for the criticism of these revolutionary films. The delay in screening *October* until after the anniversary celebrations sparked rumors that he and Aleksandrov (his codirector on *October*) were involved in Trotsky's faction and that the film was being completely reedited on Stalin's orders in order to excise all but two of the scenes featuring Trotsky.[62] It was ironic, Goodwin notes, that these most accomplished productions of revolution "as a spectacle of historical genesis and utopian potential" also exposed the decline of support for these avant-garde innovations.[63] At issue with *October*, and the other revolutionary films, was the meaning that audiences might derive from them, as well as the party leaders' demands that their meaning be more transparent. For many critics, the reality and immediacy of the October events were lost in Eisenstein's attempt at a "film poem, a film fantasy" rather than a documentary from newsreels, notwithstanding the dearth of extant footage on the October Days.[64] They criticized him for placing too much emphasis in his film on certain events, for example the defense of the Winter Palace by the women's battalion and the sailors' smashing of wine bottles in the cellars, and this overemphasis had rendered the film's *revolutionary* message inaccessible. His depiction of the latter incident could have been justified, his critics wrote, if he "had been able to discover some symbolic method of depicting this affair such as, let us say, showing that proletarian consciousness did in the final analysis cope with this wine."[65] Eisenstein was also criticized for depicting the masses in *October* as "extras" rather than as the "living, active, organized masses."[66]

Lunacharsky's review of Eisenstein's latest work was extremely positive, contrasting the "poem" or "symphony" of *October* with the "sonnet" or "musical étude" of the earlier *Potemkin*.[67] Still, while critics deemed individual episodes to be effective, they believed the "general plan" of the film suffered at the expense of such individual episodes.[68] Unwittingly evoking an earlier search for *October's* Bastille, a critic noted that the depiction of the Winter Palace in *October* was more convincing than that of Smolny, because Eisenstein had found "brighter colors" for the former.[69] Still, his films were criticized for excessive symbolism, awkward juxtaposition of images, eccentric casting, or outright camera trickery, as well as a flagrant disregard for narrative flow. Adrian Piotrovskii called for *October* to be reedited to cut down "tedious passages," such as the scenes of the White terror and the events in the wine cellar, or to correct the omission of "a number of important historical events," such as the growth of the workers' movement. In short, the "basic raw material," which was of "exceptionally high quality," had been put together poorly.[70] It had failed to create, in the opinion of many critics, the requisite meaning. T. Rokotov suggested adding a libretto to a reedited version of the film to help audiences understand it.[71]

Other directors were criticized for similar reasons. Tret'iakov called Pudovkin's *End of St. Petersburg* "insufficiently clear" and panned Barnet's *Moscow in October* for creating the "sensation of strange, almost mystical events, involving very few people and carried out in a vacuum."[72] The First All-Union Party Cinema Conference in 1928 called for films that were "intelligible to millions," contrasting them with the early "formally artistic directions and trends" of early Soviet cinema.[73] More intertitles were needed, wrote Shklovsky, as a guide to meaning, the "whole sense" of newsreels in particular deriving from "date, time, and place."[74] Critics singled out Shub's *Fall of the Romanov Dynasty*, however, as an example of a film that was compiled of old film sequences and yet "produces a much more coherent impression because its thematic and montage plan has been carefully devised."[75] Shub herself argued that fiction films should give way to newsreels, to "film the here and now, contemporary people, contemporary events," which could be as "emotionally affecting" as the former.[76] At issue for many of these critics was whether the "facts" should be allowed to speak for themselves, or whether they were merely a step on the path to a greater truth. Brik argued that it was wrong to believe that the "fact in itself provides too little" and that truth or reality somehow had to be *synthesized* from a collection of facts.[77]

Among Eisenstein's defenders was Pudovkin who praised *October* precisely for the greater truth Eisenstein was able to tease from his materials, and for the coherence of the effect it exerted on audiences. The "more powerful and more complete effect" was achieved by the montage of multiple shots of a single event (in this case the raising of the bridge) to produce a "single rhythm of a slow and powerful movement."[78] Coming to Eisenstein's defense, also, Aleksei Popov faulted the critics and the audiences for not preparing themselves enough before they viewed the film. He implied, though, that the desired goal of coherence, the task of trying to depict the "epic-heroic canvas of the October Revolution with all the strictness of the historical succession [*posledovatel'nost'*] of its stages and political atmosphere," as well as clearly delineated "motive forces of the revolution (proletariat, peasantry, army)," was a daunting one. He left unanswered his own question about whether the director was justified in trying to convey the whole process of the October Revolution on the basis of a single stage of it.[79]

In a sense, the entire project to write October had been caught in the conflict between truth and poetry, a conflict among revolutionaries about the most legitimate and effective way to tell the story of the October Revolution. The medium of film provided merely the most vivid expression of this conflict. Many of those involved in the project to write the history of October and the Bolshevik Party believed that the objective truth of this history could be found only at the local level, although they mistrusted the subjective nature of the sources (most often reminiscences) on which this truth had to depend. Others believed that October's essential spirit could best be captured not in dry documents but in the poetic flights it inspired in the population's imaginations. All of the myriad manifestations and representations of October were evaluated to some degree in these terms. The German correspondent who had watched the demonstrations in Moscow in 1927 compared the "masses, organization, discipline, [and] order" of October's tenth anniversary celebrations unfavorably with the "very revolutionary, even personal magic" of earlier celebrations.[80] The ineffable and intangible qualities of revolution had undeniably inspired many of those (Bolsheviks and non-Bolsheviks alike) who had embraced this earlier telling of October. Capturing this magic had surely been behind the perennial efforts to solicit appropriate scripts for the theater and cinema and to inspire the writing of revolutionary poetry. Over time, however, leading Bolsheviks began to regard these impulses as counterproductive to their efforts to produce a coherent October of unequivocal meaning. This surely informed Pokrovskii's observation in 1924 that "truth," not "poetry," was required here, and that the writing of memoirs about October ("the mass of factual inaccuracies" left behind by "witnesses of great events") and the writing of history were quintessentially different tasks conditioned by a subjective and an objective experience of the events respectively.[81]

Many of the materials produced for the tenth jubilee exasperated the officials of Istpart and the Bolshevik Party alike. Reviewing the materials in 1927, Nevskii acknowledged significant problems, including the perennial opposition to Istpart's endeavors, the still piecemeal coverage of certain critical moments in the history of the revolutionary movement, and the difficulties of producing "any kind of synthetic work on the history of the October Revolution."[82] In Essen's view, the uncontrolled flood of publications from both the 1905 and October jubilees threatened the coherence and transparency that were two major objectives for the history of October. Citing Lenin's "golden words" that "less is more [men'she da luchshe]," Essen implied that less literature, and more control of it, might stop the "paper spontaneity [bumazhnaia stikhiia]."[83] In a familiar refrain, reviews complained about works that seemed to "advertise" the Mensheviks or Whites.[84] One local study revealed a "yawning gap" where the party organization should have been, a gap that made much of the work "incomprehensible." "What kind of 'timid Bolshevik voice' is this?" the reviewer asked.[85]

While they had again found the local publications wanting, leading Bolsheviks at the center had themselves begun to tell a quite coherent tale of October and the party. Iaroslavskii wrote the Party of the Bolsheviks in 1917 (Partiia bol'shevikov v 1917 g.) for those "many comrades who do not know what our party was about before the Revolution of 1917." He traced the origin of the party not to a particular date or congress but rather to the moment "when the working class of Russia, deprived of rights and oppressed by the tsarist autocracy and capitalists, entered into a resolute struggle with their class enemies." This definition, though vague, rendered the party synonymous with the Russian revolutionary movement. The "Bolsheviks, headed by Lenin" preserved "our underground Bolshevik Party," sustaining it often from afar through the post-1905 reaction, the revival of political activity up until the World War, and the tribulations of the war into 1917. Even though the party organization during the war years was moribund at best, it was the only organization that kept faith with the "interests of the proletarian revolution." Although Iaroslavskii acknowledged the enormous and endemic dissatisfaction that led to the February Revolution, the "Bolsheviks earnestly prepared the masses for the action [*vystuplenie*]." In the months up to October, "the party" firmly and resolutely prepared for the workers' revolution. Although some comrades did not correctly understand the nature of the overthrow being prepared, only "individual comrades" (identified as Kamenev and Zinoviev) strayed from the path.[86]

In Iaroslavskii's and others' works, Lenin became the prophet and guide of October, the Bolshevik Party its avatar. Savel'ev wrote that while "purely external manifestations of Vladimir Il'ich's part in the revolution" were few, Lenin was "in our party the great practical man [*praktik*]," and even cited the anathematized Zinoviev several years earlier on Lenin: "If Lenin is the classic type of proletarian revolutionary, Trotsky is the 'classic' type of intelligentsia revolutionary."[87] On the day of festivities in November 1927, Molotov offered that "Lenin more than once called the October Revolution *the Bolshevik Revolution*, so closely, enduringly, and irrevocably was the party of the Bolsheviks linked with the revolution"[88] (Molotov's emphasis).

These works were of a different order from the works published earlier in the project to tell October. They did not draw on the policy of *obshchestvennost'* that had so informed and energized it in this first decade. Only rarely would this kind of endeavor be seen again in the Soviet Union.[89] Nor did they represent the kinds of personal recollections that had brought so much vitality to the project and exasperation to its framers. They represented blueprints for transparency of meaning, and as such they would have more in common with the sterile formulations of the 1930s and beyond than with the works of the early 1920s. In a sense, they heralded the deep institutional changes to the body politic that accompanied the policies of rapid industrialization and forced collectivization at the end of the 1920s, and which would have such severe repercussions for all realms of political and cultural life in the Soviet Union.

EXPERIENCING OCTOBER

The storyteller is a man who has counsel for his readers . The storyteller takes what he tells from experience his own or that reported by others. And he in turn makes it the experience of those who are listening to his tale.
—Walter Benjamin, "The Storyteller," 1936

Clearly, the project to write October was not realized in a way that satisfied its framers' aspirations and dreams. A single narrative of the October Revolution did not emerge in this first decade, at least not as it was conceived by those involved in Istpart or the jubilee commissions. The art of storytelling, for which the Soviet regime provided so many stages, proved to be immensely difficult to harness. Nonetheless, in the first decade after October 1917, the tale of the October Revolution was the primary language within which the former citizens of the tsarist empire came to articulate *and conceive of* themselves as members of the new Communist polity, a polity that presented its citizens with a radically transformed political and linguistic landscape. The October Revolution could only be experienced as such from within this landscape, one defined not in geographic but conceptual terms. Outside of it, October did not exist as revolution but as coup d'état. It is, therefore, in the act of storytelling that the power of October as a foundation tale should be measured. The scale of the project, and the absence of a viable and consistently told counternarrative inside the Soviet Union, ensured that many people had multiple opportunities to experience the events of October 1917 as revolution. It was, as the American radical journalist Albert Rhys Williams wrote in 1921, "an insistent fact, assailing us in eye and ear with banners and battle-cries, parades and assemblages."[1] This concluding chapter represents an effort to imagine some of these encounters with October, from seemingly direct experiences to more dynamic interactions. As we shall see, the depth and authenticity of one's experience of October did not rely on being present at the historical events.

BEING THERE

The tale of October might be heard simply by walking along the streets renamed for the revolution in the first years of the Bolshevik regime. To traverse the Petrogradskii district of Petrograd, it was now necessary to walk along the newly named Karl Liebknecht Avenue and Red Dawn Street that bisected it. Workers now crossed from their districts into the city center over the Bridge of Equality on their way to the Square of the Victims of the Revolution, where their attention might be caught by the new monument to the "Fighters of the Revolution" put up in 1919. Turning south along the embankment to Uritskii Square in front of the Winter Palace, they would come face to face with a monument to Karl Liebknecht and Rosa Luxemburg erected there in 1920, or the nearby bust of A. N. Radishchev. Their walk might take them from Uprising Square down Soviet Avenue to Smolny, where they might look up at the smoothly hewn features of Karl Marx. If the biographies of these personalities were not always clear to these passersby, these new monuments, by their presence and often by their style and form, were markers of times changed, reminders to the favored of the power and possibilities of the new regime. The reminders might take quite explicit form: for example, the new statue of Marx and Engels in Moscow was unveiled on the first anniversary of October, with Lenin speaking from the pedestal. How novel the passersby must have found these statues at that time, before their gypsum features dissolved in the Petrograd rain, or were rendered invisible by familiarity. These new monuments, and the empty spaces left by the obliterated monuments of the tsarist period, were also dark reminders to the formerly privileged strata that there had been a radical change in their own place in society. Gone from buildings and monuments were the old two-headed eagles, gone were the names of the Troitskii Bridge, Palace Square, Znamenskii Square, Suvorovskii Avenue—the features of an earlier regime's quite different portrait of its history on the canvas of Petersburg. Even if the names persisted in popular usage, these acts of official oblivion should not be underestimated. These changes told tales of both new and old regimes.

Many people encountered the October Revolution during this period through the official processions, demonstrations, and celebrations that formally marked the sites of the revolution in many urban centers. Indeed, these carefully scripted events may well have been for many their first points of contact with the new regime, the official closing of most shops and the increased presence of security forces on the streets being visible signs of an important day, priming the individual for the significance of this ceremony. Benjamin has observed that films of these kinds of parades and mass rallies all across Europe in the modern era brought the masses "face to face with themselves" in a way previously unknown.[2] The most emotive of these official rituals, the red funerals, tapped into a traditional custom. Some watchers undoubtedly disliked their secular nature, a "conservative intellectual's distaste" perhaps, as Merridale has pointed out of Got'e's reaction.[3] They may have contrasted these red funerals with the treatment of the fallen junkers and students at their funerals, or with the new regime's general treatment of the "unrevolutionary" dead. Others may have welcomed the message conveyed through these red funerals, their new language and structure perhaps casting the fallen victims in a wholly new light. The shiver of emotion felt by a young Komsomol at the red funeral in November 1917 at the sight of the unfurling red party banner and the sound of a triumphal march was the product of her experiencing her friend's death both in traditional terms and in terms of the specifically revolutionary incarnation of the funeral.[4]

The experience of such events was inevitably enriched by the associations that they consciously and subconsciously evoked in the individual. Watching the mass spectacle of the *Storming of the Winter Palace* in November 1920, a spectator might have been reminded of the earlier Romanov tercentenary celebrations in 1913, the grandiosity and pomp of the latter enacting a quite different drama of power. The noise, gunfire, smoke, and crowds inevitably impressed some of the people, at least to the extent that they felt a great event was being celebrated here. "When people say 'October,'" wrote Piotrovskii on the occasion of Evreinov's *Storming of the Winter Palace*, "they remember giddy autumn nights, angry crowds, fires, and the rattle of machine-guns."[5] A participant in one of the anniversary processions in celebration of October may well have been present at an earlier mass gathering in January 1905 that ended in an infamous massacre of the participants by the military. This individual might have been struck by the difference in symbols at these various mass gatherings, the earlier religious symbols of Father Gapon's march to the Winter Palace contrasting with the imperial symbols of the tsarist march, and these in turn contrasting with the political symbols of the revolutionary march.

THE EXPERIENCE OF MEMORY

In revolutionary Russia in the 1920s, many people experienced October in an act of recollection of some form, most often elicited and framed by the state. The young schoolboys who were asked in November and December 1917 to write essays on the theme "What I Know about the Russian Revolution" produced a range of impressions: "Everyone was very cheerful in the days of the revolution. I shall never forget the Russian Revolution"; "Those people who followed Lenin were called Bolsheviks, and those who followed the Provisional Government were called socialists"; the "recently arrived émigré Lenin, a very unsatisfactory and nasty person."[6] The children's innocence or lack of political awareness did not increase the authenticity or reliability of their impressions, although the instigator of this exercise claimed otherwise. Like everyone else, the children articulated their experiences in terms of the revolutionary lexicon of the time, their essays reflecting the uncertainties of the new political labels and the public contestation over the meaning of Bolshevik actions in October 1917. They were *both* authentic, personal experiences *and* expressions of the dominant political culture of the period.

In this sense, Podvoiskii's experience of the October Revolution as expressed in his repeated recollections of his role in the taking of the Winter Palace is no more authentic than these children's experiences of the October Revolution, and no less authentic than the experiences of a "common" worker or soldier. The October Revolution only emerged as such in the course of the process of "telling" October. It could be experienced and remembered only as part of this process. As the tale of October took shape, so Podvoiskii's recollections assumed the features of that tale, becoming "more dynamic and picturesque," as one Soviet scholar put it, as he tried to "bring the historical events closer to the artistic narrative."[7] His series of recollections from 1919 to 1927 did not so much change the specific details of the tale as embellish them with increasing drama and passion. Thus from the bare facts he recalled in 1919 of the taking of the Winter Palace did his much richer and *meaning-full* tale of the storming of the Winter Palace emerge in 1927 as *the* central event of both the October Revolution and his own life of revolution.

As this "total event" for October emerged, Podvoiskii's role in it emerged in the act of recollection. As the Bolshevik Party became a major actor in October, Podvoiskii became a major actor in the Bolshevik Party. He was often in charge of initiatives by the Soviet regime to commemorate October, culminating in his role as head of the Tenth Jubilee Commission, when he was able to sponsor some of the major cinematographic incarnations of the revolution, most notably Eisenstein's *October*. He was one of the guides in March 1927 for Eisenstein and Aleksandrov on their scouting tour of Leningrad.[8] His personal part in October was validated once more by his appearance in this film, and by this and other films' tendency to immortalize and heroicize certain individuals. He, and other leading Bolsheviks, literally saw themselves, or actors playing them, in the revolutionary roles of history.[9] This film, von Geldern writes, overrode Podvoiskii's original memories of his part in the taking of the Winter Palace in 1917.[10] Although Eisenstein's films certainly produced revolutionary images of enormous power and influence, these images and Podvoiskii's increasingly vivid recollections of

October might better be understood as evolving in a complex relationship to one another.

The dynamic of Eisenstein's experience of October, as a function of his film *October*, also merits closer scrutiny. Although Eisenstein had been in Petrograd throughout 1917, and had even witnessed the events of the July Days, he did not claim the cachet of personal participation that lent such authority to Podvoiskii's articulations. Eisenstein's experience was, however, no less vivid or personal than Podvoiskii's. Indeed, they were strikingly similar in tone and content, for each articulated his experiences as part of the larger process of the production of October as a foundation event, a process to which they were committed as revolutionaries. Each saw their part in it as a battle, an argument that had to be made actively. When the 1905 Jubilee Commission suggested the *Potemkin* mutiny as a focus for his planned film on the 1905 Revolution, Eisenstein was unfamiliar with that episode, recalling from childhood rather the mutiny aboard the cruiser *Ochakov* in the Sevastopol' uprising. He saw no problem in making the *Potemkin* mutiny his focus, however, particularly because it was "hardly remembered, and discussed even less." Inspired by this desire to recover this "lost memory," Eisenstein read up on the mutiny, consulting sources compiled from sponsored recollections taken in the mid-1920s as part of the effort to profile the *Potemkin* mutiny as an event of heroic proportion. For him, the episode quite easily became a distillation point for October's "dress rehearsal":

> And the episode is really such that it contains echoes of almost all the motives characteristic of the great year. The triumph on the Odessa steps and the brutal violence summon up the Ninth of January. The refusal to fire on "brothers," the squadron letting the mutinous battleship through, the general mood of common solidarity—all this summons up the numerous episodes of this year in all corners of the Russian Empire that conveyed the shaking of its foundations.[11]

Similarly, Aleksandrov and Eisenstein frequently noted the obstacles they had to overcome to make *October*, adding that they had had to approach its making as a "storming" in its own right.[12] Aleksandrov recalled disagreements among prominent artistic and political figures over the appropriateness of an actor or a look-alike playing Lenin in the film, or over how his movements should be depicted (calm or energetic). On one occasion, a staged street demonstration for a scene from the February Revolution was stopped by local Bolsheviks because of the bourgeois slogans on the banners.[13] On April 26, 1928, the directors expressed their belief that the "pathos of the struggle" of the October Revolution had been lost in the struggle to make the picture:

Instead of active leadership, we had to encounter in the best case "non-resistance" to our initiative, and from the vast majority even a lack of assistance. We therefore found ourselves in a condition of constant struggle with passivity for the chance to film at all, and to constantly have to appeal for aid from social and party organizations.[14]

Eisenstein's experience of the October Revolution as *October* was defined and articulated as a collective act. Work on a scenario began formally when Kalinin handed Eisenstein a copy of Reed's *Ten Days That Shook the World* in the fall of 1926, although he was apparently already familiar with it.[15] *October* indeed resonated with the powerful narrative imagery of Reed's work and of Mayakovsky's poem *Vladimir Il'ich Lenin*. The head of political enlightenment in the Soviet Union sent Eisenstein a list of memoir literature in August 1926 to aid his preparation for the film. The historian A. V. Efimov wrote a short essay entitled "October" as a guide for the scenario.[16] Aleksandrov recalled sifting through "mountains of materials," screening a multipart film covering February 1917 through the end of the Civil War, and meeting with historians, as well as with the novelist Aleksandr Serafimovich, "in order to be able to conceive of the material more fully."[17] Both Aleksandrov and Eisenstein read various drafts of the scenario to gatherings of participants and spent evenings with members of the Society of Old Bolsheviks looking for details of, among other episodes, Lenin's reception at the Finland Station.[18] Eisenstein consulted with Shub, who showed his group the original footage she had collected, and he and his collaborators examined hundreds of news photographs.[19] His group toured the streets and squares of Leningrad with large groups of "participants in the revolutionary events," discussing pivotal moments with them.[20] The broader formative narrative ensured that during the scouting tour of Leningrad with Podvoiskii as guide, Eisenstein saw Smolny, the Winter Palace, and Petropavlovsk, the "traces of the revolution," as he called them in his diary at the time.[21] It also determined how he would select, from the forty thousand meters of footage he shot, the two to three thousand meters that would comprise *October*.

Eisenstein's work on *October* drew in ever larger circles of people, in both the preparation, enactment, and, ultimately, the viewing of the film, providing these people in turn with their own reason to articulate their experiences as a function of the October Revolution. He wrote in his diary in June 1927, as he prepared for the scenes of the storming of the Winter Palace, how "the actual fighting was re-called" during the meetings convened by Istpart, by party committees, and through the exchange of information in newspapers: "The participants had heated arguments, passionately strove for the accuracy of the events. Several variants were sketched out—they agreed on one."22 Aleksandrov recalled how Sokolov, who played Antonov-Ovseenko in the film, slowed down work by constantly offering his advice and refuting everything, and how he had to be kept "in check."23 Aleksandrov was well aware of the diversity of opinions and experiences evoked by every stage of the film's preparation, having attended a conference of "Participants of the October Overthrow" on October 10, 1927, to whom he read the scenario drawn up by Eisenstein and himself.24 At this gathering, some people disputed various details in the scenario, including the difficulty in getting the *Aurora* to fire its shells at the Winter Palace at the right moment, the timing of certain episodes depicted in the scenario, the presence of certain individuals at certain moments, the need for more scenes depicting the July Days. More generally, they objected to the scenario's poor reflection of the spontaneity of certain military units in driving on the revolution, pointing out that they were ready, trained, and "not waiting for any kind of order to go and take power."25 In similar vein, the role of sailors was felt to be underplayed, one individual recalling their "measured inexorable steps" and their "very resolute revolutionary appearance" during the uprising.26 Others felt that the role of women in the October Revolution (in contrast to the February Revolution) was treated weakly. Some argued over the very leadership of the revolution. Trotsky received too prominent a role in the scenario, noted one man, adding that Trotsky had ordered his garrison to retreat in the heady July Days. Lenin was not featured enough in the scenario, objected Kudelli, seeding her arguments with her own experiences of having seen Lenin watching things "seriously" at key moments. "I think," she added, "he was taking account of the mood of the worker masses."27 One noted that, notwithstanding Trotsky's mistakes, if the film showed Lenin, it should show Trotsky too, adding—to laughter from the assembled—that "they will probably call me a Trotskyist."28 Others pointed out that the role of the masses in the revolution deserved an even higher priority than that of the leaders, one individual objecting to the use of the phrase "little worker person [*malen'kii rabochii chelovek*]" in the scenario in reference to the masses, because it suggested Russian workers were inferior to their "tall and strapping" comrades in Europe.29 Most often, those present at this evening objected to the absence of a clearly articulated role in the scenario for the Bolshevik Party: "We do not see any Bolsheviks in it…. Where are the Bolshevik masses there?"30 Some suggested moments that could be used to convey this role, including the persecution of the party after the July Days, the Bolshevik press, the mass meetings and Bolshevik agitation in the factories and military units. Aleksandrov recalled later how in one scene someone was carrying a banner proclaiming the "Faction [*fraktsiia*] of the Bolsheviks." "The united, tempered party of the Bolsheviks practically headed the revolutionary people [*narod*]," he wrote, "and in the frame looms 'Faction of the Bolsheviks'." Eisenstein shared his concerns and wrote to him in August 1927, "There's no stopping 'that faction' [*i "fraktsiia" pret kak chert te chto*]," and suggested the scene be reshot.[31] Clearly, both Eisenstein and Aleksandrov regarded these criticisms of their scenario as sincerely meant and potentially valuable improvements to it.

After a decade of telling October, the major elements of the October narrative were in place, as these exchanges showed. Indeed, many argued that an event as "great and weighty" as the October Revolution required a series of films costing millions of rubles on a par with Fritz Lang's recent epic *The Nibelungs*, rather than the planned eighty-minute film costing a quarter million.[32] Nobody challenged the integrity or purpose of the exercise itself, and the very act of correcting the details of this scenario affirmed the October Revolution as a given. "We are shown beyond any doubt that a certain event occurred," as Halbwachs writes of such communal acts of reminiscence, "that we were present and actively participated in it."[33]

The assembled were, of course, well aware of the *political* boundaries of the possible in this socialist state in 1927, the identification of which was intrinsic to the entire process of telling October. To articulate one's experience of October, by definition, meant to learn the limits of the politically acceptable. This was as true for our imaginary worker touring Petrograd's new political landscape in 1919 or 1920 as it was for a Bolshevik participating at an evening of reminiscences in 1927. These limits could be conveyed quite subtly through a new revolutionary monument barely noticed by passersby. They could come from the pens of those who edited the myriad texts of October prior to their compilation into published collections.[34] They could come directly from the mouth of Stalin ordering Eisenstein to cut the scenes of *October* featuring Trotsky.[35]

Trotsky's experience of October illustrated well the dangers of pushing these limits. He believed that the revolutionary apotheosis had been betrayed in this first decade, and he staked his political career on a thorny reevaluation of the October Revolution that openly tested the limits of the emerging narrative. Even when cast out, however, Trotsky continued to defend the authenticity of his experience of October from within the organization that gave that experience meaning, the Bolshevik Party. The depth of his heresy within party circles might be conveyed not so much by his excommunication from the party and eventual exile from the Soviet Union in January 1929 as by the return to him in October 1927 of the questionnaire Istpart has sent to him as one of the "active participants of October." These recollections of the October Revolution were denounced by Istpart as nothing but "the crudest factional attacks against the party."[36] Trotsky's memory of October had been rendered illegitimate, his experience no longer part of the valid communal experience of October.

More often, the limits of the October narrative were not seriously tested, and individuals often showed themselves ready to accommodate their experiences within those limits. In December 1926, Boris Pinson proposed to the central Istpart a study of the revolution and the Civil War in the North Caucasus. Pinson had arrived there at the start of 1918 as a member of the All-Russian Executive Committee of the Soviets, attached to the Commissariat of Labor (Narkomtrud) to set up a network of food supply organs. He did not intend his work to be a "reminiscence" but rather a "serious treatment of the materials." He arrived in the Caucasus, as he put it in his first letter proposing the project, at a time when Soviet power had only just arisen and when party organizations and soviets were "scarcely born, not yet established." He proposed to begin his study with the "October Revolution, which in the North Caucasus was four to five months late."[37] In a few short months, however, Pinson had clearly become aware of the necessary contours of such a study, and in the course of 1927 he sent a letter and outline to Istpart officials that were designed to allay their earlier misgivings about the content of the work:

> I absolutely understand that the entire time it is a matter of our party rebuilding itself after the February Revolution and becoming the actual leader of all the genuinely revolutionary processes that took place in the North Caucasus for the period 1917, 1918, 1919, and, in part, 1920. In the manuscript, our party will appear as the only leading political organization, in fact at the head of the workers, mountain people, and peasant masses for the years in question…. By the way, [the manuscript will take account of the] leadership that Vladimir Il'ich gave to the basic group of party comrades who worked at that time in the North Caucasus.

Pinson added that the entire work was preliminary and would be subject to "serious reworking" at various stages.[38] More important than the ultimate rejection of this project by the central Istpart was the ease with which Pinson was able to formulate and reformulate his experiences as part of the October narrative.[39] Regardless of whether his initial motives were scholarly, materialistic, self-aggrandizing, deceptive, or self-deceptive (or all of these things), he had learned both the language of articulation and the bounds of the possible in the Communist regime.[40]

REMEMBERING TOGETHER

None of these experiences of October were individual experiences. All were collective experiences in one form or another. The project to tell the history of October, however, created a quite original forum of collective remembering during this first decade. The evenings of reminiscences (*vechera vospominanii*) provide an opportunity to examine the dynamic process of experiencing October in an act of collective remembering.[41] They represent a crucial preliminary stage of the articulation of memory, before the reminiscences elicited at them were edited, supplemented, and often published in journals or in book form. They were undeniably orchestrated affairs. Preparatory meetings were often held prior to an actual evening, so that, as the head of the Moscow bureau put it, "the reminiscers come completely prepared for a particular subject."[42] Only "participants in the events" were allowed to attend the evenings about October; their numbers were sometimes limited to thirty people. The participants were asked to write down their relevant experiences beforehand and to bring paper and pencil so that they could add to their notes as things occurred to them during the evening. They were also asked to bring any relevant "newspapers, orders, photographs, draft manuscripts, notes, and so on" from the period. All of this was to be handed to the organizers of the evening as they left.[43] As a set of guidelines put it in 1925, if a participant's tale was incomplete, others should supplement it; "even the conscious omission of certain details is recommended if this serves to draw out supplementary tales from those present."[44] The evenings were generally devoted to a defined topic, at times albeit vaguely defined, such as 1905, the July Days, or the October Days. Others addressed a specific problem; for example, the Moscow bureau recommended an evening on the subject "The February Revolution in Moscow and the Participation of Our Party in It," because "the participation of our party in the February Revolution is still unclear." The bureau informed all of its district and county bureaus to do a count of "all active participants in the February overthrow and all comrades who worked in Bolshevik organizations in Moscow and the province in the immediate past," with a view to inviting them to the evening.[45]

At these evenings, the October narrative had its guardian in the form of a chair, often assigned and sent by the central Istpart. These chairs sometimes attended instructional conferences, at which they discussed how to conduct the evenings and were provided with lists of relevant questions pertaining to past events that should be discussed at them. [46] A presidium was often appointed by the chair from among the assembled, who were permitted no opportunity to object to its composition. The chair and presidium might solemnify the collective experience by having all present stand "to honor the memory of the fallen fighters of the revolution," a ritual taken up periodically by individual speakers at the evening. [47] They might be more peremptory than this. Podvoiskii, for example, at one evening cautioned the assembled not to interrupt the reading of the scenario of *October* so that they might gain a sense of Eisenstein's movie "as a whole." The interventions of the chair and presidium could unequivocally convey the limits of political acceptability in the mid-1920s. Podvoiskii weighed in on a discussion about Trotsky's role in October with the comment that Trotsky was effective in October only because Lenin played those around him "like a harp," anticipating and preventing their mistakes. [48] Reminiscers were left in little doubt about the political significance of their work at these evenings. The evening of reminiscence, one chair pointed out, was "a special kind of party work, a party job of its own kind, a party duty for party members and class work for nonparty workers." [49] "Correct" or "incorrect" behavior was a frequent criterion for evaluating past actions. [50]

Together, the chair and the presidium kept the reminiscers on track. This often entailed the chair's delivery to the assembled of a narrative synopsis of October. At an evening in celebration of the ninth anniversary, Kudelli expounded at length on the need for "perspective" for those reminiscers who had been selected because of their active participation in the events of April 21, June 18, the July Days, and so on. She reminded them "how gradually the revolution in Leningrad had developed in general and how the October overthrow had come to a head." In order that their reminiscences not be "too diffuse," Kudelli ran down a list of the "stages" of the October Revolution, beginning with Lenin's arrival in Petrograd; the revolutionary demonstrations of April 21 and 22, 1917 over Miliukov's pledge to continue Russia's part in the war; the "revolutionary awakening" in the plants and factories; and so on. She asked those present to devote "the most serious attention" to the Red Guards in particular:

> It must be stated definitely and firmly that in the February Revolution workers above all took up arms. Since there was still no Red Guard at that time, they got hold of weapons from individual regiments, individual soldiers; and later a workers' militia arose specifically to protect the plants; and later this became very quickly a workers' Red Guard, which played the most enormous role in the October Revolution.

Finally, Kudelli made sure to mention by name Zinoviev, Kamenev, Aleksei Rykov, and Nogin, who had believed Lenin's call for an uprising to be premature and had left the Central Committee as a result. "If we can focus our attention on these stages," Kudelli told them, "we will be able to present a clear picture." [51]

The true power of the storytelling process, however, lay in its ability to make storytellers of the listeners, a point understood intuitively by one of the inspirers of the evenings of reminiscences. At a preparatory meeting about Eisenstein's scenario for *October*, Podvoiskii acknowledged the dynamic process of the communal act of remembering, singling out one of the reminiscers as exemplary of the process:

Let's take this comrade. I do not remember your name: it is a fact that around him, as soon as he begins to recollect, an entire audience forms, which listens to him, and on the other hand around him forms an entire army of those who also begin to recollect: "Aha, it was so. And remember how in this or that corner I did this or that, I spoke about this or that, I kept this or that to myself, supported this or that at one time or another, etc." And it turns out that workers who never thought that they might take part in the writing of history, having united around this active participant, thus join the special army of elementary, primitive practitioners of history.

The act of communal recollection, in Podvoiskii's view, could provide the script not only with historical detail but with "the most complete, juicy [*sochnyi*], and colorful material." [52] As a published guide to these activities put it at the time, these evenings would see "bright, colorful, captivating" recollections, the creation of a "canvas" of personal experiences. [53]

The tale of October grew with the familiarity of repetition by both the chair and those who took up their own parts of the story. Reminiscers were bound by certain communal identities or experiences, which were reinforced by the collective act of storytelling at the evenings. The evenings brought together groups of people who had worked in party organizations at the same time, or in the same plant, or in the same district. [54] Such groups recalled how their party organizations grew from an insignificant group into a powerful party committee in the course of 1917, and invariably pointed out the moment when the committee expelled the Mensheviks and Socialist Revolutionaries from the organization, often after the Kornilov affair. [55] Women workers were brought together from a single district on the evening of June 6, 1927, many from the same factory. They created through their recollections a sense of revolutionary consciousness for both their group and their gender, by setting themselves apart from the bulk of women workers in 1917 who they generally represented as politically backward. "We will also be great like the men," said one such woman, to applause from the audience.[56] At another evening in October 1926, reminiscers elevated themselves by noting the revolutionary unimpeachability of their past actions, for example, by intervening with comrades who were getting drunk on wine after the Bolshevik takeover: "There was only a small group of conscious communards, who persuaded them not to drink."[57]

Reminiscers found common ground at these evenings by recounting their experiences from the recent or more distant past. They shared tales of their suffering at the hands of local peasants or Cossacks during the Civil War.[58] They recalled shared persecution at the hands of the unified committees of Mensheviks, SRs, and Kadets, which persisted into 1918 and which denounced them as "spies, provocateurs, madmen."[59] Alternatively, they recalled past collaboration with some of these groups. One reminiscer noted that prior to October the Bolsheviks, Mensheviks, and SRs in the underground had been "as if unified against the common foe."[60] Their experiences in the prerevolutionary underground even found common ground across party lines at this later date, at least for a while, as some bureaus invited local Mensheviks and nonparty people to participate in their evenings, although this sometimes met with objections from other participants or from local party organizations.[61] Those who had been living in exile at the time of October recalled their experiences in the emigration as a time of common cause in the face of intense hostility from their countries of exile to the news of the October Revolution.[62]

In interesting ways, these kinds of recollections reinforced existing group identities with the sense that their experiences were intimate, even exclusive. At an evening at the Komintern club in October 1926, participants recalled the prerevolutionary period in terms of small groups of three or four people meeting wherever they could on the city's outskirts, arguing heatedly late into the night, teaching their members "to march, to sing songs, to master weapons." They recalled the difficult, conspiratorial conditions in 1905, in particular the danger of police raids and the need for absolute vigilance.[63] At such evenings, reminiscers evaluated past actions in terms of their present coherent political identities, the better to contrast their mood against the "colorful" or "anarchistic" moods among the workers of Petrograd in 1917.[64] They recalled slogans they saw and heard in 1917 as Bolshevik or otherwise. A reminiscer at an evening on October 15, 1927, remembered seeing a banner in an anti-tsarist demonstration in March 1917 with the slogan "Bread, War against War," adding, "Now we understand that this slogan was not truly Leninist, not truly Bolshevik, because at that time Lenin had coined the slogan 'Transform the Imperialist War into a Civil War.' "[65] If they were already declared members of the Bolshevik Party prior to October, they emphasized their beleaguered status in plant committees or unified organizations, as tiny minorities surrounded by the majority Mensheviks and SRs.[66] If they were not members at that time, they invariably pointed out the general scarceness in 1917 of "independent, firm Bolsheviks." [67] If they were undecided in their party affiliation, they noted the plethora of parties vying for popular support in the course of 1917, and inevitably they stressed the point of epiphany at which individuals realized where their true interests lay (and thus joined the Bolsheviks, often switching from other parties): "After the July overthrow they [in the Provisional Government] revealed themselves, and the workers began to comprehend what

Bolshevik meant and what Menshevik meant, or what anarchist meant."[68] Individuals did not merely join the party in 1917, but, as one reminiscer noted, they had to go through a process of recommendation and vetting of credentials.[69] Thus was the impression conveyed that the party was discerning in its recruitment, and not opportunistic like other parties. Indeed, they represented their, at the time, numerically stronger opponents as less steadfast and ideologically inconsistent, one individual referring to the "porridge [*kasha*]" of Mensheviks, Socialist Revolutionaries, and anarchists, who quarreled with one another at every turn.[70] Indeed, their very numbers were testament to their inconsistency. In one plant in Petrograd in 1917, recalled one person, "there was a mass of SRs there, of course, but these SRs subsequently would have to be considered in quotation marks [*v kovych-kakh*]."[71]

Individual reminiscers at these evenings identified themselves as the legitimate bearers of this new Soviet polity in various ways. They established their class credentials by identifying themselves by their occupations. For example, a female worker introduced her recollections at the evening in June 1927 thus: "I worked as a cleaner [*uborshchitsa*] in the International Bank. Many think that I was a clerk [*kontorshchitsa*], but this was not so, I was a cleaner."[72] Class credentials could be invoked in the absence of the desired party credentials: "I was nonparty, but I held party views because I was the son of a peasant and took into account the situation of the workers" said a worker at a different evening.[73] The authenticity of their claims to being a part of this new order was, of course, already advanced by their presence at these evenings. More than this, many revealed in their acts of recollection a sense of superiority over other members of society, often setting themselves apart from the ignorant or passive masses of 1917: "In Smolny it was clear that something had to happen, but on the street it was not noticeable." [74] Many identified their own moments of revolutionary epiphany; one individual who was present at Lenin's arrival at the Finland Station on April 16, 1917, recalled hearing Lenin say " 'Long Live the Socialist Republic!' and in these words it was necessary to understand that the revolution was continuing and preparing itself for October 25." [75] Even those who asserted that they had poorly understood at the time the significance of what they were experiencing ("I even was a little confused," said a reminiscer at one evening, and a voice from the audience commented, "And how!") did so from the vantage point of their present state of revolutionary consciousness. [76] Indeed, this present state of grace was often at the root of condemnations at these meetings of Zinoviev and Kamenev for their past vacillations. Despite one person's claim that "comrade Zinoviev's declaration [against an armed uprising] was like an exploding bombshell for us" at the time, such sentiments had far more to do with *present* political concerns, as shown by this same individual's observation that the same "disease" was afflicting these comrades again nine years later. He contrasted such uncertain behavior with the steadfast behavior of "advanced fighters" like himself, "small screws in our greatest machine, the Leninist Party." [77]

Participants laid their most concrete claims to a place in the new order by locating themselves physically within the October foundation tale, noting their presence at key "moments" of the revolutionary struggle. A soldier pointed out repeatedly to his fellow reminiscers his presence as a besieging soldier at the Winter Palace on the eve of its "storming [*shturm*]." [78] Some noted their access to certain revolutionary sites or icons (most coveted were Smolny and Lenin), to which the general public had only limited access. A personal encounter with Lenin, or being present at one of his speeches, became a badge of revolutionary credentials. Reminiscers organized their autobiographies around these and future such moments. [79] Lesser Bolsheviks might also be invoked in this vein. [80] Participants often first established their whereabouts in 1917, then worked backward or forward from that date. Not infrequently, they noted their presence in Petrograd at a key revolutionary moment; indeed, their *absence* from Petrograd at such a key moment might be noted as a significant personal fact. If they were from the provinces they noted where "the revolution found me." [81] Sometimes, reminiscers would expand the definition of revolutionary action in order to be able to include their own actions in it. At the Aleksandrov evening, a number of people who had defended a munitions factory at the time of the Kornilov mutiny argued that, although they were not fighting directly against Kornilov, they were nonetheless engaged in the revolutionary protection of property: "We, we in the Arsenal, selected our best comrades to safeguard property.... We were fighting on two fronts. There was fighting with bullets and fighting to preserve property." [82]

At best, these individuals derived a sense of political and social validation from their acts of recollection. They articulated their memories consciously as self-proclaimed participants in the October Revolution, bound together by a shared sense of historical and historic immediacy. Even more than this, their reminiscences acquired additional power from the texture and depth of the tellings. The shared moments of drama, pathos, even sexist humor, at these evenings bound the assembled together in profound ways. At an evening for women workers from the Volodarskii District in June 1927, one speaker told a touching tale of searching endlessly for her young daughter who had gone off to serve as a nurse for the Bolsheviks in 1918. She eventually found her daughter at a railway station, performing the difficult task of ministering to the wounded, driven by revolutionary duty to continue doing so. [83] At another evening, a female worker told of an encounter at a congress of female workers in Moscow in December 1918 between Lenin and a female peasant. On his being told that her village regarded him as the devil, the worker recalled (to laughter and applause from the assembled),

Lenin told the woman to go back to the village and tell them that she had seen Lenin "and he has neither horns nor a tail." [84] Another individual recalled the rumors that members of the women's battalion had been raped by those who had stormed the Winter Palace. To the laughter of those present, he reported how the insurgents had merely told the women to change from the men's clothing they were wearing to skirts and then sent them home unharmed, although the skirts were too short. [85]

As the tales acquired coherence and texture in the telling at these evenings, so too did the articulated experiences and identities of the tellers. [86] Reminiscers literally wrote themselves into history as actors of significance. In some cases, this self-heroicization could be quite overt and brazen, not unlike those iconic characters transfigured by the revolutionary moment in Reed's *Ten Days That Shook the World* and given visual form by Eisenstein. In other cases, it was more complex. One woman recalled a mass meeting of 1,800 workers at her plant in Petrograd in 1917, at which the Socialist Revolutionary Viktor Chernov and others maligned the Bolsheviks so as to inflame the masses. Although young and inexperienced, she, together with several others, addressed the crowd, bringing the wrath of the crowd on her and eventually being saved by several workers. The most interesting aspect here was not the rather cliched tale of the heroic revolutionary individual haranguing the hostile, politically ignorant masses but the implied threat of sexual violence that lent the tale a sinister edge: "I stand red-faced and want to speak again, but having got to the platform we do not manage to open our mouths, as several hands grab me, pull off my skirt, and give me several slaps." [87]

In his seminal study of the dynamics of collective remembering, Halbwachs explored the genesis of seemingly personal memories in their complex interrelationship with a multitude of group frameworks in any given culture:

> Often we deem ourselves the originators of thoughts and ideas, feelings and passions, actually inspired by some group. Our agreement with those about us is so complete that we vibrate in unison, ignorant of the real source of the vibrations. How often do we present, as deeply held convictions, thoughts borrowed from a newspaper, book, or conversation? They respond so well to our way of seeing things that we are surprised to discover that their author is someone other than ourself. [88]

All of these formative mechanisms at play in the group dynamic of memory articulation were, of course, themselves shaped by the broader formative process of telling the tale of October. This ambitious effort to construct a foundation event for the new Soviet state was at its core an ideological project, consciously intended by the new state's leaders to change the very way of thinking of the Soviet population by changing their modes of articulation. The population was not only required to mouth the new terms and categories of the Communist project but they were invited, perhaps forced by the entire social environment, to use them to make sense of and to *articulate* their very experiences. At this point, ideology and personal experience were inseparable. The recent past literally took shape *within* these various individuals as they became October's storytellers.

Now I live in an explained world. I understand the causes. I am filled with enormous gratitude   when I think of those who died to make the world explained.
—Yuri Olesha, 1935

In 1960, the dissident writer Andrei Sinyavsky (using the pseudonym Abram Tertz), who would soon be found guilty of committing "crimes" against the Soviet state, wrote:

> The memory of the Revolution is as sacred, both to those who took part in it and to those who were born after it, as the image of a dead mother. It is easier for us to grant that everything that happened after the Revolution was its betrayal than to insult its memory by reproaches and suspicions. Unlike the party, the state, the Ministry of State Security, collectivization, Stalin, etc., the Revolution... is self-justified emotionally, like love or inspiration.... For we accomplished the Revolution. How then can we blame it or blaspheme against it? We are caught in this psychological squeeze. In itself, we may like it or not. But both before us and behind us stand temples so splendid that we could not bear to attack them.[1]

Siniavsky's words are revealingly dismissive of the party. The Soviet state's difficulties in integrating the Bolshevik Party into the story of October ensured that the party did not achieve as mythic a place as the October Revolution in Soviet society. Although the party's primacy was never seriously challenged (at least after the Civil War), its own sense of its leading role was undermined by the litany of criticism within its own ranks, which dogged it from October on. At a gathering of leading Bolsheviks in 1928 to discuss the party's origins, some dated it from a particular work by Lenin, from the *Iskra* period, or from the Second Congress of the RSDRP in 1903. Others marked the Prague Conference in 1912 as the "real start of Bolshevik self-determination," and still others said the party originated with the final split between the Mensheviks and Bolsheviks in 1917, when the Bolsheviks "formed a completely separate party." [2] These differences of opinion were not trivial, for each signified a quite distinct conception of the party. The story of the Bolshevik Party now seems best captured by the sterile and canonic *History of the All-Russian Communist Party (Bolshevik): Short Course* of 1936, a work framed mostly by Stalin's ego. [3]

In the case of the October Revolution, however, Sinyavsky's sentiments reveal a complex psychological bond that made it extremely difficult to reject the Soviet system, even in the face of enormous personal suffering and loss. For those who built its temples, October was an intensely subjective experience, raised to myth by their own revolutionary dreams. For subsequent generations, too, October proved to be an extremely resilient and formative foundation event. Soviet citizens turned out every year to celebrate it. [4] They articulated their aspirations and their complaints within the new terms and categories, indeed within the new historical chronology it had enshrined. [5] They made sense of the Second World War as one more stage in the "permanent, unfolding socialist revolution." [6] The stuttering process of de-Stalinization that followed the leader's death in 1953 was cast by Soviet politicians, beginning with Nikita Khrushchev, as a return to the purer ideals of October. In the final years of Soviet Russia, Mikhail Gorbachev claimed that his radical policies of perestroika (restructuring) and glasnost (openness), far from undermining the Communist way of life, were a rededication to Soviet Russia's founding principles, a continuation of the revolutionary spirit of October.[7]

In the words of historian Alan Kimball, the still unrealized "dream" of revolution in Soviet Russia ensured that the October epic had to be "sung and sung again" in the pursuit of ultimate success. [8] All those who tried to harness October to new ends were animated by a belief in the need to maintain its mythic stature among the Soviet people. Like all polities that regularly conjure their foundation events through ritual and symbol, in summoning October the USSR's politicians were primarily invoking not a set of historical and historic events but rather an atavistic spirit. Even if they did so for self-serving political ends, they still understood this spirit to comprise commitment, purity of ideals, and clarity of meaning, although they may not have fully grasped the complexities and contradictions of the early efforts to forge it.

Today, Western critics repeatedly and insistently pronounce the revolution dead, along with the revolutionary idea itself. [9] In the early 1990s, the public trial of the CPSU seemed a last, vain attempt, in the words of one author, to "salvage socialism from bolshevism." [10] Communists are evidently no longer even Communists in post-Soviet Russia; "Today's Reds," as historian Vladimir Buldakov puts it, "are not revolutionary extremists at all and not even utopians. They are… the most hopeless of the conservatives." [11] Lenin's corpse remains in its mausoleum in Red Square (minus the honor guard and the November parades), one suspects, more for reasons of government inertia than Communist mystique. [12] But can October ever be over? Its reduction and distillation to a symbol surely fixes its place in Russia's and the world's historical memory. In future crises, this symbol may well find itself invoked once more, to be embraced or denied. Indeed, perhaps October is still with us, if by another name. The passions and certainties that so energized that first generation of revolutionary storytellers in Russia might today be animating quite different sets of self-legitimizing and self-mythologizing tales of epiphany and purification elsewhere in the world.

Notes

INTRODUCTION

1. Isaac Babel, *1920 Diary* (New Haven: Yale University Press, 1995), 35.

2. Joan Scott, "The Evidence of Experience," *Critical Inquiry* 17, no. 4 (1991): 777.

3. The *Historikerstreit* of the mid-1980s was precisely about the kinds of stories Germans thought they could legitimately tell about themselves and their country's history (*Forever in the Shadow of Hitler?: Original Documents of the Historikerstreit, the Controversy Concerning the Singularity of the Holocaust,* trans. James Knowlton and Truett Cates [Atlantic Highlands, N.J.: Humanities Press, 1993], 17; *Reworking the Past: Hitler, Holocaust, and the Historians' Debate,* ed. Peter Baldwin [Boston: Beacon, 1990]). On Vichy and French identity, see Henry Rousso, *The Vichy Syndrome: History and Memory in France since 1944* (Cambridge: Harvard University Press, 1991).

4. Clerics and conquistadors of late medieval Iberia, it has been argued, could have imagined pre-Hispanic Philippines only in terms of their own social classifications and categories, thereby literally constituting the very object of their attentions (Benedict Anderson, *Imagined Communities: Reflections on the Origin and Spread of Nationalism* [London: Verso, 1991], 166 ff). The Inka myth of origin, and the very notion of Inka kingship, may also have much to do with the imposition by the Spanish of European dynastic models onto Peru (Gary Urton, *The History of a Myth: Pacariqtambo and the Origin of the Inkas* [Austin: University of Texas Press, 1990], 6). The role of war in the making of the myths of England has been brilliantly explored by Paul Fussell, *The Great War and Modern Memory* (Oxford: Oxford University Press, 1975), and by Angus Calder, *The Myth of the Blitz* (London: Jonathan Cape, 1991).

5. On the role of language and rhetoric in the constitution and reconstitution of the French Revolution, see François Furet, *Interpreting the French Revolution* (Cambridge: Cambridge University Press, 1981). On the role of memory, see Patrick H. Hutton, "The Role of Memory in the Historiography of the French Revolution," *History and Theory* 15, no. 1 (1991): 66; Pierre Nora, *Les Lieux de mémoire* (Paris: Gallimard, 1984–).

6. Michel-Rolph Trouillot, *Silencing the Past: Power and the Production of History* (Boston: Beacon, 1995).

7. William J. Bouwsma, "Intellectual History in the 1980s: From History of Ideas to History of Meaning," *Journal of Interdisciplinary History* 12, no. 2 (1981): 284–87; Peter L. Berger and Thomas Luckmann, *The Social Construction of Reality: A Treatise in the Sociology of Knowledge* (New York: Doubleday, 1966), 3.

8. Keith Michael Baker, *Inventing the French Revolution* (Cambridge: Cambridge University Press, 1990), 13, 41.

9. The ways in which individuals are drawn into the systematic and regular construction of meanings around certain events is explored in Stuart Hall's "The Rediscovery of 'Ideology': Return of the Repressed in Media Studies," in *Culture, Society and the Media,* ed. Michael Gurevitch and others (London: Methuen, 1982), 56–90; "The Narrative Construction of Reality: An Interview with Stuart Hall," *Southern Review* (Adelaide) 17, no. 1 (1984): 3–17.

10. Henry Tudor, *Political Myth* (New York: Praeger, 1972), 139. Myth has been called a "system of communication" (Roland Barthes, *Mythologies* [New York: Noonday, 1972], 109). Governments use "tradition" in a similar fashion to legitimate an ideology or to maintain social and cultural hierarchies (Jack Zipes, "The Utopian Function of Tradition," *Telos* 94 [1993–94]: 25–29; *The Invention of Tradition*, ed. Eric Hobsbawm and Terence Ranger [Cambridge: Cambridge University Press, 1983]).

11. Iwona Irwin-Zarecka, *Frames of Remembrance: The Dynamics of Collective Memory* (New Brunswick, N.J.: Transaction, 1994), 15.

12. Louis O. Mink, "Narrative Form as a Cognitive Instrument," in *The Writing of History: Literary Form and Historical Understanding*, ed. Robert H. Canary and Henry Kozicki (Madison: University of Wisconsin Press, 1978), 131.

13. The narrative form, it has been argued, invites scholars to present a complete and coherent picture of the past, while remaining unaware of the role in this played by their personal desire for coherence and completeness (see Hayden White's "The Question of Narrative in Contemporary Historical Theory" in his book *The Content of the Form: Narrative Discourse and Historical Representation* [Baltimore: Johns Hopkins University Press, 1987], 26–57; David Harlan, "Intellectual History and the Return of Literature," *American Historical Review* 94, no. 3 [1989]: 592; Hans Kellner, *Language and Historical Representation: Getting the Story Crooked* [Madison: University of Wisconsin Press, 1989]). By unconsciously masking their own role in the construction of the narrative, historians often merely reinforce the conventions of the narrative form, and they believe that they need only listen as history "seems to tell itself" (Roland Barthes, "The Discourse of History," in *The Rustle of Language* [New York: Hill and Wang, 1986], 131).

14. Martin Malia, "Why Amalrik Was Right," *Times Literary Supplement* 4675 (November 6, 1992): 9.

15. Alexander Rabinowitch, *Prelude to Revolution: The Petrograd Bolsheviks and the July 1917 Uprising* (Bloomington: Indiana University Press, 1968); Alexander Rabinowitch, *The Bolsheviks Come to Power: The Revolution of 1917 in Petrograd* (New York: W. W. Norton, 1978). Soviet historians have had it both ways, vaunting Lenin and the Bolsheviks as superb organizers and propagandists, while implying at the same time that the inherent popular appeal of the Bolshevik Party's policies was the deciding factor in the October Revolution (Peter Kenez, *The Birth of the Propaganda State: Soviet Methods of Mass Mobilization, 1917–1929* [Cambridge: Cambridge University Press, 1985], 3).

16. Graeme Gill, *The Origins of the Stalinist Political System* (Cambridge: Cambridge University Press, 1990); Malvin Magnus Helgesen, "The Origins of the Party State Monolith in Soviet Russia: Relations between the Soviets and Party Committees in the Central Provinces, October 1917–March 1921," Ph.D. diss., State University of New York at Stony Brook, 1980; Sheila Fitzpatrick, "The Civil War as a Formative Experience," Occasional Paper no. 134, Kennan Institute for Advanced Russian Studies (1981): 1–35.

17. Leonard Schapiro, *The Communist Party of the Soviet Union*, 2d ed. (Norfolk, UK: Methuen, 1970); Vladimir Brovkin, *Russia after Lenin: Politics, Culture, and Society, 1921–1929* (London: Routledge, 1998); John Keep, *The Russian Revolution: A Study in Mass Mobilization* (New York: W. W. Norton, 1976).

18. Martin Malia, *The Soviet Tragedy: A History of Socialism in Russia, 1917–1991* (New York: Free Press, 1994), 270, 314.

19. Jeffrey Brooks, "Socialist Realism in *Pravda*: Read All about It!" *Slavic Review* 53, no. 4 (1994): 978. In his 1970 Nobel Prize speech, Alexander Solzhenitsyn called on his fellow writers to "vanquish the lie!" (A. Solzhenitsyn, *Nobelevskaia lektsiia po literature 1970 g.* [Paris: YMCA, 1972], 29). For an examination of this genre that accepts it on its own terms, see Katerina Clark, *The Soviet Novel: History as Ritual*, 2nd ed. (Chicago:

University of Chicago Press, 1985). On the Soviet historical profession in its early years, see John Barber, *Soviet Historians in Crisis, 1928–1932* (Basingstoke: Macmillan, 1981).

20. Geoffrey A. Hosking, "Memory in a Totalitarian Society: The Case of the Soviet Union," in *Memory: History, Culture, and the Mind*, ed. Thomas Butler (Oxford: Blackwell, 1989), 118. Also, *À l'Est: La Mémoire retrouvée*, ed. Alain Brossat and Sonia Combe (Paris: Éditions la découverte, 1990).

21. For a survey of this trend for the 1930s in Western historiography, see Lynne Viola, "Popular Resistance in the Stalinist 1930s: Soliloquy of a Devil's Advocate," *Kritika* 1, no. 1 (2000): 45–69. Also Vladimir Kozlov, *Massovye besporiadki v SSSR pri Khrushcheve i Brezhneve, 1953–nachalo 1980–kh gg.* (Novosibirsk: Sibirskii khronograf, 1999); *Kommunisticheskii rezhim i narodnoe soprotivlenie v Rossii 1917–1991* (Moscow: Posev, 1998).

22. *Memory, History, and Opposition under State Socialism*, ed. Rubie S. Watson (Santa Fe: School of American Research Press, 1994).

23. Richard Pipes, *The Russian Revolution* (New York: Vintage, 1990); idem., "Seventy-five Years On: The Great October Revolution as a Clandestine Coup d'État," *Times Literary Supplement* 4675 (November 6, 1992): 3–4. For a critique of Pipes's approach, see Peter Kenez, "The Prosecution of Soviet History: A Critique of Richard Pipes' *The Russian Revolution*," *Russian Review* 50 (1991): 345–51; Peter Kenez, "The Prosecution of Soviet History, Volume 2," *Russian Review* 54 (1995): 265–69.

24. Ronald Grigor Suny, "Toward a Social History of the October Revolution," *American Historical Review* 88, no. 1 (1983): 43.

25. A few scholars have examined the processes of reification of the February Revolution. The influence of the intraparty struggles of the 1920s and of tsarist police reports, it has been argued, helped preserve this notion of the first legitimate revolution among both Western and Soviet historians (James D. White, "The Sormovo-Nikolaev Zemlyachestvo in the February Revolution," *Soviet Studies* 31, no. 4 [1979]: 475–504; D. A. Longley, "Iakovlev's Question, or the Historiography of the Problem of Spontaneity and Leadership in the Russian Revolution of February 1917," in *Revolution in Russia: Reassessments of 1917*, ed. J. Frankel and B. Knei Paz [Cambridge: Cambridge University Press, 1992], 366). Also, Michael Melancon, "Rethinking Russia's February Revolution: Anonymous Spontaneity or Socialist Agency?" *Carl Beck Papers in Russian and East European Studies* 1408 (June 2000).

26. François Furet, *The Passing of an Illusion: The Idea of Communism in the Twentieth Century* (Chicago: University of Chicago Press, 1999), chap. 3.

27. Ibid., 144.

28. V. P. Buldakov, "Istoriograficheskie metamorfozy 'Krasnogo Oktiabria,'" in *Istoricheskie issledovaniia v Rossii. Tendentsii poslednykh let*, ed. G. A. Bordiugov (Moscow: AIRO-20, 1996), 179.

29. In this vein, the socialist culture of the city of Magnitogorsk in the 1930s has been examined in terms of "what the party and its programs . . . made possible, intentionally and unintentionally," rather than what they prevented (Stephen Kotkin, *Magnetic Mountain: Stalinism as a Civilization* [Berkeley: University of California Press, 1995], 22). Cf. Simonetta Falasca-Zamponi, *Fascist Spectacle: The Aesthetics of Power in Mussolini's Italy* (Berkeley: University of California Press, 1997).

30. Keith Michael Baker, "Revolution," in *The Political Culture of the French Revolution*, ed. Colin Lucas, vol. 2 of *The French Revolution and the Creation of Modern Political Culture*, ed. Keith Michael Baker (Oxford: Pergamon, 1994), 50. On the emergence of the term "revolution" as one connoting a political and progressive event, see Ilan Rachum, *"Revolution": The Entrance of a New Word into Western Political Discourse* (New York: University Press of America, 1999).

31. The classic work is Lynn Hunt's *Politics, Culture, and Class in the French Revolution* (Berkeley: University of California Press, 1984).

32. Priscilla Parkhurst Ferguson, *Paris as Revolution: Writing the Nineteenth-Century City* (Berkeley: University of California Press, 1994), 1.

33. Furet, *Interpreting the French Revolution*, 6. Astrid von Borcke, *Die Ursprünge des Bolschewismus: Die Jakobinische Tradition in Rußland und die Theorie der Revolutionären Diktatur* (Munich: Johannes Berchmans, 1977).

34. G. I. Il'ina, "Obraz evropeiskikh revoliutsii i russkaia kul'tura (mart 1917 g.—noiabr' 1918 g.)," in *Anatomiia revoliutsii: 1917 g. v Rossii: massy, partii, vlast'*, ed. V. Iu. Cherniaev, and others (St. Petersburg: Glagol', 1994), 383–93; Dmitry Shlapentokh, *The Counter-Revolution in Revolution: Images of Thermidor and Napoleon at the Time of the Russian Revolution and Civil War* (New York: St. Martin's, 1999).

35. Tamara Kondratieva, *Bolcheviks et Jacobins: Itinéraire des analogies* (Paris: Payot, 1989), 248. Also Michel Vovelle, "1789–1917: The Game of Analogies," in *The French Revolution and the Creation of Modern Political Culture*, ed. Keith Michael Baker, vol. 4, *The Terror* (Oxford: Pergamon, 1994), 349–78.

36. The Paris Commune, it has been argued, was invested by succeeding generations of revolutionaries with the hopes "for what it might have been" (Patrick H. Hutton, *The Cult of the Revolutionary Tradition: The Blanquists in French Politics, 1864–1893* [Berkeley: University of California Press, 1981], 13).

37. V. I. Lenin, "Uroki kommuny," in *Sochineniia*, vol. 12, 3rd ed. (Moscow-Leningrad, 1929), 162–64.

38. V. I. Lenin, *What Is to Be Done?* (Moscow, 1973), 40–43; cf. V. I. Lenin, "Proletarskaia revoliutsiia i renegat Kautskii," in *Sochineniia*, vol. 23, 220 ff.

39. Orlando Figes and Boris Kolonitskii, *Interpreting the Russian Revolution: The Language and Symbols of 1917* (New Haven: Yale University Press, 1999), 182.

40. V. I. Lenin, "Rech' po voprosu o pechati," in *Sochineniia*, vol. 22, 43.

41. For a subtle treatment of Bolshevik propaganda, see Kenez, *Birth of the Propaganda State*.

42. Lenin developed this argument in 1899 in various pamphlets (Lenin, *Sochineniia*, vol. 2, 513–26).

43. Lenin, *What Is to Be Done?*, 109, 119, 122. Lenin's tract, it has been argued, indicated a desire to control the entire RSDRP, rather than a narrow plan to create the Bolshevik Party per se (James D. White, *Lenin: The Theory and Practice of Revolution* [Basingstoke, England: Palgrave, 2001], 178–79).

44. J. Martow, *Geschichte der Rußischen Sozialdemokratie* (Berlin: J. H. W. Dietz Nachfolger, 1926), 77.

45. In exile in Vienna after 1905, Lev Trotsky published an illegal newspaper, *Pravda*, in an effort to provide a sense of cohesion to the fragmented party organizations inside Russia (Frederick Corney, "Trotskii and the Vienna *Pravda*, 1908–1912," *Canadian Slavonic Papers* 27, no. 3 [1985]: 248–68).

46. Claims to ownership of the RSDRP took various forms over the years: Menshevik-inspired efforts to bring the party's wayward trends together at the Unification Congress in Stockholm in 1906, at the party's Central Committee in Paris in 1910, and again on the eve of World War One in Brussels; efforts by Lenin to speak in the name of the entire party at the "All-Party" Prague Conference in 1912 and again in 1914; and the Trotsky-inspired effort to counter the Prague conference with a "genuine" nonfactionalist meeting of the RSDRP in Vienna (see, respectively, *Resolutions and Decisions of the Communist Party of the Soviet Union*, ed. R. C. Elwood, vol. 1, *The Russian Social Democratic Labour Party, 1898–October 1917* [Toronto: University of Toronto Press, 1974], 92–104, 134–40; R. C. Elwood, "Lenin and the Brussels 'Unity' Conference of July 1914," *Russian Review* 39, no

1 [1980]: 32–49; *Resolutions and Decisions of the Communist Party*, 146–57; idem., "The Congress That Never Was: Lenin's Attempt to Call a 'Sixth' Party Congress in 1914," *Soviet Studies* 31, no. 3 [1979]: 343–63; *Vserossiiskaya Konferentsiya Ros. Sots.-Dem. Rab. Partii 1912 goda*, ed. R. C. Elwood [New York: Kraus, 1982]).

47. André Liebich, *From the Other Shore: Russian Social Democracy after 1921* (Cambridge: Harvard University Press, 1997), 60; Abraham Ascher, *Pavel Axelrod and the Development of Menshevism* (Cambridge: Harvard University Press, 1972), 382; Vilen Khaimovich Tumarinson, "Men'sheviki i Bol'sheviki: Nesostoiavshiisia konsensus (Opyt istoricheskoi rekonstruktsii)" (Ph.D. diss., Moscow, Moskovskii avtomobil'no-dorozhnyi institut, 1995); *The Making of Three Russian Revolutionaries*, ed. Leopold H. Haimson, in collaboration with Ziva y Galili Garcia and Richard Wortman (Cambridge: Cambridge University Press, 1987), 312–13. A study of several local RSDRP organizations through 1907 argues that local Bolshevik, Menshevik, and SR party allegiances depended far less on factional differences than on regional, generational, and cultural influences (David Lane, *The Roots of Russian Communism: A Social and Historical Study of Russian Social Democracy, 1898–1907* [Assen, The Netherlands: Van Gorcum, 1969].

48. Leopold H. Haimson, "The Problem of Social Identities in Early Twentieth-Century Russia," *Slavic Review* 47, no. 1 (1988), esp. 8–14. The ways in which lower-class Russians translated for their own use this language of revolutionary politics can be examined in the documents collected in *Voices of Revolution, 1917*, ed. Mark D. Steinberg (New Haven: Yale University Press, 2001). On the emergence of the new language of state in the Soviet era, see Michael S. Gorham, *Speaking in Soviet Tongues: Language Culture and the Politics of Voice in Revolutionary Russia* (DeKalb: Northern Illinois University Press, 2003).

49. Stephen Kotkin, " 'One Hand Clapping': Russian Workers and 1917," *Labor History* 32, no. 4 (1991): 618. Peasants confused the word "Bol'shevik" Russia prime with "bol'shaki" (peasant elders) and "bol'shie" (big people), and the term "revoliutsiia" with "revutsia," "levoliutsiia," and "levorutsia" (Figes and Kolonitskii, *Interpreting the Russian Revolution*, 131–37); cf. the confusion of a Moscow textile worker: "What is a Bolshevik? A large person?" (cited in Diane Koenker, *Moscow Workers and the 1917 Revolution* [Princeton: Princeton University Press, 1981], 187). On the meanings of the term "bourgeois" [*burzhui*] in 1917, see Boris I. Kolonitskii, "Antibourgeois Propaganda and Anti-'Burzhui' Consciousness in 1917," *Russian Review* 53, no. 2 (1994): 183–96; on the term "man in the street" [*obyvatel'*], see I. L. Arkhipov, "Obshchestvennaia psikhologiia Petrogradskikh obyvatelei v 1917 g.," *Voprosy istorii* 7 (1994): 49–58.

50. Oliver Henry Radkey, *Russia Goes to the Polls: The Election to the All-Russian Constituent Assembly, 1917* (Ithaca: Cornell University Press, 1990), 74.

51. Stephen Kotkin, "One Hand Clapping," 618–19.

52. Michael Hanne, *The Power of the Story: Fiction and Political Change* (Oxford: Berghahn, 1994), 11.

53. The quote refers to the social bond created by French revolutionaries through the anniversary festivals they staged (Mona Ozouf, *Festivals and the French Revolution* [Cambridge: Harvard University Press, 1988], 9). For the Russian example, see James von Geldern, *Bolshevik Festivals, 1917–1920* (Berkeley: University of California Press, 1993).

54. The changing inflections of the Storming of the Bastille, and its long path into the popular imagination as the symbolic defining "total event" of the French Revolution are examined in Hans-Jürgen Lüsebrink and Rolf Reichardt, "La Prise de la Bastille comme 'Événement total': Jalons pour une théorie historique de l'événement à l'époque moderne," *L'Événement* (Actes du colloque organisé à Aix-en-Provence par le Centre Meridional d'Histoire Sociale, September 16–18, 1983), 77–102.

55. Anderson, *Imagined Communities*, 80–81.

56. Robert A. Rosenstone argues that such abstractions as revolution, progress, modernization, Manifest Destiny, the Resistance, and the working class are essential if the past is to have meaning for individuals (*Revisioning History: Film and the Construction of a New Past* [Princeton: Princeton University Press, 1995], 8).

57. Robert F. Berkhofer, *Beyond the Great Story: History as Text and Discourse* (Cambridge: Harvard University Press, 1995), 70.

58. John E. Toews, "Intellectual History after the Linguistic Turn: The Autonomy of Meaning and the Irreducibility of Experience," *American Historical Review* 92, no. 4 (1987): 884; Stuart Hall, "Notes on Deconstructing 'the Popular,' " in *People's History and Socialist Theory*, ed. Raphael Samuel (London: Routledge and Kegan Paul, 1981), 233.

59. Matt K. Matsuda, *The Memory of the Modern* (New York: Oxford University Press, 1996), 36.

60. The now common attitude toward memory or remembering as an intricate process of social and cultural construction rather than as an act of retrieval began with the "rediscovery" of the work of a sociologist and a psychologist from the early twentieth century (see Maurice Halbwachs, *Les Cadres sociaux de la mémoire* [Paris: Librairie Félix Alcan, 1925]; Frederick C. Bartlett, *Remembering: A Study in Experimental and Social Psychology* (Cambridge: Cambridge University Press, 1964). On the narrative form as the "typical form of framing experience (and our memory of it)," see Jerome Bruner, *Acts of Meaning* (Cambridge: Harvard University Press, 1990), 56.

61. Bartlett, *Remembering*, 205. On the dynamics at play in such groups and the methods involved in framing group memories, see Elizabeth Tonkin, *Narrating Our Pasts: The Social Construction of Oral History* (Cambridge: Cambridge University Press, 1992), 90; Alessandro Portelli, "The Peculiarities of Oral History," *History Workshop* 12 (1981): 96–107. On the role of visual and auditory stimuli in anchoring an event in an individual's memory, see John Kotre, *White Gloves: How We Create Ourselves through Memory* (New York: Free Press, 1995), 93–106. On the pivotal role of language in the articulation of an individual's perceptions, see Halbwachs, *Les Cadres sociaux de la mémoire*, 377; Bouwsma, "Intellectual History in the 1980s," 289–90.

62. Jerome Bruner, "The Autobiographical Process," in *The Culture of Autobiography: Constructions of Self-Representation*, ed. Robert Folkenflik (Stanford: Stanford University Press, 1993), 38–39.

63. Tonkin, *Narrating Our Pasts*, 97. Memory is the "tool" we have to give our lives meaning, writes Luisa Passerini in *Memory and Totalitarianism*, ed. Luisa Passerini (Oxford: Oxford University Press, 1992), 3.

CHAPTER 1: THE POWER OF THE STORY

1. Part of this chapter appears in Frederick C. Corney, "Narratives of October and the Issue of Legitimacy," in *Russian Modernity: Politics, Knowledges, Practices*, ed. David L. Hoffmann and Yanni Kotsonis (New York: St. Martin's, 2000), 185–203.

2. A recent study stresses the present-minded dynamism of the early Communist system, in contrast to the postponed futures of "bourgeois Utopian" ideologies (Stephen E. Hanson, *Time and Revolution: Marxism and the Design of Soviet Institutions* [Chapel Hill: University of North Carolina Press, 1997], 202).

3. *Rabochii put'*, October 26, 1917, 1–2.

4. Baker, "Revolution," 56. Baker is referring to the journal *Révolutions de Paris*, which appeared in Paris in 1789. It began as a daily chronicle of events, but its emphasis soon shifted to defining more clearly "their structure and meaning" (ibid., 55).

5. The importance of pamphlets in the construction and propagation of certain revolutionary conceptions in America and France has been explored in a number of studies

(Bernard Bailyn, *The Ideological Origins of the American Revolution* [London: Harvard University Press, 1967], 33; Hunt, *Politics, Culture, and Class,* 129 ff.; Christian Jouhaud, "Printing the Event: From La Rochelle to Paris," in *The Culture of Print: Power and the Uses of Print in Early Modern Europe,* ed. Roger Chartier [Oxford: Polity, 1989], 290).

6. Patrick Wright, *On Living in an Old Country: The National Past in Contemporary Britain* (London: Verso, 1985), 141–42.

7. A. I. Shingarev, *The Shingarev Diary* (Royal Oak, Mich.: Strathcona, 1978), 67.

8. On this, see Peter Burke, "History as Social Memory," in *Memory: History, Culture, and the Mind,* ed. Thomas Butler (Oxford: Blackwell, 1989), 97; Norman R. Brown, Steven K. Shevell, and Lance J. Rips, "Public Memories and Their Personal Context," in *Autobiographical Memory,* ed. David C. Rubin (Cambridge: Cambridge University Press, 1986), 137–58.

9. V. I. Vernadskii, *Dnevniki, 1917–1921* (Kiev: Naukova Dumka, 1994), 28.

10. For a discussion of the attitudes of various political groups to Bolshevism, see Jane Burbank, *Intelligentsia and Revolution: Russian Views of Bolshevism, 1917–1922* (Oxford: Oxford University Press, 1986).

11. Leopold H. Haimson, "The Parties and the State: The Evolution of Political Attitudes," in *The Structure of Russian History: Interpretive Essays,* ed. Michael Cherniavsky (New York: Random House, 1970), 336. Also Michael Melancon, " 'Marching Together!' Left Bloc Activities in the Russian Revolutionary Movement, 1900 to February 1917," *Slavic Review* 49, no. 2 (1990): 239–52. One interesting study depicts the parties, the Bolshevik Party in particular, as the ultimate beneficiaries of a surging labor movement in Petrograd in 1917, although peripheral to it for much of the time (S. A. Smith, *Red Petrograd: Revolution in the Factories, 1917–18* [Cambridge: Cambridge University Press, 1983]).

12. *Making of Three Russian Revolutionaries,* 423.

13. For a rather typical picture of Lenin's triumphant return to Russia drawn mostly from sources commissioned in the 1920s, and especially for the tenth jubilee of October, see E. H. Carr, *The Bolshevik Revolution, 1917–1932,* vol. 1 (Harmondsworth: Penguin, 1950), 88–90.

14. Stepan Sletov, *K istorii vozniknoveniia partii sotsialistov-revoliutsionerov* (Petrograd, 1917), 6.

15. Hickey's work is highly suggestive about the conduct of radical politics at the local level in general (Michael C. Hickey, "The Rise and Fall of Smolensk's Moderate Socialists: The Politics of Class and the Rhetoric of Crisis in 1917," in *Provincial Landscapes: Local Dimensions of Soviet Power, 1917–1953,* ed. Donald J. Raleigh [Pittsburgh: University of Pittsburgh Press, 2001], 14–35).

16. On membership figures, see T. H. Rigby, *Communist Party Membership in the USSR, 1917–1967* (Princeton: Princeton University Press, 1968), chap. 1.

17. "Komitetam RSDRP v Vendene, Moskve, Khar'kove, Odesse, Kieve, Ekaterinoslave, Rostove-na-Donu, Tiflise, Viatke, Bol'shom Tokmake," in *Perepiska Sekretariata TsK RSDRP(b) s mestnymi partiinymi organizatsiiami,* ed. G. D. Obichkin, A. A. Struchkov, and M. D. Stuchebnikova, vol. 1 (Moscow, 1957), 22.

18. See the kinds of detailed questions asked of delegates in a questionnaire at a RSDRP(b) congress in July 1917 ("Oprosnyi list dlia delegatov Vserossiiskogo s"ezda RSDRP(b)," in *Perepiska,* vol. 1, 25–27), and the center's attempts to micromanage local organizations via a stream of memoranda (e.g., "Tsirkuliarnoe pis'mo mestnym partiinym organizatsiiam po voprosu 10% otchislenii," in *Perepiska,* vol. 1, 50).

19. I. G. Tsereteli, *Vospominaniia o fevral'skoi revoliutsii,* vol. 2 (Paris: Mouton, 1963), 171.

20. Cited in L. D. Trotskii, *O Lenine: Materialy dlia biografa* (Moscow, n.d.), 54.

21. On the effect Lenin's various calls to action up to October had on party leaders, see Schapiro, *Communist Party of the Soviet Union*, 165 ff; William Henry Chamberlin, *The Russian Revolution, 1917–1918: From the Overthrow of the Czar to the Assumption of Power by the Bolsheviks*, vol. 1 (New York: Universal, 1935), 159–60.

22. *Den'*, July 25, 1917, 6. For examples of anti-Bolshevik resolutions, also see August 11, 2; August 12, 1; October 19, 4; October 21, 4. *Den'* also documented the persecution of the Bolshevik press (August 11, 1917, 2).

23. Ibid., October 24, 1917, 4.

24. Ibid., September 7, 1917, 1; September 20, 1917, 1; October 12, 1917, 1.

25. P. Golikov, "To, o chem ne dogovarivaiut bol'sheviki," *Rabochaia gazeta*, October 19, 1917, 1. The only difference, Golikov argued, between anarchism and Bolshevism was that the latter exhibited everywhere a noticeable "absence of boldness of thought, a refusal to give a direct answer . . . equivocation."

26. *Rabochii put'*, October 1, 1917, 1. The claims of electoral gains were disputed in *Iskra*, October 14, 1917, 1.

27. V. I. Lenin, "Uderzhat li bol'sheviki gosudarstvennuiu vlast'?" in Lenin, *Sochineniia* 21, 251. In 1920, Lenin again wrote of the "hounding" of the Bolsheviks by the Kadets, especially from June 1917 onward, which "helped the masses to make an appraisal of Bolshevism; apart from the newspapers, all public life was full of discussions about Bolshevism." The foreign powers, Lenin continued, were now doing the Bolsheviks the same favor (V. I. Lenin, *"Left-Wing" Communism, an Infantile Disorder* [Moscow, 1975], 84).

28. Cited in Sergei Hackel, *The Poet and the Revolution: Aleksandr Blok's "The Twelve"* (Oxford: Clarendon, 1975), 65.

29. Figes and Kolonitskii, *Interpreting the Russian Revolution*, 172–73.

30. Zinaida Gippius, *Peterburgskie dnevniki, 1914–1919* (New York: Teleks, 1990), 194–95. Gippius often expressed her skepticism of the new order by placing key terms in quotation marks, including "Bolshevism," "Bolshevik," "parties," "comrade-socialists," "revolutionaries." Korolenko shared her mistrust of the masses, so much "human dust, blown around by any winds!" (V. G. Korolenko, "Dnevniki, 1917–1921," *Voprosy literatury* 5 [June 1990]: 213).

31. M. M. Prishvin, *Dnevniki, 1914–1917* (Moscow: Moskovskii rabochii, 1991), 366.

32. *Rabochii put'*, October 17, 1917, 4.

33. See the recurrent feature on party life ("Partiinaia zhizn' ") and related articles in *Rabochii put'*: September 26, 1917, 4; September 27, 1917, 4; October 1, 1917, 4; October 3, 1917, 4; October 4, 1917, 4, announcing the *first* conference on October 1 of all Bolshevik organizations in Petrograd province; October 6, 1917, 4; October 10, 1917, 3; and October 11, 1917, 3; *Sotsial-demokrat*, October 21, 1917, 2. See also the voluminous correspondence between the center and local organizations in the last months of 1917 published in *Perepiska*, vols. 1 and 2.

34. Vl. Nevskii, *Chto takoe bol'sheviki?* (Petrograd, 1917), 3, 4–6.

35. Cited in Rabinowitch, *Bolsheviks Come to Power*, 179–80. The best accounts of these events can be found in Rabinowitch, 172–208, and in Robert V. Daniels, *Red October: The Bolshevik Revolution of 1917* (Boston: Beacon, 1967), chap. 6.

36. On the rumors, see *Trudovaia kopeika*, October 20, 1917, 2; *Gazeta dlia vsekh*, October 20, 1917, 1. The latter quote is from D. B. Riazanov, cited in Daniels, *Red October*, 88.

37. Cited in Robert V. Daniels, *The Conscience of the Revolution: Communist Opposition in Soviet Russia* (Cambridge: Cambridge University Press, 1960), 61.

38. For Zinoviev's and Kamenev's views, see "Zaiavlenie G. Zinov'eva i Iu. Kameneva 24 (11) Oktiabria," in Lenin, *Sochineniia*, vol. 21, 494–98. For a broader discussion of their

views, see Daniels, *Conscience of the Revolution*, esp. 60–63. Notwithstanding his very public polemic with Zinoviev and Kamenev, Lenin had no shortage of otherwise ardent supporters ready to communicate similar misgivings in private (see Daniels, *Red October*, 101–2; Rabinowitch, *Bolsheviks Come to Power*, 202–4).

39. Cited in Daniels, *Red October*, 99.

40. *Pravda*, November 8, 1917, 2. In the 1920s, such statements would be used against him and other leaders. Further evidence would be furnished from the frequent local condemnations of the "treachery" of Zinoviev and Kamenev vis-à-vis Lenin and the October Revolution that appeared in the "Party Life" feature of *Pravda* (November 25, 1917, 4).

41. *Novaia zhizn'*, October 17, 1917, 1; October 18, 1917, 3; and Lenin's responses in *Rabochii put'*, October 19, 20, 21, 1917.

42. *Rabochaia gazeta*, October 19, 1917, 1.

43. See *Den'*, October 15, 1917, 4; *Rabochaia gazeta*, October 19, 1917, 3. Indeed, critics were able to draw on published denials by the Bolsheviks of the "disturbing rumors" of a Bolshevik "action" (*Sotsial-demokrat*, October 18, 1917, 3; this denial was moved to the front page of *Sotsial-demokrat*, October 20, 1917, 1). One article called the talk about the Bolsheviks appointing a day for an uprising "childish prattle. We are not preparing an uprising. *We will simply rise up*" (*Rabochii put'*, October 17, 1917, 2 [emphasis in original]).

44. "To seize power is doubtless possible, to hold it for long is more than difficult" (*Iskra*, October 27, 1917, 1).

45. *Rabochaia gazeta*, November 4, 1917, 1. Gorky's paper *Novaia zhizn'* was vocal in predicting the internal demise of the Bolshevik Party; see *Novaia zhizn'*, October 25, 1917, 1.

46. *Rabochaia gazeta*, November 6, 1917, 1.

47. *Delo naroda*, October 10, 1917, 1.

48. On October 17, the Provisional Government sent representatives of the militia to tour Petrograd to gauge the mood of the masses, particularly the workers and soldiers, producing "quite reassuring results" (*Rabochaia gazeta*, October 18, 1917, 2). For more "reassuring results" on the mood of soldiers, see ibid., October 18, 1917, 1; *Den'*, October 19, 1917, 4. Even after October 25, *Rabochaia gazeta* reported that the front had not given the Bolsheviks a single soldier, despite all their requests (*Rabochaia gazeta*, November 4, 1917, 3).

49. Gippius, *Petersburgskie dnevniki*, 194–95.

50. *Iskra*, October 14, 1917, 1.

51. *Den'*, October 24, 1917, 4.

52. *Rech'*, October 14, 1917, 2 and October 18, 1917, 1, respectively.

53. *Utro Rossii*, November 10, 1917, 1; November 10, 1917, 2; *Rech'*, October 26, 1917, 2.

54. Ibid., November 14, 1917, 1.

55. *Utro Rossii*, November 10, 1917, 3; November 15, 1917, 2; November 16, 1917, 3; November 18, 1917, 5; November 19, 1917, 5; *Nasha rech'*, November 16, 1917, 2.

56. *Utro Rossii*, December 7, 1917, 4; November 14, 1917, 4; November 15, 1917, 2.

57. Ibid., November 14, 1917, 4; November 16, 1917, 1. Also *Rech'*, October 15, 1917, 2.

58. *Vtoroi Vserossiiskii S"ezd Sovetov Rabochikh i Soldatskikh Deputatov (25–26 oktiabria 1917 g.): Sbornik dokumentov i materialov* (Moscow: Arkheograficheskii tsentr, 1997), 41.

59. *Rabochaia gazeta*, October 28, 1917, 1; November 7, 1917, 2.

60. The Mensheviks in particular had long been responding to moves by Lenin and their Bolshevik cousins (see Leopold Haimson's preface to Solomon M. Schwarz, *The Russian Revolution of 1905: The Workers' Movement and the Formation of Bolshevism and Menshevism* [Chicago: University of Chicago Press, 1967]).

61. This reluctance has been called a "self-denying ordinance" (Israel Getzler, "Marxist Revolutionaries and the Dilemma of Power," in *Revolution and Politics in Russia: Essays in Memory of B. I. Nicolaevsky*, ed. Alexander Rabinowitch, Janet Rabinowitch, with Ladis Kristof [Bloomington: Indiana University Press, 1972], 101).

62. Ascher, *Pavel Axelrod*, 382; Schapiro, *Communist Party of the Soviet Union*, 134–35. On the effects of Bolshevik power on the situation inside the Party of Socialist Revolutionaries, see *Partiia Sotsialistov Revoliutsionerov posle Oktiabr'skogo perevorota 1917 g.: Dokumenty iz arkhiva P.S.-R.*, selected and annotated by Marc Jansen (Amsterdam: Stichting Beheer IISG, 1989), documents 6 to 24.

63. For the Menshevik resolution, which the SRs joined prior to the walkout, see *Vtoroi Vserossiiskii S"ezd*, 69–70.

64. Ibid., 41–42.

65. *Rabochii put'*, October 25, 1917, 1; *Rabochaia gazeta*, October 26, 1917, 1; *Bor'ba*, November 10, 1917, 1.

66. *Rabochaia gazeta*, October 26, 1917, 1.

67. Ibid., November 9, 1917, 2; *Iskra*, December 4, 1917, 2.

68. *Rabochaia gazeta*, October 26, 1917, 4.

69. Ibid., October 27, 1917, 1.

70. *Delo naroda*, October 26, 1917, 1.

71. Ibid., October 28, 1917, 1.

72. *Rabochaia gazeta*, November 8, 1917, 2.

73. "Delo o samoubiistve Rossii: Iz dnevnika Leonida Andreeva," *Istochnik* 2 (1994): 42.

74. *Pravda (Rabochii put')*, October 31, 1917, 1.

75. *Sotsial-demokrat*, November 2, 1917, 2.

76. *Pravda (Rabochii put')*, November 1, 1917, 2.

77. *Rabochaia gazeta*, October 28, 1917, 1.

78. Ibid., October 26, 1917, 1.

79. *Delo naroda*, October 28, 1917, 1.

80. *Rabochaia gazeta*, November 1, 1917, 1. For a similar SR view, see *Delo naroda*, October 28, 1917, 1.

81. *Rabochaia gazeta*, November 4, 1917, 3.

82. Ibid., November 2, 1917, 1.

83. *Den'*, October 28, 1917, 1.

84. *Rabochii put'*, October 22, 1917, 1.

85. *Pravda (Rabochii put')*, October 28, 1917, 1.

86. *Rabochaia gazeta*, October 28, 1917, 1.

87. *Novaia zhizn'*, November 4, 1917, 1.

88. *Pravda (Rabochii put')*, October 31, 1917, 1.

89. *Rabochaia gazeta*, November 2, 1917, 1. Also, ibid., October 20, 1917, 2; October 25, 1917, 1; October 26, 1917, 1. Lenin had written in 1908 on the Paris Commune, in which he had praised the proclamation of the "Commune and civil war," which had "democratized the social order, [and] abolished the bureaucracy" ("Uroki kommuny," in Lenin, *Sochineniia*, vol. 12, 163).

90. *Delo naroda*, November 11, 1917, 4; *Rabochaia gazeta*, November 6, 1917, 1.

91. Petr Struve, "V chem revoliutsiia i kontr-revoliutsiia? Neskol'ko zamechanii po povodu stat'i I. O. Levina," *Russkaia mysl'*, book 11/12 (1917), 58.

92. Radkey, *Russia Goes To The Polls*, 18.

93. Leopold H. Haimson, "The Mensheviks after the October Revolution: Part III: The Constituent Assembly Meets," *Russian Review* 39, no. 4 (1980), 462–83.

94. S. V. Iarov, *Proletarii kak politik. Politicheskaia psikhologiia rabochikh Petrograda v 1917–1923 gg.* (St. Petersburg: "Dmitrii Bulanin," 1999), 170; idem., *Gorozhanin kak politik. Revoliutsiia, voennyi kommunizm i NEP glazami Petrogradtsev* (St. Petersburg: "Dmitrii Bulanin," 1999), 20; idem., *Krest'ianin kak politik. Krest'ianstvo Severo-Zapada Rossii v 1918–1919 gg. Politicheskoe myshlenie i massovyi protest* (St. Petersburg: "Dmitrii Bulanin," 1999), 19. By 1921, the Constituent Assembly had all but disappeared from the political lexicon of the workers (idem, *Proletarii*, 114).

95. Oliver H. Radkey, *The Sickle under the Hammer: The Russian Socialist Revolutionaries in the Early Months of Soviet Rule* (New York: Columbia University Press, 1963), 448–50. Even the short-lived Committee of Members of the Constituent Assembly (Komuch), set up in Samara by SRs in June 1918, enjoyed little popular support (Donald J. Raleigh, *Experiencing Russia's Civil War: Politics, Society, and Revolutionary Culture in Saratov, 1917–1922* [Princeton: Princeton University Press, 2002], 47–48).

96. Gippius, *Peterburgskie dnevniki*, 207.

97. A. Blok, "Intelligentsiia i revoliutsiia," in A. Blok, *Iskusstvo i revoliutsiia* (Moscow, 1979), 221.

98. P. S. Kogan, "Aleksandr Blok i revoliutsiia: Pamiati poeta," *Pechat' i revoliutsiia*, bk. 2 (August–October 1921) 5.

99. Cited in Robert C. Williams, *Artists in Revolution: Portraits of the Russian Avant-Garde, 1905–1925* (Bloomington: Indiana University Press, 1977), 137.

100. Avril Pyman, "Russian Poetry and the October Revolution," *Revolutionary Russia* 3, no. 1 (1990), 6–9.

101. Alexander Blok, *The Twelve and the Scythians*, translated by Jack Lindsay (London: Journeyman, 1982), 69.

102. Cited in Victor Erlich, *Modernism and Revolution: Russian Literature in Transition* (Cambridge: Harvard University Press, 1994), 17.

103. Cited in *Pod sozvezdiem topora: Petrograd 1917 g. Znakomyi i neznakomyi* (Moscow: Sovetskaia Rossiia, 1991), 54.

104. Gippius, *Peterburgskie dnevniki*, 192. On the persistent juxtaposition of light and darkness in the poetry and literature on revolution, see the introduction by V. A. Chalmaev to *Pod sozvezdiem topora*, 5 ff.

105. Prishvin, *Dnevnik*, 380.

106. Korolenko, "Dnevniki," 215, 216.

107. Matil'da Kshesinskaia, *Vospominaniia* (Moscow: Kul'tura, 1992), 199–200.

108. Noted in the introduction to Blok, *The Twelve*, 8. All quotations from "The Twelve" are from this volume, although I have taken the liberty of making small changes, where I thought the translation misleading.

109. Hackel, *The Poet and the Revolution*, 65.

110. Blok, "Intelligentsiia i revoliutsiia," 227.

111. Written in 1917 and cited in Andrei Sinyavsky, *Soviet Civilization: A Cultural History* (New York: Arcade, 1990), 8.

112. Natasha Templeton, "The October Revolution and the Poets," *Landfall* 21, no. 84 (1967): 386–87.

113. *Pravda*, November 3, 1917, 2.

114. *Delo naroda*, October 27, 1917, 1.

115. *Rabochaia gazeta*, October 26, 1917, 3.

116. *Novaia zhizn'*, October 26, 1917, 2.

117. *Rabochaia gazeta*, October 26, 1917, 3.

118. *Novaia zhizn'*, October 30, 1917, 2; *Delo naroda*, October 29, 1917, 1–2.

119. V. A. Amfiteatrov-Kadashev, "Iz dnevnika 1917 g.," *Literaturnaia gazeta* 29 (July 20, 1994): 6.

120. *Rabochaia gazeta,* October 27, 1917, 2.

121. P. N. Maliantovich, "V Zimnem dvortse 25–26 oktiabria 1917 g.," *Byloe* 12, June 1918, 113–14, 129.

122. *Utro Rossii,* November 14, 1917, 3.

123. *Fakel',* November 25, 1917, 2. The description that follows is drawn from this article and the following: N. R., "Pod znamenem revoliutsii," *Rabochaia gazeta,* November 1, 1917, 3; "Razgrom Zimniago dvortsa," *Delo naroda,* November 26, 1917, 3; "Orgiia v Zimnem dvortse," *Polnoch',* November 25, 1917, 2; "Orgiia v Zimnem dvortse," *V glukhuiu noch',* November 26, 1917, 3; Larisa Reisner, "V Zimnem dvortse," *Novaia zhizn',* November 11, 1917, 6.

124. Amfiteatrov-Kadashev, "Iz dnevnika 1917 g.," 6. On the rape of the women's battalion, see *Delo naroda,* November 2, 1917, 4; November 5, 1917, 4.

125. Ibid., October 28, 1917, 1.

126. Lenin, "V khvoste u monarchicheskoi burzhuazii ili vo glave revoliutsionnogo i krest'ianstva," in Lenin, *Sochineniia,* vol. 8, 166–75.

127. *Pravda,* October 27, 1917, 1.

128. Ibid., November 8, 1917, 2.

129. Ibid., October 30, 1917, 1. Even in later pitched battle with the junkers, the Bolsheviks stressed their readiness to show them revolutionary mercy and guarantee their safety if they surrendered (*Pravda,* October 30, 1917, 1).

130. *Izvestiia,* November 5, 1917, 6.

131. von Geldern, *Bolshevik Festivals,* 23.

132. Lüsebrink and Reichardt, "La prise de la Bastille," 85. The authors argue that protracted reporting in the press prior to 1789 on imprisonings in the Bastille (including such colorful touches as Alexandre Dumas's "Man in the Iron Mask") helped create this myth of the Bastille as a redoubt of tyranny (ibid., 78). They argue elsewhere that the Storming of the Bastille was, therefore, a "prophesied, expected event, predicted by philosophers and writers as a prerequisite of a new age of freedom" (Hans-Jürgen Lüsebrink and Rolf Reichardt, *Die Bastille: Zur Symbolgeschichte von Herrschaft und Freiheit* [Frankfurt-am-Main: Fischer, 1990], 259).

133. Analogies between the Bastille and Russian fortresses such as the Petropavlovsk and Schlissel'burg are not common (see Eugene Petit, *Une Bastille Russe: La Forteresse de Schlüsselbourg* [Paris, 1906]). The destruction and liberation of tsarist prisons was apparently a major feature of the February Days of 1917 (see Figes and Kolonitskii, 55–56). M. Kozlovskii recalled the taking of the prisons in Petrograd soon after the October overthrow as encountering sympathy rather than opposition from the old prison commandants ("Vospominaniia ob Oktiabr'skom perevorote," *Proletarskai revoliutsiia* 10 (1922), 67). Interestingly, the anarchist Emma Goldman in her memoirs recollected the "dread and awe" that the "heavy mass of stone, dark and sinister" of Petropavlovsk inspired in her when she arrived in Petrograd at the age of thirteen (see Emma Goldman, *My Disillusionment in Russia* [New York: Thomas Y. Crowell, 1970], 80–83). Pitirim Sorokin, an SR member of the Constituent Assembly arrested by the Bolsheviks, referred in his diary to the Petropavlovsk Fortress, where he was being held, as the "Bastille of Petrograd" (Pitirim Sorokin, *Leaves from a Russian Diary* [New York: Dutton, 1924], 118).

134. Cited in Bengt Jangfeldt, "Russian Futurism, 1917–1919," in *Art, Society, Revolution, 1917–1921,* ed. Nils Åke Nilsson (Stockholm: Almqvist and Wiksell, 1979), 123. Cf. the ambivalent place of the Bolsheviks in Vladimir Mayakovsky's early paeans to the October Revolution, e.g., "Oda revoliutsii," [Ode to Revolution], "Nash marsh" [Our March], "Geroi i zhertvy revoliutsii" [Heroes and Victims of Revolution].

135. *Pravda,* November 2, 1917, 1.

136. Ibid., December 16, 1917, 2; November 16, 1917, 1; *Petrogradskaia pravda*, September 29, 1918, 3. Cf. G. Zinov'ev, "Velikaia godovshchina: Chto zhe budet dal'she?" *God proletarskoi revoliutsii*, no. 1, November 7, 1918, 1. *Novyi luch* criticized these parallels, pointing out the shortcomings of the "state-commune" boasted by the Bolsheviks and emphasizing the inclusive nature of the Paris Commune, its universal election by all of Paris (rather than the "class organization" and election of the soviets of workers' and soldiers' deputies), the "truly revolutionary order" in Paris at the time, and the absence in the Paris Commune of the "bloody words" so often in the mouths of the Committee of Public Safety (and, the paper added, heard also within the walls of the Smolny Institute) (*Novyi luch*, December 14, 1917, 3).

137. A report on the fortunes of the Moscow Region Bureau of the RSDRP between its July and December conferences gave the impression of highly volatile support, despite the report's efforts to link support to periods of Bolshevik agitation (*Sotsial-demokrat*, December 15, 1917, 2).

138. *Rabochii put'*, October 26, 1917, 3; *Pravda*, October 31, 1917, 4; November 9, 1917, 4.

139. *Pravda*, December 2, 1917, 4. Blurring party lines, the author observed that while he had until now considered himself to be a Left SR, his sympathies to Bolshevism had long been known to the Central Committee. He had, he wrote, always voted Bolshevik as a member of the Petrograd Soviet, sided with the Bolsheviks of his locality, and sent money to the Central Committee. Cf. Martov's rueful observation in October 1918 of defections of Mensheviks, "avec les armes et les baggages," to the Bolshevik Party (letter to A. N. Stein, in *Dear Comrades: Menshevik Reports on the Bolshevik Revolution and the Civil War*, ed. Vladimir N. Brovkin [Stanford: Hoover Institution Press, 1991], 126).

140. *Rabochii put'*, October 26, 1917, 3. See also the section "Partiinaia zhizn' " in *Pravda*: October 27, 1917, 4; October 28, 1917, 4; October 31, 1917, 4; December 9, 1917, 4.

141. *Izvestiia*, November 12, 1917, 2. On further ambivalence about party labels, see ibid., November 3, 1917, 2.

142. *Rabochaia gazeta*, November 10, 1917, 2.

143. *Pravda*, November 2, 1917, 4; November 13, 1917, 4; November 16, 1917, 4.

144. *Sotsial-demokrat*, December 21, 1917, 3. E. D. Kuskova would also use the word "zoologicheski" in 1922 to describe the conduct of the "Russian Revolution," although I. A. Bunin would take issue with this term, observing that "in the animal world there is no such senseless savagery,—savagery for savagery's sake, as occurred in the human world and especially during the revolution" (I. A. Bunin, "Iz 'Vospominanii,' " in *Pod sozvezdiem topora*, 403).

145. *Izvestiia*, November 15, 1917, 1.

146. *Sotsial-demokrat*, November 1, 1917, 1.

147. Ibid., November 25, 1917, 1.

148. Ibid., November 1, 1917, 1.

149. *Pravda*, November 3, 1917, 2.

150. *Sotsial-demokrat*, October 4, 1917, 3.

151. Ibid., November 25, 1917, 1.

152. *Pravda*, November 7, 1917, 2. Cf. *Rabochaia gazeta*, November 9, 1917, 2.

153. *Sotsial-demokrat*, December 8, 1917, 2.

154. *Pravda*, December 12, 1917, 2.

155. Walter Benjamin, "The Storyteller," in *Illuminations: Essays and Reflections* (New York: Schocken, 1968), 94.

156. Catherine Merridale, *Night of Stone: Death and Memory in Russia* (London: Granta, 2000), 104–6. On the "cult of the fallen" in the February Days, see Figes and Kolonitskii, *Interpreting the Russian Revolution*, 75; Merridale, *Night of Stone*, 118–21.

157. The film in question was *The Anniversary of the Revolution* [*Godovshchina revoliutsii*] (*Pravda* 238, November 2, 1918, 3); for the draft plans for the film, see Gosudarstvennyi Arkhiv Rossiiskoi Federatsii (hereinafter GARF), f. 1235, op. 94, d. 151, ll. 291–95).

158. *Sotsial-demokrat*, November 4, 1917, 1.

159. *Pamiatnik bortsam proletarskoi revoliutsii pogibshim v 1917–1921 g.g.*, 3d ed. (Moscow-Leningrad, 1925). The first edition appeared in 1922.

160. *Pravda*, November 11, 1917, 4; *Izvestiia*, November 2, 1917, 8.

161. *Den'*, November 17, 1917, 1; *Novyi den'*, November 19, 1917, 1; *Polnoch'*, November 24, 1917, 1; November 25, 1917, 1; *Den'*, December 2, 1917, 1. The Bolshevik press also published the contributions donated to families of fallen sailors by the crews of various naval vessels (*Pravda*, December 8, 1917, 4).

162. This description is drawn from *Sotsial-demokrat*, November 9, 1917, 4; *Gazeta dlia vsekh*, November 12, 1917, 2.

163. The original slogan, *Zhertvam-predvestnikam mirovoi sotsial'noi revoliutsii* [To the Victim-Heralds of the World Social Revolution], captured in a filming of the funeral, found its way into John Reed's work as "To The Martyrs of the Avant-garde of the World Socialist Revolution" (*Muchenikam avangarda mirovoi sotsialisticheskoi revoliutsii*) (V. S. Listov, "Priemy istochnikovedcheskogo analiza kinoskriptov dokumental'nogo kino perioda Oktiabr'skoi revoliutsii i grazhdanskoi voiny," in *Trudy Moskovskogo Gosudarstvennogo Istoriko-Arkhivnogo Instituta*, vol. 24, *Voprosy istochnikoveniia istorii SSSR, vyp. 2* [Moscow,-1966], 247). As we shall see, the change from victims to martyrs, from heralds to avantgarde, and from social to socialist revolution in Reed's memory were the product of the evolving narrative of October over the next few years.

164. Figes and Kolonitskii, *Interpreting the Russian Revolution*, 63–64.

165. *Pravda*, November 18, 1917, 3.

166. Ibid., November 21, 1917, 2.

167. *Sotsial-demokrat*, November 10, 1917, 3.

168. Cited in *Storming the Heavens: Voices of October*, ed. Mark Jones (London: Atlantic Highlands, 1987), 136.

169. *Pravda*, November 9, 1917, 4. Cf. ibid., November 24, 1917, 3.

170. *Izvestiia*, December 19, 1917, 6.

171. *Delo naroda*, November 11, 1917, 4; *Gazeta dlia vsekh*, November 14, 1917, 3.

172. *Gazeta dlia vsekh*, November 12, 1917, 2.

173. *Rabochaia gazeta*, November 7, 1917, 4; *Edinstvo*, November 8, 1917, 4; *Delo naroda*, November 8, 1917, 3.

174. *Gazeta dlia vsekh*, November 14, 1917, 3; November 12, 1917, 2; *Utro Rossii*, November 14, 1917, 3.

175. The citation refers to the funerals of the Bolsheviks V. Volodarskii and M. S. Uritskii, killed in Petrograd in the summer of 1918 (Merridale, *Night of Stone*, 182). Cf. the obituary of Vera Slutskaia, a long-standing member of the RSDRP, written as a litany of tribulations at the hands of the tsars and eventual death from "the traitorous hands of this adventurist [Kerensky]" (actually by a shell fired from Kerensky's armored train) (*Izvestiia*, November 2, 1917, 1).

176. Louise Bryant, *Six Red Months in Russia: An Observer's Account of Russia before and during the Proletarian Dictatorship* (New York: George H. Doran, 1918), 191, 188–89. Foreign observers often failed to see the organized aspect of the red funerals: "It was so simple, so spontaneous and so elemental. It came straight out of the heart of the people" (Albert Rhys Williams, *Through the Russian Revolution* [New York: Boni and Liveright, 1921], 258).

177. *Pravda*, November 21, 1917, 2.

178. *Novaia zhizn'*, November 8, 1917, 2. On these kinds of rumors, see Iarov, *Gorozhanin*, 29–31. Cf. the role of rumors in changing popular attitudes toward the monarchy prior to 1917 (Figes and Kolonitskii, *Interpreting the Russian Revolution*, chap. 1).

179. *Sotsial-demokrat*, November 19, 1917, 1; November 21, 1917, 3. His position was endorsed by the editorial board in a footnote.

180. Trouillot, *Silencing the Past*, 158, n. 4.

CHAPTER 2: THE DRAMA OF POWER

1. *Bor'ba*, November 10, 1917, 4. On the rising sense of panic among Bolshevik critics, see *Rabochaia gazeta*, November 1, 1917, 1; November 9, 1917, 2.

2. A. V. Blium, *Za kulisami "Ministerstva pravdy": Tainaia istoriia sovetskoi tsenzury, 1917–1929* (St. Petersburg: Akademicheskii proekt, 1994), 34–41.

3. *Sotsial-demokrat*, October 31, 1917, 1. This particular ban was lifted several days later, see ibid., November 8, 1917, 1. Arguments that the bourgeois press in 1917 had also periodically repressed the fledgling socialist press were also a regular feature (ibid., November 9, 1917, 1).

4. *The Debate on Soviet Power: Minutes of the All-Russian Central Executive Committee of Soviets, Second Convocation, October 1917–January 1918*, ed. John L. H. Keep (Oxford: Clarendon, 1979), 70.

5. *Rabochaia gazeta*, October 28, 1917, 1.

6. *Sotsial-demokrat*, November 3, 1917, 1; *Pravda*, October 29, 1917, 2; November 5, 1917, 1; *Sotsial-demokrat*, November 5, 1917, 1; *Pravda*, December 10, 1917, 1.

7. On the oppression of the Mensheviks, and their internal inability to muster meaningful political responses to the Bolsheviks, see Vladimir N. Brovkin, *The Mensheviks after October: Socialist Opposition and the Rise of the Bolshevik Dictatorship* (Ithaca: Cornell University Press, 1987), 298; also Vera Broido, *Lenin and the Mensheviks: The Persecution of Socialists under Bolshevism* (Aldershot, England: Gower/Maurice Temple Smith, 1987); S. P. Mel'gunov, *Krasnyi terror v Rossii* (New York: Brandy, 1979). On the Soviet approach to Bolshevik censorship as a necessary and legitimate response to "bourgeois slander," see A. Z. Okorokov, *Oktiabr' i krakh russkoi burzhuaznoi pressy* (Moscow, 1970). For examples of the post-Soviet approach that come closer to the above Western attitude, see Blium, *Za kulisami "Ministerstva pravdy"*; E. G. Gimpel'son, *Formirovanie sovetskoi politicheskoi sistemy, 1917–1923 gg.* (Moscow: Nauka, 1995).

8. On the constructive intent of censors, see Michael Holquist, "Corrupt Originals: The Paradox of Censorship," PMLA (January 1994): 22.

9. Richard Stites attributes to this failure, along with prolonged fighting in Moscow and the still tentative nature of Soviet power outside of the capitals, the absence of "spontaneous," festive celebrations of October (of the kind seen in the February "Days of Revolution" celebrations) (*Revolutionary Dreams: Utopian Vision and Experimental Life in the Russian Revolution* [Oxford: Oxford University Press, 1989], 83).

10. Orlando Figes, *Peasant Russia, Civil War: The Volga Countryside in Revolution, 1917–1921* (Oxford: Clarendon Press, 1989). On the Civil War in general, Evan Mawdsley, *The Russian Civil War* (Boston: Allen and Unwin, 1987).

11. Peter Holquist, " 'Information Is the Alpha and Omega of Our Work': Bolshevik Surveillance in Its Pan-European Context," *Journal of Modern History* 69 (September 1997): 435.

12. Raleigh, *Experiencing Russia's Civil War*, 94, 105.

13. Vladimir Brovkin, "The Mensheviks' Political Comeback: The Elections to the Provincial City Soviets in Spring 1918," *Russian Review* 42, no. 1 (1983): 1–50; *Men'sheviki*

v bol'shevistskoi Rossii, 1918–1924. Men'sheviki v 1918 g. ed. Ziva Galili and Al'bert Nen-arokov (Moscow: ROSSPEN, 1999); Brovkin, The Mensheviks after October; idem., "Workers' Unrest and the Bolsheviks' Response in 1919," *Slavic Review* 49, no. 3 (1990): 350–73.

14. Raleigh, *Experiencing*, 110.

15. Daniel Peris, *Storming the Heavens: The Soviet League of the Militant Godless* (Ithaca: Cornell University Press, 1998), 1–2; Elizabeth A. Wood, *The Baba and the Comrade: Gender and Politics in Revolutionary Russia* (Bloomington: Indiana University Press, 1997); Stites, *Revolutionary Dreams*; James C. McClelland, "The Utopian and the Heroic: Divergent Paths to the Communist Educational Ideal," in *Bolshevik Culture: Experiment and Order in the Russian Revolution*, ed. Abbott Gleason, Peter Kenez, and Richard Stites (Blooming-ton: Indiana University Press, 1985), esp. 114–30.

16. Christopher A. P. Binns, "The Changing Face of Power: Revolution and Accom-modation in the Development of the Soviet Ceremonial System: Part I," *Man* (N.S.) 14 (1979): 588–89; Jennifer McDowell, "Soviet Civil Ceremonies," *Journal for the Scientific Study of Religion* 13, no. 3 (1974): 165–279.

17. Robert Service, *The Bolshevik Party in Revolution, 1917–1923: A Study in Organisa-tional Change* (Basingstoke, England: Macmillan, 1979); esp. chaps. 4 and 5; K. Shelavin, "Ubyl' ili usilenie?" *God proletarskoi revoliutsii* 1, November 7, 1918, 3.

18. *Pravda*, January 3, 1918, 1.

19. *Sed'moi s"ezd Rossiiskoi Kommunisticheskoi Partii: Stenograficheskii otchet 6–8–go marta 1918 g.* (Moscow-Petrograd, 1923), 10–12, 58.

20. "Iz arkhivov partii," *Izvestiia TsK KPSS* 4, 1989, 148-49.

21. Tsentr Dokumentatsii Noveishei Istorii Iaroslavskoi Oblasti [hereinafter TsDNIIaO]," f. 394, op. 1, d. 30, ll.28–29. Also, *Izvestiia TsK KPSS* 4 (1989), 150–51; *Pravda*, November 9, 1918, 4.

22. *Pravda*, June 6, 1918, 1.

23. *Vos'moi s"ezd RKP (b): 18-23 marta 1919 g.* (Moscow, 1933), 166, 169, 170, 178-79, 167.

24. A. Lunacharskii, "Prazdnik nashei partii," *God proletarskoi revoliutsii* 1, November 7, 1918, 1. Cf. the attitudes of discomfort toward party members expressed during the Civil War years in S. Fedorchenko, *Narod na voine* (Moscow, 1990), 154. Thanks to Michael Gorham for pointing this out.

25. *Sed'moi s"ezd Rossiiskoi Kommunisticheskoi Partii*, 176.

26. *Sed'moi s"ezd*, 179. For similar reasons, Iurii Larin proposed retaining the word "worker [*rabochaia*]" in the name, because this was a "quality [of our party] we in no way want to hide" (177).

27. G. Zinov'ev, *Chego khotiat sotsial-demokraty bol'sheviki? (V voprosakh i otvetakh)* (Moscow, 1918), 3.

28. G. Zinov'ev, *Bespartiinyi ili kommunist?* (Petrograd, 1919), 5, 7. For more on popular negative perceptions of Bolsheviks and Communists, see S. K. Minin, *Kto takie kommunisty?* (Moscow, 1919), 3.

29. Zinov'ev, *Bespartiinyi ili kommunist?* 7.

30. Zinov'ev, *Chego khotiat sotsial-demokraty bol'sheviki?* (Moscow, 1918), 3. Cf. the discussion of Bolshevik Party history as a function of its historical and ideological differences with the Mensheviks and the Right SRs in B. Shumiatskii, *Chego khotiat bol'sheviki? (K program partii)* (n.p., 1919).

31. von Geldern, *Bolshevik Festivals*, 28, 72. On Proletkult, see Lynn Mally, *Culture of the Future: the Proletkult Movement in Revolutionary Russia* (Berkeley: University of Cali-fornia Press, 1990).

32. Stefan Plaggenborg, *Revolutionskultur: Menschenbilder und Kulturelle Praxis in Sowjetrussland zwischen Oktoberrevolution und Stalinismus* (Cologne: Böhlau, 1996), 274–75.

33. Christel Lane, *The Rites of Rulers: Ritual in Industrial Society—The Soviet Case* (Cambridge: Cambridge University Press, 1981), 25.

34. Florencia E. Mallon, *Peasant and Nation: The Making of Postcolonial Mexico and Peru* (Berkeley: University of California Press, 1995), 283.

35. Such redefinition of social relations was continued throughout the 1920s, as Katerina Clark argues, in the "proletarianization" and "sovietization" of intellectual life ("The 'Quiet Revolution' in Soviet Intellectual Life," in *Russia in the Era of NEP: Explorations in Soviet Society and Culture,* ed. Sheila Fitzpatrick, Alexander Rabinowitch, and Richard Stites [Bloomington: Indiana University Press, 1991], 210-30).

36. von Geldern, *Bolshevik Festivals,* 177.

37. The quote refers specifically to the way in which censorship is used by "the powerful" not only to restrict "the powerless," but also to "inform and instruct" them. The insight has wider application to other manifestations of power (Sue Curry Jansen, *Censorship: The Knot That Binds Power and Knowledge* [Oxford: Oxford University Press, 1988], 7).

38. Claudio Fogu is referring to the tightly regimented fiftieth anniversary celebration of the death of the hero of the Italian Risorgimento, Giuseppe Garibaldi (Claudio Fogu, "Fascism and Historic Representation: The 1932 Garibaldian Celebrations," *Journal of Contemporary History* 31 [1996]: 319).

39. On the common practice of filming these events, see V. S. Listov, "Priemy istochnikovedcheskogo analiza kinoskriptov dokumental'nogo kino perioda Oktiabr'skoi Revoliutsii i grazhdanskoi voiny," in *Trudy Moskovskogo Gosudarstvennogo Istoriko-Arkhivnogo Instituta,* vol. 24, *Voprosy istochnikovedeniia istorii SSSR, Vyp. 2* (Moscow, 1966), 235–49. They were staples of the regular newsreels directed by Dziga Vertov under the title *Kinonedelia (Sovetskaia kinokhronika 1918–1925 gg. Annotirovannyi katalog. 1 chast'* [Moscow, 1965], 8–38).

40. Cf. Michel Hastings, "Identité culturelle locale et politique festive communiste: Halluin la Rouge, 1920–1934," *Le Mouvement social* 139 (April–June 1987): 7–25.

41. On the celebrations in Saratov Province, see Raleigh, *Experiencing Russia's Civil War,* 215 ff. On the spread of committees throughout Russia charged with organizing local celebrations, see *Pravda,* November 1, 1918, 4; *Izvestiia,* October 27, 1918, 6.

42. *Pravda,* November 1, 1918, 3; *Izvestiia,* October 24, 1918, 6; *Zhizn' iskusstva* 3, October 31, 1918, 5.

43. *Pravda,* November 5, 1918, 4.

44. Cited in Iarov, *Gorozhanin,* 31.

45. *Izvestiia,* October 29, 1918, 6.

46. *Pravda,* November 1, 1918, 3.

47. *Izvestiia,* November 2, 1918, 6.

48. *Pravda,* November 1, 1918, 3.

49. Ibid., October 31, 1918, 3.

50. *Izvestiia,* October 31, 1918, 6. The distribution of food and presents, especially for children, was also a priority in the provinces (*Pravda,* November 1, 1918, 4).

51. *Izvestiia,* November 2, 1918, 2.

52. Ibid., October 30, 1918, 6.

53. *Pravda,* November 2, 1918, 3; *Izvestiia,* November 2, 1918, 6; *Zhizn' iskusstva* 5, November 2, 1918, 5.

54. *Zhizn' iskusstva* 4, November 1, 1918, 4. Also, *Pravda,* November 1, 1918, 3; *Izvestiia,* November 3, 1918, 5.

55. *Petrogradskaia pravda,* November 5, 1918, 2.

56. *Izvestiia*, November 2, 1918, 6. One of the plays planned was Rollands' *The Taking of the Bastille*.

57. *Pravda*, November 5, 1918, 3.

58. *Izvestiia*, October 29, 1918, 6. Also ibid., November 2, 1918, 6.

59. *Pravda*, October 29, 1918, 4.

60. One especially large mass meeting, it was announced, would feature Lev Kamenev, Aleksei Rykov, Iakov Sverdlov, Iurii Steklov, Emel'ian Iaroslavskii, N. Osinskii, Aleksandra Kollontai, and many others (*Pravda*, October 31, 1918, 1; also announced in *Izvestiia* on October 31 and November 1, 1918, 1).

61. *Zhizn' iskusstva* 9, November 9, 1918, 2.

62. See *Pravda*, November 1, 1918, 1; November 3, 1918, 1; November 10, 1918, 1; November 14, 1918, 2.

63. V. Bystrianskii, "Oktiabr'skaia revoliutsiia—velichaishee sobytie v mirovoi istorii," *God proletarskoi revoliutsii* 1, November 7, 1918, 1. See also G. Zinov'ev, "Velikaia godovshchina: Chto zhe budet dal'she?" ibid.

64. Vatin [V. Bystrianskii], "Oktiabr'skaia godovshchina—prazdnik mezhdunarodnogo proletariata," *God proletarskoi revoliutsii* 1, November 7, 1918, 1.

65. *Izvestiia*, November 10, 1918, 4.

66. von Geldern, *Bolshevik Festivals*, 73.

67. *Izvestiia TsIK* (April 14, 1918), 3; L. I. Koroleva, "Dokumenty TsGAOR SSSR o Leninskom plane monumental'noi propagandy (1918–1920 g.)," *Sovetskie arkhivy* 2 (1977): 16–19. Also Catriona Kelly, "Iconoclasm and Commemorating the Past," in *Constructing Russian Culture in the Age of Revolution: 1881–1940*, ed. Catriona Kelly and David Shepherd (Oxford: Oxford University Press, 1998), 227–37.

68. Hunt examines the hierarchical network of revolutionary officials in France established between 1792 and 1794 specifically to teach the public how to read the "new symbolic text of revolution." She also traces changes in the meanings of various symbols over time, for example the remaking of the figure of Hercules between 1789 and 1799 from a symbol of the monarchy to a symbol of the people (Hunt, *Politics, Culture, and Class*, 94–116). The Taking of the Bastille was also refashioned in the same period from the epitome of brutality into the "key founding event of national identity" (Lüsebrink and Reichardt, "La Prise de la Bastille," esp. 29–47).

69. *Izvestiia*, November 2, 1918, 6. See also *Pravda*, November 3, 1918, 3; *Izvestiia*, November 6, 1918, 9. Typical was the article written eulogizing Rodin, whose art "directly contradicted the decrepit bourgeois art and pathetic attempts of the innovators, the slaves of the bourgeois world" (*Izvestiia*, November 9, 1917, 3).

70. *Pravda*, November 9, 1918, 3

71. "V krasnom Pitere (Vpechatleniia)," *God proletarskoi revoliutsii* 3, November 9, 1918, 4.

72. *Pravda*, November 1, 1918, 3.

73. Cited in "Pervaia godovshchina Oktiabr'skoi revoliutsii: Dokumenty," *Istoriia SSSR* 6 (1987): 126.

74. "Pereimenovanie ulits," *God proletarskoi revoliutsii* 2, November 8, 1918, 3.

75. "Oktiabr'skie torzhestva v Moskve (Po telefonu)," *God proletarskoi revoliutsii* 3, November 9, 1918, 1.

76. *Izvestiia*, October 25, 1918, 2; *God proletarskoi revoliutsii* 2, November 8, 1918, 3; 3, November 9, 1918, 4.

77. Victoria Bonnell examines the varying use of color in Soviet political posters, noting the contrast between the heavy reds and blacks of wartime iconography with the more muted pastel colors of less militant periods (Victoria E. Bonnell, *Iconography of Power:*

Soviet Political Posters under Lenin and Stalin [Berkeley: University of California Press, 1997], 258).

78. *God proletarskoi revoliutsii* 2, November 8, 1918, 4.

79. Ibid. 1, November 7, 1918, 1.

80. Ibid. 3, November 9, 1918, 4.

81. *Zhizn' iskusstva* 4, November 1, 1918, 4.

82. *God proletarskoi revoliutsii* 2, November 8, 1918, 3.

83. For the published routes, see ibid. 1, November 7, 1918, 1.

84. Ibid. 2, November 8, 1918, 3.

85. *Pravda*, November 1, 1918, 3.

86. Ibid., November 5, 1918, 4.

87. Ibid., November 2, 1918, 3.

88. Ibid., November 1, 1918, 3.

89. Ibid., November 5, 1918, 4.

90. For examples of the slogans, see *Pravda*, November 1, 1918, 1; November 2, 1918, 1; November 5, 1918, 1; for slogans suggested by the Moscow Council of Trade Unions, see *Pravda*, November 2, 1918, 3; November 5, 1918, 4.

91. *God proletarskoi revoliutsii* 1, November 7, 1918, 1.

92. Cited in "Pervaia godovshchina," 131.

93. The workers' commission in the Palace of Labor (*Dvorets Truda*), for example, "finally" decided to decorate the Square of the Uprising (*Ploshchad' Vosstaniia*) "where the first Russian Revolution began" (*Zhizn' iskusstva* 284–85, November 5, 1919, 3). Also *Pravda*, November 6, 1919, 4.

94. A competition was announced by the Artistic Section of the Trade Union of Workers of the Arts (*Profsoiuz rabotnikov iskusstv*) in Petrograd involving eighteen artists and architects who were to come up with draft plans to decorate Smolny, the Square of the Uprising, and the Square of the Victims of the Revolution (*Ploshchad' Zhertv Revoliutsii*). Four other artists were to design posters, the best to be awarded monetary prizes (*Zhizn' iskusstva* 268, October 15, 1919, 3). Other projects included the making of ceremonial plates bearing such unwieldy slogans as "Every time that a great idea penetrates the consciousness of the age, it spreads around the same horror that is spat out on the streets and in the market" (*Zhizn' iskusstva* 267, October 14, 1919, 3).

95. *Krasnaia gazeta*, November 5, 1919, 4.

96. Ibid., November 7, 1919, 1.

97. *Pravda*, November 6, 1919, 4; *Krasnaia gazeta*, November 5, 1919, 4. Ten thousand rubles were assigned by the Organizing Committee to the regions for the children's meal (*Petrogradskaia* pravda, November 7, 1919, 4).

98. *Krasnaia gazeta*, November 5, 1919: 4; November 7, 1919, 4.

99. *Petrogradskaia pravda*, November 9, 1919, 2. For the planned routes of the processions, see November 6, 1919, 1.

100. Ibid., November 6, 1919, 1.

101. Cf. "Forward to victory over all enemies of the Communist revolution," "Hunger, cold, and the ruin of the economy we will vanquish only through the friendly work of female and male workers" (*Pravda*, November 6, 1919, 4, 3).

102. *Petrogradskaia pravda*, October 26, 1919, 2; *Krasnaia gazeta*, November 7, 1919, 6.

103. *Pravda*, October 31, 1919, 1; November 6, 1919, 1; November 7, 1919, 2.

104. *Petrogradskaia pravda*, November 7, 1919, 1. Trotsky also placed the city center stage (*Pravda*, November 7, 1919, 1).

105. *Petrogradskaia pravda*, November 7, 1919, 1.

106. *Pravda*, November 7, 1919, 1. Also *Petrogradskaia pravda*, November 7, 1919, 4; *Pravda*, November 7, 1919, 3; *Krasnaia gazeta*, November 9, 1919, 1.

107. *Krasnaia gazeta*, November 9, 1919, 1.

108. Raleigh, *Experiencing Russia's Civil War*, 222.

109. Binns, "The Changing Face of Power," 588. For a more nuanced evaluation of the difficulties of discerning popular reactions to the 1918 celebrations, see von Geldern, *Bolshevik Festivals*, 97–102.

110. *Pravda*, November 9, 1918, 3. The object of one such symbolic burning was apparently a dummy representing a kulak (*Izvestiia*, November 9, 1918, 5). A particularly ambitious example of such a burning in Moscow's Dinamo Stadium involved hundreds of (Young) Pioneers attacking a gigantic scarecrow representing the enemies of the Soviet Union (Nicolas Evreinoff, *Histoire du théatre Russe* [Paris: Éditions du Chêne, 1947], 425).

111. *God proletarskoi revoliutsii* 1, November 7, 1918, 5.

112. Ibid. 3, November 9, 1918, 4.

113. *Izvestiia*, November 9, 1918, 5.

114. Ibid., November 10, 1918, 7.

115. "Nastroenie mass v dni prazdnika," *God proletarskoi revoliutsii* 3, November 9, 1918, 1. The "ordinary man in the street [*obyvatel'*]," who had hidden during the May demonstrations of the proletariat, was also included in this category of people who were involuntarily caught up in the atmosphere (*Izvestiia*, November 9, 1918, 5).

116. "V Krasnom Pitere (Vpechatleniia)," *God proletarskoi revoliutsii* 3, November 9, 1918, 4.

117. *Pravda*, November 12, 1918, 1. Cf. A. Vyborgskaia, "Nash prazdnik," *God proletarskoi revoliutsii* 2, November 8, 1918, 1; A. Lunacharskii, "Prazdnik," ibid. 1, November 7, 1918, 2; *Krasnaia gazeta*, November 9, 1919, 2.

118. *Gazeta dlia vsekh*, December 19, 1917, 1.

119. "V velikie dni," *God proletarskoi revoliutsii* 3, November 9, 1918, 1. Cf. the references to people "sniggering" at the worn and tattered red banners that had been hanging outside of Petrograd buildings for the entire year (*Krasnaia gazeta*, November 12, 1918, 4).

120. *Time of Troubles: The Diary of Iurii Vladimirovich Got'e*, edited and translated by Terence Emmons (Princeton: Princeton University Press, 1988), 209, 211.

121. John Pollock, *The Bolshevik Adventure* (London: Constable, 1919), 128–30.

122. *Time of Troubles*, 315–16.

123. Soviet historians measured the artistic products of this time by their success or failure in conveying the necessary revolutionary elements. One scholar criticized certain elements of the celebrations—for example, the revolutionary panels "The Storming of the Winter Palace" by V. Volkov and "Revolution" by I. Vladimirov—precisely for their lack of "poster gaudiness and festive emotional expressiveness." Typically, the author attributed the "facelessness of the images" of this first anniversary to the fact that too little time had passed since the October Revolution for the artists to "come to a deep understanding of the essence of the events that had taken place" (O. Nemiro, *V gorod prishel prazdnik: Iz istorii khudozhestvennogo oformleniia sovetskikh massovykh prazdnestv* [Leningrad, 1973], 22 and 24).

124. *Iskusstvo kommuny* 1, December 7, 1918, 2; also *Plamia* 35, January 5, 1919, 11.

125. *Plamia* 35, January 5, 1919, 11; similar sentiments were expressed by V. Kerzhentsev in an unpublished manuscript dated February 10, 1919 (see "Iz stat'i V. Kerzhentseva 'Uprek khudozhnikam,' " reproduced in *Agitatsionno-massovoe iskusstvo: Oformlenie prazdnestv* [Moscow, 1984], 83–84). For a discussion of the various new manifestations of post-October art, see *Tvorchestvo* 10–11, 1919, 38–45.

126. *Iskusstvo kommuny* 2, December 15, 1918, 1–2.

127. For more on this, see Nils Åke Nilsson, "Spring 1918: The Arts and the Commissars," in *Art, Society, Revolution, 1917–1921*, ed. Nils Åke Nilsson, 9–53.

128. von Geldern, *Bolshevik Festivals*, 93. On artistic disputes in the realm of the theater, see Katerina Clark, *Petersburg: Crucible of Cultural Revolution* (Cambridge: Harvard University Press, 1995), chap. 4; on disputes pertaining to the 1918 anniversary celebrations, see von Geldern, *Bolshevik Festivals*, 93–102.

129. Clark, *Petersburg*, 100–101.

130. For example, Bengt Jangfeldt, "Russian Futurism, 1917–1919," in *Art, Society, Revolution, 1917–1921*, 111.

131. *Partiinoe Soveshchanie R. S-D R. P 27 dekabria 1918 g.—1 ianvaria 1919 g. Rezoliutsii* (Moscow, 1919), 4.

132. *Petrogradskaia pravda*, November 5, 1918, 2.

133. V. V. Maiakovskii, "*Misteriia-Buff: Geroicheskoe, epicheskoe, i satiricheskoe izobrazhenie nashei epokhi*," in *Sobranie sochinenii v vos'mi tomakh*, vol. 1 (Moscow, 1968), 258.

134. For a description of the plot, see *Zhizn' iskusstva* 1, October 29, 1918, 4. For interesting discussions of the aesthetics and style of the play, see von Geldern, *Bolshevik Festivals*, 63–71; Clark, *Petersburg*, 116–17.

135. von Geldern, *Bolshevik Festivals*, 67–68.

136. Cited in Clark, *Petersburg*, 117. On the "popular" reception of the play, especially its "inaccessibility," see Aleksandr Fevral'skii, *Pervaia sovetskaia p"esa: 'Misteriia-buff' V. V. Maiakovskogo* (Moscow, 1971), 62 ff.

137. von Geldern, *Bolshevik Festivals*, 63–64.

138. Bonnell, *Iconography of Power*, 27–28.

139. *God proletarskoi revoliutsii* 1, November 7, 1918, 8.

140. *Petrogradskaia pravda*, September 22, 1918, 2; *Izvestiia*, October 25, 1918, 1.

141. *God proletarskoi revoliutsii* 1, November 7, 1918, 2. The author accused those who had earlier opposed the new revolutionary regime of long-standing emptiness and lack of commitment, best illustrated by their calls during the elections to the Constituent Assembly to choose "For God's sake, not the Bolsheviks."

142. Requests from 1919 to 1920 from non-Bolshevik radicals (including internationalists, revolutionary Communists, SRs, Mensheviks, and so on) for resources to publish their own newspapers and collections of articles, for permission to speak at mass meetings or agitate at the front, for permission to teach at Moscow State University, were considered, and often rejected, at the highest levels of the Communist Party, namely the Politburo (*Rossiiskii Gosudarstvennyi Arkhiv Sotsial'no-Politicheskoi Istorii* (hereinafter RGASPI), f. 17, op. 3, d. 4, ll. 1–2; d. 5, l. 2; d. 6, l. 3; d. 29, l. 1; d. 33, ll. 1–2; d. 37, ll. 1–3; d. 43, l. 1; d. 48, l. 3; d. 49, l. 1; d. 58, l. 3; d. 75, l. 2; d. 84, l. 1; d. 85, l. 2; d. 88, l. 3; d. 89, l. 3; d. 108, l. 2; d. 125, l. 2).

143. On political passivity and the prevalence of nonparty sentiments in the plants and factories of Petrograd between 1917 and 1921, see Iarov, *Gorozhanin*, 24, 86–88; Iarov, *Proletarii*, 6 ff, 53–55, 62; T. L. Levina, "Pervye bespartiinye krest'ianskie konferentsii (po materialam Permskoi i Ekaterinburgskoi gubernii)," *Permskii Gosudarstvennyi Universitet im. A. M. Gor'kogo. Uchenye zapiski* 133 (1965), 30–56.

144. *Petrogradskaia pravda*, September 21, 1918, 1.

145. Ibid. 212, September 29, 1918, 4; see also I. V. Potemkin, "K nesoznatel'nomu tovarishchu," *Iaroslavskii sbornik* (November 7, 1918), 18; Vlad. Korolev, "Eto—Ia!" ibid., 23.

146. *Krasnaia gazeta*, November 30, 1918, 4.

147. *Petrogradskaia pravda*, November 1, 1919, 1.

148. *Pravda*, November 4, 1919, 1. In this vein, see ibid., November 2, 1919, 1; November 11, 1919, 1. For a folksy tale of exemplary courage and bravery by Communist Red Army men during an attack on Iudenich, see *Petrogradskaia pravda*, December 7, 1919, 1. Also, the Red Army soldier and Communist were explicitly linked in an article about the upsurge of popular poetry as a sign of a "revolution in consciousness" since October 1917: one such poem was written by a Red Army man who used the pseudonym "Kommunist" who was "evidently proud of this probably recently acquired name" (*Ural'skii rabochii*, November 7, 1919, supplement p. 6).

149. *Izvestiia*, November 6, 1919, 2. The author added that Bolshevik members of the soviet executive committees (*ispolkomy*) broke down according to party membership as follows: 4 percent had a pre-1905 pedigree, 18 percent had worked underground between 1905 and 1917, 14 percent joined after February but before October 1917, 65 percent joined after October (ibid.). For a similar linkage of trade union good fortunes to the party, see *Petrogradskaia pravda*, November 7, 1919, 2. By contrast, compare the brochure on the gains of the three years since October 1917 as a function of "Soviet power" with scarcely a mention of the party (V. I. Nevskii, *Kak obrazovalas' sovetskaia vlast' i chto eiu sdelano za tri goda* [Moscow, 1920]).

150. A. Terne, *V tsarstve Lenina: Ocherki sovremennoi zhizni v RSFSR.* (Berlin: Izd. Ol'gi D'iakovoi i K-o., 1922), 64.

151. *Pravda*, October 14, 1919, 2.

152. *Ural'skii rabochii*, November 7, 1919, supplement p. 2.

153. *Petrogradskaia pravda*, October 30, 1919, 1. See also Minin, *Kto takie kommunisty?* Such appeals to the uncommitted even included the "evangelical Christians," of which there were several thousand in Petrograd, whom the Bolsheviks referred to as "sectarian Communists" (*Petrogradskaia pravda*, November 11, 1919, 4).

154. *Pravda*, November 6, 1919, 3.

155. *Ural'skii rabochii*, November 7, 1919, supplement p. 6.

156. Ibid., November 7, 1919, supplement p. 2. For similar sentiments, see *Pravda*, October 31, 1919, 1; November 7, 1919, 3.

CHAPTER 3: APOTHEOSIS OF OCTOBER

1. Leonard Schapiro, *The Origin of the Communist Autocracy. Political Opposition in the Soviet State. First Phase, 1917–1922* (Cambridge: Harvard University Press, 1966), 108–10, 235–52; Charles Bettelheim, *Class Struggles in the USSR. First Period: 1917–1923* (New York: Monthly Review, 1976), 156–59.

2. On these intraparty conflicts, see Daniels, *Conscience of the Revolution*, chaps. 4 and 5.

3. *Deviataia konferentsiia RKP(b), Sentiabr' 1920 g. Protokoly* (Moscow, 1972), 139–67.

4. L. Trotskii, "Oktiabr'skaia revoliutsiia (broshiura 1918 g.)," in *Sochineniia*, vol. 3, pt. 2 [Moscow, n.d.], 257, 263–64. The brochure was quickly translated and published by Western socialists as Leon Trotzky, *From October to Brest-Litovsk* (New York: Socialist Publication Society, 1919).

5. Trotskii, "Oktiabr'skaia revoliutsiia," 259. In the emigration, he had devoted much of his publicist energies to nonpartisan agitation among local workers inside Russia. Similarly, his Inter-District Organization (Mezhraionka) that existed from 1913–1917 was intended to bridge the divide between the leaders (*verkhy*) and the rank and file (*nizy*).

6. Ibid., 275.

7. Ibid., 265.

8. Ibid., 288.

9. N. Bukharin and E. Preobrazhensky, *The ABC of Communism*, ed. E. H. Carr (Harmondsworth, England: Pelican, 1970), 215.

10. Ibid., 63–64.

11. N. Lenin, "Detskaia bolezn' 'levizny' v kommunizme," in *Sochineniia*, vol. 25, 3d ed. (Moscow-Leningrad, 1929), 174–75, 180–81. Cf. the inexorable development of the Bolshevik Party in defined stages from 1902 to 1917 offered in G. Zinov'ev, "V. I. Lenin i nasha partiia," *Petrogradskaia pravda*, April 23, 1920, 1.

12. Leon Trotsky, *My Life* (New York: Pathfinder, 1970), 213.

13. Lenin, "Detskaia bolezn'," 181.

14. This rewriting signaled a reevaluation of the Paris Commune, its failure now attributed to the absence of a strong guiding party (i.e., like the Bolshevik Party). For example, see the special issue devoted to the Paris Commune, *Krasnoarmeets* 36–38, 1920, esp. 14.

15. Nina Tumarkin, *Lenin Lives! The Lenin Cult in Soviet Russia* (Cambridge: Harvard University Press, 1983), chap. 3.

16. M. Khodorovskii, *Partiinye i bespartiinye* (Kazan', 1920), 20, 28. Also *Pravda*, December 24, 1920, 1; December 26, 1920, 2.

17. *Petrogradskaia pravda*, November 14, 1920, 4; November 23, 1920, 4; *Pravda*, November 21, 1920, 4; December 19, 1920, 4. Even the writer Lev Tolstoy was deemed by *Izvestiia* to have "declared himself a fervent supporter of communism" in a letter of support he had sent to the *dukhobors*, a persecuted Russian religious sect that had fled to Canada in the late nineteenth century and had "in tsarism practiced communism in their lives" (*Izvestiia*, November 24, 1920, 1).

18. Hostile foreign newspaper reports attesting to this were excerpted in the official press (e.g., *Izvestiia*, November 6, 1920, 3).

19. Ibid., November 6, 1920, 2; November 7, 1920, 1; *Pravda*, November 7, 1920, 3; October 29, 1920, 1; *Izvestiia*, November 6, 1920, 2, 3.

20. *Izvestiia*, November 3, 1920, 2.

21. A Red Army theater group staged *The Fall of the Autocracy* in March 1919 in Petrograd, reprising it 250 times over the next seven months at various venues around the city (Stites, *Revolutionary Dreams*, 94).

22. Michel Aucouturier, "Theatricality as a Category of Early Twentieth-Century Russian Culture," in *Theater and Literature in Russia, 1900–1930: A Collection of Essays*, ed. Lars Kleberg and Nils Åke Nilsson (Stockholm: Almqvist and Wiksell, 1984), 18.

23. On the divergent trends among these radical artists, see Julie A. Cassiday, *The Enemy on Trial: Early Soviet Courts on Stage and Screen* (DeKalb: Northern Illinois University Press, 2000), 10–19; Lars Kleberg, "Vjaceslav Ivanov and the Idea of Theater," in *Theater and Literature in Russia, 1900–1930*, 57–70. On the limits of "Theatrical October," see Konstantin Rudnitsky, *Russian and Soviet Theater, 1905–1932* (New York: Abrams, 1988), 59–64.

24. Clark, *Petersburg*, 126.

25. Robert Leach, *Revolutionary Theatre* (London: Routledge, 1994), 23.

26. Anatolii Lunacharsky, "Revolution and Art, 1920–1922," in *Russian Art of the Avant-Garde*, ed. John E. Bowlt (New York: Thames and Hudson, 1988), 191.

27. A. I. Mazaev, *Prazdnik kak sotsial'no-khudozhestvennoe iavlenie* (Moscow, 1978), 329.

28. For creative readings of these spectacles, see von Geldern, *Bolshevik Festivals*, 156–63, 185–93; Clark, *Petersburg*, 126–31; František Deák, "Russian Mass Spectacles," *Drama Review* 19, no. 2 (1975): 8–15.

29. The scenarios of *Mystery* and of *Commune* are reprinted respectively in *Russkii-sovetskii teatr, 1917–1921*, ed. A. Z. Iufit (Leningrad, 1968), 263–64; *Istoriia Sovetskogo*

Teatra, vol. 1, *Petrogradskie teatry na poroge Oktiabria i v epokhu voennogo kommunizma, 1917–1921* (Leningrad, 1933), 272–75.

30. In posters, the factory—or even the Soviet state—was often represented as a fortress, complete with crenellated towers, and sometimes in the embrace of a serpent of imperialism or under attack from foreign powers, hunger, or plunder (Stephen White, *The Bolshevik Poster* [New Haven: Yale University Press, 1988], 45, 44; Viacheslav Polonskii, *Russkii revoliutsionnyi plakat* [Moscow, 1924], 34, 38, 40, 48, 134; *Sovetskii politicheskii plakat/The Soviet Political Poster* [Moscow, 1984], posters 19, 28, 37); cf. the storming of the "yellow fortress" of the Moscow Union of Printworkers that was required to make it a revolutionary union (*Pravda*, November 7, 1920, 8). A rare reference to the Winter Palace as the Bastille of capitalism can be found in a poem at the bottom of one poster from 1920 (*Sovetskii politicheskii plakat*, poster 15).

31. *Zhizn' iskusstva* 442, May 4, 1920, 1.

32. *Petrogradskaia pravda*, October 31, 1920, 2.

33. The term "total event" was coined by Lüsebrink and Reichardt, in relation to the French Revolution ("La Prise de la Bastille," 77–102). Although the more literal translation of the word *vziatie* is "taking," a more faithful translation of the term given its cultural context of the time would be "storming." One newspaper referred to the spectacle as the *Siege of the Winter Palace* (*Osada Zimnego dvortsa*) (*Zhizn' iskusstva* 562–63, September 21 and 22, 1920, 3).

34. The most creative readings of this spectacle can be found in von Geldern, *Bolshevik Festivals*, 199–207, 122–24; Deák, "Russian Mass Spectacles," 15–21; Leach, *Revolutionary Theatre*, 46–50. See also the accounts in the memoirs of Iurii Annenkov, *Dnevnik moikh vstrech: Tsikl tragedii*, vol. 2 (New York: Inter-Language Literary Associates, 1966), 118–28.

35. "Libretto instsenirovki *Vziatie Zimnego dvortsa,* " in *Sovetskii teatr*, 272.

36. *Krasnyi militsioner* 14, 1920, 4.

37. Cited in *Istoriia sovetskogo teatra*, 280.

38. *Zhizn' iskusstva* 596–97, October 31, 1920, 1.

39. Ibid. 607, November 12, 1920, 2.

40. *Petrogradskaia pravda*, November 7, 1920, 4.

41. Evreinoff, *Histoire du théatre Russe*, 426.

42. *Petrogradskaia pravda*, November 10, 1920, 2. By the mid-1920s, the spectacle was couched in explicitly Bolshevik terms. The White and Red stages now represented the "Kerensky regime" and "Bolshevism," and the "Bolshevization of the masses" was identified as a pivotal instrument in the making of October ("Stat'ia K. N. Derzhavina 'Vziatie Zimnego dvortsa' v 1920 g. [k piatiletiiu instsenirovki] [7–10 noiabria 1925 g.]," in *Sovetskii teatr*, 274

43. *Zhizn' iskusstva* 596–97, October 31, 1920, 1.

44. *Petrogradskaia pravda*, November 4, 1920, 2.

45. *Zhizn' iskusstva* 607, November 12, 1920, 2.

46. A. V. Lunacharskii, "O narodnykh prazdnestvakh," in *A. V. Lunacharskii o massovykh prazdnestvakh, estrade i tsirke* (Moscow, 1981), 84.

47. "Stat'ia neustanovlennogo avtora *Vziatie Zimnego dvortsa* (vpechatleniia)," in *Sovetskii teatr*, 273.

48. Deák, "Russian Mass Spectacles," 21.

49. *Petrogradskaia pravda*, November 7, 1920, 3.

50. *Krasnyi militsioner* 14, 1920, 4.

51. *Petrogradskaia pravda*, October 17, 1920, 1; "Libretto instsenirovki *Vziatie Zimnego dvortsa,* " in *Sovetskii teatr*, 273.

52. *Krasnyi militsioner* 14, 1920, 5. Another dramatic description of the *Storming* was offered by Arthur Holitscher, *Drei Monate in Sowjet-Russland* (Berlin: Fischer, 1921),

130–32. His and Evreinov's representations are frequently cited extensively, presumably in an effort to convey the "inherent" drama of the original (Huntley Carter, *The New Theatre and Cinema of Soviet Russia* [London: Chapman and Dodd, 1924], esp. 106–9; cf. Deák, "Russian Mass Spectacles," 7–22).

53. *Krasnyi militsioner* 14, 1920, 4.

54. Lüsebrink and Reichardt, *Die Bastille*, 78, 241, 37.

55. Still, one eyewitness mentioned prisons, "large, red, scenic constructions with barred windows," opening their doors during the performance of the *Storming* to disgorge large crowds (Artur Holitscher, *Das Theater im Revolutionären Rußland* (Berlin: Volksbühnen-verlags- und Vertriebs-GMBH, n.d.), 20.

56. A. Suslov, *Zimnii dvorets, 1754–1927 gg. Istoricheskii ocherk* (Leningrad, 1928), 62–63.

57. *Petrogradskaia pravda*, November 7, 1920, 3.

58. *Krasnyi militsioner* 14, 1920, 4. The invalids were ready to give Kerensky the "last of their energies" (*Petrogradskaia pravda*, November 10, 1920, 2).

59. Ibid., October 31, 1920, 2.

60. Ibid., November 7, 1920, 4.

61. A. V. Lunacharskii, "O narodnykh prazdnestvakh," 87.

62. Ibid., 85. Cf. A. V. Lunacharskii, "O starykh i novykh formakh teatra," ibid., 118–19. For another critical voice on the mass spectacles, see Sergei Kozakevich, "V masshtabakh otkrytogo neba," *Zhizn' iskusstva* 600–601, November 5, 1920, 1. Others argued against the notion that the spectator and actor could in some way be merged, Radlov, for example, asserting that "*always* in the theater the spectator is passive" (ibid., 536–37, August 22, 1920, 1). Cf. René Fueloep-Miller's comments in 1926 on the mass spectacles: "These compositions are not the work of proletarians, but of the intelligentsia and merely betray what a poor opinion the Bolshevik leaders have of the level of this 'mass man' " (René Fueloep-Miller, *The Mind and Face of Bolshevism: An Examination of Cultural Life in Soviet Russia* [New York: Harper Torchbooks, 1965], 151).

63. Cited in Mazaev, *Prazdnik*, 343.

64. Annenkov, *Dnevnik moikh vstrech*, 120–22.

65. Cited in Mazaev, *Prazdnik*, 341.

66. Andrew Lass, "From Memory to History: The Events of November 17 Dis/Membered," in *Memory, History, and Opposition under State Socialism*, 91.

67. N. N. Sukhanov, *Zapiski o revoliutsii*, vol. 1 (Moscow, 1991), 44.

68. *Sotsial-demokrat*, November 4, 1917, 1.

69. *Izvestiia*, November 1, 1918, 1.

70. The Publishing Department of the Moscow Soviet envisaged print runs of 50,000 copies for one such collection at a cost of 400,000 rubles (*Izvestiia* 240, November 2, 1918, 6). Similar plans for jubilee publications were made in the provinces (*Pravda*, November 1, 1918, 4).

71. He is referring to Hitler's beer hall putsch of 1923 (Paul Connerton, *How Societies Remember* [Cambridge: Cambridge University Press, 1989], 43).

72. *Petrogradskaia pravda*, November 7, 1919, 2.

73. M. Gor'kii, *Nesvoevremennyia mysli: Zametki o revoliutsii i kul'ture* (Moscow: Sovetskii pisatel', 1990), 7; also *Krasnaia gazeta*, November 30, 1918, 1.

74. *Krasnoarmeets* 10–15, 1919, 43.

75. John Reed, *Ten Days That Shook the World* (Harmondsworth, England: Penguin, 1982), 119. Historians, such as A. J. P. Taylor, criticize Reed's work for its unreliability or bias, and at the same time they praise its ability to "*recapture* the spirit of those stirring days" (Reed, *Ten Days*, ix [emphasis added]). Cf. the comment that it was "justly famous for its drama, if not always for its accuracy" (Daniels, *Red October*, 251).

76. James D. White, "Early Soviet Historical Interpretations of the Russian Revolution, 1918–1924," *Soviet Studies* 37, no. 3 (1985): 334–37.

77. Reed, *Ten Days*, 9.

78. "Predislovie k knige Dzhona Rida: *10 dnei, kotorye potriasli mir*," Lenin, *Sochineniia*, vol. 24, 661. Lenin's comments formed the introduction to the Russian edition of Reed's work in 1923.

79. *Pravda*, November 7, 1919, 3; November 6, 1919, 3.

80. Fedotov, "Dvintsy," in *Moskva v Oktiabre 1917 g.*, ed. N. Ovsiannikov (Moscow, 1919), 25.

81. N. Norov, "Nakanune," in *Moskva v Oktiabre 1917 g.*, 16; Fedotov, "Dvintsy," ibid., 19.

82. *Pravda*, November 7, 1919, 3.

83. Ibid., November 6, 1919, 3.

84. Ibid., October 9, 1919, 3; also A. Beriushina, *Pochemu ia stala kommunistkoi?* (Moscow, 1919). Such testimonials invariably stressed the long-standing coherence and distinctness (especially vis-à-vis the Menshevik Party) of the Bolsheviks as a factor in their decision.

85. Reed, *Ten Days*, 102–3.

86. *Pravda*, November 6, 1919, 3.

87. M. Ol'minskii, "Khod sobytii," in *Moskva v Oktiabre 1917 g.*, 37. Bonch-Bruevich also recalled the formation, "rapidly and distinctly," during these days of a "single class association" of proletarians, peasants, and soldiers (*Izvestiia*, November 10, 1918, 7).

88. White, "Early Soviet Historical Interpretations," 334–37.

89. Reed, *Ten Days*, 82.

90. Ibid., 67–68, 91.

91. *Moskva v Oktiabre 1917 g.*, 13.

92. M. Ol'minskii, "Khod sobytii," in *Moskva v Oktiabre 1917 g.*, 37.

93. Fedotov, "Dvintsy," in *Moskva v Oktiabre 1917 g.*, 27.

94. Ol'minskii, "Khod sobytii," in *Moskva v Oktiabre 1917 g.*, 36.

95. Reed, *Ten Days*, 117.

96. Trotskii, "Oktiabr'skaia revoliutsiia," 295.

97. *Petrogradskaia pravda*, November 7, 1919, 1. Also *God proletarskoi revoliutsii* 3, November 9, 1918, 4.

98. Reed, *Ten Days*, 87.

99. *God proletarskoi revoliutsii* 2, November 8, 1918, 3. For other reminiscences that chose Smolny as the site of all the major decisions, see the articles by Podvoiskii, Kamenev, and Antonov-Ovseenko in *Izvestiia*, November 6, 1918, 3; November 10, 1918, 7; *Krasnoarmeets* 10–15, 1919, 29–30.

100. *Izvestiia*, November 10, 1918, 7; *Pravda*, November 6, 1918, 2; *Izvestiia*, November 6, 1918, 3.

101. Trotskii, "Oktiabr'skaia revoliutsiia," 298.

102. *Izvestiia*, November 6, 1918, 3.

103. *Pravda*, November 7, 1919, 1. For a similar representation of events in Moscow, see Iurii Sablin's piece in *Pravda*, November 9, 1919, 1.

104. *Izvestiia*, November 10, 1918, 7.

105. Ibid., November 6, 1918, 3; see also V. I. Nevskii's article in *Krasnoarmeets* 10–15, 1919, 34–44.

106. *Pravda*, November 6, 1918, 2; *Izvestiia*, November 6, 1918, 4.

107. Compare the muted reports of the taking of the palace offered in the loose chronological narrative of the October Revolution drawn from source materials (*Oktiabr'skii*

perevorot: Fakty i dokumenty, compiled by A. L. Popov, edited by N. A. Rozhkova [Petrograd, 1918], 184–85).

108. Trotskii, "Oktiabr'skaia revoliutsiia," 300–301.

109. Reed, *Ten Days*, 93.

110. Ibid., 162.

111. Ibid., 107–8. For a similar treatment written already on November 17, 1917, see Reed's dispatch to *The Liberator* ("Red Russia: The Triumph of the Bolsheviki," in *John Reed and the Russian Revolution: Uncollected Articles, Letters, and Speeches on Russia, 1917–1920*, ed. Eric Homberger and John Biggart [New York: St. Martin's, 1992], 74–95).

112. *Izvestiia,* November 6, 1918, 3; also Antonov-Ovseenko in *Krasnoarmeets* 10–15, 1919, 30–31.

113. *Izvestiia,* November 6, 1918, 3.

114. *Proletarskaia revoliutsiia* 10 (1922), 79–80, 82.

115. Peter Holquist, *Making War, Forging Revolution: Russia's Continuum of Crisis, 1914–1921* (Cambridge: Harvard University Press, 2002), 5. Holquist observes that the term "Russian Civil War" is the result of a later process of homogenization of what he prefers to call "civil wars and national conflicts."

116. Only in the 1920s did the female worker emerge as the iconic New Soviet Woman. The Bolsheviks attempted retroactively to display their party's long commitment to women's rights, by "enshrin[ing] in history" a "Bolshevik women's movement," notably through festive rituals that celebrated rather than ignored or belittled women (Choi Chatterjee, *Celebrating Women: Gender, Festival Culture, and Bolshevik Ideology, 1910–1939* [Pittsburgh: University of Pittsburgh Press, 2002], 60 and 18).

117. *Petrogradskaia pravda,* November 4, 1920, 2. A short film was indeed made, complete with explanatory subtitles. It is not known how widely it was shown in Russia. My thanks to Alma Law for allowing me to view her copy of the film.

118. Unrealized planned mass spectacles included one entitled *The Storming of the Bastille* and Vsevolod Meyerhold's *Struggle and Victory of the Soviets* (*Istoriia sovetskogo teatra,* 271; Leach, *Revolutionary Theatre,* 102–3).

119. For celebratory evaluations by these artists of their own achievements in the new regime, see *Proletarische Kulturrevolution in Sowjetrussland, 1917–1921*, ed. Richard Lorenz (Munich: Deutscher Taschenbuch Verlag, 1969), 108–78.

120. Cassiday, *The Enemy on Trial,* 21.

121. Anatolii Lunacharsky and Yuvenal Slavinsky, "Theses of the Art Section of Narkompros and the Central Committee of the Union of Art Workers Concerning Basic Policy in the Field of Art, 1920," in *Russian Art of the Avant-Garde,* 185.

122. On the demise in the early 1920s of such spearheads of the "October in the Theater" movement as Proletkult and the Theater of Revolutionary Satire (TEREVSAT), see Leach, *Revolutionary Theatre,* chap. 4.

123. Clark argues that Eisenstein parodied the scene of the storming of the Stock Exchange in *The Mystery of Liberated Labor* in his Odessa steps massacre scene in *Battleship Potemkin* (Clark, *Petersburg,* 129).

124. *Petrogradskaia pravda,* November 10, 1920, 4.

125. Clark, *Petersburg,* 123.

126. Regular reports on celebrations in local towns stressed these meeting activities (*Petrogradskaia pravda,* November 10, 1920, 2; *Izvestiia,* November 11, 1920, 2; November 12, 1920, 3; November 13, 1920, 2). For a description of the drab and humdrum November 1920 celebrations in Rostov-on-the-Don through the eyes of an observer disgusted with the habits and pretensions of what he called the "Soviet bourgeoisie," see Terne, *V Tsarstve Lenina,* 304–5. An exception was the planned performance in several cities of northern

Russia of a theatrical production rather prosaically entitled *The History of the Revolution from February to October 1917* (*Petrogradskaia pravda*, November 5, 1920, 2).

127. See the special jubilee issue of a local Urals newspaper (*Ural'skii rabochii*, supplement to no. 81, November 7, 1919). Also, *Dokumenty sotsialisticheskoi revoliutsii: noty, dekrety, rechi vozhdei Sovetskoi vlasti* (Samara, 1919); cf. *Kratkii ocherk revoliutsionnogo dvizheniia i razvitiia proletarskoi revoliutsii v Rossii* (Kaluga, 1919).

128. *Proletarskaia revoliutsiia* 10 (1922), 58.

129. *Ural'skii rabochii*, supplement to no. 81, November 7, 1919, 6.

130. Cited in Robert A. Maguire, "Literary Conflicts in the 1920s," *Survey* 18, no. 82 (1972): 103. Maguire points out that the literature of the 1920s also reflected the notion that the hope generated by the transcendent meaning and purpose of the early revolutionary years had given way to the despair of gloomy mundanity (103–4).

131. Michael David-Fox, *Revolution of the Mind: Higher Learning among the Bolsheviks, 1918–1929* (Ithaca: Cornell University Press, 1997), 12.

132. Lenin, *Sochineniia*, vol. 25, 477.

133. For example, the Central Committee decided that the fourth anniversary celebrations in 1921 would be about economic reconstruction and "the insoluble link between the NEP and the basic line of the October overthrow" (RGASPI, f. 17, op. 60, ed. khr. 38, l. 2). The theme for 1922 was the Congress of the Comintern and making workers and peasants more aware of the Third International (RGASPI, f. 17, op. 60, ed. khr. 163, l. 21).

134. David-Fox, *Revolution of the Mind*; Vera Tolz, *Russian Academicians and the Revolution: Combining Professionalism and Politics* (Basingstoke, England: Macmillan, 1997).

135. On these, see G. D. Alekseeva, *Oktiabr'skaia revoliutsiia i istoricheskaia nauka, 1917–1923* (Moscow, 1968), chap. 1; L. V. Ivanova, *U istokov sovetskoi istoricheskoi nauki (podgotovka kadrov istorikov-marksistov, 1917–1929)* (Moscow, 1968), pt. 3.

CHAPTER 4: ISTPART AND THE INSTITUTIONALIZATION OF MEMORY

1. Cited in Figes, *Peasant Russia*, 321. See also *Za sovety bez kommunistov: Krest'ianskoe vosstanie v Tiumenskoi gubernii 1921. Sbornik dokumentov* (Novosibirsk: Sibirskii khronograf, 2000).

2. On Bolshevik surveillance, see Holquist, "Information," 415–50.

3. Scholars have recently argued that the scale of this unrest and the seriousness of its challenge to the Bolshevik state has been underestimated in the historiography (Jonathan Aves, *Workers against Lenin: Labour Protest and the Bolshevik Dictatorship* [London: I. B. Tauris, 1996], chap. 4; Donald J. Raleigh, "A Provincial Kronstadt: Popular Unrest in Saratov at the End of the Civil War," in *Provincial Landscapes*, 82–104).

4. Lenin, *Sochineniia*, vol. 26, 284.

5. "Obrashchenie kronshtadtskogo VRK po radio k rabochim, krasnoarmeitsam i matrosam s prizyvom prisoedinit'sia i ustanovit' sviaz' s vosstavshimi," in *Kronshtadtskaia tragediia 1921 g.: Dokumenty v dvukh knigakh*, ed. V. K. Vinogradov and L.V. Dvoinykh, vol. I (Moscow: Rosspen, 1999), 254; "Obrashchenie Vremennogo Revoliutsionnogo Komiteta k krest'ianam, rabochim i krasnoarmeitsam," in *Kronshtadt 1921. Dokumenty*, ed. V. P. Naumov and A. A. Kosakovskii (Moscow: "Demokratiia," 1997), 55. One participant described his decision to leave the "despicable Yid [*zhidovskaia*] party of Communists" ("Zaiavleniia o vykhode iz partii," in *Kronshtadtskaia tragediia 1921 g.*, vol. 1, 361).

6. *Pravda*, March 16, 1921, 1. Three-quarters of the mutineers had apparently served in the fleet at least since the World War (Evan Mawdsley, "The Baltic Fleet and the Kronstadt Mutiny," *Soviet Studies* 24, no. 4 [1973], 508–9). A steady stream of RKP members serving in Kronstadt left the party in 1920, apparently disillusioned with the bureaucratiz-

ation of the party and with the "band of careerists and robbers [*razboiniki*]" running it ("Zaiavleniia o vykhode iz partii," in *Kronshtadtskaia tragediia 1921 g.*, vol 1, 360).

7. "Iz stenograficheskogo otcheta zasedaniia plenuma Petrosoveta—Doklad predsedatelia PGChK N. P. Komarova o prichinakh i urokakh Kronshtadtskikh sobytii i preniia po dokladu," in *Kronshtadtskaia tragediia 1921 g.*, vol. 1, 622–23.

8. *Pravda*, March 16, 1921, 1.

9. According to the Menshevik Fedor Dan, who shared a detention cell in Petrograd with some of the sailors, the uprising was completely unexpected even by them (Fedor Dan, *Dva goda skitanii 1919–1921* [Berlin, 1922], 154). Kronstadt energized various émigré groups, such as the National Center and the SRs, yet failed to become a common cause for them (Paul Avrich, *Kronstadt 1921* [Princeton: Princeton University Press, 1970], 88–130).

10. *Sotsialisticheskii vestnik* 5, April 5, 1921, 3.

11. Ibid., March 18, 1921, 3. Cf. also the comparison in L. Martow, "Zum 50: Jahrestag der Pariser Commune," *Freiheit*, March 18, 1921, 1. The Menshevik Raphael Abramovich later likened the sailors to the Paris communards and stressed the spontaneous nature of their uprising (Raphael R. Abramovich, *The Soviet Revolution, 1917–1939* [New York: International Universities Press, 1962], 201). In the historiography, Kronstadt has tended to be romanticized by scholars who seek signs of "legitimate" popular expression in early Soviet society. Getzler called it a "self-governing, egalitarian and highly politicized Soviet democracy, the like of which had not been seen in Europe since the days of the Paris Commune" (Israel Getzler, *Kronstadt, 1917–1921: The Fate of a Soviet Democracy* [Cambridge: Cambridge University Press, 1983], 246).

12. "Iz stenograficheskogo otcheta," in *Kronshtadtskaia tragediia 1921 g.*, vol. 1, 638.

13. Avrich, *Kronstadt*, 213.

14. *Sotsialisticheskii vestnik* 5, April 5, 1921, 4.

15. Ibid. 2, February 16, 1921, 2, 3.

16. Schapiro, *Origin*, 231–34.

17. Lenin, *Sochineniia*, vol. 26, 87.

18. RGASPI, f. 17, op. 60, ed. khr. 36, ll. 13–26.

19. RGASPI, f. 91, op. 1, ed. khr. 231, l. 4.

20. Soviet historians, particularly from the 1960s onward, generated a cottage industry of studies of the central Istpart and its local affiliates, written, as one critic put it, "as if to a single plan, a single schema" (V. E. Korneev, *Mestnye biuro Istparta TsK VKP(b): Sozdanie istochnikovoi bazy istoriko-partiinoi nauki 1920–1929 gg. Uchebnoe posobie* [Moscow, 1986], 7). Little serious study of Istpart has been undertaken in the West, in part because the party archives where these materials are located were until glasnost not open to Western scholars, and in part because of prevailing assumptions that these kinds of institutions were about the manipulation of historical information for political ends and thus did not constitute legitimate or reliable sources about Soviet reality. A rare Western treatment examines Istpart as a losing battle between independent scholarly voices and ascendant political forces within the party (Larry E. Holmes and William Burgess, "Scholarly Voice or Political Echo? Soviet Party History in the 1920s," *Russian History* 9, no. 2–3 (1982): 378–98; William Francis Burgess, "The Istpart Commission: The Historical Department of the Russian Communist Party Central Committee, 1920–1928" [Ph.D. diss., Yale University, 1981]). A more recent study of the Russian Revolution concluded with an examination of Istpart. This symbolic separation of the "actual" revolution from the writing of its history highlighted the Bolsheviks' "subordination of Marxist ideology to their current political objectives" (James D. White, *The Russian Revolution, 1917–1921: A Short History* [London: Edward Arnold, 1994], 253).

21. Maurice Halbwachs, *The Collective Memory* (New York: Harper and Row, 1980), 43.

22. Maurice Halbwachs, *La Topographie légendaire des évangiles en Terre Sainte* (Paris: Presses universitaires de France, 1971), 118.

23. *Rabochaia gazeta*, October 13, 1917, 1; on the *kruzhkovshchina* and its effects, see Theodor Dan, "Die Sozialdemokratie Rußlands nach dem Jahre 1908," in Martow, *Geschichte*, 236.

24. Cited in *Vladimir Akimov on the Dilemmas of Russian Marxism, 1895–1903*, ed. Jonathan Frankel (Cambridge: Cambridge University Press, 1969), 14.

25. *Making of Three Russian Revolutionaries*, 4. On the persistence of *kruzhok* culture in literary circles, and how its reemergence in the early Soviet period provided some conduits of influence for literary figures in their relationship with the Soviet state, see Barbara Walker, "*Kruzhok* Culture: The Meaning of Patronage in the Early Soviet Literary World," *Contemporary European History* 11, no. 1 (2002): 107–23.

26. Dan, "Die Sozialdemokratie Rußlands," 236.

27. Some had already attempted histories of their movement, including Nikolai Baturin, *Ocherk istorii sotsial-demokratii v Rossii* (Moscow, 1906), and Martyn Liadov, *Istoriia Rossiiskoi Sotsialdemokraticheskoi Rabochei Partii* (St. Petersburg, 1906).

28. In mid-1921, Ol'minskii complained that Riazanov did not attend the meetings, Bystrianskii was living in Petrograd, Baturin was ill, Nevskii had little time for the work, Bubnov had gone to Rostov, Lepeshinskii was soon leaving, Pokrovskii only attended the meetings, and Adoratskii only did administrative work. Piontkovskii was working, but he had been a Menshevik for ten years, had become a Bolshevik in 1919, and produced one work in a "Kadet-Menshevik spirit" that was destroyed. He himself, Ol'minskii noted, was not capable of a great deal of work (RGASPI, f. 91, op. 1, ed. khr. 177, l. 7). In April 1923, Lepeshinskii told the First All-Russian Conference of Istpart Workers (*Vserossiiskoe soveshchanie rabotnikov Istparta*) that although the staff of the central Istpart eventually settled around thirty-five people, many of them were unable to discharge their duties due to ill-health (*Biulleten' Istparta* 2 [1924]: 5). In January 1924, Ol'minskii complained to the Central Committee that illness severely impeded his efforts, and that most of the personnel were working at 20 to 40 percent of their capacity (RGASPI, f. 70, op. 1, ed. khr. 94, l. 3).

29. The interesting relationship between the "Red archivists," who saw their archival duties as a weapon in the revolutionary struggle, and the hostile prerevolutionary archivists, who often persisted in these institutions in supervisory roles into the early 1920s, is examined in Antonella Salomoni, "Un Savoir historique d'état: Les Archives Soviétiques," *Annales HSS* 1 (January–February 1995): 3–27.

30. *Deviataia konferentsiia RKP(b)*, 98.

31. *Petrogradskaia pravda*, October 26, 1920, 1.

32. RGASPI, f. 70, op. 1, ed. khr. 17, l. 21.

33. *Pravda*, June 6, 1918, 1; *Vechernie izvestiia*, November 9, 1919, 1.

34. *Deviataia konferentsiia RKP(b)*, 102.

35. *Pravda*, February 22, 1919, 1.

36. *Ko vsem chlenam partii* (Moscow, 1920), 2–3. At the Ninth Party Conference, Pokrovskii cited examples from the French Revolution of the shape certain episodes acquired in the "wrong" hands (*Deviataia konferentsiia RKP(b)*, 100).

37. RGASPI, f. 70, op. 2, d. 5, l. 22.

38. *Deviataia konferentsiia RKP(b)*, 98.

39. Ibid., 100.

40. *Ko vsem chlenam partii*, 15.

41. RGASPI, f. 70, op. 1, ed. khr. 17, l. 27.

42. By 1925, explicit approval was required from the central Istpart for the publication of any documents from party archives (RGASPI, f. 70, op. 1, ed. khr. 94, l. 104).

43. *Deviataia konferentsiia RKP(b)*, 101.

44. This counternarrative, told through émigré publications such as the Menshevik *Sotsialisticheskii vestnik* (*Socialist Herald*) and the SR *Revoliutsionnaia Rossiia* (*Revolutionary Russia*), was deeply formative of Western perceptions of Soviet Russia. Tantalizing glimpses of that story can be seen in Liebich, *From the Other Shore* (see my review in *The Harriman Review* 12, no. 1 (1999), 31–32) and Haimson's introduction in *The Making of Three Russian Revolutionaries*). Its resilience underpinned the increased scholarly interest (in the West from the 1960s and in glasnost and post-Soviet Russia) in those parties that opposed the Bolsheviks during and after October. This practice by former Soviet historians of the CPSU has been described as the "mindless apologia" of the opponents of Bolshevism (Buldakov, "Istoriograficheskie metamorfozy," 180).

45. *Deviataia konferentsiia RKP(b)*, 101.

46. Ibid., 102.

47. RGASPI, f. 70, op. 2, ed. khr. 217, l. 7.

48. *Revoliutsionnoe byloe* 1 (1923), 7. A history primer from 1910 used in training courses for gendarmes included a series of 180 questions and answers intended to provide them with answers to such questions as "Who is the main enemy of the tsar and fatherland?" (the correct answer being "Bolsheviks, Yids, and students") ("Revoliutsionnoe dvizhenie v Rossii," in *Neizvestnaia Rossiia. 20 vek*, vol. 2 [Moscow: Istoricheskoe nasledie, 1992], 352).

49. These rules were needed, as Stalin put it, to prevent information from reaching "our enemies" (cited in Vladimir Lebedev, "Praviashchaia partiia ostavalas' podpol'noi," *Istochnik* 4–5 [1993], 88). These rules, sent by the Central Committee to local party organizations, are reproduced in ibid., documents 1–4, 11, 13.

50. RGASPI, f. 70, op. 1, ed. khr. 17, l. 21.

51. *Protokoly 10 s"ezda RKP(b)* (Moscow, 1933), 135.

52. *Petrogradskaia pravda*, November 11, 1920, 1.

53. Ibid., October 10, 1920, 2.

54. RGASPI, f. 70, op. 1, ed. khr. 16, l. 1, 10.

55. Ibid., l. 10.

56. N. S. Komarov, "Sozdanie i deiatel'nost' Istparta, 1920–1928 gg.," *Voprosy istorii KPSS* 5 (1958), 154.

57. The Moscow bureau of Istpart also had separate sections (*sektsii*) for the history of the revolution and the history of the party (RGASPI, f. 70, op. 2, ed. khr. 216, l. 3).

58. RGASPI, f. 70, op. 1, d. 45, l. 21.

59. RGASPI, f. 70, op. 2, ed. khr. 406, l. 1.

60. *Biulleten' Istparta* 1, 1921, 4.

61. N. M. Mikhailova, "M. S. Ol'minskii ob istochnikakh po istorii Kommunisticheskoi Partii i Oktiabr'skoi Revoliutsii" in *Istoriia i istoriki: Istoriograficheskii ezhegodnik, 1972* (Moscow, 1973), 218–19.

62. *Petrogradskaia pravda*, November 11, 1920, 1.

63. *Protokoly 10 s"ezda RKP(b)*, 133–34.

64. *Ko vsem chlenam partii*, 5.

65. RGASPI, f. 70, op. 2, ed. khr. 206, l. 90.

66. *Deviatyi s"ezd Rossiiskoi Kommunisticheskoi Partii: Stenograficheskii otchet, 19 marta–4 aprelia 1920 g.* (Moscow, 1920), 10.

67. *Iskra* 6, October 27, 1917, 2–3. Nikolaevskii, unwittingly presaging the kinds of problems this project would entail, criticized local reminiscers in Samara for not adequately identifying themselves, for limiting their reminiscences to "superficial remarks," and for making factual errors about the party's history.

68. *Zhizn' iskusstva* 291, November 13, 1919, 1.

69. *Protokoly 10 s"ezda RKP(b)*, 133.

70. *Deviataia konferentsiia RKP(b)*, 99.

71. *Iz epokhi "Zvezdy" i "Pravdy," 1911–1914 gg.* (Moscow, 1921), 4. He repeated these views at the Tenth Party Congress (*Protokoly 10 s"ezda RKP(b)*, 135).

72. It claimed to have learned of the creation of Istpart only from the first issue of the Istpart bulletin (*Biulleten' Istparta* 2, 1924, 14).

73. The first bureaus were set up in Petrograd, Ekaterinburg, Perm', Tver', Nizhegorod, Voronezh-Don, Omsk, North Caucasus, Ivanovo-Voznesensk, Gomel', Briansk, Odessa, Ekaterinoslav, Minsk, Smolensk, Samara, Novgorod, Iaroslavl', Kaluga, Siberia, and the Tatar bureau; these were followed by the Archangel, Astrakhan, Bashkir, Vologda, Far Eastern, Kuban-Black Sea, Kursk, and Riazan' bureaus a year later. Most of the union republics also had branches (Korneev, *Mestnye biuro Istparta TsK VKP(b)*, 14–16).

74. RGASPI, f. 70, op. 2, ed. khr. 1, l. 1.

75. RGASPI, f. 70, op. 1, ed. khr. 3, l. 9.

76. *Ko vsem chlenam partii*, 8.

77. *Petrogradskaia pravda*, October 26, 1920, 1.

78. RGASPI, f. 70, op. 2, ed. khr. 1, l. 1; f. 17, op. 60, ed. khr. 36, l. 37.

79. *Deviataia konferentsiia RKP(b)*, 100.

80. *Protokoly 10 s"ezda RKP(b)*, 136.

81. RGASPI, f. 70, op. 2, ed. khr. 3, l. 42, 46, 53, 66, 66a.

82. RGASPI, f. 17, op. 60, ed. khr. 36, l. 37.

83. Trouillot, *Silencing the Past*, 52.

84. *Pravda*, February 22, 1919, 1.

85. For more on these early efforts, see V. E. Korneev, *Arkhivy RKP(b) v 1917–1925 gg. Uchebnoe posobie* (Moscow, 1979); V. V. Maksakov, *Istoriia i organizatsiia arkhivnogo dela v SSSR, 1917–1945 gg.* (Moscow, 1969).

86. *Ko vsem chlenam partii*, 7.

87. RGASPI, f. 70, op. 2, ed. khr. 1, l. 1.

88. *Ko vsem chlenam partii*, 14–16.

89. RGASPI, f. 70, op. 2, ed. khr. 206, l. 24.

90. Kovalenko, the chairman of the Group of Former Russian Prisoners-of-War Abroad (Gruppa byvshikh russkikh voennoplennykh za granitsei) suggested these latter materials to the Istpart board as a source on the revolutionary movement. Varentsova was assigned to this work (RGASPI, f. 70, op. 1, ed. khr. 2, l. 1). The archive of Georgii Plekhanov, one of the founders of Russian Social Democracy, was brought from Paris to Moscow after negotiations with his wife (Komarov, "Sozdanie," 164).

91. RGASPI, f. 70, op. 1, ed. khr. 4, l. 5.

92. By April 1924, the archive contained 2,000 illegal and rare books; 18,000 brochures and journals, mainly from the pre-October period; 10,674 leaflets; and 57 newspapers, some in complete runs (Komarov, "Sozdanie," 163).

93. RGASPI, f. 17, op. 84, ed. khr. 765, l. 29.

94. RGASPI, f. 70, op. 1, ed. khr. 161, l. 37.

95. RGASPI, f. 70, op. 2, ed. khr. 206, l. 37.

96. RGASPI, f. 70, op. 2, ed. khr. 216, l. 1. Cf. the following periodization agreed upon by the Petrograd bureau: 1874–1880; 1881–1894; 1894–1903; 1903–1905; 1905–1906; 1906–1912; 1912–1914; 1914–1917 (RGASPI, f. 70, op. 2, ed. khr. 206, l. 24).

97. The Tver' bureau believed that the "lack of system to the work, the fragmentariness" could best be rectified by a "known plan" and by division of its work into several time periods (RGASPI, f. 17, op. 84, ed. khr. 539, l. 27). It proposed the following broad periodization in late 1922: the period of illegal work before the February Revolution of 1917; February 1917 to the October Revolution; the history of the party and Soviet power from October to the present (RGASPI, f. 70, op. 2, ed. khr. 5, l. 11).

98. In early 1923, the Irkutsk bureau used the following periodization: the period up to the February Revolution of 1917; the February Revolution; the October Revolution; the initial period after October, including the intervention of Czech troops; the Kolchakovshchina; and the organization of stable Soviet power in Siberia. These periods were subdivided into the following departments (*otdely*): underground work of the RSDRP (Bolsheviks and Mensheviks) up to 1917; the split in this party; exile and hard labor in Irkutsk; the Czechoslovak movement; the partisan movement; the formation of soviet power; party building; agitprop work; the development of the trade union movement; the role of the peasantry in the proletarian revolution; the cooperative movement and its role in the proletarian revolution; the activity of other parties; green banditism ("Greens" referred to deserters from Red and White armies during the Civil War, who could end up raiding either side); and so on (RGASPI, f. 70, op. 2, ed. khr. 5, l. 21).

99. In its first three years, the Saratov bureau examined the files of the Saratov provincial gendarme administration for the period 1883–1898 for materials showing the "evolution in the program and tactics of provincial revolutionary circles and their gradual transition from anarchism and populism to Marxism and social democratic ideas." They also combed these and the Okhrana files for the 1898–1907 period for information on the activities of the Saratov organization of the RSDRP and the labor movement during these years (RGASPI, f. 70, op. 2, ed. khr. 5, ll. 6–7).

100. RGASPI, f. 70, op. 1, ed. khr. 3, l. 1.

101. Ibid., ed. khr. 4, l. 1, 8.

102. *Izvestiia*, November 6, 1918, 9.

103. *Zhizn' iskusstva* 286–288, November 9, 1919, 2.

104. He soon became disillusioned by the encroachments on the "independent, non-partisan character" of the museum by Istpart, which was "hostile to free initiative and best effort" (Alexander Berkman, *The Bolshevik Myth: Diary 1920–1922* [London: Hutchinson and Co., 1925), 157–63). See also Emma Goldman, *My Disillusionment in Russia* (New York: Thomas Y. Crowell, 1970), 75–79.

105. RGASPI, f. 70, op. 2, ed. khr. 2, l. 4.

106. RGASPI, f. 70, op. 1, ed. khr. 3, ll. 13–15. Lepeshinskii informed the Istpart conference in 1923 that eighty-two excursions (about 2,500 people) a year had visited the exhibition (*Biulleten' Istparta* 2, 1924, 6).

107. Komarov, "Sozdanie," 160.

108. RGASPI, f. 70, op. 2, ed. khr. 217, l. 35.

109. RGASPI, f. 70, op. 2, ed. khr. 5, l. 4.

110. RGASPI, f. 70, op. 1, ed. khr. 2, l. 1.

111. RGASPI, f. 70, op. 2, ed. khr. 2, l. 6, 7; ed. khr. 5, l. 15

112. *Biulleten' Istparta* 2, 1924, 13.

113. Ibid. 2 [1924]: 17 and 13.

114. RGASPI, f. 70, op. 2, ed. khr. 5, ll. 1a-2; *Biulleten' Istparta* 2, 1924, 15. Cf. the exhibition organized by the Istpart of the Ukraine, comprising 2,700 exhibits and visited by 2,200 people (ibid., 12).

115. RGASPI, f. 70, op. 2, ed. khr. 5, l. 2.

116. In Moscow, courses on the history of the party were organized by the Museum of the Revolution and intended for groups of sixty to seventy people (RGASPI, f. 70, op. 2, ed. khr. 216, l. 19).

117. *Biulleten' Istparta* 2, 1924: 15.

118. *Ko vsem chlenam partii*, 4.

119. *Iz epokhi*, 190.

120. *Protokoly 10 s"ezda RKP(b)*, 136.

121. RGASPI, f. 70, op. 2, ed. khr. 216, l. 42.

122. *Biulleten' Istparta* 2, 1924, 17.

123. RGASPI, f. 70, op. 2, ed. khr. 216, l. 42.

124. *Iz epokhi*, 3.

125. *Zhizn' iskusstva* 291, November 13, 1919, 1.

126. *Deviataia konferentsiia RKP(b)*, 99.

127. *Petrogradskaia pravda*, October 23, 1920, 1.

128. *Deviataia konferentsiia RKP(b)*, 99.

129. RGASPI, f. 70, op. 1, ed. khr. 17, l. 26.

130. RGASPI, f. 70, op. 2, ed. khr. 1, l. 1.

131. *Iz epokhi*, 4.

132. *Ko vsem chlenam partii*, 9.

133. RGASPI, f. 70, op. 2, ed. khr. 206, l. 97.

134. *Petrogradskaia pravda*, November 11, 1920, 1.

135. *Pechat' i revoliutsiia* 2 (1921), 246. This list included Inessa Armand, Vera Bonch-Bruevich, A. A. Bogdanov, among others.

136. RGASPI, f. 17, op. 60, ed. khr. 36, l. 37.

137. V. Iu. Korovainikov, "'Ankety' kak istochnik po istorii Oktiabr'skogo perevorota," in *Mir istochnikovedeniia* (Moscow and Penza, 1995), 167–70; Z. N. Tikhonova, "Ankety uchastnikov Velikoi Oktiabr'skoi Sotsialisticheskoi Revoliutsii—istoricheskii istochnik," *Voprosy Istorii KPSS* 11 (1964), 99–103.

138. *Biulleten' Istparta* 2, 1924, 12, 16–17.

139. TsDNIIaO, f. 394, op. 1, d. 30, ll. 23–24; *Petrogradskaia pravda*, November 11, 1920, 1.

140. TsDNIIaO, f. 394, op. 1, d. 30, ll. 23–24.

141. RGASPI, f. 70, op. 1, d. 69, l. 239.

142. RGASPI, f. 70, op. 2, ed. khr. 406, ll. 33–39.

143. Ibid.

144. Ibid., l. 40.

145. Ibid., l. 41; *Ko vsem chlenam partii*, 10–13.

146. RGASPI, f. 70, op. 2, ed. khr. 406, ll. 33–41; *Ko vsem chlenam partii*, 10–13.

147. *Krasnaia byl'* 1 (1922), 118–20. Cf. the similar structure of a questionnaire on Iaroslavl' (TsDNIIaO, f. 394, op. 1, d. 64, ll. 40–41). 325

CHAPTER 5:   HOW NOT TO WRITE THE HISTORY OF OCTOBER

1. Rex A. Wade, "The Revolution in the Provinces: Khar'kov and the Varieties of Response to the October Revolution," *Revolutionary Russia* 4, no. 1 (1991): 132–42; Roger William Pethybridge, *The Spread of the Russian Revolution: Essays on 1917* (London: Macmillan, 1972); John Keep, "October in the Provinces," in *Revolutionary Russia*, ed. Richard Pipes (Cambridge: Harvard University Press, 1968), 180–223.

2. Douglas T. Northrop, "*Hujum*: Unveiling Campaigns and Local Responses in Uzbekistan, 1927," in *Provincial Landscapes*, 125–45; Michael C. Hickey, "Paper, Memory, and a Good Story: How Smolensk Got Its 'October'," *Revolutionary Russia* 13, no. 1 (2000): 1–19.

3. As with much Soviet historiography, scholars looked back from the 1930s to the 1920s as a kind of Golden Age of local studies *(kraevedenie)*, in which individuals were able to articulate a more autonomous accounting of their past and present experiences. As this study attempts to show, studies of October at the local level were already, by definition, a function of the revolutionary metanarrative being developed from the center. This did not, however, preclude local inflections of the revolutionary tale (cf. the introductory remarks in *Provincial Landscapes*, 4–6). Indeed, as Mark Steinberg shows in his study of proletarian poets who put their feelings into writing through the 1920s, the metanarrative

both framed and fired their imagination (Mark D. Steinberg, *Proletarian Imagination: Self, Modernity, and the Sacred in Russia, 1910–1925* [Ithaca, New York: Cornell University Press, 2002]).

4. RGASPI, f. 17, op. 60, ed. khr. 388, ll. 26–34.

5. V. I. Nevskii, *Bol'shevik, kommunist, i rabochii* (Petrograd, 1921), 26, 27.

6. Cf. the letters sent to various local bureaus, RGASPI, f. 70, op. 2, ed. khr. 3, l. 42, 53, 66, 66a.

7. RGASPI, f. 70, op. 2, ed. khr. 3, l. 46.

8. As happened with the Crimean and Saratov bureaus (respectively, RGASPI, f. 17, op. 84, ed. khr. 539, l. 27; f. 70, op. 2, ed. khr. 5, l. 6).

9. RGASPI, f. 70, op. 2, ed. khr. 2, 1. 3, 7; ed. khr. 5, l. 1a, 3, 9–15; 12; ed. khr. 59, l. 28; ed. khr. 248, l. 10; f. 17, op. 84, ed. khr. 539, l. 27; also *Biulleten' Istparta* 2, 1924, 11–17. The "office" of the Kostroma bureau was one table in an anteroom of Agitprop (RGASPI, f. 70, op. 2, ed. khr. 5, l. 9).

10. RGASPI, f. 70, op. 2, ed. khr. 5, ll. 6–8, 12, 17; *Biulleten' Istparta* 2, 1924, 11.

11. RGASPI, f. 70, op. 2, ed. khr. 2, l. 3.

12. RGASPI, f. 70, op. 2, ed. khr. 248, l. 2, l. 4.

13. *Biulleten' Istparta* 1, 1921, 5–6.

14. RGASPI, f. 70, op. 2, ed. khr. 5, l. 11.

15. RGASPI, f. 70, op. 2, ed. khr. 5, l. 10; f. 17, op. 84, ed. khr. 368, l. 4; f. 70, op. 1, ed. khr. 2, l. 2.

16. RGASPI, f. 70, op. 2, ed. khr. 216, l. 13. At the district level these plenipotentiaries existed mostly only on paper.

17. RGASPI, f. 70, op. 2, ed. khr. 216, ll. 22–23; ed. khr. 5, l. 10.

18. RGASPI, f. 70, op. 2, ed. khr. 206, ll. 36–37.

19. RGASPI, f. 70, op. 2, ed. khr. 206, ll. 41–43.

20. RGASPI, f. 70, op. 2, ed. khr. 210, l. 36.

21. RGASPI, f. 70, op. 2, ed. khr. 206, ll. 40, 46 ff.

22. RGASPI, f. 70, op. 2, ed. khr. 216, ll. 22–23, 28–29.

23. RGASPI, f. 70, op. 2, ed. khr. 216, l. 12; ed. khr. 217, l. 19.

24. RGASPI, f. 70, op. 2, ed. khr. 217, ll. 34–35.

25. RGASPI, f. 70, op. 1, ed. khr. 2, l. 8.

26. *Dvenadtsaty s"ezd Rossiiskoi Kommunisticheskoi Partii (bol'shevikov). 17–25 aprelia 1923 g.* (Moscow, 1923), 503.

27. *Trinadtsatyi s"ezd Rossiiskoi Kommunisticheskoi Partii (bol'shevikov): Stenograficheskii otchet 23–31 maia 1924 g.* (Moscow, 1924), 703.

28. *Biulleten' Istparta* 2, 1924, 5.

29. RGASPI, f. 70, op. 1, ed. khr. 94, l. 3. Lev Kamenev and Emel'ian Iaroslavskii were singled out by Ol'minskii as having sent material to Istpart for publication in its journal.

30. RGASPI, f. 70, op. 1, ed. khr. 3, l. 8. Nevskii had been ordered in late 1922 to split his time between the Central and Petrograd Istparts so as to promote closer links between them (RGASPI, f. 70, op. 1, ed. khr. 2, l. 8).

31. RGASPI, f. 70, op. 1, ed. khr. 2, l. 7.

32. N. S. Komarov, "Sozdanie i deiatel'nost' Istparta (1920–1928 gg.)," *Voprosy istorii KPSS* 5 (1958): 158.

33. *Biulleten' Istparta* 2, 1924, 8.

34. RGASPI, f. 70, op. 1, ed. khr. 2, l. 3.

35. RGASPI, f. 70, op. 2, ed. khr. 3, l. 39; ed. khr. 5, l. 8.

36. *Biulleten' Istparta* 2, 1924, 12.

37. RGASPI, f. 70, op. 2, ed. khr. 5, l. 5.

38. *Biulleten' Istparta* 2, 1924, 14.

39. RGASPI, f. 70, op. 2, ed. khr. 5, ll. 2–4.

40. *Biulleten' Istparta* 2, 1924, 12; RGASPI, f. 70, op. 2, ed. khr. 60, l. 3.

41. *Biulleten' Istparta* 2, 1924, 14.

42. Ibid., 15.

43. Ibid., 5.

44. RGASPI, f. 70, op. 1, ed. khr. 187, l. 4.

45. *Rybinsk v revoliutsii, 1917–1922* (Rybinsk, 1922).

46. *Iz proshlogo: Vtoroi sbornik vospominanii. Krest'ianskie vosstaniia v 1918 g. v Kungurskom uezde* (Kungur, 1922); *K piatoi godovshchine proletarskoi revoliutsii v Prikam'e (sbornik statei)* (Izhevsk, 1922).

47. *Sibirskie ogni* 5 (1922): 225.

48. *Krot* 6, October 1923, 1.

49. *Proletarskaia revoliutsiia na Donu* 3 (1922): 2.

50. *Krasnaia byl'* 1 (1922): 1.

51. Ibid., 2 (1922): 15–45.

52. N. Krasil'nikov, "Istoriia Sovetskoi vlasti v Krasnom-Khol'mu i ego uezde," *Rybinsk v revoliutsii*, 58.

53. Kashnikov, "Perevorot v Myshkine," ibid., 47.

54. *Krot* 4, August 1923, 4–5.

55. *Revoliutsionnoe byloe* 1 (1923): 34–36.

56. Sergeev, "Politicheskie partii i Oktiabr'skie sobytiia v Izhevske" in *K piatoi godovshchine*, 17.

57. *Rybinsk v revoliutsii*, 3.

58. *Proletarskaia revoliutsiia na Donu* 2 (1922): 35, 46, 45. Also *Oktiabr'skaia Revoliutsiia, Memuary*, ed. S. A. Alekseev and A. I. Usagina (Moscow–Leningrad: "Orbita," 1926, reprinted 1991).

59. *Rybinsk v revoliutsii*, 49, 25, 9, 52, 49, 10, 30.

60. RGASPI, f. 70, op. 1, ed. khr. 2, l. 9.

61. *Kratkii ocherk revoliutsionnogo dvizheniia i razvitiia proletarskoi revoliutsii v Rossii* (Kaluga, 1919).

62. Ia. Iakovlev, *Ob istoricheskom smysle Oktiabria* (Moscow, 1922). On this, see White, *Russian Revolution*, 257.

63. *Proletarskaia revoliutsiia* 3 (1921): 29.

64. M. Ol'minskii, "Probel v nashei istorii," in *Ot gruppy Blagoeva k "Soiuzu Bor'by": 1886–1894 gg.* (Rostov-on-Don, 1921), 3 and 5.

65. *Krasnaia byl'* 2 (1923): 7.

66. RGASPI, f. 70, op. 2, ed. khr. 5, l. 6. The Urals bureau organized a local exhibition on the occasion of the jubilee of the local party organization; the Ukraine bureau published an illustrated album of "RKP activists" (*Biulleten' Istparta* 2, 1924, 12 and 16).

67. RGASPI, f. 70, op. 2, ed. khr. 216, l. 13. Of the forty authors who were asked to contribute to the reader, only six sent articles, and these articles covered "far from all periods" in the development of the Moscow organization (RGASPI, f. 70, op. 2, ed. khr. 216, l. 31).

68. *Krot* 8, December 1923, 16. A drawing of the group's official stamp was included as proof of the vitality of the Kungur group of the Perm' committee of the RSDRP.

69. Ibid., 7, November 1923, 13; 8, December 1923, 11.

70. *Revoliutsionnoe byloe* 1 (1923): 8.

71. RGASPI, f. 70, op. 2, ed. khr. 216, l. 18.

72. RGASPI, f. 70, op. 2, ed. khr. 5, ll. 4–5.

73. *Biulleten' Istparta* 2, 1924, 13.

74. K. Bukharin, "Stranichka iz istorii Rybinskoi organizatsii RSDR Partii (bol'shevikov) v 1917 g.," in *Rybinsk v revoliutsii*, 12; and V. Varkholov, "Vospominaniia zheleznodorozhnika," ibid., 26.

75. N. Kornev, "Moi vospominanii," in ibid., 7–11.

76. *Proletarskaia revoliutsiia na Donu* 2 (1922): 34–35.

77. Ibid., 2 (1922): 58.

78. Ibid., 36.

79. Mazin, "Iz istorii 1–go Trudovogo raiona (kratkii ocherk)," *Rybinsk v revoliutsii*, 20.

80. *Puti revoliutsii* 3 (1923): 86–92.

81. *Proletarskaia revoliutsiia na Donu* 2 (1922) 39.

82. See V. Potanin, "Pred'utrennii son," *Rybinsk v revoliutsii*, 30; *Proletarskaia revoliutsiia na Donu* 2 (1922): 39.

83. Mazin, "Iz istorii 1–go Trudovogo raiona (kratkii ocherk)," *Rybinsk v revoliutsii*, 23–24.

84. *Revoliutsionnoe byloe* 1 (1923): 34; also ibid., 37–38.

85. At a meeting of the Moscow provincial bureau in January 1922, someone from Sergievsk commented that no underground organization of any kind existed before the February Revolution. Bobrovskaia responded that she recalled that there was an organization there at the time, and that it was necessary to trace the old comrades (RGASPI, f. 70, op. 2, ed. khr. 216, l. 10).

86. RGASPI, f. 70, op. 2, ed. khr. 211, l. 11.

87. *Krot* 5, September 1923, 1.

88. Ibid., 11–12.

89. *Rybinsk v revoliutsii, 1917–1922*, 5.

90. N. Kornev, "Moi vospominaniia," in *Rybinsk v revoliutsii*, 7.

91. *Krot* 5, September 1923, 1; 7, November 1923, 5.

92. *Iz proshlogo. Vtoroi sbornik vospominanii. Krest'ianskie vosstaniia v 1918 g. v Kungurskom uezde* (Kungur, 1922), 4.

93. *Krot* 1, May 1923, 1–5; 2, June 1923, 1–2.

94. Ibid., 4, August 1923, 1–2. When *Golos* ceased publication, the circle subscribed to the Menshevik *Permskaia zhizn' (Perm' Life)* (ibid., 3).

95. *Krot* 4, August 1923, 3.

96. Ibid., 3, July 1923, 1–2.

97. Ibid., 1, May 1923, 11–13.

98. One obituary in the Kungur journal carried the following exchange in 1918 between a political prisoner (now deceased) of the Whites and his jailor: " 'What are you, a Bolshevik?' Baiderin replied: 'No, I am not yet numbered in the ranks of the Bolsheviks, I have not managed to sign up, but I am a Bolshevik sympathizer!" (ibid., 4, August 1923, 11).

99. Ibid., 5, September 1923, 9–11.

100. A. Martsinovskii, *Zapiski Rabochego-Bol'shevika* (Saratov, 1923), 1, 4, 11, 29, 38–39, 40, 77, 90.

101. *Biulleten' Istparta* 2, 1924, 5, 12.

102. *Proletarskaia revoliutsiia* 4 (1923): 288.

103. RGASPI, f. 70, op. 2, ed. khr. 263, l. 32.

104. The bureau cited this kind of criticism as one of its reasons for ceasing publication of its journal, *Krot*, after only eight issues (*Krot* 8, December 1923, 18–19).

105. RGASPI, f. 70, op. 2, ed. khr. 61, l. 6. The Orenburg bureau complained at this time that it had almost no materials for 1917, 1918, and 1919 and "no official material on the October events in Orenburg" (RGASPI, f. 70, op. 2, ed. khr. 248, l. 4).

106. *Biulleten' Istparta* 2, 1924, 5. The Saratov bureau, for example, by 1923 had sources on the 1890s and the early 1900s, when "a strong RSDRP organization already existed" in Saratov (RGASPI, f. 17, op. 60, ed. khr. 633, l. 112). The Tatar bureau had collected materials by individuals relating to the Kazan' organization of the RSDRP, mostly relating to the underground and the period of the October Revolution (*Biulleten' Istparta* 2, 1924, 16). The Samara bureau by 1923 had some memoirs covering 1904–1908 and 1914–1916, but very little else (RGASPI, f. 70, op. 2, ed. khr. 5, l. 12).

107. RGASPI, f. 70, op. 2, ed. khr. 59, l. 28.

108. *Proletarskaia revoliutsiia* 4 (1923): 289–96.

109. RGASPI, f. 70, op. 1, ed. khr. 183, ll. 148–49. The work was *Moskva v 1917 g.*, by Rozova.

110. RGASPI, f. 70, op. 2, ed. khr. 217, l. 39.

111. Lev Trotskii, "Uroki Oktiabria," in *Ob "Urokakh Oktiabria"* (Leningrad, 1924), 220–62. The article first appeared in October 1924 as the introduction to two volumes of writings on the first year of the revolution, entitled *1917*. Criticism also included two other works by Trotsky, published at the same time, in which he touched on similar themes (see Trotskii, "O Lenine"; idem., "Novyi kurs," in L. D. Trotskii, *K istorii russkoi revoliutsii* [Moscow, 1990], 164–203).

112. See the special issue on the Red Army of *Krasnaia niva* 8, February 23, 1923.

113. *The Trotsky Papers: 1917–1922*, ed. Jan M. Meijer, vol. 2 (The Hague: Mouton, 1971), 643. Trotsky's opponents ensured that this letter was often included in published compilations of critiques of his *Lessons of October* as proof of his heresy. By the late 1920s, however, compilations of writings on the "discussion" did not include Trotsky's direct voice, the term "Trotskyism" taking its place (e.g., *Diskussiia 1925 g. Materialy i dokumenty* (Moscow-Leningrad, 1929).

114. Trotskii, "Uroki," 240.

115. White, *Russian Revolution*, 258.

116. Trotskii, "Uroki," 220, 221, 222.

117. S. A. Piontkovskii, "Oshibki v 'Urokakh Oktiabria' tov. Trotskogo," *Proletarskaia revoliutsiia* 1 (1925): 220.

118. D. Lebed', "O nedopustimom iskazhenii istoricheskikh faktov," in *Za Leninizm: Sbornik statei* (Moscow-Leningrad, 1925), 259, 260.

119. Trotskii, "Uroki," 250.

120. E. Kviring, "Lenin, zagovorshchestvo, Oktiabr'," in *Ob "Urokakh Oktiabria"*, 145 and 147. The author was critiquing Trotsky's *O Lenine*.

121. Lebed', "O nedopustimom iskazhenii," 261.

122. Trotskii, *O Lenine: Materialy dlia biografa* (Moscow, n.d.), resp. 56, 61.

123. Trotskii, "Novyi kurs," 167–68.

124. Ibid., 167.

125. G. Sokol'nikov, "Kak podkhodit' k istorii Oktiabria?: Po povodu 'Urokov Oktiabria' tov. Trotskogo," in *Za Leninizm*, 157.

126. L. Kamenev, "Leninizm ili trotskizm," in *Ob "Urokakh Oktiabria"*, 18. Elsewhere, it was argued that the newspaper published by Trotsky from 1908 to 1912, the Vienna *Pravda*, a nonfactional newspaper, had depicted Bolshevism as "a narrow, isolated doctrinaire group" (Lebed', "O nedopustimom iskazhenii," 259).

127. G. Zinov'ev, "O fraktsionnosti i o stat'e tov. Trotskogo," in *Za partiiu, za Leninizm* (Petrograd, 1924), 132.

128. N. Bukharin, "Kak ne nuzhno pisat' istoriiu Oktiabria: po povodu knigi Trotskogo '1917'," in *Za Leninizm*, 14–15.

129. Ibid., 10, 12–13.

130. I. Stepanov, "Kto sovershil Oktiabr'skuiu Revoliutsiiu? Po povodu 'Istorii' Oktiabria v knige L. Trotskogo '1917'," in *Za Leninizm*, 267, 271, 272.

131. RGASPI, f. 70, op. 1, ed. khr. 94, l. 3.

132. RGASPI, f. 17, op. 84, ed. khr. 539, l. 15.

133. Stepanov, "Kto sovershil Oktiabr'skuiu revoliutsiiu?" 266.

134. I. Gelis, "Kak nado pisat' vospominaniia (metodologicheskii ocherk)," *Proletarskaia revoliutsiia* 7 (1925): 197.

135. RGASPI, f. 17, op. 84, ed. khr. 765, ll. 154–155, 158.

CHAPTER 6: THE LESSONS OF OCTOBER: THE TWENTIETH ANNIVERSARY OF 1905

1. RGASPI, f. 70, op. 2, ed. khr. 429, ll. 5, 14; f. 17, op. 85, ed. khr. 319, l. 25; ed. khr. 37, l. 3.

2. RGASPI, f. 70, op. 1, ed. khr. 4, l. 8.

3. RGASPI, f. 70, op. 1, d. 96, l. 129.

4. These biographical details are drawn from Burgess, "The Istpart Commission," 149–51.

5. *Proletarskaia revoliutsiia* 1, no. 36 (1925): 5, 8–9, 13; also Holmes and Burgess, "Scholarly Voice or Political Echo?" 393 ff.

6. RGASPI, f. 17, op. 84, ed. khr. 765, l. 81. Local bureaus responded positively to such calls (RGASPI, f. 70, op. 2, ed. khr. 429, l. 14).

7. RGASPI, f. 70, op. 1, ed. khr. 187, l. 4.

8. RGASPI, f. 70, op. 1, ed. khr. 12, l. 10. The commission, comprised Ol'minskii, Elizarova, Baturin, Nevskii, Varentsova, Liadov, and Mitskevich, and was confirmed on December 18, 1923 (RGASPI, f. 70, op. 1, ed. khr. 4, l. 1, l. 10). At Istpart's urging, the Society of Old Bolsheviks also set up a commission on 1905 (RGASPI, f. 17, op. 84, ed. khr. 539, l. 16).

9. RGASPI, f. 17, op. 84, ed. khr. 539, l. 16.

10. RGASPI, f. 70, op. 1, d. 96, l. 128.

11. RGASPI, f. 70, op. 1, ed. khr. 187, l. 3.

12. RGASPI, f. 70, op. 1, ed. khr. 4, l. 11, 12.

13. *Proletarskaia revoliutsiia* 1 (1925): 149, 151–53.

14. Ibid., 2 (1925): 213–15, 216.

15. Ibid., 7 (1925): 197–99, 207.

16. RGASPI, f. 70, op. 1, ed. khr. 12, l. 15.

17. RGASPI, f.70, op. 2, ed. khr. 411, l. 18. The literary subcommission was intended as the clearinghouse for all publications on 1905 that eventually appeared under the imprint of the State Publishing House (Gosizdat), the commission under TSIK SSSR, and Istpart (RGASPI, f. 70, op. 1, ed. khr. 12, l. 17).

18. RGASPI, f. 17, op. 84, ed. khr. 876, l. 224; ed. khr. 765, l. 141; f. 70, op. 1, ed. khr. 12, l. 15.

19. RGASPI, f. 70, op. 2, ed. khr. 430, l. 6.

20. Kanatchikov referred the matter to the Central Committee's Orgbiuro for adjudication (RGASPI, f. 70, op. 1, ed. khr. 94, l. 98).

21. RGASPI, f. 17, op. 84, ed. khr. 765, l. 127.

22. RGASPI, f. 70, op. 1, ed. khr. 185, l. 1.

23. *Proletarskaia revoliutsiia* 12 (1925): 251–53.

24. RGASPI, f. 70, op. 1, ed. khr. 185, l. 1.

25. *Biulleten' Istparta* 1, 1921, 12–14.

26. RGASPI, f. 70, op. 1, ed. khr. 4, l. 1–3.

27. Jonathan Frankel, "Party Genealogy and the Soviet Historians (1920–1938)," *Slavic Review* 25, no. 4 (1966): 569–78.

28. The documents were selected from the archives to show an inexorably evolving Bolshevik identity, emphasizing Bolshevik distinctness (from the Mensheviks in particular) dating back to the 1903 split in the RSDRP. The collection aimed to show that these Bolsheviks, who had burst from the underground into the open political arena in February 1917 "with such noise," and about whom now "millions were speaking," brought with them a distinct identity that had evolved over many years (M. A. Tsiavlovskii, ed., *Bol'sheviki: Dokumenty po istorii bol'shevizma s 1903 po 1916 g. byvsh. Moskovskago Okhrannago Otdeleniia* [Moscow, 1918], iii). The fervent police interest in all radical groups up to 1917 should not be equated with the popular standings of those groupings. The Okhrana's role at this time was to locate identifiable causes of the political unrest and to evaluate the potential threat posed by revolutionaries, a threat sometimes oddly measured in the physical weight of antigovernment literature ("Revoliutsionnoe dvizhenie v Rossii," in *Neizvestnaia Rossiia. 20 Vek,* vol. 2 [Moscow: "Istoricheskoe nasledie," 1992], 353).

29. *Pechat' i revoliutsiia* 2 (1921): 246–47.

30. *Biulleten' Istparta* 2, 1924, 5–6. Volumes on the fate of populism to 1900, the *Iskra* period, and the reaction of 1907–1910 were already in the final stages of editing. Work was also under way on the 1905–1906 period and the years of the war, the latter volume extending up to the 1917 February revolution. Curiously, the reader would not cover the revolutions of 1917 because, according to Lepeshinskii, "there is already extensive literature on the February and October Revolutions" (ibid.).

31. Baturin had been tasked in 1922 with presenting such a plan for the reader within a week, and Lepeshinskii a plan for the primer within two; neither did so (RGASPI, f. 70, op. 1, ed. khr. 2, l. 3, 4, 7). After a report by Baturin on the progress of the reader, Istpart decided to take "extreme measures" to publish the first volume as soon as possible (RGASPI, f. 70, op. 1, ed. khr. 3, l. 1).

32. RGASPI, f. 70, op. 1, ed. khr. 2, l. 4.

33. *Biulleten' Istparta* 2, 1924, 6.

34. *Rossiiskaia Kommunisticheskaia Partii (bol'shevikov) v rezoliutsiiakh ee s"ezdov i konferentsii (1898–1921 g.g.)* (Moscow, 1922), iii. The publication in question was *Rossiiskaia Kommunisticheskaia Partiia (bol'shevikov) v postanovlenniiakh ee s"ezdov 1903–1921 g.g.* (Petersburg, 1921).

35. *Rossiiskaia Kommunisticheskaia Partii (bol'shevikov) v rezoliutsiiakh,* iii–iv.

36. It decided to include, among other issues, the Democratic Conference and comrade Rykov's Rightist position on it; Lenin's declaration of September 20, 1917, on the exclusion of Kamenev and Zinoviev; the position of the Rightists on permitting Mensheviks and Socialist Revolutionaries into the government; Lenin's stand against the editorship of Bukharin in *Pravda* and for Trotsky; Stalin's declaration on the eve of the October overthrow that he was leaving *Pravda*; Kamenev's proposal to destroy all copies of Lenin's letters on the uprising and Stalin's proposal to distribute them among the organizations (RGASPI, f. 70, op. 2, d. 484, l. 4).

37. *Tretii ocherednoi s"ezd Rossiiskoi Sotsial–Demokraticheskoi Rabochei Partii 1905 g. Polnyi tekst protokolov* (Moscow, 1924), 7–8.

38. Ibid., 13–14.

39. Ibid., 12.

40. RGASPI, f. 70, op. 1, ed. khr. 3, l. 5.

41. RGASPI, f. 70, op. 1, ed. khr. 3, l. 2.

42. RGASPI, f. 70, op. 1, ed. khr. 3, l. 1.

43. RGASPI, f. 70, op. 1, ed. khr. 49, ll. 87–88.

44. In the winter of 1923–24, the Moscow bureau, following a directive of the Moscow Committee of the party, decided to bring in students of the Institute of Red Professors and other Communists to compile scholarly popular sketches of the history of the revolutionary movement and the RKP (RGASPI, f. 70, op. 2, ed. khr. 217, l. 18). The Simbirsk

bureau dated its existence only from the twenty-fifth jubilee of the party (*Biulleten' Istparta* 2, 1924, 13).

45. Tsentral'nyi Gosudarstvennyi Arkhiv Obshchestvennykh Dvizhenii g. Moskvy (hereinafter TsGAOD g.M), f. 3, op. 11, d. 134, l. 1. The commission also planned party meetings jointly with Komsomol and other groups at the rural district level (ibid., l. 2); and drew up a list of literature to be published for the jubilee (ibid., l. 15; l. 23).

46. TsGAOD g.M, f. 3, op. 11, d. 134, l. 15.

47. RGASPI, f. 70, op. 2, ed. khr. 216, l. 18.

48. White, *Lenin*, 178–79.

49. Major studies on the cult of Lenin stress either the continuing impact of Russian popular religiosity on the success of this mythmaking (Tumarkin, *Lenin Lives!*), or the Bolshevik use of religious metaphors to facilitate the path of the myth into Soviet public opinion (Benno Ennker, "Leninkult und Mythisches Denken in der Sowjetischen Öffentlichkeit 1924," *Jahrbücher für Geschichte Osteuropas* 44, no. 3 [1996]: 431–55; Benno Ennker, *Die Anfänge des Leninkults in der Sowjetunion* [Cologne: Böhlau, 1997]).

50. RGASPI, f. 70, op. 1, ed. khr. 26, l. 6.

51. *Trinadtsatyi s"ezd*, 560–73.

52. "Ot redaktsii," *Leninskii sbornik*, vol. 2 (Moscow-Leningrad, 1924), 3. Compare L. Kamenev, "Literaturnoe nasledstvo i sobranie sochinenii Vladimira Lenina," ibid., vol. 1 (Moscow-Leningrad, 1924), 5–23.

53. RGASPI, f. 70, op. 2, ed. khr. 217, l. 13. The Iaroslavl' bureau brought in a group of fifteen students from the local pedagogical institute to participate in a seminar on 1905, although the head of the bureau complained that the students were left without guidance and produced only superficial work (RGASPI, f. 70, op. 2, ed. khr. 431, ll. 28–29).

54. RGASPI, f. 70, op. 2, ed. khr. 248, l. 2. The bureau declared that its first task would be to bring some order to the party archive (RGASPI, f. 70, op. 2, ed. khr. 248, l. 10). It also very quickly published a collection of reminiscences and organized an exhibition on 1905 (RGASPI, f. 70, op. 2, ed. khr. 248, l. 8).

55. RGASPI, f.70, op. 2, ed. khr. 410, ll. 29–36.

56. RGASPI, f. 70, op. 2, ed. khr. 210, l. 35. The Iaroslavl' bureau reported beginning work organizing the "chaotic" archival materials on 1905 in its region, as well as organizing a library of six hundred books according to the following sections: "History of the Party," "Marxism-Leninism," "Sociology," and so on (RGASPI, f. 70, op. 2, ed. khr. 431, l. 24).

57. RGASPI, f. 70, op. 2, ed. khr. 248, l. 10, 12.

58. RGASPI, f. 70, op. 2, ed. khr. 431, ll. 24–25.

59. RGASPI, f. 70, op. 2, ed. khr. 248, l. 2, 4.

60. Lebed', "O nedopustimom iskazhenii," 264.

61. RGASPI, f. 70, op. 2, ed. khr. 12, l. 6. On the groups of assistance, see V. Iu. Korovainikov, "Gruppy sodeistviia Istpartu TsK VKP(b)," *Voprosy istorii KPSS* 1 (1991): 112–23.

62. RGASPI, f. 70, op. 2, d. 8, ll. 58–59. The most productive groups had already produced verified reminiscences on the revolution in their areas, including Dnepropetrovsk, Odessa, Kostroma, and Minsk.

63. *Proletarskaia revoliutsiia* 6 (1925): 259.

64. RGASPI, f. 70, op. 1, ed. khr. 135, l. 9.

65. RGASPI, f. 70, op. 2, ed. khr. 429, l. 5; RGASPI, f. 70, op. 2, ed. khr. 429, l. 14.

66. By fall 1927, thirty-three groups of assistance encompassing 728 people had produced 149 transcripts (*stenogrammy*) of evenings of reminiscences (V. Iu. Korovainikov, "Stenogrammy vecherov vospominanii kak istochnik po istorii Velikoi Oktiabr'skoi Sotsialisticheskoi Revoliutsii," *Sovetskie arkhivy* 5, 1990, 75).

67. *Biulleten' Istparta* 2, 1924, 12.

68. RGASPI, f. 70, op. 2, ed. khr. 2, l. 3.

69. RGASPI, f. 70, op. 2, ed. khr. 5, l. 12. Similarly, the head of the Simbirsk bureau noted in 1923 the "haphazard" organization of the evenings (*Biulleten' Istparta* 2, 1924, 13).

70. A. Terne, *V tsarstve Lenina*, 65–66.

71. RGASPI, f. 17, op 3, d. 84, l. 1.

72. It initiated a similar process of self-definition among the accused SRs on trial (see their defense speeches in *Partiia Sotsialistov-Revoliutsionerov. Dokumenty i materialy. Oktiabr' 1917 g.–1925 g.* [Moscow: ROSSPEN, 2000], 855–921).

73. In 1919 the Politburo allowed a collection of articles on the Right SR Komuch to be published only if it did not receive "broad, mass distribution" (RGASPI, f. 17, op. 3, d. 4, l. 2; cf. ibid., d. 33, l. 2; d. 37, l. 2). Cf. similar Politburo decisions in 1919 on Menshevik and other publications (ibid., d. 29, l. 1; d. 33, l. 1; d. 33, l. 2), and a decision by the Central Committee in 1924 that memoirs by Mensheviks could be published by Gosizdat only with the sanction *in each case* of the Istpart board (RGASPI, f. 70, op. 1, ed. khr. 4, l. 9).

74. Only fifty copies of the first three issues of *Vestnik* reached Russia in 1921. The numbers increased to one hundred to one hundred fifty copies of later issues. By late 1922, about three hundred to four hundred copies of each issue were being received (Boris Dvinov, *Ot legal'nosti k podpol'iu, 1921–1922* [Stanford: Hoover Institution, 1968], 34, 127).

75. Kamenev, "Leninizm ili Trotskizm," 6–7, 19, 7, 17.

76. RGASPI, f. 70, op. 1, ed. khr. 94, l. 3.

77. *Kak rozhdalas' partiia Bol'shevikov: Literaturnaia polemika 1903–04 gg. Sbornik* (Leningrad, 1925), 5–8.

78. *Pravda*, October 17, 1926, 1.

79. Ibid., October 20, 1926, 1.

80. Ibid., October 17, 1926, 3.

81. Ibid., 1.

82. *Pravda*, October 12, 1927, 7; October 20, 1927, 6; October 26, 1927, 1; November 1, 1927, 2.

83. Cited in Daniels, *Conscience of the Revolution*, 275.

84. *Biulleten' oppozitsii* 9 (1930): 31–32.

85. RGASPI, f. 70, op. 2, ed. khr. 431, ll. 29–31.

86. RGASPI, f. 70, op. 1, ed. khr. 49, l. 96.

87. Ol'minskii argued that the jubilee had to have the official imprimatur of the Central Committee of the party, had to be sufficiently funded, and had to be able to draw on the resources and authority of the Central Executive Committee of the Republic, the Agitation and Propaganda Department of the Central Committee of the party, Istpart, the Institute of Lenin, the Central Archive, the Society of Former Political Exiles and Prisoners, and the Society of Old Bolsheviks (RGASPI, f. 17, op. 84, ed. khr. 539, l. 17).

88. RGASPI, f. 70, op. 2, ed. khr. 430, l. 6.

89. RGASPI, f. 70, op. 1, ed. khr. 91, ll. 33–34.

90. RGASPI, f. 70, op. 2, ed. khr. 210, l. 15, 35.

91. *Kalendar'. Khronika sobytii 1905 goda s ianvaria 1905 g. po mart 1906 g.*, ed. E. A. Morokhovets (Moscow-Leningrad, 1926), 11.

92. RGASPI, f. 70, op. 1, ed. khr. 49, l. 92.

93. RGASPI, f. 70, op. 2, ed. khr. 12, l. 5.

94. RGASPI, f. 70, op. 1, ed. khr. 160, ll. 2–4.

95. RGASPI, f. 70, op. 1, d. 91, ll. 11–12.

96. *Proletarskaia revoliutsiia* 8 (1925): 272–73.

97. RGASPI, f. 70, op. 2, ed. khr. 411, l. 24.

98. RGASPI, f. 70, op. 2, ed. khr. 411, l. 11.

99. *1905. Revoliutsionnye sobytiia 1905 g. v g. Ufe i Ural'skikh zavodakh (Bashrespublika)* (Ufa, 1925), 113. A plan of publications for the 1905 jubilee, drawn up by the official Iaroslavl' jubilee committee, was divided into distinct themes: Bolshevik Party work in 1904–1907 and the activities of the "bourgeois and petite bourgeois" parties; the economic condition of the province; the peasant movement; and the course of strikes during these years (RGASPI, f. 70, op. 2, ed. khr. 431, l. 25).

100. M. Verkhotorskii, "1905 god," in *1905. Revoliutsionnye sobytiia 1905 g.*, 1.

101. RGASPI, f. 70, op. 2, ed. khr. 248, l. 8; ed. khr. 411, l. 24.

102. RGASPI, f.70, op. 2, ed. khr. 411, l. 11.

103. "Pervaia konferentsiia voennykh i boevykh organizatsii R.S.-D.R.P.," in *1905. Revoliutsionnye sobytiia 1905 g.*, 175.

104. *Pravda* 184, August 15, 1924, 3.

105. Ibid., 203, September 7, 1924, 2. Savel'ev identified this article as required reading for all who wanted to know about 1905 and the history of the party, and particularly for those who worked at local Istpart bureaus (RGASPI, f. 70, op. 1, ed. khr. 185, l. 1).

106. *1905. Istoriia revoliutsionnogo dvizheniia v otdelnykh ocherkakh*, ed. M. N. Pokrovskii, vol. 1, *Predposylki revoliutsii* (Moscow-Leningrad, 1925), v–vii. The second volume, chronicling the January to October period, in fact devoted much space to the RSDRP (see *1905*, vol. 2, *Ot ianvaria k Oktiabriu* (Moscow-Leningrad, 1925).

107. RGASPI, f. 70, op. 1, ed. khr. 49, l. 89.

108. RGASPI, f. 70, op. 1, ed. khr. 49, l. 144 (emphasis added).

109. RGASPI, f. 70, op. 1, ed. khr. 13, l. 3. The deputy director of the Central Committee's Agitation and Propaganda Department, Mal'tsev, proposed to Bukharin and Molotov a detailed plan of assignment of duties (by a planned five-man presidium) to the members of the jubilee commission (RGASPI, f. 17, op. 85, ed. khr. 14, l. 4).

110. *Pravda* 47 (3579), February 26, 1927, 5.

111. RGASPI, f. 70, op. 3, ed. khr. 960, ll. 1–3.

112. RGASPI, f. 17, op. 85, ed. khr. 14, l. 2, 8, 1, 6–7.

113. RGASPI, f. 17, op. 85, ed. khr. 107, ll. 1–2.

114. RGASPI, f. 17, op. 85, ed. khr. 107, l. 34.

115. *Biulleten' Komissii pri Prezidiume TsIK Soiuza SSR po organizatsii i provedeniiu prazdnovaniia 10–letiia Oktiabr'skoi Revoliutsii* 1 (July 1927): 12.

116. RGASPI, f. 70, op. 1, ed. khr. 36, ll. 54–55.

117. RGASPI, f. 70, op. 1, ed. khr. 119, l. 192.

118. *Pravda*, September 27, 1927, 5; *Izvestiia*, November 1, 1927, 2.

119. RGASPI, f. 70, op. 2, ed. khr. 8, ll. 64–65.

120. RGASPI, f. 70, op. 1, ed. khr. 119, l. 93.

121. RGASPI, f. 70, op. 1, ed. khr. 119, l. 180.

122. RGASPI, f. 70, op. 1, ed. khr. 119, l. 192.

123. RGASPI, f. 17, op. 85, ed. khr. 14, l. 27.

124. RGASPI, f. 17, op. 84, ed. khr. 765, ll. 105–41.

125. RGASPI, f. 70, op. 2, d. 8, l. 59.

126. *Pravda*, September 7, 1927, 5; September 14, 1927, 5; September 16, 1927, 5.

127. Ibid., September 17, 1927, 3.

128. V. A. Nevskii, *Massovaia polit.-prosvet: Rabota revoliutsionnykh let* (Moscow-Leningrad, 1925), 14.

129. M. Danilevskii, *Prazdniki obshchestvennogo byta. Organizatsiia, metodika, praktika* (Moscow-Leningrad, 1927), 5–8. Also, *Novyi lef* 7 (1927): 46–48.

130. *Novyi lef* 4 (1927): 35.

131. RGASPI, f. 17, op. 85, ed. khr. 107, l. 7. By early October, the section had produced twenty-nine plays and productions (*instsenirovki*), many of them translated into the national languages of the Soviet Union (*Pravda*, October 2, 1927, 6).

132. *Izvestiia*, November 5, 1927, 5.

133. By late September, preparations were well underway for a series of films, e.g., *Armored Cars* [*Broneviki*], *General Line*, *Moscow in October*, *Petersburg-Petrograd-Leningrad*, *Ten Years*, among many others (*Pravda*, September 29, 1927, 5).

134. *Pravda*, September 7, 1927, 5.

135. Nevskii, *Massovaia polit.-prosvet. rabota*, 42, 88–89.

136. *Pravda*, September 30, 1927, 5.

137. N. I. Podvoiskii and A. R. Orlinskii, *Massovoe deistvo: Rukovodstvo k organizatsii i provedeniiu prazdnovaniia 10–letiia Oktiabria i drugikh revoliutsionnykh prazdnikov* (Moscow-Leningrad, 1927), 3.

CHAPTER 7: TRUTH AND POETRY: THE TENTH ANNIVERSARY OF OCTOBER

1. *Pravda*, October 6, 1927, 5; October 11, 1927, 5; October 27, 1927, 4. Visitors returned to their home countries to set up local organizations in support of the Soviet project: e.g., the International Society for Friends of the Soviet Union in Cologne (Sophie Coeure, "Les 'Fêtes d'Octobre' 1927 à Moscou: La Dynamique des structures d'influence Soviétique et Kominterniennes autour d'un anniversaire," *Communisme* 42–44 (1995): 63–69).

2. *Pravda*, September 8, 1927, 5.

3. Ibid., October 27, 1927, 4.

4. Ibid., September 3, 1927, 6.

5. Ibid., November 10, 1927, 1; also, *Izvestiia*, November 10, 1927, 4.

6. *Leningradskii rabochii*, November 26, 1927, 7.

7. *Izvestiia*, November 11, 1927, 3.

8. *Pravda*, October 26, 1927, 3.

9. *Izvestiia*, November 4, 1927, 3–4; *Pravda*, November 15, 1927, 1.

10. *Pravda*, September 21, 1927, 3; September 25, 1927, 3; October 1, 1927, 3; October 4, 1927, 3; October 7, 1927, 3.

11. Trotsky, *My Life*, 531–33.

12. See Coeure, "Les 'Fêtes d'Octobre' 1927 à Moscou, 66.

13. Paul Scheffer, *Augenzeuge im Staate Lenins: Ein Korrespondent Berichtet aus Moskau, 1921–1930* (Munich: Piper, 1972), 293.

14. *Leningradskii rabochii*, November 26, 1927, 7.

15. *Pravda*, November 10, 1927, 6.

16. Ibid., November 11, 1927, 1.

17. Ibid., November 10, 1927, 6.

18. *Izvestiia*, November 10, 1927, 3; *Pravda*, November 10, 1927, 6.

19. For example, *Pravda*, November 11, 1927, 4; November 15, 1927, 4.

20. Ibid., November 11, 1927, 2.

21. Podvoiskii and Orlinskii, *Massovoe deistvo*, 258–73.

22. R. R. Suslovich, "Zritel' massovogo prazdnika," in *Massovye prazdnestva* (Leningrad, 1925), 190–91.

23. *Leningradskii rabochii* 22, November 26, 1927, 11. Cf. *Pravda*, September 8, 1927, 5.

24. *Pravda*, October 23, 1927, 3; October 25, 1927, 2; October 27, 1927, 3; October 28, 1927, 3; November 1, 1927, 5; November 2, 1927, 2; November 3, 1927, 3; November 4, 1927, 3; November 5, 1927, 2; November 6–7, 1927, 8.

25. Ibid., October 14, 1927, 7. Compare another such list that included a play entitled *Ten Days*, which was based on John Reed's work, and another production entitled *October Episode* (ibid., September 24, 1927, 5).

26. *Izvestiia*, November 1, 1927, 2.

27. Ibid., November 4, 1927, 5.

28. Ibid., November 5, 1927, 6; cf. Pokrovskii's account in *Pravda*, November 6–7, 1927, 6.

29. *Izvestiia*, November 4, 1927, 5.

30. *Pravda*, November 6–7, 1927, 6.

31. P. E. Dybenko, *Iz nedr tsarskogo flota k Velikomu Oktiabriu: Iz vospominanii o revoliutsii, 1917–1927* (Moscow, 1928), 161.

32. *Izvestiia*, November 2, 1927, 3.

33. Nikolai Podvoiskii, *Krasnaia gvardiia v Oktiabr'skie dni (Leningrad i Moskva)* (Moscow-Leningrad, 1927), 6.

34. *Izvestiia*, November 6–7, 1927, 9; November 5, 1927, 3.

35. Ibid., November 5, 1927, 6. This episode appeared almost verbatim as a climactic episode in a book-length treatment of his experiences (Podvoiskii, *Krasnaia gvardiia v Oktiabr'skie dni*, 41).

36. According to Aleksandrov's voice-over at the beginning of the version of *October* that he reworked for worldwide distribution in 1967, Podvoiskii played himself in the film (also Iu. Krasovskii, "Kak sozdaval'sia fil'm *Oktiabria*," in *Iz istorii kino: Dokumenty i materialy* [Moscow, 1965], 49).

37. A. A. Khanzhonkov, *Pervye gody russkoi kinematografii* (Moscow-Leningrad, 1937), 104. In the first days of March 1917, the Union of Cinema Workers (*Soiuz kinodeiatelei*) promised to show all "free citizens" the film *The Great Days of Revolution in Moscow* [Velikie dni revoliutsii v Moskve] (ibid.).

38. "Udostoverenie E. M. Modzelevskomu na pravo kinematograficheskikh s"emok v Petrograde i ego okrestnostiakh vydaiushchikhskia revolutsionnykh sobytii," in *Petrogradskii voenno-revoliutsionnyi komitet*, vol. 2 (Moscow, 1966), 124. For similar authorization to the filmmaker G. M. Boltianskii, see "Udostoverenie," in *Bol'shevistskie voenno-revoliutsionnye komitety* (Moscow, 1958), 117. Not all requests for filming permission were granted; see "Protokol vechernego zasedaniia Petrogradskogo voenno-revoliutsionnogo komiteta," in *Oktiabr'skoe vooruzhennoe vosstanie v Petrograde* (Moscow, 1957), 740.

39. V. Listov, "Iz istorii dvukh s"emok," *in Leniniana: poiski i nakhodki* (Moscow, 1970), 51; Jay Leyda, *Kino: A History of Russian and Soviet Film*, 3d ed. (Princeton: Princeton University Press, 1983), 132–33, 142; "Obiazatel'noe postanovlenie," *Petrogradskaia pravda*, October 27, 1920, 4.

40. G. Boltianskii, *Lenin i kino* (Moscow-Leningrad, 1925), 35.

41. G. Boltianskii, *Kino-khronika i kak ee snimat'* (Moscow, 1926), 8, 49.

42. Leon Trotsky, "Vodka, the Church, and the Cinema," in Leon Trotsky, *Problems of Everyday Life and Other Writings on Culture and Science* (New York: Monad, 1973), 31–35.

43. David Bordwell, "The Idea of Montage in Soviet Art and Film," *Cinema Journal* 11, no. 2 (1972): 10.

44. Sergei Eisenstein, *Notes of a Film Director* (London: Lawrence and Wishart, 1959), 23.

45. Sergei Eisenstein, "The Method of Making Workers' Films," in *Bolshevik Visions: First Phase of the Cultural Revolution in Soviet Russia*, ed. William G. Rosenberg (Ann Arbor: University of Michigan Press, 1990), 110–11.

46. The films by Shub and Barnet were not available to me and will not be included in the following discussion of the jubilee films.

47. One scholar argues that Eisenstein's *October* was an acknowledgment of Stalin's policy of Socialism in One Country in 1926 and represented not a "hymn to the conquering revolution" but rather to the conquest of a "space beyond the reach of foreign influences" (Pierre Sorlin, *The Film in History: Restaging the Past* [Totowa, N.J.: Barnes and Noble,

1980], 178–79). More often, these films are analyzed in terms of their historical accuracy (D. J. Wenden, "Battleship Potemkin: Film and Reality," in *Feature Films as History*, ed. K. R. M. Short [Knoxville: University of Tennessee Press, 1981], 37–61). The dangers of using "reconstructed films" are discussed in Marc Ferro, "1917: History and Cinema," *Journal of Contemporary History* 3, no. 4 (1968): 46. Even scholars who approach these films in terms of their mythic structure and function find it hard to resist the temptation to measure them against the "real" events being represented (James Goodwin, *Eisenstein, Cinema, and History* [Urbana: University of Illinois Press, 1993], 58, 83–84; David Bordwell, *The Cinema of Eisenstein* [Cambridge: Harvard University Press, 1993], 79–84). For a critique of this tendency and an argument for studying *October* in its own terms, namely as invention, see Robert A. Rosenstone, "*October* as History," *Rethinking History* 5, no. 2 (2001): 255–74.

48. Shub planned a trilogy of films. *Fall of the Romanov Dynasty* and *The Great Way* were completed, but no trace remains of the third, *The Russia of Nicholas II and Lev Tolstoy (Rossiia Nikolai II i Lev Tolstoi)* (Graham Roberts, *Forward Soviet! History and Non-Fiction Film in the USSR* [London: I. B. Tauris, 1999], 157, n. 14). Eisenstein intended a seven-part cycle of films entitled *Toward the Dictatorship (K diktature)*, of which only the fifth part, *Strike* [*Stachka*, 1925], was completed. *October* also started out as a seven-parter (Iu. Krasovskii, "Kak sozdaval'sia fil'm *Oktiabria*," in *Iz istorii kino*, 42). Pudovkin's films were also born from scripts of ambitious reach (Leyda, *Kino*, 222–23).

49. Goodwin, *Eisenstein, Cinema, and History*, 41. In *Potemkin*, Eisenstein juxtaposed the muscular and burly form of the sailors against the slender and effete form of the officers, and the sailors' open and candid gazes against the officers' devious and squinting glares (ibid., 65).

50. Goodwin, *Eisenstein, Cinema, and History*, 66.

51. On Eisenstein's use of the shock effect in *Potemkin*, see Goodwin, *Eisenstein, Cinema, and History*, 74–78.

52. Roberts, *Forward Soviet!*, 56.

53. Ibid., 59.

54. Michèle Lagny, Marie-Claire Ropars-Wuilleumier, and Pierre Sorlin, *La Révolution figurée: Inscription de l'histoire et du politique dans un film* (Paris: Albatros, 1979), 154. The occurrences and significance of these markers in this film receive detailed examination in ibid., 153–60.

55. Iurii Tsiv'ian has remarked on the use of the "motif of petrification [*okamenenie*] of power" in Eisenstein's films (*Istoricheskaia retseptsiia kino: Kinematograf v Rossii, 1896–1930* [Riga: Zinatne, 1991], 334).

56. Bordwell, *Cinema of Eisenstein*, 45.

57. *Novyi lef* 10 (1927): 29.

58. Marie-Claire Ropars-Wuilleumier, *L'Écran de la mémoire: Essais de lecture cinématographique* (Paris: Éditions du Seuil, 1970), 200. The recurrence of certain objects and graphic patterns throughout Eisenstein's work added to the internal coherence of the narrative (Bordwell, *Cinema of Eisenstein*, 48).

59. "The Lef Ring: Comrades! A Clash of Views!" in *The Film Factory: Russian and Soviet Cinema in Documents, 1896–1939*, ed. Richard Taylor and Ian Christie (London: Routledge and Kegan Paul, 1988), 232. As Stites notes, for such reasons the episode of the storming of the Winter Palace has remained "a truncated narrative lacking the orgiastic release that drama would require" (Stites, *Revolutionary Dreams*, 83).

60. Cited in Bordwell, *Cinema of Eisenstein*, 91. For Bordwell's general discussion of this motif, see ibid., 90–91.

61. "Vladimir Mayakovsky: Speech in Debate on 'The Paths and Policy of Sovkino,' " in *Film Factory*, 173.

62. Leyda, *Kino*, 238–39.

63. Goodwin, *Eisenstein, Cinema, and History*, 80.

64. Early cameramen were able to produce only "several hundred meters of old film of poor quality," showing such sites as Smolny, the Winter Palace, Tsarskoe Selo, and Gatchina. Even these contained little "material on events." Generally, the lack of footage of the storming is blamed on the technical problems of shooting at night or the bureaucratic problems presented by the military conditions of the period (V. Listov, *Istoriia smotrit v ob"ektiv* [Moscow, 1973], 51), even on the cunning of the Bolsheviks in staging their coup under cover of dark (Richard Pipes, "Seventy-Five Years On," 3).

65. "The Lef Ring: Comrades! A Clash of Views!" in *Film Factory*, 227, 230.

66. *Zhizn' iskusstva* 13 (March 27, 1928): 12.

67. Anatoli Lunacharsky, "Review of *October*," in *Film Factory*, 216.

68. *Zhizn' iskusstva* 13, March 27, 1928, 12.

69. *Vecherniaia Moskva* 59 (March 9, 1928): 3.

70. Adrian Piotrovsky, "October Must Be Re-edited!" in *Film Factory*, 216–17.

71. *Zhizn' iskusstva* 15, April 10, 1928, 16–17; also "*October*: The Results of the Discussion," in *Film Factory*, 232–34.

72. *Novyi lef* 10 (1927): 29, 27.

73. "Materialy 1 Vsesoiuznogo Partiinogo Kino-Soveshchaniia," *Kommunisticheskaia revoliutsiia* 8 (1928): 87. At least one radical director, Aleksandr Dovzhenko, responding to criticism that his work was inaccessible to audiences, suggested that the fault lay with the audience rather than with his films (ibid., 8, 1928, 68–69).

74. Viktor Shklovsky, "Where Is Dziga Vertov Striding?" in *Film Factory*, 152. Cf. Viktor Shklovsky, "The Cine-Eyes and Intertitles," in *Film Factory*, 153–54.

75. "The Lef Ring: Comrades! A Clash of Views!" in *Film Factory*, 225–26.

76. Esfir Shub, "We Do Not Deny the Element of Mastery," in *Film Factory*, 187.

77. *Novyi lef* 2 (1927): 32.

78. *Zhizn' iskusstva* 7, February 14, 1928, 2–3. *Battleship Potemkin* had received similar praise for its fusing of "form and content… into a powerful unity" (Alexei Gvozdev, "A New Triumph for Soviet Cinema: *The Battleship Potemkin* and the 'Theatrical October'," in *Film Factory*, 140).

79. *Zhizn' iskusstva* 14, April 3, 1928, 16; "*October*: The Results of the Discussion," in *Film Factory*, 232–34.

80. Scheffer, *Augenzeuge*, 291.

81. *Pravda*, September 7, 1924, 2; November 6–7, 1927, 6.

82. *Pechat' i revoliutsiia* 8 (December 1927): 68.

83. RGASPI, f. 70, op. 3, ed. khr. 960, l. 2, 3. Lenin was referring, in 1923, to the need to take time to improve the state apparatus, to focus not on its size but on its quality (V. I. Lenin, "Luchshe men'she, da luchshe," in *Sochineniia*, vol. 27, 406–18).

84. RGASPI, f. 70, op. 1, ed. khr. 178, ll. 1–4. Also, RGASPI, f. 139, op. 1, ed. khr. 18, l. 1.

85. RGASPI, f. 70, op. 3, ed. khr. 962, ll. 19–22. For similar complaints, see *Proletarskaia revoliutsiia* 5 (1928): 184–87, 188.

86. E. Iaroslavskii, *Partiia bol'shevikov v 1917 g.* (Moscow-Leningrad, 1927), 3, 10, 16, 18, 23.

87. M. Savel'ev, *Lenin i Oktiabr'skoe vooruzhennoe vosstanie* (Moscow-Leningrad, 1927), 4, 5, 34, 60.

88. *Izvestiia*, November 6–7, 1927, 3.

89. In 1931, Gorky initiated a project to write the history of factory life, particularly the ways in which it had improved under Communism (*A. M. Gor'kii i sozdanie istorii fabrik i zavodov: Sbornik dokumentov i materialov v pomoshch' rabotaiushchim nad istoriei*

fabrik i zavodov SSSR [Moscow, 1959]. Gorky complained in 1934 that the circles at the plants produced little and spent too much time in meetings discussing how to write, what to write, and how much to write ("Ne nravitsia mne eto—i Gripp, i Diuma," *Istochnik* 1 (1994): 18).

CONCLUSION: EXPERIENCING OCTOBER

1. Albert Rhys Williams, *Through The Russian Revolution* (New York: Boni and Liveright, 1921), 197.

2. Walter Benjamin, "The Work of Art in the Age of Mechanical Reproduction," in *Illuminations: Essays and Reflections* (New York: Schocken, 1968), 251, n. 21.

3. Merridale, *Night of Stone*, 184.

4. Cited in *Storming the Heavens*, 136.

5. *Zhizn' iskusstva* 602–4, November 8, 1920, 1.

6. " 'Ia stal ochen' boiattsa vsekh liudei…'," Ogonek 44–46 (November 1992): 31–32.

7. L. G. Borozinets, "Memuary N. I. Podvoiskogo kak istoricheskii istochnik," in *Gorod Lenina v dni Oktiabria i Velikoi Otechestvennoi Voiny, 1941–1945 gg. Sbornik statei* (Moscow-Leningrad, 1964), 60. For a comparison of the various versions of Antonov-Ovseenko's reminiscences by his son, see A. V. Antonov-Ovseenko, "Memuary V. A. Antonov-Ovseenko kak istochnik po istorii revoliutsionnykh sobytii 1917 g.," in *Trudy Moskovskogo Gosudarstvennogo Istoriko-Arkhivnogo Instituta*, vol. 24, *Voprosy istochnikoveniia istorii SSSR, Vyp.2* (Moscow, 1966), 203–19.

8. Krasovskii, "Kak sozdaval'sia fil'm *Oktiabria*," 45.

9. Advertisements for Barnet's *Moscow in October* made the following promise: "To be seen in the film: Stalin, Rykov, Bukharin, Yaroslavsky, Ulanov [sic], Skvortzev-Stepanov." Leyda writes that Eisenstein found doubles for all the well-known participants, even the members of Kerensky's cabinet (Leyda, *Kino*, 237).

10. von Geldern, *Bolshevik Festivals*, 3.

11. Sergei Eizenshtein, "S ekrana v zhizn'," 120–21. For one of the most prominent sources on the *Potemkin* created at the time, see *Vosstanie na bronenostse "Kniaz Potemkin Tavricheskii." Vospominaniia, materialy i dokumenty*, ed. V. I. Nevskii (Moscow-Petrograd, 1924).

12. *Vecherniaia Moskva*, March 8, 1928, 3.

13. G. V. Aleksandrov, *Epokha i kino*, 2d ed. (Moscow, 1983), 101–4.

14. Krasovskii, "Kak sozdaval'sia fil'm *Oktiabria*," 53.

15. Aleksandrov, *Epokha i kino*, 99.

16. Krasovskii, "Kak sozdaval'sia fil'm *Oktiabria*," 41.

17. Aleksandrov, *Epokha i kino*, 99–100.

18. Ibid., 107.

19. Leyda, *Kino*, 231. One such news photo of fleeing July demonstrators in Petrograd was duplicated so vividly by Eisenstein in *October* that the still of the episode is reproduced as often as the original photograph to portray the historical event (ibid., 232).

20. Aleksandrov, *Epokha i kino*, 107.

21. Cited in Krasovskii, "Kak sozdaval'sia fil'm *Oktiabria*," 45.

22. Cited in ibid., 50.

23. Aleksandrov, *Epokha i kino*, 111.

24. TsGAIPD SPb, f. 4000, op. 6, d. 63, ll. 27–54.

25. Ibid., l. 32.

26. Ibid., l. 36.

27. Ibid., l. 34.

28. Ibid., l. 44.

29. Ibid., l. 41.

30. Ibid., l. 35.

31. Aleksandrov, *Epokha i kino*, 107–9. My thanks to Aleksandr Burak for suggesting this translation of the colloquialism.

32. TsGAIPD SPb, f. 4000, op. 6, d. 63, ll. 50–51.

33. Maurice Halbwachs, *Collective Memory*, 24.

34. At an evening of reminiscences in November 1920, Savel'ev recalled thinking during the July Days that "we cannot be masters of this mass." An anonymous editor altered the transcript to read "the mass is seizing and carrying us along" (RGASPI, f. 70, op. 3, ed. khr. 81, l. 4).

35. Aleksandrov, *Epokha i kino*, 117.

36. RGASPI, f. 70, op. 1, ed. khr. 119, l. 288.

37. RGASPI, f. 70, op. 1, ed. khr. 5, l. 13, 11, 12. Pinson was granted one thousand rubles by Istpart to assist his research work (RGASPI, f. 70, op. 1, ed. khr. 5, l. 6).

38. RGASPI, f. 70, op. 1, ed. khr. 5, l. 10. This was indeed reflected in the attached outline (RGASPI, f. 70, op. 1, ed. khr. 5, ll. 15–25).

39. The project was cancelled after the manuscript was rejected for publication by the regional committee (*kraikom*) of the party in the North Caucasus (RGASPI, f. 70, op. 1, ed. khr. 5, l. 9; RGASPI, f. 70, op. 1, ed. khr. 5, l. 28).

40. For a similar example from Smolensk, see Hickey, "Paper, Memory, and a Good Story," 1–19; also Larry E. Holmes, "Soviet Rewriting of 1917: The Case of A. G. Shliapnikov," *Slavic Review* 38, no. 2 (1979): 224–42.

41. The following analysis is drawn from unpublished transcripts of several evenings of reminiscences held in 1926 and 1927 (TsGAIPD SPb, f. 4000, op. 5, d. 2103, ll. 1–5; op. 6, d. 43, ll. 1–40; d. 70, ll. 1–17; d. 42, ll. 1–18; d. 90, ll. 1–39, ll. 40–77).

42. *Biulleten' Istparta* 2, 1924, 11.

43. RGASPI, f. 70, op. 1, ed. khr. 17, l. 30.

44. Nevskii, *Massovaia polit. prosvet. rabota*, 62.

45. RGASPI, f. 70, op. 2, ed. khr. 216, l. 41.

46. RGASPI, f. 70, op. 2, ed. khr. 248, l. 8.

47. TsGAIPD SPb, f. 4000, op. 6, d. 43, l. 1.

48. TsGAIPD SPb, f. 4000, op. 6, d. 63, l. 44, 45.

49. TsGAIPD SPb, f. 4000, op. 5, d. 2103, l. 2.

50. TsGAIPD SPb, f. 4000, op. 6, d. 90, l. 14.

51. TsGAIPD SPb, f. 4000, op. 5, d. 2103, ll. 2–12.

52. TsGAIPD SPb, f. 4000, op. 5, d. 2103, l. 4, 1.

53. Nevskii, *Massovaia polit. prosvet. rabota*, 62.

54. RGASPI, f. 70, op. 2, ed. khr. 216, l. 42; TsGAIPD SPb, f. 4000, op. 6, d. 90, l. 40.

55. TsGAIPD SPb, f. 4000, op. 6, d. 90, ll. 29–30.

56. TsGAIPD SPb, f. 4000, op. 6, d. 70, l. 14.

57. TsGAIPD SPb, f. 4000, op. 6, d. 42, l. 9.

58. Ibid., l. 3, 8.

59. Ibid., l. 3.

60. Ibid., l. 15.

61. At one such gathering, a delegate interjected that "there were no Mensheviks in the local organization [*okruzhka*]." The Petrograd Committee of the RKP objected to the inclusion of "nonparty fellows" at an evening of reminiscences about the Gapon movement (*Biulleten' Istparta* 2, 1924, 9–11).

62. TsGAIPD SPb, f. 4000, op. 6, d. 42, l. 1.

63. Ibid., l. 11, 15.

64. TsGAIPD SPb, f. 4000, op. 6, d. 90, l. 3, 4.

65. Ibid., l. 13. Compare TsGAIPD SPb, f. 4000, op. 6, d. 42, l. 10.

66. TsGAIPD SPb, f. 4000, op. 6, d. 90, l. 13.

67. Ibid., l. 54.

68. Ibid., l. 6.

69. Ibid., l. 2.

70. Ibid., l. 36.

71. Ibid., l. 2.

72. TsGAIPD SPb, f. 4000, op. 6, d. 70, l. 6.

73. TsGAIPD SPb, f. 4000, op. 6, d. 90, l. 52.

74. TsGAIPD SPb, f. 4000, op. 6, d. 42, l. 12.

75. TsGAIPD SPb, f. 4000, op. 6, d. 43, l. 20.

76. TsGAIPD SPb, f. 4000, op. 6, d. 70, l. 1.

77. TsGAIPD SPb, f. 4000, op. 6, d. 43, ll. 12–18.

78. Ibid., ll. 21–23.

79. One reminiscer recalled how he had made sure the coast was clear for Lenin's escape from the police in 1905, noting that he did not see him again until 1919 (TsGAIPD SPb, f. 4000, op. 6, d. 42, l. 15). A female worker recalled how she had demanded, "in the name of the workers," to see the heavily guarded Lenin in Smolny in 1917 and was allowed to meet with him (TsGAIPD SPb, f. 4000, op. 6, d. 90, l. 32).

80. TsGAIPD SPb, f. 4000, op. 6, d. 90, l. 4.

81. TsGAIPD SPb, f. 4000, op. 6, d. 70, l. 5.

82. TsGAIPD SPb, f. 4000, op. 6, d. 63, ll. 47–48.

83. TsGAIPD SPb, f. 4000, op. 6, d. 70, l. 11.

84. Ibid., l. 3, 9.

85. TsGAIPD SPb, f. 4000, op. 6, d. 63, l. 41, 38.

86. This assumption stamps a study of the revolutionary tales told by Russian students about themselves (Susan K. Morrissey, *Heralds of Revolution: Russian Students and the Mythologies of Radicalism* [New York: Oxford University Press, 1998]).

87. TsGAIPD SPb, f. 4000, op. 6, d. 70, ll. 8–9.

88. Halbwachs, *Collective Memory*, 44–45

EPILOGUE

1. Abram Tertz, *The Trial Begins and On Socialist Realism* (Berkeley: University of California Press, 1960), 203–4.

2. RGASPI, f. 70, op. 1, ed. khr. 15, l. 3–4. A summary was published in *Proletarskaia revoliutsiia* 4 (April 1928): 219–23.

3. N. N. Maslov, "*Short Course of the History of the All-Russian Communist Party (Bolshevik):* An Encyclopedia of Stalin's Personality Cult," *Soviet Studies in History* 28, no. 3 (1989–90): 51–67.

4. Karen Petrone, *Life Has Become More Joyous, Comrades! Celebrations in the Time of Stalin* (Bloomington: Indiana University Press, 2000).

5. Igal Halfin, *From Darkness to Light: Class, Consciousness, and Salvation in Revolutionary Russia* (Pittsburgh, Penn.: University of Pittsburgh Press, 2000); *Tagebuch aus Moskau, 1931–1939*, edited by Jochen Hellbeck (Munich: Deutscher Taschenbuch Verlag, 1996), 9–73; *Intimacy and Terror: Soviet Diaries of the 1930s*, ed. Véronique Garros, Natalia Korenevskaya, and Thomas Lahusen (New York: New Press, 1995).

6. Amir Weiner, *Making Sense of War: The Second World War and the Fate of the Bolshevik Revolution* (Princeton: Princeton University Press, 2001), 8.

7. "Oktiabr' i perestroika: Revoliutsiia prodolzhaetsia," *Kommunist* 17 (1987): 3–40.

8. Alan Kimball, "I. I. Mints and the Representation of Reality in History," *Slavic Review* 35, no. 4 (1976): 719.

9. On these kinds of obituaries, see Tim Snyder, " 'Coming to Terms with the Charm and Power of Soviet Communism,' " *Contemporary European History* 6, no. 1 (1997): 133–44.

10. Joseph Bradley, "Introduction," *Russian Studies in History* 33, no. 3 (1994–95): 3. On the trial of the CPSU, see F. M. Rudinskii, *"Delo KPSS" v Konstitutsionnom Sude: Zapiski, uchastnika, protsessa* (Moscow: Bylina, 1999).

11. V. Buldakov, *Krasnaia smuta: Priroda i posledstviia revoliutsionnogo nasiliia* (Moscow: ROSSPEN, 1997), 357.

12. Benno Ennker, "Ende des Mythos? Lenin in der Kontroverse," in *Die Umwertung der Sowjetischen Geschichte*, ed. Dietrich Geyer (Göttingen: Vandenhoeck and Ruprecht, 1991), 54–74; Frederick C. Corney, "Rethinking a Great Event: The October Revolution as Memory Project," *Social Science History* 22, no. 4 (1998): 389–414.

Bibliography

ARCHIVES

Rossiiskii Gosudarstvennyi Arkhiv Sotsial'no-Politicheskoi Istorii (RGASPI)
fond 17	TsK VKP(b)
opis' 3	(Politburo)
opis' 60	Department of Agitation and Propaganda of the CC VKP(b)
opis' 71	(Collection of Documents on the Oppositions)
opis' 84	(Bureau of the Secretariat)
opis' 85	(Secret Department)
fond 70	Istpart TsK VKP(b)
fond 91	Personal file on M. S. Ol'minskii
fond 139	Personal file on P. N. Lepeshinskii

Tsentral'nyi Gosudarstvennyi Arkhiv Istoriko-politicheskikh Dokumentov Sankt Peterburga) (TsGAIPD SPb)
fond 1	Petrograd Committee of the RKP(b)
fond 461	Leningrad Department of Istpart of the Leningrad obkom
fond 4000	Institute of the History of the Party under the Leningrad Obkom of the CPSU
opis' 5	(Personal Reminiscences)
opis' 6	(Stenograms and Protocols of Evenings of Reminiscences)

Tsentral'nyi Gosudarstvennyi Arkhiv Obshchestvennykh Dvizhenii g. Moskvy (Ts-GAODg.M)
fond 3	Moscow Committee of the VKP(b)

Tsentr Dokumentatsii Noveishei Istorii Iaroslavskoi Oblasti (TsDNIIaO)
fond 394	Istpart

CONTEMPORARY NEWSPAPERS AND JOURNALS

(all published in Moscow or Petrograd, unless otherwise indicated)

Birzhevye vedomosti
Biulleten' Istparta
Biulleten' Komissii pri Prezidiume TsIK Soiuza SSR po organizatsii i provedeniiu prazdnovaniia 10–letiia Oktiabr'skoi Revoliutsii
Biulleten' oppozitsii (Berlin)
Bor'ba
Byloe
Delo naroda
Den'
Edinstvo
Fakel'
Freiheit (Berlin)
Gazeta dlia vsekh

Novaia zhizn'
Novyi den'
Novyi lef
Novyi luch
Pechat' i revoliutsiia
Petrogradskaia pravda
Plamia
Polnoch'
Pravda
Proletarskaia revoliutsiia
Proletarskaia revoliutsiia na Donu (Rostov)
Puti revoliutsii (Kazan')
Rabochaia gazeta
Rabochii put'

God proletarskoi revoliutsii
Iaroslavskii sbornik (Iaroslavl')
Iskra
Iskusstvo kommuny
Izvestiia
Izvestiia TsIK
Kommunisticheskaia revoliutsiia
Krasnaia byl' (Samara)
Krasnaia gazeta
Krasnaia niva
Krasnoarmeets
Krasnyi militsioner
Krot (Kungur, Perm')
Leningradskii rabochii
Nasha rech'

Rech'
Revoliutsionnoe byloe (Tula)
Russkaia mysl'
Sibirskie ogni (Novosibirsk)
Sotsial-demokrat
Sotsialisticheskii vestnik (Berlin)
Trudovaia kopeika
Tvorchestvo
Ural'skii rabochii (Ekaterinburg)
Utro Rossii
Vecherniaia Moskva
Vechernie izvestiia
Vestnik kul'tury i politiki
V glukhuiu noch'
Zhizn' iskusstva

PUBLISHED MATERIALS

1905. Istoriia revoliutsionnogo dvizheniia v otdel'nykh ocherkakh. 3 volumes. Edited by M. N. Pokrovskii. Moscow-Leningrad, 1925–27.

1905. Revoliutsionnye sobytiia 1905 g. v g. Ufe i Ural'skikh zavodakh (Bashrespublika). Ufa, 1925.

Abramovich, Raphael R. *The Soviet Revolution, 1917–1939.* New York: International Universities Press, 1962.

Agitatsionno-massovoe iskusstvo: Oformlenie prazdnestv. Moscow, 1984.

Aleksandrov, G. V. *Epokha i kino.* 2d ed. Moscow, 1983.

Alekseeva, G. D. *Oktiabr'skaia revoliutsiia i istoricheskaia nauka, 1917–1923.* Moscow, 1968.

À *l'est, la mémoire retrouvée,* ed. Alain Brossat and Sonia Combe. Paris: Éditions la Découverte, 1990.

Amfiteatrov-Kadashev, V. A. "Iz dnevnika 1917 g." *Literaturnaia gazeta* 29 (5509) (20 July 1994): 6.

A. M. Gor'kii i sozdanie istorii fabrik i zavodov: Sbornik dokumentov i materialov v pomoshch' rabotaiushchim nad istoriei fabrik i zavodov SSSR. Moscow, 1959.

Anderson, Benedict. *Imagined Communities: Reflections on the Origin and Spread of Nationalism.* London: Verso, 1991.

Annenkov, Iurii. *Dnevnik moikh vstrech: Tsikl tragedii.* Vol. 2 of two volumes. New York: Inter-Language Literary Associates, 1966.

Antonov-Ovseenko, A. V. "Memuary V. A. Antonov-Ovseenko kak istochnik po istorii revoliutsionnykh sobytii 1917 goda." In *Voprosy istochnikovedeniia istorii SSSR, Vyp. 2.* Vol. 24 of *Trudy Moskovskogo Gosudarstvennogo Istoriko-Arkhivnogo Instituta,* 203–19. Moscow, 1966.

Arkhipov, I. L. "Obshchestvennaia psikhologiia Petrogradskikh obyvatelei v 1917 godu." *Voprosy istorii* 7 (1994): 49–58.

Ascher, Abraham. *Pavel Axelrod and the Development of Menshevism.* Cambridge: Harvard University Press, 1972.

Autobiographical Memory. Edited by David C. Rubin, 137–58. Cambridge: Cambridge University Press, 1986.

Aves, Jonathan. *Workers against Lenin: Labour Protest and the Bolshevik Dictatorship.* London: I. B. Tauris, 1996.

A. V. Lunacharskii o massovykh prazdnestvakh, estrade, i tsirke. Moscow, 1981.

Avrich, Paul. *Kronstadt 1921.* Princeton: Princeton University Press, 1970.

Babel, Isaac. *1920 Diary.* New Haven: Yale University Press, 1995.

Bailyn, Bernard. *The Ideological Origins of the American Revolution.* London: Belknap at Harvard University Press, 1967.

Baker, Keith Michael. *Inventing the French Revolution.* Cambridge: Cambridge University Press, 1990.

——. "Revolution." In *The Political Culture of the French Revolution,* edited by Colin Lucas. Vol. 2 of *The French Revolution and the Creation of Modern Political Culture,* edited by Keith Michael Baker. Oxford: Pergamon, 1994.

Barber, John. *Soviet Historians in Crisis, 1928–1932.* Basingstoke, England: Macmillan, 1981.

Barnes, Julian. *England, England.* New York: Vintage Books, 1998.

Barthes, Roland. *Mythologies.* New York: Noonday, 1972.

——. "Writing the Event." In *The Rustle of Language.* New York: Hill and Wang, 1986.

Bartlett, Frederic C. *Remembering: A Study in Experimental and Social Psychology.* Cambridge: Cambridge University Press, 1964.

Baturin, Nikolai. *Ocherk istorii sotsial–demokratii v Rossii.* Moscow, 1906.

Benjamin, Walter. *Illuminations: Essays and Reflections.* New York: Schocken, 1968.

Berger, Peter L., and Thomas Luckmann. *The Social Construction of Reality: A Treatise in the Sociology of Knowledge.* New York: Doubleday, 1966.

Beriushina, A. *Pochemu ia stala kommunistkoi?* Moscow, 1919.

Berkhofer, Robert F. *Beyond the Great Story: History as Text and Discourse.* Cambridge: Harvard University Press, 1995.

Berkman, Alexander. *The Bolshevik Myth: Diary 1920–1922.* London: Hutchinson and Co., 1925.

Bettelheim, Charles. *Class Struggles in the USSR: First Period, 1917–1923.* New York: Monthly Review Press, 1976.

Binns, Christopher A. P. "The Changing Face of Power: Revolution and Accommodation in the Development of the Soviet Ceremonial System: Part I." *Man (N.S.)* 14 (1979): 585–606.

Blium, A. V. *Za kulisami "Ministerstva pravdy": Tainaia istoriia sovetskoi tsenzury, 1917–1929.* St. Petersburg: "Akademicheskii proekt," 1994.

Blok, Alexander. *The Twelve and the Scythians.* Translated by Jack Lindsay. London: Journeyman, 1982.

Bolshevik Culture: Experiment and Order in the Russian Revolution. Edited by Abbott Gleason, Peter Kenez, and Richard Stites. Bloomington: Indiana University Press, 1985.

Bol'sheviki: Dokumenty po istorii bol'shevizma s 1903 po 1916 god byvsh. Moskovskago Okhrannago Otdeleniia. Edited by M. A. Tsiavlovskii. Moscow, 1918.

Bolshevik Visions. First Phase of the Cultural Revolution in Soviet Russia. Edited by William G. Rosenberg. Ann Arbor: University of Michigan Press, 1990.

Bol'shevistskie voenno-revoliutsionnye komitety. Moscow, 1958.

Boltianskii, G. *Kinokhronika i kak ee snimat'.* Moscow, 1926.

——. *Lenin i kino.* Moscow-Leningrad, 1925.

Bonnell, Victoria E. *Iconography of Power: Soviet Political Posters under Lenin and Stalin.* Berkeley: University of California Press, 1997.

Bordwell, David. *The Cinema of Eisenstein.* Cambridge: Harvard University Press, 1993.

——. "The Idea of Montage in Soviet Art and Film." *Cinema Journal* 11, no. 2 (1972): 9–17.

Bouwsma, William J. "Intellectual History in the 1980s: From History of Ideas to History of Meaning." *Journal of Interdisciplinary History* 12, no. 2 (1981): 279–91.

Bradley, Joseph. "Introduction." *Russian Studies in History* 33, no. 3 (1994–95): 3.

Broido, Vera. *Lenin and the Mensheviks: The Persecution of Socialists under Bolshevism.* Aldershot, England: Gower/Maurice Temple Smith, 1987.

Brooke, Rupert. *The Bastille. A Prize Poem.* Rugby, England: Lawrence, 1905.

Brooks, Jeffrey. "Socialist Realism in *Pravda*: Read All about It!" *Slavic Review* 53, no. 4 (1994): 973–91.

Brovkin, Vladimir. *The Mensheviks after October: Socialist Opposition and the Rise of the Bolshevik Dictatorship.* Ithaca: Cornell University Press, 1987.

——. "The Mensheviks' Political Comeback: The Elections to the Provincial City Soviets in Spring 1918." *Russian Review* 42, no. 1 (1983): 1–50.

——. *Russia After Lenin. Politics, Culture and Society, 1921–1929.* London and New York: Routledge, 1998.

——. "Workers' Unrest and the Bolsheviks' Response in 1919." *Slavic Review* 49, no. 3 (1990): 350–73.

Bruner, Jerome. *Acts of Meaning.* Cambridge: Harvard University Press, 1990.

Bryant, Louise. *Six Red Months in Russia: An Observer's Account of Russia before and during the Proletarian Dictatorship.* New York: George H. Doran, 1918.

Bukharin, N., and E. Preobrazhensky. *The ABC of Communism.* Edited by E. H. Carr. Harmondsworth, England: Pelican, 1970.

Buldakov, V. "Istoriograficheskie metamorfozy 'Krasnogo Oktiabria'." In *Istoricheskie issledovaniia v Rossii. Tendentsii poslednykh let,* edited by G. A. Bordiugov. Moscow: <<AIRO-XX>>, 1996.

——. *Krasnaia smuta. Priroda i posledstviia revoliutsionnogo nasiliia.* Moscow: ROSSPEN, 1997.

Burbank, Jane. *Intelligentsia and Revolution: Russian Views of Bolshevism, 1917–1922.* Oxford: Oxford University Press, 1986.

Burgess, William Francis. "The Istpart Commission: The Historical Department of the Russian Communist Party Central Committee, 1920–1928." Ph.D. diss., Yale University, 1981.

Calder, Angus. *The Myth of the Blitz.* London: Jonathan Cape, 1991.

Carr, E. H. *The Bolshevik Revolution, 1917–1932.* 3 volumes. Harmondsworth, England: Penguin, 1950–1953.

Carter, Huntley. *The New Theatre and Cinema of Soviet Russia.* London: Chapman and Dodd, 1924.

Cassiday, Julie A. *The Enemy on Trial: Early Soviet Courts on Stage and Screen.* DeKalb: Northern Illinois University Press, 2000.

Chamberlin, William Henry. *The Russian Revolution, 1917–1918: From the Overthrow of the Czar to the Assumption of Power by the Bolsheviks.* Vol. 1. New York: Universal, 1935.

Chatterjee, Choi. *Celebrating Women: Gender, Festival Culture, and Bolshevik Ideology, 1910–1939.* Pittsburgh: University of Pittsburgh Press, 2002.

Clark, Katerina. *Petersburg: Crucible of Cultural Revolution.* Cambridge: Harvard University Press, 1995.

——. *The Soviet Novel: History as Ritual.* 2d ed. Chicago: University of Chicago Press, 1985.

——. "The 'Quiet Revolution' in Soviet Intellectual Life." In *Russia in the Era of NEP. Explorations in Soviet Society and Culture,* edited by Sheila Fitzpatrick, Alexander Rabinowitch, and Richard Stites. Bloomington: Indiana University Press, 1991.

Coeure, Sophie. "Les 'Fêtes d'Octobre' 1927 à Moscou. La Dynamique des structures d'influence Soviétique et Kominterniennes autour d'un anniversaire." *Communisme* 42–44 (1995): 57–74.

Connerton, Paul. *How Societies Remember.* Cambridge: Cambridge University Press, 1989.

Corney, Frederick C. "Rethinking a Great Event: The October Revolution as Memory Project." *Social Science History* 22, no. 4 (1998): 389–414.

———. "Trotskii and the Vienna *Pravda*, 1908–1912." *Canadian Slavonic Papers* 37, no. 3 (1985): 248–68.

The Culture of Autobiography: Constructions of Self-Representation. Edited by Robert Folkenflik. Stanford: Stanford University Press, 1993.

Dan, Fedor. *Dva goda skitanii, 1919–1921*. Berlin, 1922.

Daniels, Robert V. *Red October: The Bolshevik Revolution of 1917*. Boston: Beacon, 1967.

———. *The Conscience of the Revolution: Communist Opposition in Soviet Russia*. Cambridge, Mass.: Harvard University Press, 1960.

Danilevskii, M. *Prazdniki obshchestvennogo byta: Organizatsiia, metodika, praktika*. Moscow-Leningrad, 1927.

David-Fox, Michael. *Revolution of the Mind: Higher Learning among the Bolsheviks, 1918–1929*. Ithaca: Cornell University Press, 1997.

Deák, František. "Russian Mass Spectacles." *Drama Review* 19, no. 2 (1975): 7–22.

Dear Comrades: Menshevik Reports on the Bolshevik Revolution and the Civil War. Edited by Vladimir N. Brovkin. Stanford: Hoover Institution Press, 1991.

The Debate on Soviet Power. Minutes of the All-Russian Central Executive Committee of Soviets. Second Convocation, October 1917–January 1918. Edited by John L. H. Keep. Oxford: Clarendon, 1979.

"Delo o samoubiistve Rossii: Iz dnevnika Leonida Andreeva." *Istochnik* 2 (1994): 40–50.

Deviataia konferentsiia RKP(b): Sentiabr' 1920 goda. Protokoly. Moscow, 1972.

Deviatyi s"ezd Rossiiskoi Kommunisticheskoi Partii: Stenograficheskii otchet (19 marta–4 aprelia 1920 g.). Moscow, 1920.

Diskussiia 1925 goda: Materialy i dokumenty. (Moscow-Leningrad, 1929).

Dokumenty sotsialisticheskoi revoliutsii (noty, dekrety, rechi vozhdei sovetskoi vlasti). Samara, 1919.

Dvenadtsatyi s"ezd Rossiiskoi Kommunisticheskoi Partii (bol'shevikov): 17–25 aprelia 1923 g. Moscow, 1923.

Dvinov, Boris. *Ot legal'nosti k podpol'iu, 1921–1922*. Stanford: Hoover Institution Press, 1968.

Dybenko, P. E. *Iz nedr tsarskogo flota k Velikomu Oktiabriu: Iz vospominanii o revoliutsii, 1917–1927*. Moscow, 1928.

Eisenstein, Sergei. *Notes of a Film Director*. London: Lawrence and Wishart, 1959.

Eizenshtein, Sergei. *Izbrannye proizvedeniia v shesti tomakh*. Moscow, 1964.

Elwood, R. C. "The Congress That Never Was. Lenin's Attempt to Call a 'Sixth' Party Congress in 1914." *Soviet Studies* 31, no. 3 (1979): 343–63.

———. "Lenin and the Brussels 'Unity' Conference of July 1914." *Russian Review* 39, no. 1 (1980): 32–49.

Ennker, Benno. *Die Anfänge des Leninkults in der Sowjetunion*. Cologne: Böhlau, 1997.

———. "Ende Des Mythos? Lenin in der Kontroverse." In *Die Umwertung der Sowjetischen Geschichte*, edited by Dietrich Geyer. Göttingen: Vandenhoeck and Ruprecht, 1991.

———. "Leninkult und mythisches Denken in der Sowjetischen Öffentlichkeit 1924." *Jahrbücher für Geschichte Osteuropas* 44, no. 3 (1996): 431–55.

Erlich, Victor. *Modernism and Revolution: Russian Literature in Transition*. Cambridge: Harvard University Press, 1994.

Evreinoff, Nicolas. *Histoire du théatre Russe*. Paris: Éditions du Chêne, 1947.

Falasca-Zamponi, Simonetta. *Fascist Spectacle: The Aesthetics of Power in Mussolini's Italy*. Berkeley: University of California Press, 1997.

Fedorchenko, S. *Narod na voine*. Moscow, 1990.

Ferguson, Priscilla Parkhurst. *Paris as Revolution: Writing the Nineteenth-Century City*. Berkeley: University of California Press, 1994.

Ferro, Marc. "1917: History and Cinema." *Journal of Contemporary History* 3, no. 4 (1968): 45–61.

Fevral'skii, A. *Pervaia sovetskaia p"esa: "MisteriiaBuff" V. V. Maiakovskogo.* Moscow, 1971.

Figes, Orlando. *Peasant Russia, Civil War: The Volga Countryside in Revolution, 1917–1921.* Oxford: Clarendon Press, 1989.

Figes, Orlando, and Boris Kolonitskii. *Interpreting the Russian Revolution: The Language and Symbols of 1917.* New Haven: Yale University Press, 1999.

The Film Factory: Russian and Soviet Cinema in Documents, 1896–1939. Edited by Richard Taylor and Ian Christie. London: Routledge and Kegan Paul, 1988.

Fitzpatrick, Sheila. "The Civil War as a Formative Experience." Occasional Paper No. 134. Kennan Institute for Advanced Russian Studies (1981).

Fogu, Claudio. "Fascism and *Historic* Representation: The 1932 Garibaldian Celebrations." *Journal of Contemporary History* 31 (1996): 317–45.

Forever in the Shadow of Hitler? : Original Documents of the Historikerstreit, the Controversy Concerning the Singularity of the Holocaust. Translated by James Knowlton and Truett Cates. Atlantic Highlands, N. J.: Humanities Press, 1993.

Frankel, Jonathan. "Party Genealogy and the Soviet Historians (1920–1938)." *Slavic Review* 25, no. 4 (1966): 563–603.

Fueloep-Miller, René. *The Mind and Face of Bolshevism: An Examination of Cultural Life in Soviet Russia.* New York: Harper Torchbooks, 1965.

Furet, François. *Interpreting the French Revolution.* Cambridge: Cambridge University Press, 1981.

——. *The Passing of an Illusion: The Idea of Communism in the Twentieth Century.* Chicago: University of Chicago Press, 1999.

Fussell, Paul. *The Great War and Modern Memory.* Oxford: Oxford University Press, 1975.

Getzler, Israel. *Kronstadt, 1917–1921: The Fate of a Soviet Democracy.* Cambridge: Cambridge University Press, 1983.

——. "Marxist Revolutionaries and the Dilemma of Power." In *Revolution and Politics in Russia. Essays in Memory of B.I. Nicolaevsky,* edited by Alexander Rabinowitch, Janet Rabinowitch, and Ladis Kristof. Bloomington: Indiana University Press, 1972.

Gill, Graeme. *The Origins of the Stalinist Political System.* Cambridge: Cambridge University Press, 1990.

Gimpel'son, E. G. *Formirovanie sovetskoi politicheskoi sistemy, 1917–1923 gg.* Moscow: Nauka, 1995.

Gippius, Zinaida. *Peterburgskie dnevniki, 1914–1919.* New York: Teleks, 1990.

Goldman, Emma. *My Disillusionment in Russia.* New York: Thomas Y. Crowell, 1970.

Goodwin, James. *Eisenstein, Cinema, and History.* Urbana: University of Illinois Press, 1993.

Gorham, Michael S. *Speaking in Soviet Tongues: Language Culture and the Politics of Voice in Revolutionary Russia.* DeKalb: Northern Illinois University Press, 2003.

Gor'kii, M. *Nesvoevremennyia mysli. Zametki o revoliutsii i kul'ture.* Moscow: Sovetskii pisatel', 1990.

Gorod Lenina v dni Oktiabria i Velikoi Otechestvennoi Voiny 1941–1945 gg.Sbornik statei. Moscow-Leningrad, 1964.

Hackel, Sergei. *The Poet and the Revolution: Aleksandr Blok's "The Twelve".* Oxford: Clarendon, 1975.

Haimson, Leopold H. "The Mensheviks after the October Revolution: Part III: The Constituent Assembly Meets." *Russian Review* 39, no. 4 (1980): 462–83.

——. "The Parties and the State: The Evolution of Political Attitudes." In *The Structure of Russian History. Interpretive Essays,* edited by Michael Cherniavsky. New York: Random House, 1970.

——. "The Problem of Social Identities in Early Twentieth-Century Russia." *Slavic Review* 47, no. 1 (1988): 1–20.

Halbwachs, Maurice. *The Collective Memory.* New York: Harper & Row, 1980.

——. *La Topographie légendaire des évangiles en Terre Sainte.* Paris: Presses Universitaires de France, 1971.

——. *Les Cadres sociaux de la mémoire.* Paris: Librairie Félix Alcan, 1925.

Halfin, Igal. *From Darkness to Light: Class, Consciousness, and Salvation in Revolutionary Russia.* Pittsburgh: University of Pittsburgh Press, 2000.

Hall, Stuart. "Notes on Deconstructing 'the Popular'." In *People's History and Socialist Theory,* edited by Raphael Samuel. London: Routledge & Kegan Paul, 1981.

——. "The Rediscovery of 'Ideology': Return of the Repressed in Media Studies." In *Culture, Society and the Media,* edited by Michael Gurevitch and others. London and New York: Methuen, 1982.

Hanne, Michael. *The Power of the Story: Fiction and Political Change.* Oxford: Berghahn, 1994.

Hanson, Stephen E. *Time and Revolution: Marxism and the Design of Soviet Institutions.* Chapel Hill: University of North Carolina Press, 1997.

Harlan, David. "Intellectual History and the Return of Literature." *American Historical Review* 94, no. 3 (1989): 581–609.

Hastings, Michel. "Identité culturelle locale et politique festive communiste: Halluin la Rouge, 1920–1934." *Le Mouvement Social* 139 (April–June 1987): 7–25.

Helgesen, Malvin Magnus. "The Origins of the Party-State Monolith in Soviet Russia: Relations between the Soviets and Party Committees in the Central Provinces, October 1917–March 1921." Ph.D. diss., State University of New York at Stony Brook, 1980.

Hickey, Michael C. "Paper, Memory, and a Good Story: How Smolensk Got Its 'October'." *Revolutionary Russia* 13, no. 1 (2000): 1–19.

Holitscher, Arthur. *Drei Monate in SowjetRussland.* Berlin: Fischer, 1921.

——. [Artur Holitscher]. *Das Theater im Revolutionären Russland.* Berlin: Volksbühnen-verlags und Vertriebs-GMBH, n.d.

Holmes, Larry E. "Soviet Rewriting of 1917: The Case of A. G. Shliapnikov." *Slavic Review* 38, no. 2 (1979): 224–42.

Holmes, Larry E., and William Burgess. "Scholarly Voice or Political Echo? Soviet Party History in the 1920s." *Russian History* 9, no. 2–3 (1982): 378–98.

Holquist, Michael. "Corrupt Originals: The Paradox of Censorship." *PMLA* (January 1994): 14–24.

Holquist, Peter. " 'Information Is the Alpha and Omega of Our Work': Bolshevik Surveillance in Its Pan-European Context." *Journal of Modern History* 69 (September 1997): 415–50.

——. *Making War, Forging Revolution: Russia's Continuum of Crisis, 1914–1921.* Cambridge: Harvard University Press, 2002.

Hosking, Geoffrey A. "Memory in a Totalitarian Society: The Case of the Soviet Union." In *Memory. History, Culture and the Mind,* edited by Thomas Butler. Oxford: Blackwell, 1989.

Hunt, Lynn. *Politics, Culture, and Class in the French Revolution.* Berkeley: University of California Press, 1984.

Hutton, Patrick H. *The Cult of the Revolutionary Tradition: The Blanquists in French Politics, 1864–1893.* Berkeley: University of California Press, 1981.

——. "The Role of Memory in the Historiography of the French Revolution." *History and Theory* 30, no. 1 (1991): 56–69.

Iakovlev, Ia. *Ob istoricheskom smysle Oktiabria.* Moscow, 1922.

Iaroslavskii, E. *Partiia bol'shevikov v 1917 godu.* Moscow-Leningrad, 1927.

Iarov, S. V. *Gorozhanin kak politik: Revoliutsiia, voennyi kommunizm, i NEP glazami Petro-gradtsev.* St. Petersburg: Dmitrii Bulanin, 1999.

——. *Krest'ianin kak politik. Krest'ianstvo Severo-Zapada Rossii v 1918–1919 gg.: Politicheskoe myshlenie i massovyi protest.* St. Petersburg: Dmitrii Bulanin, 1999.

——. *Proletarii kak politik: Politicheskaia psikhologiia rabochikh Petrograda v 1917–1923 gg.* St. Petersburg: Dmitrii Bulanin, 1999.

" 'Ia stal ochen' boiattsa vsekh liudei…' " *Ogonek* 44–46 (November 1992): 31–32.

Il'ina, G. I. "Obraz evropeiskikh revoliutsii i russkaia kul'tura (mart 1917 g.–noiabr' 1918 g.)." In *Anatomiia revoliutsii. 1917 g. v Rossii: massy, partii, vlast'*, edited by V. Iu. Cherniaev, and others. St. Petersburg: Glagol, 1994.

Intimacy and Terror: Soviet Diaries of the 1930s. Edited by Véronique Garros, Natalia Korenevskaya, and Thomas Lahusen. New York: New Press, 1995.

The Invention of Tradition. Edited by Eric Hobsbawm and Terence Ranger. Cambridge: Cambridge University Press, 1983.

Irwin-Zarecka, Iwona. *Frames of Remembrance: The Dynamics of Collective Memory.* New Brunswick, N.J.: Transaction, 1994.

Iskusstvo i revoliutsiia. Edited by A. Blok. Moscow, 1979.

Istoricheskie issledovaniia v Rossii: Tendentsii poslednykh let. Edited by G. A. Bordiugov. Moscow: "AIRO-20," 1996.

Istoriia i istoriki: Istoriograficheskii ezhegodnik 1972. Moscow, 1973.

Istoriia sovetskogo teatra. Vol. 1. Leningrad, 1933.

Ivanova, L. V. *U istokov sovetskoi istoricheskoi nauki (podgotovka kadrov istorikov-marksistov v 1917–1929 gg.).* Moscow, 1968.

"Iz arkhivov partii." *Izvestiia TsK KPSS* 4 (1989): 140–56.

Iz epokhi "Zvezdy" i "Pravdy," 1911–1914 gg. Moscow, 1921.

Iz istorii kino: Dokumenty i materialy. Moscow, 1965.

Iz proshlogo. Vtoroi sbornik vospominanii. Krest'ianskie vosstaniia v 1918 g. v Kungurskom uezde. Kungur, 1922.

Jangfeldt, Bengt. "Russian Futurism, 1917–1919." In *Art, Society, Revolution 1917–1921*, edited by Nils Åke Nilsson. Stockholm: Almqvist and Wiksell, 1979.

Jansen, Sue Curry. *Censorship: The Knot That Binds Power and Knowledge.* New York: Oxford University Press, 1988.

John Reed and the Russian Revolution: Uncollected Articles, Letters, and Speeches on Russia, 1917–1920. Edited by Eric Homberger and John Biggart. New York: St. Martin's, 1992.

Jouhaud, Christian. "Printing the Event: From La Rochelle to Paris." In *The Culture of Print. Power and the Uses of Print in Early Modern Europe*, edited by Roger Chartier. Oxford, UK: Polity Press, 1989.

Kak rozhdalas' partiia Bol'shevikov. Literaturnaia polemika 1903–04 gg. Sbornik. Leningrad, 1925.

Kalendar'. Khronika sobytii 1905 goda s ianvaria 1905 g. po mart 1906 g. Edited by E. A. Morokhovets. Moscow-Leningrad, 1926.

Karpovich, Michael. "The Russian Revolution of 1917." *Journal of Modern History* 2, no. 2 (1930): 258–80.

Keep, John. *The Russian Revolution. A Study in Mass Mobilization.* New York: Norton, 1976.

——. "October in the Provinces." In *Revolutionary Russia*, edited by Richard Pipes. Cambridge, Mass.: Harvard University Press, 1968.

Kellner, Hans. *Language and Historical Representation: Getting the Story Crooked.* Madison: University of Wisconsin Press, 1989.

Kelly, Catriona. "Iconoclasm and Commemorating the Past." In *Constructing Russian Culture in the Age of Revolution: 1881–1940*, edited by Catriona Kelly and David Shepherd. Oxford: Oxford University Press, 1998.

Kenez, Peter. *The Birth of the Propaganda State: Soviet Methods of Mass Mobilization, 1917–1929*. Cambridge: Cambridge University Press, 1985.

——. "The Prosecution of Soviet History: A Critique of Richard Pipes' *The Russian Revolution*." *Russian Review* 50 (1991): 345–51.

——. "The Prosecution of Soviet History, Volume 2." *Russian Review* 54 (1995): 265–69.

Khanzhonkov, A. A. *Pervye gody russkoi kinematografii*. Moscow-Leningrad, 1937.

Khodorovskii, M. *Partiinye i bespartiinye*. Kazan', 1920.

Kimball, Alan. "I. I. Mints and the Representation of Reality in History." *Slavic Review* 35, no. 4 (1976): 715–23.

Koenker, Diane. *Moscow Workers and the 1917 Revolution*. Princeton: Princeton University Press, 1981.

Kogan, P. S. "Aleksandr Blok i revoliutsiia: Pamiati poeta." *Pechat' i revoliutsiia*. Bk 2, August–October 1921, 3–7.

Kolonitskii, Boris I. "Antibourgeois Propaganda and Anti-'Burzhui' Consciousness in 1917." *Russian Review* 53, no. 2 (1994): 183–96.

Komarov, N. S. "Sozdanie i deiatel'nost' Istparta (1920–1928 gg.)." *Voprosy istorii KPSS* 5 (1958): 153–65.

Kommunisticheskii rezhim i narodnoe soprotivlenie v Rossii, 1917–1991. Moscow: Posev, 1998.

Kondratieva, Tamara. *Bolcheviks et Jacobins: Itinéraire des analogies*. Paris: Payot, 1989.

Korneev, V. E. *Arkhivy RKP(b) v 1917–1925 gg. Uchebnoe posobie*. Moscow, 1979.

——. *Mestnye biuro Istparta TsK VKP(b): Sozdanie istochnikovoi bazy istoriko-partiinoi nauki, 1920–1929 gg. Uchebnoe posobie*. Moscow, 1986.

Korolenko, V. G. "Dnevniki, 1917–1921." *Voprosy literatury* 5 (1990): 193–218.

Koroleva, L. I. "Dokumenty TsGAOR SSSR o Leninskom plane monumental'noi propagandy, 1918–1920 gody." *Sovetskie arkhivy* 2 (1977): 16–19.

Korovainikov, V. Iu. " 'Ankety' kak istochnik po istorii Oktiabr'skogo perevorota." In *Mir istochnikovedeniia*. Moscow and Penza, 1995.

——. "Gruppy sodeistviia Istpartu TsK VKP(b)." *Voprosy istorii KPSS* 1 (1991): 112–23.

——. "Stenogrammy vecherov vospominanii kak istochnik po istorii Velikoi Oktiabr'skoi Sotsialisticheskoi Revoliutsii." *Sovetskie arkhivy* 5 (1990): 75–79.

Kotkin, Stephen. *Magnetic Mountain: Stalinism as a Civilization*. Berkeley: University of California Press, 1995.

——. " 'One Hand Clapping': Russian Workers and 1917." *Labor History* 32, no. 4 (1991): 604–20.

Kotre, John. *White Gloves: How We Create Ourselves through Memory*. New York: Free Press, 1995.

Ko vsem chlenam partii. Moscow, 1920.

Kozlov, Vladimir. *Massovye besporiadki v SSSR pri Khrushcheve i Brezhneve, 1953–nachalo 1980–kh gg*. Novosibirsk: Sibirskii khronograf, 1999.

K piatoi godovshchine proletarskoi revoliutsii v Prikam'e (sbornik statei). Izhevsk, 1922.

Kratkii ocherk revoliutsionnogo dvizheniia i razvitiia proletarskoi revoliutsii v Rossii. Kaluga, 1919.

Kronshtadt 1921: Dokumenty. Edited by V. P. Naumov and A. A. Kosakovskii, Moscow: "Demokratiia," 1997.

Kronshtadtskaia tragediia 1921 goda: Dokumenty v dvukh knigakh. Edited by V. K. Vinogradov and L. V. Dvoinykh. Moscow: Rosspen, 1999.

Kshesinskaia, Matil'da. *Vospominaniia*. Moscow: Kul'tura, 1992.

Lagny, Michèle, Marie-Claire Ropars-Wuilleumier, and Pierre Sorlin. *La Révolution figurée: Inscription de l'histoire et du politique dans un film.* Paris: Albatros, 1979.

Lane, Christel. *The Rites of Rulers: Ritual in Industrial Society—The Soviet Case.* Cambridge: Cambridge University Press, 1981.

Lane, David. *The Roots of Russian Communism: A Social and Historical Study of Russian Social Democracy, 1898–1907.* Assen, The Netherlands: Van Gorcum, 1969.

Lass, Andrew. "From Memory to History. The Events of November 17 Dis/Membered." *In Memory, History, and Opposition Under State Socialism,* edited by Rubie S. Watson. Santa Fe, New Mexico: School of American Research Press, 1994.

Leach, Robert. *Revolutionary Theatre.* London: Routledge, 1994.

Lebedev, Vladimir. "Praviashchaia partiia ostavalas' podpol'noi." *Istochnik* 4–5 (1993): 88–95.

Lenin, V. I. *"Left-Wing" Communism, an Infantile Disorder.* Moscow, 1975.

——. *Sochineniia.* 3d ed. 30 volumes. Moscow-Leningrad, 1926–1932.

——. *The State and Revolution: The Marxist Theory of the State and the Tasks of the Proletariat in the Revolution.* Moscow: Progress, 1985.

——. *What Is to Be Done?* Moscow, 1973.

Leniniana: poiski i nakhodki. Moscow, 1970.

Leninskii sbornik. Edited by L. B. Kamenev. 2d ed. 11 volumes. Moscow-Leningrad, 1924–1932.

Levina, T. L. "Pervye bespartiinye krest'ianskie konferentsii (po materialam Permskoi i Ekaterinburgskoi gubernii)." *Permskii Gosudarstvennyi Universitet im A. M. Gor'kogo. Uchenye zapiski* 133 (1965): 30–56.

Leyda, Jay. *Kino: A History of Russian and Soviet Film.* 3d ed. Princeton: Princeton University Press, 1983.

Liadov, M. *Istoriia Rossiiskoi Sotsial-demokraticheskoi Rabochei Partii.* St. Petersburg, 1906.

——. "Predislovie." In *Tretii ocherednoi s"ezd Rossiskoi Sotsial-Demokraticheskoi Rabochei Partii 1905 goda. Polnyi tekst protokolov,* 7–14. Moscow, 1924.

Liebich, André. *From the Other Shore: Russian Social Democracy after 1921.* Cambridge: Harvard University Press, 1997.

Lih, Lars T. "The Mystery of the *ABC.*" *Slavic Review* 56, no. 1 (1997): 50–72.

Listov, V. *Istoriia smotrit v ob"ektiv.* Moscow, 1973.

——. "Priemy istochnikovedcheskogo analiza kinoskriptov dokumental'nogo kino perioda Oktiabr'skoi Revoliutsii i grazhdanskoi voiny." In *Voprosy istochnikoveniia istorii SSSR,* vyp. 2. Vol. 24 of *Trudy Moskovskogo Gosudarstvennogo Istoriko-Arkhivnogo Instituta.* Moscow, 1966.

Longley, D. A. "Iakovlev's Question, or the Historiography of the Problem of Spontaneity and Leadership in the Russian Revolution of February 1917." In *Revolution in Russia: Reassessments of 1917,* edited by J. Frankel and B. Knei-Paz. Cambridge, UK: Cambridge University Press, 1992.

Lüsebrink, Hans-Jürgen, and Rolf Reichardt. *Die Bastille: Zur Symbolgeschichte von Herrschaft und Freiheit.* Frankfurt am Main: Fischer, 1990.

——. "La Prise de la Bastille comme 'événement total': Jalons pour une théorie historique de l'événement à l'époque moderne." *L'Événement (Actes du Colloque Organisé à Aix-en-Provence par le Centre Meridional d'Histoire Sociale),* September 16–18, 77–102. Aix-en-Provence.

Maguire, Robert A. "Literary Conflicts in the 1920s." *Survey* 18, no. 82 (1972): 98–127.

The Making of Three Russian Revolutionaries. Edited by Leopold H. Haimson, in collaboration with Ziva Galili y Garcia and Richard Wortman. Cambridge: Cambridge University Press, 1987.

Maiakovskii, V. V. *Sobranie sochinenii v vos'mi tomakh.* 8 volumes. Moscow, 1968.

Maksakov, V. V. *Istoriia i organizatsiia arkhivnogo dela v SSSR, 1917–1945 gg.* Moscow, 1969.

Malia, Martin. *The Soviet Tragedy: A History of Socialism in Russia, 1917–1991.* New York: Free Press, 1994.

——. "Why Amalrik Was Right." *Times Literary Supplement* 4675 (November 6, 1992): 9.

Mallon, Florencia E. *Peasant and Nation: The Making of Postcolonial Mexico and Peru.* Berkeley: University of California Press, 1995.

Mally, Lynn. *Culture of the Future: The Proletkult Movement in Revolutionary Russia.* Berkeley: University of California Press, 1990.

——. *Revolutionary Acts: Amateur Theater and the Soviet State, 1917–1938.* Ithaca: Cornell University Press, 2000.

Martow, J. *Geschichte der Russischen Sozialdemokratie.* Berlin: J. H. W. Dietz Nachfolger, 1926.

Martsinovskii, A. *Zapiski Rabochego-Bol'shevika.* Saratov, 1923.

Marx, Karl. *The Class Struggles in France, 1848–50.* New York: International Publishers, 1964.

Maslov, N. N. "*Short Course of the History of the All-Russian Communist Party (Bolshevik)*—An Encyclopedia of Stalin's Personality Cult." *Soviet Studies in History* 28, no. 3 (1989–90): 51–67.

Massovye prazdnestva. Leningrad, 1925.

Matsuda, Matt K. *The Memory of the Modern.* Oxford: Oxford University Press, 1996.

Mawdsley, Evan. "The Baltic Fleet and the Kronstadt Mutiny." *Soviet Studies* 24, no. 4 (1973): 506–21.

——. *The Russian Civil War.* Boston: Allen and Unwin, 1987.

Mazaev, A. I. *Prazdnik kak sotsial'no-khudozhestvennoe iavlenie.* Moscow, 1978.

McDowell, Jennifer. "Soviet Civil Ceremonies." *Journal for the Scientific Study of Religion* 13, no. 3 (1974): 165–279.

Melancon, Michael. " 'Marching Together!': Left Bloc Activities in the Russian Revolutionary Movement, 1900 to February 1917." *Slavic Review* 49, no. 2 (1990): 239–52.

——. "Rethinking Russia's February Revolution: Anonymous Spontaneity or Socialist Agency?" *Carl Beck Papers in Russian and East European Studies* 1408 (June 2000).

Mel'gunov, S. P. *Krasnyi terror v Rossii.* New York: Brandy, 1979.

Memory: History, Culture, and the Mind. Edited by Thomas Butler. Oxford: Blackwell, 1989.

Memory, History, and Opposition under State Socialism. Edited by Rubie S. Watson. Santa Fe: School of American Research Press, 1994.

Men'sheviki v bol'shevistskoi Rossii, 1918–1924. Men'sheviki v 1918 godu. Edited by Ziva Galili and Al'bert Nenarokov. Moscow: ROSSPEN, 1999.

Merridale, Catherine. *Night of Stone: Death and Memory in Russia.* London: Granta, 2000.

Minin, S. K. *Kto takie kommunisty?* Moscow, 1919.

Mink, Louis O. "Narrative Form as a Cognitive Instrument." In *The Writing of History: Literary Form and Historical Understanding*, edited by Henry Kozicki and Robert H. Canary, 129–49. Madison: University of Wisconsin Press, 1978.

Morrissey, Susan K. *Heralds of Revolution: Russian Students and the Mythologies of Radicalism.* New York: Oxford University Press, 1998.

Moskva v Oktiabre 1917 g. Edited by N. Ovsiannikov. Moscow, 1919.

Nabokov, Vladimir. *Speak, Memory: An Autobiography Revisited.* New York: G. P. Putnam's Sons, 1966.

Namer, Gérard. "Affectivité et temporalité de la mémoire." *L'Homme et la société* 90, no. 4 (1988): 9–14.

"The Narrative Construction of Reality: An Interview with Stuart Hall." *Southern Review* (Adelaide) 17, no. 1 (1984): 3–17.

Nemiro, O. *V gorod prishel prazdnik: Iz istorii khudozhestvennogo oformleniia sovetskikh massovykh prazdnestv.* Leningrad, 1973.

"Ne nravitsia mne eto—i Gripp, i Diuma," *Istochnik* 1 (1994): 6–20.

Nevskii, V. A. *Massovaia polit.-prosvet. Rabota revoliutsionnykh let.* Moscow-Leningrad, 1925.

Nevskii, V. I. *Bol'shevik, kommunist i rabochii.* Petrograd, 1921.

———. *Chto takoe bol'sheviki?* Petrograd, 1917.

———. *Kak obrazovalas' sovetskaia vlast' i chto eiu sdelano za tri goda.* Moscow, 1920.

Nilsson, Nils Åke. "Spring 1918. The Arts and the Commissars." In *Art, Society, Revolution 1917–1921,* edited by Nils Åke Nilsson. Stockholm: Almqvist and Wiksell International, 1979.

Nora, Pierre. *Les Lieux de mémoire.* 3 volumes. Paris: Gallimard, 1984–1986.

Ob "Urokakh Oktiabria". Leningrad, 1924.

Okorokov, A. Z. *Oktiabr' i krakh russkoi burzhuaznoi pressy.* Moscow, 1970.

"Oktiabr' i perestroika: Revoliutsiia prodolzhaetsia." *Kommunist* 17 (1987): 3–40.

Oktiabr'skaia Revoliutsiia. Memuary. Edited by S. A. Alekseev and A. I. Usagina. Moscow-Leningrad: "Orbita," 1926 and 1991.

Oktiabr'skii perevorot: Fakty i dokumenty. Compiled by A. L. Popov. Edited by N. A. Rozhkova. Petrograd, 1918.

Oktiabr'skoe vooruzhennoe vosstanie v Petrograde. Moscow, 1957.

Orwell, George. *1984.* New York: New American Library, 1981.

Ot gruppy Blagoeva k "Soiuzu bor'by" (1886–1894 gg.). Rostov-on-Don, 1921.

Ozouf, Mona. *Festivals and the French Revolution.* Cambridge: Harvard University Press, 1988.

Pamiatnik bortsam proletarskoi revoliutsii pogibshim v 1917–1921 gg. 3d ed. Moscow-Leningrad, 1925.

Partiia Sotsialistov-Revoliutsionerov. Dokumenty i materialy. Oktiabr' 1917 g.–1925 g. Moscow: ROSSPEN, 2000.

Partiia Sotsialistov-Revoliutsionerov posle Oktiabr'skogo perevorota 1917 goda: Dokumenty iz arkhiva PSR. Selected and annotated by Marc Jansen. Amsterdam: Stichting Beheer IISG, 1989.

Partiinoe soveshchanie RS-DRP 27 dekabria 1918 g.: 1 ianvaria 1919 g. Rezoliutsii. Moscow, 1919.

Passerini, Luisa, ed. *Memory and Totalitarianism.* Oxford: Oxford University Press, 1992.

Perepiska sekretariata TsK RSDRP(b) s mestnymi partiinymi organizatsiiami. Edited by G. D. Obichkin, A. A. Struchkov, and M. D. Stuchebnikova. 8 volumes. Moscow, 1957–1974.

Peris, Daniel. *Storming the Heavens: The Soviet League of the Militant Godless.* Ithaca: Cornell University Press, 1998.

"Pervaia godovshchina Oktiabr'skoi revoliutsii: Dokumenty." *Istoriia SSSR* 6 (1987): 121–34.

Pethybridge, Roger William. *The Spread of the Russian Revolution: Essays on 1917.* London: Macmillan, 1972.

Petit, Eugene. *Une Bastille Russe: La Forteresse de Schlüsselbourg.* Paris, 1906.

Petrogradskii voenno-revoliutsionnyi komitet. Vol. 2. Moscow, 1966.

Petrone, Karen. *Life Has Become More Joyous, Comrades! Celebrations in the Time of Stalin.* Bloomington: Indiana University Press, 2000.

Piontkovskii, S. *Oktiabr' 1917 g.* Moscow-Leningrad, 1927.

Pipes, Richard. *The Russian Revolution.* New York: Vintage, 1990.

——. "Seventy-Five Years On: The Great October Revolution as a Clandestine Coup d'État." *Times Literary Supplement* 4675 (November 6, 1992): 3–4.

Plaggenborg, Stefan. *Revolutionskultur: Menschenbilder und Kulturelle Praxis in Sowjetrussland Zwischen Oktoberrevolution und Stalinismus.* Cologne: Böhlau, 1996.

Pod sozvezdiem topora: Petrograd 1917 goda. Znakomyi i neznakomyi. Moscow: Sovetskaia Rossiia, 1991.

Podvoiskii, Nikolai I. *Krasnaia gvardiia v Oktiabr'skie dni (Leningrad i Moskva).* Moscow-Leningrad, 1927.

Podvoiskii, Nikolai I., and A. R. Orlinskii. *Massovoe deistvo. Rukovodstvo k organizatsii i provedeniiu prazdnovaniia 10–letiia Oktiabria i drugikh revoliutsionnykh prazdnikov.* Moscow and Leningrad, 1927.

Pollock, John. *The Bolshevik Adventure.* London: Constable, 1919.

Polonskii, V. *Russkii revoliutsionnyi plakat.* Moscow, 1924.

Portelli, Alessandro. *The Death of Luigi Trastulli and Other Stories: Form and Meaning in Oral History.* Albany: State University of New York Press, 1991.

——. "The Peculiarities of Oral History." *History Workshop* 12 (1981): 96–107.

Prishvin, M. M. *Dnevniki, 1914–1917.* Moscow: Moskovskii rabochii, 1991.

Proletarische Kulturrevolution in Sowjetrussland, 1917–1921. Edited by Richard Lorenz, 108–78. Munich: Deutscher Taschenbuch Verlag, 1969.

Protokoly 10 s"ezda RKP(b). Moscow, 1933.

Provincial Landscapes: Local Dimensions of Soviet Power, 1917–1953. Edited by Donald J. Raleigh. Pittsburgh: University of Pittsburgh Press, 2001.

Pyman, Avril. "Russian Poetry and the October Revolution." *Revolutionary Russia* 3, no. 1 (1990): 5–54.

Rabinowitch, Alexander. *The Bolsheviks Come to Power: The Revolution of 1917 in Petrograd.* New York: Norton, 1978.

——. *Prelude to Revolution: The Petrograd Bolsheviks and the July 1917 Uprising.* Bloomington: Indiana University Press, 1968.

Rachum, Ilan. *"Revolution": The Entrance of a New Word into Western Political Discourse.* New York: University Press of America, 1999.

Radkey, Oliver Henry. *Russia Goes to the Polls: The Election to the All-Russian Constituent Assembly, 1917.* Ithaca: Cornell University Press, 1990.

——. *The Sickle Under the Hammer. The Russian Socialist Revolutionaries in the Early Months of Soviet Rule.* New York: Columbia University Press, 1963.

Raleigh, Donald J. *Experiencing Russia's Civil War: Politics, Society, and Revolutionary Culture in Saratov, 1917–1922.* Princeton: Princeton University Press, 2002.

Reed, John. *Ten Days That Shook the World.* Harmondsworth, England: Penguin, 1982.

"Revoliutsionnoe dvizhenie v Rossii." *Neizvestnaia Rossiia. 20 vek* (Moscow) 2 (1992): 351–79.

Reworking the Past: Hitler, Holocaust, and the Historians' Debate. Edited by Peter Baldwin. Boston: Beacon, 1990.

Rigby, T. H. *Communist Party Membership in the USSR, 1917–1967.* Princeton: Princeton University Press, 1968.

Roberts, Graham. *Forward Soviet! History and Non-Fiction Film in the USSR.* London: I.B. Tauris, 1999.

Ropars-Wuilleumier, Marie-Claire. *L'Écran de la mémoire: Essais de lecture cinématographique.* Paris: Éditions du Seuil, 1970.

Rosenstone, Robert A. *"October* as History." *Rethinking History* 5, no. 2 (2001): 255–74.

——. *Revisioning History: Film and the Construction of a New Past.* Princeton: Princeton University Press, 1995.

Rossiiskaia Kommunisticheskaia Partii (bol'shevikov) v postanovleniiakh ee s"ezdov 1903–1921 gg. Petrograd, 1921.

Rossiiskaia Kommunisticheskaia Partii (bol'shevikov) v rezoliutsiiakh ee s"ezdov i konferentsii 1898–1921 gg. Moscow, 1922.

Rousso, Henry. *The Vichy Syndrome: History and Memory in France since 1944.* Cambridge: Harvard University Press, 1991.

Rudinskii, F. M. *"Delo KPSS" v Konstitutsionnom sude: Zapiski, uchastnika, protsessa.* Moscow: Bylina, 1999.

Rudnitsky, Konstantin. *Russian and Soviet Theater, 1905–1932.* New York: Harry N. Abrams, 1988.

Russian Art of the Avant-Garde. Edited by John E. Bowlt. New York: Thames and Hudson, 1988.

Russian Modernity: Politics, Knowledges, Practices. Edited by David L. Hoffmann and Yanni Kotsonis. New York: St. Martin's, 2000.

The Russian Social Democratic Labour Party, 1898–October 1917. Vol. 1 of *Resolutions and Decisions of the Communist Party of the Soviet Union.* Edited by R. C. Elwood. Toronto: University of Toronto Press, 1974.

Russkii-sovetskii teatr, 1917–1921. Edited by A. Z. Iufit. Leningrad, 1968.

Rybinsk v revoliutsii, 1917–1922. Rybinsk: Izdanie Istparta Rybinskogo gubkoma RKP(b), 1922.

Salomoni, Antonella. "Un Savoir historique d'état: Les Archives Soviétiques." *Annales HSS* 1 (January–February 1995): 3–27.

Savel'ev, M. *Lenin i Oktiabr'skoe vooruzhennoe vosstanie.* Moscow-Leningrad, 1927.

Schapiro, Leonard. *The Communist Party of the Soviet Union.* 2d ed. Norfolk, England: Methuen, 1970.

——. *The Origin of the Communist Autocracy: Political Opposition in the Soviet State. First Phase, 1917–1922.* Cambridge: Harvard University Press, 1966.

Scheffer, Paul. *Augenzeuge im Staate Lenins: Ein Korrespondent Berichtet aus Moskau, 1921–1930.* Munich: Piper, 1972.

Schwarz, Solomon M. *The Russian Revolution of 1905: The Workers' Movement and the Formation of Bolshevism and Menshevism.* Chicago: University of Chicago Press, 1967.

Scott, Joan. "The Evidence of Experience." *Critical Inquiry* 17, no. 4 (1991): 773–97.

Sebald, W. G. *The Rings of Saturn.* New York: New Directions Books, 1998.

Sed'moi s"ezd Rossiiskoi Kommunisticheskoi Partii: Stenograficheskii otchet 6–8-go marta 1918 goda. Moscow-Petrograd, 1923.

Service, Robert. *The Bolshevik Party in Revolution, 1917–1923: A Study in Organisational Change.* Basingstoke, England: Macmillan, 1979.

Shingarev, A. I. *The Shingarev Diary.* Royal Oak, MI: Strathcona, 1978.

Shlapentokh, Dmitry. *The Counter-Revolution in Revolution: Images of Thermidor and Napoleon at the Time of Russian Revolution and Civil War.* New York: St. Martin's, 1999.

Shumiatskii, B. *Chego khotiat bol'sheviki? (K programme partii).* N.p., 1919.

——. *Sibir' na putiakh k Oktiabriu.* Moscow, 1927.

Sinyavsky, Andrei. *Soviet Civilization: A Cultural History.* New York: Arcade, 1990.

Sletov, Stepan. *K istorii vozniknoveniia partii sotsialistov-revoliutsionerov.* Petrograd, 1917.

Smith, S. A. *Red Petrograd: Revolution in the Factories, 1917–18.* Cambridge: Cambridge University Press, 1983.

Snyder, Tim. " 'Coming to Terms with the Charm and Power of Soviet Communism.' " *Contemporary European History* 6, no. 1 (1997): 133–44.

Solzhenitsyn, Alexsandr. *Nobelevskaia lektsiia po literature 1970 goda.* Paris: YMCA-Press, 1972.

Sorlin, Pierre. *The Film in History: Restaging the Past.* Totowa, N.J.: Barnes and Noble, 1980.

Sorokin, Pitirim. *Leaves from a Russian Diary.* New York: Dutton, 1924.

Sovetskaia kinokhronika, 1918–1925 gg. Annotirovannyi katalog. 1 chast'. Moscow, 1965.

Sovetskii politicheskii plakat/The Soviet Political Poster. Moscow, 1984.

Steinberg, Mark D. *Proletarian Imagination. Self, Modernity, and the Sacred in Russia, 1910–1925.* Ithaca: Cornell University Press, 2002.

Stikhotvoreniia i poemy. Moscow, 1990.

Stites, Richard. *Revolutionary Dreams: Utopian Vision and Experimental Life in the Russian Revolution.* Oxford: Oxford University Press, 1989.

Storming the Heavens: Voices of October. Edited by Mark Jones. London: Atlantic Highlands, 1987.

Sukhanov, N. N. *Zapiski o revoliutsii.* Vol. 1. Moscow, 1991.

Suny, Ronald Grigor. "Toward a Social History of the October Revolution." *American Historical Review* 88, no. 1 (1983): 31–52.

Suslov, A. *Zimnii dvorets, 1754–1927 gg.: Istoricheskii ocherk.* Leningrad, 1928.

Tagebuch aus Moskau, 1931–1939. Edited by Jochen Hellbeck. Munich: Deutscher Taschenbuch Verlag, 1996.

Templeton, Natasha. "The October Revolution and the Poets." *Landfall* 21, no. 84 (1967): 378–87.

Terne, A. *V tsarstve Lenina. Ocherki sovremennoi zhizni v RSFSR.* Berlin: Izd. Ol'gi D'iakovoi i K-o, 1922.

Tertz, Abram. *The Trial Begins and On Socialist Realism.* Berkeley: University of California Press, 1960.

Theater and Literature in Russia 1900–1930. A Collection of Essays. Edited by Lars Kleberg and Nils Åke Nilsson. Stockholm: Almqvist and Wiksell International, 1984.

Tikhonova, Z. N. "Ankety uchastnikov Velikoi Oktiabr'skoi Sotsialisticheskoi Revoliutsii: Istoricheskii istochnik." *Voprosy Istorii KPSS* 11 (1964): 99–103.

Time of Troubles: The Diary of Iurii Vladimirovich Got'e. Edited and translated by Terence Emmons. Princeton: Princeton University Press, 1988.

Toews, John E. "Intellectual History after the Linguistic Turn: The Autonomy of Meaning and the Irreducibility of Experience." *American Historical Review* 92, no. 4 (1987): 879–907.

Tolz, Vera. *Russian Academicians and the Revolution: Combining Professionalism and Politics.* Basingstoke, England: Macmillan, 1997.

Tonkin, Elizabeth. *Narrating Our Pasts: The Social Construction of Oral History.* Cambridge: Cambridge University Press, 1992.

Tretii ocherednoi s"ezd Rossiiskoi Sotsial-Demokraticheskoi Rabochei Partii 1905 g. Polnyi tekst protokolov (Moscow, 1924).

Trinadtsatyi s"ezd Rossiiskoi Kommunisticheskoi Partii (Bol'shevikov): Stenograficheskii otchet 23–31 maia 1924 g. Moscow, 1924.

Trotskii, L. *K istorii russkoi revoliutsii.* Moscow, 1990.

———. *O Lenine: Materialy dlia biografa.* Moscow, n.d.

———. *Sochineniia.* 21 volumes. Moscow, 1925–27.

Trotsky, L. *Literature and Revolution.* New York: Russell and Russell, 1957.

———. *My Life.* New York: Pathfinder, 1970.

———. *Problems of Everyday Life and Other Writings on Culture and Science.* New York: Monad, 1973.

The Trotsky Papers, 1917–1922. Edited by Jan M. Meijer. Vol. 2. The Hague, The Netherlands: Mouton, 1971.

Trotzky, Leon. *From October to Brest-Litovsk.* New York: Socialist Publication Society, 1919.

Trouillot, Michel-Rolph. *Silencing the Past: Power and the Production of History.* Boston: Beacon, 1995.

Tsereteli, I. G. *Vospominaniia o fevral'skoi revoliutsii.* Vol. 2. Paris: Mouton, 1963.

Tsiv'ian, Iurii G. *Istoricheskaia retseptsiia Kino: Kinematograf v Rossii, 1896–1930.* Riga: Zinatne, 1991.

Tucker, Robert C. "Party History: What It Is and Is Not." *American Slavic and East European Review* 20, no. 2 (1961): 295–300.

Tudor, Henry. *Political Myth.* New York: Praeger, 1972.

Tumarinson, Vilen Khaimovich. "Men'sheviki i bol'sheviki: Nesostoiavshiisia konsensus (Opyt istoricheskoi rekonstruktsii)." Ph.D. diss., Moscow, Moskovskii avtomobil'no-dorozhnyi institut, 1995.

Tumarkin, Nina. *Lenin Lives! The Lenin Cult in Soviet Russia.* Cambridge: Harvard University Press, 1983.

Urton, Gary. *The History of a Myth: Pacariqtambo and the Origin of the Inkas.* Austin: University of Texas Press, 1990.

Viola, Lynne. "Popular Resistance in the Stalinist 1930s: Soliloquy of a Devil's Advocate." *Kritika* 1, no. 1 (2000): 45–69.

V. I. Vernadskii. Dnevniki, 1917–1921. Kiev: Naukova Dumka, 1994.

Vladimir Akimov on the Dilemmas of Russian Marxism, 1895–1903. Edited by Jonathan Frankel. Cambridge: Cambridge University Press, 1969.

Voices of Revolution, 1917. Edited by Mark D. Steinberg. New Haven: Yale University Press, 2001.

von Borcke, Astrid. *Die Ursprünge des Bolschewismus: Die Jakobinische Tradition in Russland und die Theorie der Revolutionären Diktatur.* Munich: Johannes Berchmans, 1977.

von Geldern, James. *Bolshevik Festivals, 1917–1920.* Berkeley: University of California Press, 1993.

Voprosy istochnikovedeniia istorii SSSR, Vyp. 2. Vol. 24 of *Trudy Moskovskogo Gosudarstvennogo Istoriko-Arkhivnogo Instituta.* Moscow, 1966.

Vos'moi s"ezd RKP(b). 18–23 marta 1919 g. Moscow, 1933.

Vosstanie na bronenostse "Kniaz Potemkin Tavricheskii." Vospominaniia, materialy i dokumenty. Edited by V. I. Nevskii. Moscow-Petrograd, 1924.

Vovelle, Michel. "1789–1917: The Game of Analogies." In *The Terror.* Vol. 4 of *The French Revolution and the Creation of Modern Political Culture,* edited by Keith Michael Baker. Oxford: Pergamon Press, 1994.

Vserossiiskaya Konferentsiya Ros. Sots. –Dem. Rab. Partii 1912 goda. Edited by R. C. Elwood. New York: Kraus, 1982.

Vtoroi Vserossiiskii S"ezd Sovetov Rabochikh i Soldatskikh Deputatov (25–26 oktiabria 1917 g.): Sbornik dokumentov i materialov. Moscow: "Arkheograficheskii tsentr," 1997.

Wade, Rex A. "The Revolution in the Provinces: Khar'kov and the Varieties of Response to the October Revolution." *Revolutionary Russia* 4, no. 1 (1991): 132–42.

Walker, Barbara. "*Kruzhok* Culture: The Meaning of Patronage in the Early Soviet Literary World." *Contemporary European History* 11, no. 1 (2002): 107–23.

Weiner, Amir. *Making Sense of War: The Second World War and the Fate of the Bolshevik Revolution.* Princeton: Princeton University Press, 2001.

Wenden, D. J. "Battleship Potemkin–Film and Reality." In *Feature Films as History,* edited by K. R. M. Short. Knoxville: University of Tennessee Press, 1981.

White, Hayden. *The Content of the Form: Narrative Discourse and Historical Representation.* Baltimore: Johns Hopkins University Press, 1987.

White, James D. "Early Soviet Historical Interpretations of the Russian Revolution, 1918–1924." *Soviet Studies* 37, no. 3 (1985): 330–52.

——. *Lenin: The Theory and Practice of Revolution.* Basingstoke, England: Palgrave, 2001.

——. *The Russian Revolution, 1917–1921: A Short History.* London: Edward Arnold, 1994.

——. "The Sormovo-Nikolaev Zemlyachestvo in the February Revolution." *Soviet Studies* 31, no. 4 (1979): 475–504.

White, Stephen. *The Bolshevik Poster.* New Haven: Yale University Press, 1988.

Williams, Albert Rhys. *Through the Russian Revolution.* New York: Boni and Liveright, 1921.

Williams, Robert C. *Artists in Revolution: Portraits of the Russian Avant-Garde, 1905–1925.* Bloomington: Indiana University Press, 1977.

Wood, Elizabeth A. *The Baba and the Comrade: Gender and Politics in Revolutionary Russia.* Bloomington: Indiana University Press, 1997.

Wright, Patrick. *On Living in an Old Country: The National Past in Contemporary Britain.* London: Verso, 1985.

Za Leninizm: Sbornik statei. Moscow-Leningrad, 1925.

Za partiiu, za Leninizm. Petrograd, 1924.

Za sovety bez kommunistov. Krest'ianskoe vosstanie v Tiumenskoi gubernii 1921. Sbornik dokumentov. Novosibirsk: Sibirskii khronograf, 2000.

Zinov'ev, G. *Bespartiinyi ili kommunist?* Petrograd, 1919.

——. *Chego khotiat sotsial-demokraty bol'sheviki? (V voprosakh i otvetakh).* Moscow, 1918.

Zipes, Jack. "The Utopian Function of Tradition." *Telos* 94 (1993–94): 25–29.

Index

ABC of Communism, The (Azbuka
  kommunizma), 71–72
Aberfan, xiii–xiv
About Lenin (O Lenine), 145
Adoratskii, V. V., 100, 101, 104, 108
Aleksandrov, Grigorii, 184, 195, 204, 205,
  206–7, 208
Alexander III, statue of, 190, 191, 193
All-Russian Communist Party (Bolshevik)
  [VKP(b)]. See Bolshevik Party
Amfiteatrov, Vladimir, 33, 34
Anderson, Benedict, 10
Annenkov, Iurii, 73, 74, 76, 81
Antonov-Ovseenko, V. A., 35, 89, 182, 184,
  207
Archives, 3, 10, 93, 104, 107, 108, 113–15, 129,
  131, 142, 164; and the Bolshevik Party, 105,
  106, 113–15, 142, 158, 165, 169, 262n28;
  Central Archive (Tsentroarkhiv), 131, 164;
  Historical-Revolutionary Archive, 129;
  tsarist, 107, 109, 118, 131, 153, 154, 168,
  262n28; Red archivists, 131, 252n29
Arosev, A. Ia., 101, 102, 103
Aurora, 79, 179, 181, 182, 207
Avanesov, V. A., 51
Avdeev, N. N., 101, 102, 152

Babel, Isaac, 1
Baker, Keith Michael, 3, 6
Baltic Fleet, 97, 181
Barnet, Boris, 184; and Moscow in October
  (Moskva v Oktiabre), 184, 196, 270n9
Bastille, as revolutionary motif, 2, 10, 32, 34,
  35, 47, 55, 73, 75, 80, 90, 92, 105, 196,
  227n54, 234n132
Battleship Potemkin (Bronenosets Potemkin),
  184, 187, 188, 191, 205, 249n123
Baturin, N. N., 100, 101, 102, 104, 107, 108,
  109, 121, 154
Belenkii, Grigorii, 60

Bely, Andrei, 31
Benjamin, Walter, 39, 203
Berkhofer, Robert, 10
Berkman, Alexander, 117, 118
Bezpartiinye (nonparty people), 37, 38, 65,
  67–68, 73, 106, 119, 124, 127, 138, 139,
  140–41, 159, 172, 211, 213, 214, 244n153,
  271n61
Black Hundreds, 107, 134, 142, 160, 186
Blanquism, 145
Blok, Aleksandr, 19, 30; "The Scythians," 30;
  "The Twelve," 31
Bobrovskaia (Zelikson), Ts. S., 101, 130
Bolshevik Party, Agitation and Propaganda
  Department (Agitprop), 126–27, 164, 176;
  and archives, 105, 106, 113–15, 142, 158,
  165, 169, 262n28; attitude to cinema, 184,
  195–98; attitude to reminiscences, 82–83,
  112, 115, 119–21, 142, 149, 152, 158, 159,
  165–69, 197, 210; and "bourgeois" as a
  political category, 6, 8, 20, 21, 22, 23, 35,
  41, 46–47, 51, 56, 60, 62, 63, 65, 66, 71, 72,
  75, 80, 84, 85, 105, 107, 108, 123, 124, 131,
  133, 134, 135, 139, 154, 161–62, 163, 176,
  177, 205; changes its name, 51; The
  Communist Party of the Soviet Union
  (Bolshevik). Short Course, 220; cooperation
  with Mensheviks, 8, 20, 36, 72, 142, 162,
  227n47; decree on land, 28, 56; Democratic
  Centralists, 70–71, 99; Eighth Party
  Congress (1919), 50–51, 72; and the
  February Revolution, 56, 107, 158, 209, 210,
  262n28; First All-Union Party Cinema
  Conference (1928), 196; Fourteenth Party
  Congress (1925), 162–63; Left Communists,
  70, 102; legitimacy of, 35–36, 70–73, 99,
  143; and the "literary discussion," 143–47,
  150, 153, 161, 169; local party organizations,
  17, 20, 36–37, 49–50, 57–58, 99, 101–3, 108,
  112–13, 114, 116, 118, 119, 121–24, 126–28,
  129, 136–40, 141, 142, 156, 158, 159, 166,